Bergstrand

ADVANCED TEXTS IN ECONOMETRICS

General Editors
C.W.J. Ganger   G.E. Mizon

D1595832

Other Advanced Texts in Econometrics

ARCH: Selected Readings
Edited by Robert F. Engle

Asymptotic Theory for Integrated Processes
By H. Peter Boswijk

Bayesian Inference in Dynamic Econometric Models
By Luc Bauwens, Michel Lubrano, and Jean-François Richard

Co-integration, Error Correction, and the Econometric Analysis of Non-Stationary Data
By Anindya Banerjee, Juan J. Dolado, John W. Galbraith, and David Hendry

Dynamic Econometrics
By David F. Hendry

Finite Sample Econometrics
By Aman Ullah

Generalized Method of Moments
By Alastair Hall

Likelihood-Based Inference in Cointegrated Vector Autoregressive Models
By Søren Johansen

Long-Run Econometric Relationships: Readings in Cointegration
Edited by R. F. Engle and C. W. J. Granger

Micro-Econometrics for Policy, Program, and Treatment Effect
By Myoung-jae Lee

Modelling Econometric Series: Readings in Econometric Methodology
Edited by C. W. J. Granger

Modelling Non-Linear Economic Relationships
By Clive W. J. Granger and Timo Teräsvirta

Modelling Seasonality
Edited by S. Hylleberg

Non-Stationary Times Series Analysis and Cointegration
Edited by Colin P. Hargeaves

Outlier Robust Analysis of Economic Time Series
By André Lucas, Philip Hans Franses, and Dick van Dijk

Panel Data Econometrics
By Manuel Arellano

Periodicity and Stochastic Trends in Economic Time Series
By Philip Hans Franses

Progressive Modelling: Non-nested Testing and Encompassing
Edited by Massimiliano Marcellino and Grayham E. Mizon

Readings in Unobserved Components
Edited by Andrew Harvey and Tommaso Proietti

Stochastic Limit Theory: An Introduction for Econometricians
By James Davidson

Stochastic Volatility
Edited by Neil Shephard

Testing Exogeneity
Edited by Neil R. Ericsson and John S. Irons

The Econometrics of Macroeconomic Modelling
By Gunnar Bårdsen, Øyvind Eitrheim, Eilev S. Jansen, and Ragnar Nymoen

Time Series with Long Memory
Edited by Peter M. Robinson

Time-Series-Based Econometrics: Unit Roots and Co-integrations
By Michio Hatanaka

Workbook on Cointegration
By Peter Reinhard Hansen and Søren Johansen

Micro-Econometrics for Policy, Program, and Treatment Effects

MYOUNG-JAE LEE

OXFORD
UNIVERSITY PRESS

OXFORD

UNIVERSITY PRESS

Great Clarendon Street, Oxford OX2 6DP

Oxford University Press is a department of the University of Oxford.
It furthers the University's objective of excellence in research, scholarship,
and education by publishing worldwide in

Oxford New York

Auckland Cape Town Dar es Salaam Hong Kong Karachi
Kuala Lumpur Madrid Melbourne Mexico City Nairobi
New Delhi Shanghai Taipei Toronto

With offices in

Argentina Austria Brazil Chile Czech Republic France Greece
Guatemala Hungary Italy Japan Poland Portugal Singapore
South Korea Switzerland Thailand Turkey Ukraine Vietnam

Oxford is a registered trade mark of Oxford University Press
in the UK and in certain other countries

Published in the United States
by Oxford University Press Inc., New York

British Library Cataloguing in Publication Data
Data available

Library of Congress Cataloging in Publication Data
Data available

Typeset by Newgen Imaging Systems (P) Ltd., Chennai, India
Printed in Great Britain
on acid-free paper by
Biddles Ltd., King's Lynn, Norfolk

ISBN 0-19-926768-5 (hbk.)   9780199267682
ISBN 0-19-926769-3 (pbk.)   9780199267699

1 3 5 7 9 10 8 6 4 2

To my brother, Doug-jae Lee,
and sister, Mee-young Lee

Preface

In many disciplines of science, it is desired to know the effect of a 'treatment' or 'cause' on a response that one is interested in; the effect is called 'treatment effect' or 'causal effect'. Here, the treatment can be a drug, an education program, or an economic policy, and the response variable can be, respectively, an illness, academic achievement, or GDP. Once the effect is found, one can intervene to adjust the treatment to attain the desired level of response. As these examples show, treatment effect could be the single most important topic for science. And it is, in fact, hard to think of any branch of science where treatment effect would be irrelevant.

Much progress for treatment effect analysis has been made by researchers in statistics, medical science, psychology, education, and so on. Until the 1990s, relatively little attention had been paid to treatment effect by econometricians, other than to 'switching regression' in micro-econometrics. But, there is great scope for a contribution by econometricians to treatment effect analysis: familiar econometric terms such as structural equations, instrumental variables, and sample selection models are all closely linked to treatment effect. Indeed, as the references show, there has been a deluge of econometric papers on treatment effect in recent years. Some are parametric, following the traditional parametric regression framework, but most of them are semi- or non-parametric, following the recent trend in econometrics.

Even though treatment effect is an important topic, digesting the recent treatment effect literature is difficult for practitioners of econometrics. This is because of the sheer quantity and speed of papers coming out, and also because of the difficulty of understanding the semi- or non-parametric ones. The purpose of this book is to put together various econometric treatment effect models in a coherent way, make it clear which are the parameters of interest, and show how they can be identified and estimated under weak assumptions. In this way, we will try to bring to the fore the recent advances in econometrics for treatment effect analysis. Our emphasis will be on semi- and non-parametric estimation methods, but traditional parametric approaches will be discussed as well. The target audience for this book is researchers and graduate students who have some basic understanding of econometrics.

The main scenario in treatment effect is simple. Suppose it is of interest to know the effect of a drug (a treatment) on blood pressure (a response variable) by comparing two people, one treated and the other not. If the two people are exactly the same, other than in the treatment status, then the difference between their blood pressures can be taken as the effect of the drug on blood pressure. If they differ in some other way than in the treatment status, however, the difference in blood pressures may be due to the differences other than the treatment status difference. As will appear time and time again in this book, the main catchphrase in treatment effect is *compare comparable people*, with comparable meaning 'homogenous on average'. Of course, it is impossible to have exactly the same people: people differ visibly or invisibly. Hence, much of this book is about what can be done to solve this problem.

This book is written from an econometrician's view point. The reader will benefit from consulting non-econometric books on causal inference: Pearl (2000), Gordis (2000), Rosenbaum (2002), and Shadish *et al.* (2002) among others which vary in terms of technical difficulty. Within econometrics, Frölich (2003) is available, but its scope is narrower than this book. There are also surveys in Angrist and Krueger (1999) and Heckman *et al.* (1999). Some recent econometric textbooks also carry a chapter or two on treatment effect: Wooldridge (2002) and Stock and Watson (2003). I have no doubt that more textbooks will be published in coming years that have extensive discussion on treatment effect.

This book is organized as follows. Chapter 1 is a short tour of the book; no references are given here and its contents will be repeated in the remaining chapters. Thus, readers with some background knowledge on treatment effect could skip this chapter. Chapter 2 sets up the basics of treatment effect analysis and introduces various terminologies. Chapter 3 looks at controlling for observed variables so that people with the same observed characteristics can be compared. One of the main methods used is 'matching', which is covered in Chapter 4. Dealing with unobserved variable differences is studied in Chapters 5 and 6: Chapter 5 covers the basic approaches and Chapter 6 the remaining approaches. Chapter 7 looks at multiple or dynamic treatment effect analysis. The appendix collects topics that are digressing or technical. A star is attached to chapters or sections that can be skipped. The reader may find certain parts repetitive because every effort has been made to make each chapter more or less independent.

Writing on treatment effect has been both exhilarating and exhausting. It has changed the way I look at the world and how I would explain things that are related to one another. The literature is vast, since almost everything can be called a treatment. Unfortunately, I had only a finite number of hours available. I apologise to those who contributed to the treatment effect literature but have not been referred to in this book. However, a new edition or a sequel may be published before long and hopefully the missed references will be added. Finally, I would like to thank Markus Frölich for his detailed comments, Andrew Schuller, the economics editor at Oxford University Press, and Carol Bestley, the production editor.

Contents

Abridged Contents

1

Tour of the book

Suppose we want to know the effect of a childhood education program at age 5 on a cognition test score at age 10. The program is a *treatment* and the test score is a *response* (or outcome) variable. How do we know if the treatment is effective? We need to compare two *potential* test scores at age 10, one (y_1) with the treatment and the other (y_0) without. If $y_1 - y_0 > 0$, then we can say that the program worked. However, we never observe both y_0 and y_1 for the same child as it is impossible to go back to the past and '(un)do' the treatment. The observed response is $y = dy_1 + (1 - d)y_0$ where $d = 1$ means treated and $d = 0$ means untreated. Instead of the individual effect $y_1 - y_0$, we may look at the *mean effect* $E(y_1 - y_0) = E(y_1) - E(y_0)$ to define the treatment effectiveness as $E(y_1 - y_0) > 0$.

One way to find the mean effect is a randomized experiment: get a number of children and divide them randomly into two groups, one treated (*treatment group*, 'T group', or '$d = 1$ group') from whom y_1 is observed, and the other untreated (*control group*, 'C group', or '$d = 0$ group') from whom y_0 is observed. If the group mean difference $E(y|d = 1) - E(y|d = 0)$ is positive, then this means $E(y_1 - y_0) > 0$, because

$$E(y|d = 1) - E(y|d = 0) = E(y_1|d = 1) - E(y_0|d = 0) = E(y_1) - E(y_0);$$

randomization d determines which one of y_0 and y_1 is observed (for the first equality), and with this done, d is independent of y_0 and y_1 (for the second equality). The role of randomization is to choose (in a particular fashion) the 'path' 0 or 1 for each child. At the end of each path, there is the outcome y_0 or y_1 waiting, which is not affected by the randomization. The particular fashion is that the two groups are homogenous on average in terms of the variables other than d and y: sex, IQ, parental characteristics, and so on.

However, randomization is hard to do. If the program seems harmful, it would be unacceptable to randomize any child to group T; if the program seems beneficial, the parents would be unlikely to let their child be randomized to group C. An alternative is to use observational data where the children (i.e., their parents) self-select the treatment. Suppose the program is perceived as good and requires a hefty fee. Then the T group could be markedly different from the C group: the T group's children could have lower (baseline) cognitive ability at age 5 and richer parents. Let x denote observed variables and ε denote unobserved variables that would matter for y. For instance, x consists of the baseline cognitive ability at age 5 and parents' income, and ε consists of the child's genes and lifestyle.

Suppose we ignore the differences across the two groups in x or ε just to compare the test scores at age 10. Since the T group are likely to consist of children of lower baseline cognitive ability, the T group's test score at age 10 may turn out to be smaller than the C group's. The program may have worked, but not well enough. We may falsely conclude no effect of the treatment or even a negative effect. Clearly, this comparison is wrong: we will have compared incomparable subjects, in the sense that the two groups differ in the observable x or unobservable ε. The group mean difference $E(y|d=1) - E(y|d=0)$ may not be the same as $E(y_1 - y_0)$, because

$$E(y|d=1) - E(y|d=0) = E(y_1|d=1) - E(y_0|d=0) \neq E(y_1) - E(y_0).$$

$E(y_1|d=1)$ is the mean treated response for the richer and less able T group, which is likely to be different from $E(y_1)$, the mean treated response for the C and T groups combined. Analogously, $E(y_0|d=0) \neq E(y_0)$. The difference in the observable x across the two groups may cause *overt bias* for $E(y_1 - y_0)$ and the difference in the unobservable ε may cause *hidden bias*. Dealing with the difference in x or ε is the main task in finding treatment effects with observational data.

If there is no difference in ε, then only the difference in x should be taken care of. The basic way to remove the difference (or imbalance) in x is to select T and C group subjects that share the same x, which is called 'matching'. In the education program example, compare children whose baseline cognitive ability and parents' income are the same. This yields

$$E(y|x, d=1) - E(y|x, d=0) = E(y_1|x, d=1) - E(y_0|x, d=0)$$
$$= E(y_1|x) - E(y_0|x) = E(y_1 - y_0|x).$$

The variable d in $E(y_j|x, d)$ drops out once x is conditioned on as if d is randomized given x. This assumption $E(y_j|x, d) = E(y_j|x)$ is *selection-on-observables* or ignorable treatment.

With the *conditional effect* $E(y_1 - y_0|x)$ identified, we can get an x-weighted average, which may be called a *marginal effect*. Depending on the weighting function, different marginal effects are obtained. The choice of the weighting function reflects the importance of the subpopulation characterized by x.

For instance, if poor-parent children are more important for the education program, then a higher-than-actual weight may be assigned to the subpopulation of children with poor parents.

There are two problems with matching. One is a *dimension problem*: if x is high-dimensional, it is hard to find control and treat subjects that share exactly the same x. The other is a *support problem*: the T and C groups do not overlap in x. For instance, suppose x is parental income per year and $d = 1[x \geq \tau]$ where $\tau = \$100,000$, $1[A] = 1$ if A holds and 0 otherwise. Then the T group are all rich and the C group are all (relatively) poor and there is no overlap in x across the two groups.

For the observable x to cause an overt bias, it is necessary that x alters the probability of receiving the treatment. This provides a way to avoid the dimension problem in matching on x: match instead on the one-dimensional *propensity score* $\pi(x) \equiv P(d = 1|x) = E(d|x)$. That is, compute $\pi(x)$ for both groups and match only on $\pi(x)$. In practice, $\pi(x)$ can be estimated with logit or probit.

The support problem is binding when both $d = 1[x \geq \tau]$ and x affect (y_0, y_1): x should be controlled for, which is, however, impossible due to no overlap in x. Due to $d = 1[x \geq \tau]$, $E(y_0|x)$ and $E(y_1|x)$ have a break (discontinuity) at $x = \tau$; this case is called *regression discontinuity* (or *before-after* if x is time). The support problem cannot be avoided, but subjects near the threshold τ are likely to be similar and thus comparable. This comparability leads to 'threshold (or borderline) randomization', and this randomization identifies $E(y_1 - y_0|x \simeq \tau)$, the mean effect for the subpopulation $x \simeq \tau$.

Suppose there is no dimension nor support problem, and we want to find comparable control subjects (*controls*) for each treated subject (*treated*) with matching. The matched controls are called a 'comparison group'. There are decisions to make in finding a comparison group. First, how many controls there are for each treated. If one, we get *pair matching*, and if many, we get *multiple matching*. Second, in the case of multiple matching, exactly how many, and whether the number is the same for all the treated or different needs to be determined. Third, whether a control is matched only once or multiple times. Fourth, whether to pass over (i.e., drop) a treated or not if no good matched control is found. Fifth, to determine a 'good' match, a distance should be chosen for $|x_0 - x_1|$ for treated x_1 and control x_0.

With these decisions made, the matching is implemented. There will be new T and C groups—T group will be new only if some treated subjects are passed over—and matching success is gauged by checking balance of x across the new two groups. Although it seems easy to pick the variables to avoid overt bias, selecting x can be deceptively difficult. For example, if there is an observed variable w that is affected by d and affects y, should w be included in x?

Dealing with hidden bias due to imbalance in unobservable ε is more difficult than dealing with overt bias, simply because ε is not observed. However, there are many ways to remove or determine the presence of hidden bias.

Sometimes matching can remove hidden bias. If two identical twins are split into the T and C groups, then the unobserved genes can be controlled for. If we get two siblings from the same family and assign one sibling to the T group and the other to the C group, then the unobserved parental influence can be controlled for (to some extent).

One can *check for the presence of hidden bias using multiple doses, multiple responses, or multiple control groups.* In the education program example, suppose that some children received only half the treatment. They are expected to have a higher score than the C group but a lower one than the T group. If this ranking is violated, we suspect the presence of an unobserved variable. Here, we use multiple doses $(0, 0.5, 1)$.

Suppose that we find a positive effect of stress (d) on a mental disease (y) and that the same treated (i.e., stressed) people report a high number of injuries due to accidents. Since stress is unlikely to affect the number of injuries due to accidents, this suggests the presence of an unobserved variable—perhaps lack of sleep causing stress and accidents. Here, we use multiple responses (mental disease and accidental injuries).

'No treatment' can mean many different things. With drinking as the treatment, no treatment may mean real non-drinkers, but it may also mean people who used to drink heavily a long time ago and then stopped for health reasons (ex-drinkers). Different no-treatment groups provide multiple control groups. For a job-training program, a no-treatment group can mean people who never applied to the program, but it can also mean people who did apply but were rejected. As real non-drinkers differ from ex-drinkers, the non-applicants can differ from the rejected. The applicants and the rejected form two control groups, possibly different in terms of some unobserved variables. Where the two control groups are different in y, an unobserved variable may be present that is causing hidden bias.

Econometricians' first reaction to hidden bias (or an 'endogeneity problem') is to find instruments which are variables that directly influence the treatment but not the response. It is not easy to find convincing instruments, but the micro-econometric treatment-effect literature provides a list of ingenious instruments and offers a new look at the conventional instrumental variable estimator; an *instrumental variable identifies the treatment effect for compliers*—people who get treated only due to the instrumental variable change. The usual instrumental variable estimator runs into trouble if the treatment effect is heterogenous across individuals, but the complier-effect interpretation remains valid despite the heterogenous effect.

Yet another way to deal with hidden bias is *sensitivity analysis*. Initially, treatment effect is estimated under the assumption of no unobserved variable causing hidden bias. Then, the presence of unobserved variables is parameterized by, say, γ with $\gamma = 0$ meaning no unobserved variable: $\gamma \neq 0$ is allowed to see how big γ must be for the initial conclusion to be reversed. There are different ways to parameterize the presence of unobserved variables, and thus different sensitivity analyses.

What has been mentioned so far constitutes the main contents of this book. In addition to this, we discuss several other issues. To list a few, firstly, the *mean effect is not the only effect of interest*. For the education program example, we may be more interested in lower quantiles of $y_1 - y_0$ than in $E(y_1 - y_0)$. Alternatively, instead of mean or quantiles, whether or not y_0 and y_1 have the same marginal distribution may also be interesting. Secondly, instead of matching, it is possible to *control for x by weighting the T and C group samples differently*. Thirdly, the T and C groups may be observed multiple times over time (before and after the treatment), which leads us to *difference in differences* and related study designs. Fourthly, binary treatments are generalized into *multiple treatments that include dynamic treatments* where binary treatments are given repeatedly over time. Assessing dynamic treatment effects is particularly challenging, since interim response variables could be observed and future treatments adjusted accordingly.

2

Basics of treatment effect analysis

For a treatment and a response variable, we want to know the causal effects of the former on the latter. This chapter introduces causality based on 'potential—treated and untreated—responses', and examines what type of treatment effects are identified. The basic way of identifying the treatment effect is to compare the average difference between the treatment and control (i.e., untreated) groups. For this to work, the treatment should determine which potential response is realized, but be otherwise unrelated to it. When this condition is not met, due to some observed and unobserved variables that affect both the treatment and the response, biases may be present. Avoiding such biases is one of the main tasks of causal analysis with observational data. The treatment effect framework has been used in statistics and medicine, and has appeared in econometrics under the name 'switching regression'. It is also linked closely to structural form equations in econometrics. Causality using potential responses allows us a new look at regression analysis, where the regression parameters are interpreted as causal parameters.

2.1 Treatment intervention, counter-factual, and causal relation

2.1.1 Potential outcomes and intervention

In many science disciplines, it is desired to know the effect(s) of a treatment or cause on a response (or outcome) variable of interest y_i, where $i = 1, \ldots, N$ indexes individuals; the effects are called 'treatment effects' or 'causal effects'.

The following are examples of treatments and responses:

Treatment:	exercise	job training	college education	drug	tax policy
Response:	blood pressure	wage	lifetime earnings	cholesterol	work hours

It is important to be specific on the treatment and response. For the drug/cholesterol example, we would need to know the quantity of the drug taken and how it is administered, and when and how cholesterol is measured. The same drug can have different treatments if taken in different dosages at different frequencies. For example cholesterol levels measured one week and one month after the treatment are two different response variables. For job training, classroom-type job training certainly differs from mere job search assistance, and wages one and two years after the training are two different outcome variables.

Consider a binary treatment taking on 0 or 1 (this will be generalized to multiple treatments in Chapter 7). Let y_{ji}, $j = 0, 1$, denote the *potential outcome* when individual i receives treatment j exogenously (i.e., when treatment j is forced in $(j = 1)$ or out $(j = 0)$, in comparison to treatment j self-selected by the individual): for the exercise example,

$$y_{1i}: \text{blood pressure with exercise 'forced in';}$$

$$y_{0i}: \text{blood pressure with exercise 'forced out'.}$$

Although it is a little difficult to imagine exercise forced in or out, the expressions 'forced-in' and 'forced-out' reflects the notion of intervention. A better example would be that the price of a product is determined in the market, but the government may intervene to set the price at a level exogenous to the market to see how the demand changes. Another example is that a person may willingly take a drug (self-selection), rather than the drug being injected regardless of the person's will (intervention).

When we want to know a treatment effect, we want to know the *effect of a treatment intervention, not the effect of treatment self-selection*, on a response variable. With this information, we can adjust (or manipulate) the treatment exogenously to attain the desired level of response. This is what policy making is all about, after all. Left alone, people will self-select a treatment, and the effect of a self-selected treatment can be analysed easily whereas the effect of an intervened treatment cannot. Using the effect of a self-selected treatment to guide a policy decision, however, can be misleading if the policy is an intervention. Not all policies are interventions; e.g., a policy to encourage exercise. Even in this case, however, before the government decides to encourage exercise, it may want to know what the effects of exercises are; here, the effects may well be the effects of exercises intervened.

Between the two potential outcomes corresponding to the two potential treatments, only one outcome is observed while the other (called 'counter-factual') is not, which is the fundamental problem in treatment effect analysis. In the example of the effect of college education on lifetime earnings, only one outcome (earnings with college education or without) is available per person. One may argue that for some other cases, say the effect of a drug on cholesterol, both y_{1i} and y_{0i} could be observed sequentially. Strictly speaking however, if two treatments are administered one-by-one sequentially, we cannot say that we observe both y_{1i} and y_{0i}, as the subject changes over time, although the change may be very small. Although some scholars are against the notion of counter-factuals, it is well entrenched in econometrics, and is called 'switching regression'.

2.1.2 Causality and association

Define $y_{1i} - y_{0i}$ as the *treatment (or causal) effect for subject i*. In this definition, there is no uncertainty about what is the cause and what is the response variable. This way of defining causal effect using two potential responses is *counter-factual causality*. As briefly discussed in the appendix, this is in sharp contrast to the so-called 'probabilistic causality' which tries to uncover the real cause(s) of a response variable; there, no counter-factual is necessary. Although probabilistic causality is also a prominent causal concept, when we use causal effect in this book, we will always mean counter-factual causality. In a sense, everything in this world is related to everything else. As somebody put it aptly, a butterfly's flutter on one side of an ocean may cause a storm on the other side. Trying to find the real cause could be a futile exercise. Counter-factual causality fixes the causal and response variables and then tries to estimate the magnitude of the causal effect.

Let the *observed treatment* be d_i, and the *observed response* y_i be

$$y_i = (1 - d_i) \cdot y_{0i} + d_i \cdot y_{1i}, \qquad i = 1, \ldots, N.$$

Causal relation is different from associative relation such as correlation or covariance: we need (d_i, y_{0i}, y_{1i}) in the former to get $y_{1i} - y_{0i}$, while we need only (d_i, y_i) in the latter; of course, an associative relation suggests a causal relation. Correlation, $COR(d_i, y_i)$, between d_i and y_i is an association; also $COV(d_i, y_i)/V(d_i)$ is an association. The latter shows that Least Squares Estimator (LSE)—also called Ordinary LSE (OLS)—is used only for association although we tend to interpret LSE findings in practice as if they are causal findings. More on this will be discussed in Section 2.5.

When an association between two variables d_i and y_i is found, it is helpful to think of the following three cases:

1. d_i influences y_i unidirectionally ($d_i \longrightarrow y_i$).
2. y_i influences d_i unidirectionally ($d_i \longleftarrow y_i$).

3. There are third variables w_i, that influence both d_i and y_i unidirectionally although there is not a direct relationship between d_i and y_i $(d_i \longleftarrow w_i \longrightarrow y_i)$.

In treatment effect analysis, as mentioned already, we fix the cause and try to find the effect; thus case 2 is ruled out. What is difficult is to tell case 1 from 3 which is a '*common factor*' case (w_i is the common variables for d_i and y_i). Let x_i and ε_i denote the observed and unobserved variables for person i, respectively, that can affect both d_i and (y_{0i}, y_{1i}); usually x_i is called a 'covariate' vector, but sometimes both x_i and ε_i are called covariates. The variables x_i and ε_i are candidates for the common factors w_i. Besides the above three scenarios, there are other possibilities as well, which will be discussed in Section 3.1.

It may be a little awkward, but we need to imagine that person i has $(d_i, y_{0i}, y_{1i}, x_i, \varepsilon_i)$, but shows us either y_{0i} and y_{1i} depending on $d_i = 0$ or 1; x_i is shown always, but ε_i is never. To simplify the analysis, we usually ignore x_i and ε_i at the beginning of a discussion and later look at how to deal with them. In a given data set, the group with $d_i = 1$ that reveal only (x_i, y_{1i}) is called the *treatment group* (or *T group*), and the group with $d_i = 0$ that reveal only (x_i, y_{0i}) is called the *control group* (or *C group*).

2.1.3   Partial equilibrium analysis and remarks

SUTVA
(1)

Unless otherwise mentioned, assume that the observations are independent and identically distributed (*iid*) across i, and often omit the subscript i in the variables. The *iid* assumption—particularly the independent part—may not be as innocuous as it looks at the first glance. For instance, in the example of the effects of a vaccine against a contagious disease, one person's improved immunity to the disease reduces the other persons' chance of contracting the disease. Some people's improved lifetime earnings due to college education may have positive effects on other people's lifetime earnings. That is, the iid assumption does not allow for 'externality' of the treatment, and in this sense, the iid assumption restricts our treatment effect analysis to be microscopic or of 'partial equilibrium' in nature.

The effects of a large scale treatment which has far reaching consequences does not fit our partial equilibrium framework. For example, large scale expensive job-training may have to be funded by a tax that may lead to a reduced demand for workers, which would then in turn weaken the job-training effect. Findings from a small scale job-training study where the funding aspect could be ignored (thus, 'partial equilibrium') would not apply to a large scale job-training where every aspect of the treatment would have to be considered (i.e., 'general equilibrium'). In the former, untreated people would not be affected by the treatment. For them, their untreated state with the treatment given to other people would be the same as their untreated state without the existence of the treatment. In the latter, the untreated people would be affected indirectly by the treatment (either by paying the tax or by the reduced demand for workers). For them, their untreated state when the treatment is present would not be the same as their untreated state in the absence of the treatment. As this example illustrates, partial equilibrium analysis may exaggerate the general equilibrium treatment effect which takes into account all the consequences if there is a negative externality. However, considering all the consequences would be too ambitious and would require far more assumptions and models than is necessary in partial equilibrium analysis. The gain in general equilibrium analysis could be negated by false assumptions or misspecified models. In this book, therefore, we will stick to microscopic partial-equilibrium type analysis.

This chapter is an introduction to treatment effects analysis. Parts of this chapter we owe to Rubin (1974), Holland (1986), Pearl (2000), Rosenbaum (2002), and other treatment effect literature, although it is often hard to point out exactly which papers, as the origin of the treatment effect idea is itself unclear. Before proceeding further, some explanation of notations are necessary.

Often $E(y|x = x_o)$ will be denoted simply as $E(y|x_o)$, or as $E(y|x)$ if we have no particular value x_o in mind. 'Indicator function' $1[A]$ takes 1 if A holds (or occurs) and 0 otherwise, which may be written also as $1[\omega \in A]$ or $1_A(\omega)$ where ω denotes a generic element of the sample space in use. Convergence in law is denoted with "$\rightsquigarrow$". The variance and standard deviation of ε are denoted as $V(\varepsilon)$ and $SD(\varepsilon)$. The covariance and correlation between x and ε are denoted as $COV(x, \varepsilon)$ and $COR(x, \varepsilon)$. The triple line "$\equiv$" is used for definitional equality. Define

$$y_j \amalg d|x \colon y_j \text{ is independent of } d \text{ given } x;$$

$$y_j \perp d|x \colon y_j \text{ is uncorrelated with } d \text{ given } x.$$

The single vertical line in $\perp$ is used to mean 'orthogonality', whereas two vertical lines are used in $\amalg$, for independence is stronger than zero correlation; the notation $y_j \amalg d|x$ is attributed to Dawid (1979). Dropping the conditioning part "$\cdot|x$" will be used for the unconditional independence of y_j and d and for the zero correlation of y_j and d, respectively. In the literature, sometimes $\perp$ is used for independence. Density or probability of a random vector z will be denoted typically as $f(z)/P(z)$ or as $f_z(\cdot)/P_z(\cdot)$, and its conditional version given x as $f(z|x)/P(z|x)$ or as $f_{z|x}(\cdot)/P_{z|x}(\cdot)$. Sometimes, the f-notations will also be used for probabilities.

2.2 Various treatment effects and no effects

2.2.1 Various effects

The *individual treatment effect* (of d_i on y_i) is defined as

$$y_{1i} - y_{0i},$$

which is, however, not identified. If there were two identical individuals, we might assign them to treatment 0 and 1, respectively, to get $y_{10} - y_{0i}$, but this is impossible. The closest thing would be monozygotic (identical) twins who share the same genes and are likely to grow up in similar environments. Even in this case, however, their environments in their adult lives could be quite different. The study of twins is popular in social sciences, and some examples will appear later where the inter-twin difference is used for $y_{1i} - y_{0i}$.

Giving upon observing both y_{1i} and y_{0i}, $i = 1, \ldots, N$, one may desire to know only the joint distribution for (y_0, y_1), which still is a quite difficult task (the appendix explores some limited possibilities though). A less ambitious goal would be to know the distribution of the scalar $y_1 - y_0$, but even this is hard. We could look for some aspects of $y_1 - y_0$ distribution, and the most popular choice is the mean effect $E(y_1 - y_0)$. There are other effects, however, such as the $Med(y_1 - y_0)$ or more generally the $Q_\alpha(y_1 - y_0)$, where Med and Q_α denote median and αth quantile, respectively.

Instead of differences, we may use ratios:

$$E(y_1 - y_0)/E(y_0) = \frac{E(y_1)}{E(y_0)} - 1, \quad \text{proportional effect relative to } E(y_0);$$

$$E\{(y_1 - y_0)/y_0\} = E\left(\frac{y_1}{y_0} - 1\right), \quad \text{if } y_0 \text{ does not take } 0.$$

Replacing $E(\cdot)$ with Q_α yields

$$\frac{Q_\alpha(y_1)}{Q_\alpha(y_0)} - 1 \quad \text{and} \quad Q_\alpha\left(\frac{y_1}{y_0} - 1\right).$$

Despite many treatment effects, in practice, the mean effect is the most popular. The popularity of the mean effect is owing to the important equation

$$E(y_1 - y_0) = E(y_1) - E(y_0) :$$

the mean of the difference $y_1 - y_0$ can be found from the two marginal means of the T and C groups. This is thanks to the linearity of $E(\cdot)$, which does not hold in general for other location measures of the $y_1 - y_0$ distribution; e.g., $Q_\alpha(y_1 - y_0) \neq Q_\alpha(y_1) - Q_\alpha(y_0)$ in general.

To appreciate the difference between $Q_\alpha(y_1 - y_0)$ and $Q_\alpha(y_1) - Q_\alpha(y_0)$, consider $Q_{0.5}(\cdot) = Med(\cdot)$ for an income policy:

$$Med(y_1 - y_0) > 0 \quad \text{where at least 50\% of the population} \\ \text{have } y_1 - y_0 > 0;$$

$$Med(y_1) - Med(y_0) > 0 \quad \text{where the median person's income increases.}$$

For instance, imagine five people whose y_0's are rising. With $d = 1$, their income changes such that the ordering of y_1's is the same as that of y_0's and everybody but the median person loses by one unit, while the median person gains by four units:

person	1	2	3	4	5
$y_0 \longrightarrow y_1$	$\longleftarrow$	$\longleftarrow$	$\longrightarrow\longrightarrow\longrightarrow\longrightarrow$	$\longleftarrow$	$\longleftarrow$
$\Delta y = y_1 - y_0$	-1	-1	4	-1	-1

In this case, $Med(y_1 - y_0) = -1$ but $Med(y_1) - Med(y_0) = 4$. Due to this kind of difficulty, we will focus on $E(y_1 - y_0)$ and its variations among many location measures of the $y_1 - y_0$ distribution.

A generalization (or a specialization, depending on how one sees it) of the marginal mean effect $E(y_1 - y_0)$ is a $E(y_1 - y_0 | x = x_o)$ where $x = x_o$ denotes a subpopulation characterized by the observed variables x taking x_o (e.g., male, aged 30, college-educated, married, etc). The conditional mean effect shows that the treatment effect can be heterogenous depending on x, which is also said to be 'treatment interacting with x'. It is also possible that the treatment effect is heterogenous depending on the unobservable ε.

For the x-heterogenous effects, we may present all the effects as a function x. Alternatively, we may summarize the multiple heterogenous effects with some summary measures. The natural thing to look at would be a weighted average $\int E(y_1 - y_0 | x) w(x) dx$ of $E(y_1 - y_0 | x)$ with weights $w(x)$ being the population density of x. If there is a reason to believe that a certain subpopulation is more important than the others, then we could assign a higher weight to it. That is, there could be many versions of the marginal mean effect depending on the weighting function. We could also use $E(y_1 - y_0 | x = E(x))$ instead of the integral. For ε-heterogenous effects $E(y_1 - y_0 | \varepsilon)$, since ε is unobserved, ε has to be either integrated out or replaced with a known number. Heterogenous effects will appear from time to time, but unless otherwise mentioned, we will focus on constant effects.

2.2.2 Three no-effect concepts

Having observed many effects, we could ask what it means to have no treatment effect, since, for instance, we have seen that it is possible to have a zero mean effect but a non-zero median effect. The *strongest version of no effect is* $y_{1i} = y_{0i} \ \forall i$, which is analytically convenient and is often used in the literature. For a 'weighty' treatment (e.g., college education), it is hard to imagine the response variable (e.g., lifetime earnings) being exactly the same for all i with or without the treatment. The weakest version of no effect, at least in the effects we are considering, is a zero location measure, such as $E(y_1 - y_0) = 0$ or $Med(y_1 - y_0) = 0$ where y_1 and y_0 can differ considerably, despite zero mean/median of $y_1 - y_0$.

An appealing no treatment-effect concept is where y_1 and y_0 are *exchangeable*:

$$P(y_0 \leq t_0, y_1 \leq t_1) = P(y_1 \leq t_0, y_0 \leq t_1), \qquad \forall t_0, t_1,$$

which allows for relation between y_0 and y_1 but *implies the same marginal distribution*. For instance, if y_0 and y_1 are jointly normal with the same mean, then y_0 and y_1 are exchangeable. Another example is y_0 and y_1 being iid. Since $y_0 = y_1$ implies exchangeability, exchangeability is weaker than $y_0 = y_1$. Because exchangeability implies the symmetry of $y_1 - y_0$, exchangeability is stronger than the zero mean/median of $y_1 - y_0$. In short, the implication arrows of the three no-effect concepts are

$$y_0 = y_1 \implies y_0 \text{ and } y_1 \text{ exchangeable} \implies \text{zero mean/median of } y_1 - y_0.$$

Since the relation between y_0 and y_1 can never be identified, in practice, we examine the main implication of exchangeability that y_0 *and* y_1 *follow the same distribution*: $F_1 = F_0$ where F_j denotes the marginal distribution (function) for y_j ('Distribution' is a probability measure whereas 'distribution function' is a real function, but we'll often use the same notation for both). With $F_1 = F_0$ meaning no effect, to define a positive effect, we consider the *stochastic dominance* of F_1 over F_0:

$$F_1(t) \leq F_0(t) \qquad \forall t \quad \text{(with inequality holding for some } t\text{)}.$$

Here, y_1 tends to be greater than y_0, meaning a positive treatment effect.

In some cases, only the marginal distributions of y_0 and y_1 matter. Suppose that $U(\cdot)$ is an income utility function and F_j is the income distribution under treatment j. A social planner could prefer policy 1 to 0 if, under policy 1, the mean utility is greater:

$$\int_{-\infty}^{\infty} U(y)dF_0(y) \leq \int_{-\infty}^{\infty} U(y)dF_1(y) \iff E\{U(y_0)\} \leq E\{U(y_1)\}.$$

Here, the difference $y_1 - y_0$ is not a concern, nor the joint distribution of (y_0, y_1). Instead, only the two marginal distributions matter.

So long as we focus on the mean effect, then $E(y_1 - y_0) = 0$ is the appropriate no-effect concept. But, there will be cases where a stronger version, $y_0 = y_1$ or $F_1 = F_0$, is adopted.

2.2.3   Further remarks

The effects of a drug on health can be multidimensional given the nature of health. For instance, the benefit of a drug could be a lower cholesterol level, lower blood pressure, lower blood sugar level, etc ..., while the cost of the drug could be its bad side-effects. In another example, the benefits of a job training could be measured by the length of time it took to get a job or by the post-training wage, while the cost could be the actual training cost and the opportunity cost of taking the training. Taking $E(y_1 - y_0)$ as the treatment effect is different from the traditional cost-benefit analysis which tries to account for all benefits and costs associated with the treatment. In $E(y_1 - y_0)$, the goal is much narrower, examining only one outcome measure instead of multiple outcomes. The cost side is also often ignored. If all benefits and costs could be converted into the same monetary unit, however, and if y is the net benefit (gross benefit minus cost), then the treatment effect analysis would be the same as the cost-benefit analysis.

When all benefits and costs cannot be converted into a single unit, we face *multiple response variables*. Vectors y_1 and y_0 may not be ordered, because a component of y_1 may be greater than the corresponding component in y_0, whereas another component of y_1 may be smaller than the corresponding component of y_0. Also, if treatments are more than binary, we will have *multiple treatments*.

When we talk about the distribution of $y_1 - y_0$ and write $E(y_1 - y_0)$, there are two different views. Suppose we have a population of interest consisting of N^o people, each with $(y_{0i}, y_{1i}, x_i', \varepsilon_i)$. In the first view, $(y_{0i}, y_{1i}, x_i', \varepsilon_i)$ is fixed for each i, thus $E(y_1 - y_0) = (1/N^o) \sum_{i=1}^{N^o} (y_{1i} - y_{0i})$. When a random sample of size N ($<N^o$) is drawn, there is a randomness because we do not know who will be sampled from the population. If d_i is assigned randomly for the sample, there is an additional randomness due to the treatment assignment, and only (y_i, x_i', d_i), $i = 1, \ldots, N$, are observed. If the data is a census ($N = N^o$) so that there is no sampling, then the only source of randomness is the treatment assignment. In the other view, all variables are inherently random, and even if the sample is equal to the population (i.e., the data set is a census) so that there is no sampling, each observation is still drawn from an underlying probability distribution. According to this view, there is always randomness outside sampling and treatment assignments, as the world is inherently random.

When the sample is not a census, the two views are not very different. However, if the sample is (taken as) the population of interest, the two views will have the following pros and cons. The advantage of the first view is constancy of the variables other than d_i, which is analytically convenient. The disadvantage is that what is learned from the data is applicable only to the data and not to other data in general, because the data at hand is the study population—the findings have only *internal validity*. In the second view, one is dealing with random variables, not constants, and what is learned from the data applies to the population distribution, and thus is applicable to other data drawn from the same distribution—the findings have *external validity* as well. We will tend to adopt the second view, but there may be cases where the first view is followed for its analytical convenience.

2.3   Group-mean difference and randomization

2.3.1   Group-mean difference and mean effect

Suppose that y_0 and y_1 are *mean-independent* of d:

$$E(y_j|d) = E(y_j) \iff E(y_j|d=1) = E(y_j|d=0), \qquad j = 0, 1.$$

Here, y_j and d appear asymmetrically, whereas they appear symmetrically in $y_j \perp d$:

$$COR(y_j, d) = 0 \iff E(y_j d) = E(y_j)E(d).$$

As shown in Subsection 2.7.2, if $0 < P(d=1) < 1$, then

$$E(y_j|d) = E(y_j) \iff E(y_j d) = E(y_j)E(d);$$

otherwise, the former implies the latter, but the converse does not necessarily hold. Because we will always assume $0 < P(d=1) < 1$, $E(y_j|d) = E(y_j)$ and $y_j \perp d$ will be used interchangeably in this book. When the mean independence holds, d is sometimes said to be 'ignorable' (ignorability is also used with II replacing $\perp$).

Under the mean independence, the mean treatment effect is identified with the group-mean difference:

$$E(y|d=1) - E(y|d=0) = E(y_1|d=1) - E(y_0|d=0)$$
$$= E(y_1) - E(y_0) = E(y_1 - y_0).$$

The conditions $y_j \perp d$, $j = 0, 1$, hold for randomized experimental data. Other than for randomized experiments, the condition may hold if d is forced on the subjects by a law or regulation for reasons unrelated to y_0 and y_1 ('quasi experiments'), or by nature such as weather and geography ('natural experiments'). The two expressions, quasi experiment and natural experiment, are often used interchangeably in the literature, but we will use them differently.

If we want to know the conditional effect $E(y_1 - y_0|x)$, then we need

$$\text{'overlapping } x\text{': } 0 < P(d=1|x) < 1,$$

and

$$x\text{-conditional mean independence of } d: y_j \perp d|x, \qquad j = 0, 1;$$

the former means that there are subjects sharing the same x across the T and C groups. Under these,

$$E(y|d=1,x) - E(y|d=0,x) = E(y_1|d=1,x) - E(y_0|d=0,x)$$
$$= E(y_1|x) - E(y_0|x) = E(y_1 - y_0|x):$$

the conditional effect is identified with the conditional group mean difference. The conditional mean independence holds for randomized data or for randomized data on the subpopulation x. Once $E(y_1 - y_0|x)$ is identified, we can get a marginal effect $\int E(y_1 - y_0|x)w(x)dx$ for a weighting function $w(x)$. If the conditional independence holds only for $x \in X_c$ where X_c is a subset of the x-range, then the identified marginal effect is

$$\int_{X_c} E(y_1 - y_0|x)w(x)dx \Big/ \int_{X_c} w(x)dx.$$

Rosenbaum and Rubin (1983a) define 'strong ignorability' as

$$(y_0, y_1) \amalg d|x, \quad 0 < P(d = 1|x) < 1 \qquad \forall x,$$

reserving 'ignorability' for something else. We will, however, ignore the distinction and call all of

$$y_j \perp d, \quad y_j \amalg d, \quad y_j \perp d|x, \quad y_j \amalg d|x, \quad (y_0, y_1) \amalg d, \quad (y_0, y_1) \amalg d|x$$

ignorability of d; the difference between $(y_0 \amalg d, y_1 \amalg d)$ and $(y_0, y_1) \amalg d$ will be examined in Subsection 2.7.3. Which one is being used should be clear from the context. If in doubt, take $(y_0, y_1) \amalg d$. As we assume $0 < P(d = 1) < 1$ always, we will assume $0 < P(d = 1|x) < 1 \ \forall x$ as well. If the latter holds only for $x \in X_c$, we just have to truncate x to redefine the range of x as X_c.

A caution is that $COR(y_j, d) = 0$, $j = 0, 1$ do not imply $COR(y, d) = 0$, because

$$E(dy) = E\{d(dy_1 + (1 - d)y_0)\} = E(dy_1) = E(d)E(y_1) \neq E(d)E(y);$$

$E(y)$ contains both $E(y_0)$ and $E(y_1)$. The reverse does not hold either, because $COR(y, d) = 0$ is

$$\begin{aligned}
E(yd) &= E(y)E(d) \\
&\Longleftrightarrow E(y_1 d) = E(y)E(d) \\
&\Longleftrightarrow E(y_1|d = 1) = E(y) \text{ after dividing both sides by } E(d) = P(d=1) > 0 \\
&\Longleftrightarrow E(y_1|d = 1) = E(y_1|d = 1)P(d = 1) + E(y_0|d = 0)P(d = 0) \\
&\Longleftrightarrow E(y_1|d = 1)P(d = 0) = E(y_0|d = 0)P(d = 0) \\
&\Longleftrightarrow E(y_1|d = 1) = E(y_0|d = 0) \quad \text{for } P(d = 0) > 0.
\end{aligned}$$

Hence,

$$COR(y, d) = 0 \Longleftrightarrow E(y_1|d = 1) - E(y_0|d = 0) = 0,$$

which is nothing but zero group mean difference; this equation is, however, mute on whether $E(y_j|d=1) = E(y_j)$ or not. In view of the last display,

$$COR(y,d) = 0 \iff zero\ mean\ effect \qquad \text{under } y_j \perp d.$$

All derivations still hold with x conditioned on.

2.3.2   Consequences of randomization

We mentioned that randomization assures $y_j \perp d$. In fact, randomization does more than that. In this subsection, we take a closer look at randomization.

Suppose there are two regions R_1 and R_0 in a country, and R_1 has standardized tests ($d=1$) while R_0 does not ($d=0$). We may try to estimate the effect of standardized tests on academic achievements using R_1 and R_0 as the T and C groups, respectively. The condition $COR(y_j,d) = 0$ can fail, however, if there is a third variable that varies across the two groups and is linked to y_j and d. For instance, suppose that the true effect of the standardized tests is zero but that R_1 has a higher average income than R_0, that students with higher income parents receive more education outside school, and that more education causes higher academic achievements. It is then the R_1's higher income (and thus the higher extra education), not the tests, that results in the higher academic achievements in R_1 than in R_0. The two regions are heterogenous in terms of income before the treatment is administered, which leads to a false inference. We are comparing incomparable regions. Now consider a random experiment. Had all students from both regions been put together and then randomly assigned to the T and C groups, then the income level would have been about the same across the two groups. As with the income level, *randomization balances all variables other than d and y, observed (x) or unobserved (ε), across the two groups* in the sense that the probability distribution of (x,ε) is the same across the two groups.

In a study of a treatment on hypertension, had the treatment been self-selected by the subjects, we might have seen a higher average age and education in the T group, as the older or more educated people may be more likely to seek the treatment for hypertension. Old age worsens hypertension, but education can improve it, as educated people may have a healthier life style. In this case, the T group may show a better result simply because of the higher education, even when the treatment is ineffective. These are examples of pitfalls in non-experimental data. From now on, 'experimental data' or 'randomized data' will always mean 'randomized experimental data', where both x and ε are balanced across the two groups. Because one might get the impression that randomization is a panacea, we will discuss some of the problems of randomized studies next.

For randomization to balance x and ε, a sufficient number of subjects are needed so that a law of large numbers (LLN) can work for both groups. Here we present part of a table in Rosner (1995, p. 149) on a randomized experiment for a hypertension treatment:

	N	age (SD)	education (SD)	black men (%)	black women (%)
Treatment	2365	71.6 (6.7)	11.7 (3.5)	4.9	8.9
Control	2371	71.5 (6.7)	11.7 (3.4)	4.3	9.7

Age and education in both groups match very closely whereas black men and women do not, because there were not many blacks in the samples.

If a randomization is to take place, some people may not participate in the study, for they do not like being randomized out: 'randomization (-out) problem'. If those non-participants are systematically different from the participants, then the findings from the study may not be applicable to the non-participants. For example, if relatively highly educated people are the non-participants, then the study results may be applicable only to less educated people, i.e., the participants.

Even if there is no systematic difference between the participants and non-participants, subjects in the C group may not like having been denied the treatment, and may consequently get the treatment or a similar one on their own from somewhere else: 'substitution (or noncompliance) problem'. See Heckman *et al.* (2000) for evidence. Also, treated subjects may behave abnormally (i.e., more eagerly) knowing that they are in a 'fishbowl', which can lead to a positive effect, although the true effect is zero under the normal circumstances. The effect in this case is sometimes called a 'Hawthorne effect'. These problems, however, do not occur if the subjects are 'blinded' (i.e., they do not know which treatment they are receiving). In medical science, blinding can be done with a placebo, which, however, is not available in social sciences (think of a placebo job training teaching useless knowledge!). Even in medical science, if the treatment is perceived as harmful (e.g., smoking or exposure to radio-active material), then it is morally wrong to conduct a randomized experiment. The point is that randomization has problems of its own, and even if the problems are minor, randomization may be infeasible in some cases.

2.3.3 Checking out covariate balance

It is always a good idea to check whether the covariates are balanced across the T and C groups. Even if randomization took place, it may not have been done correctly. Even if the data is observational, d may be close to having been randomized with little relation to the other variables. If the observed x is not balanced across the two groups, imbalance in the unobservable ε would be suspect as well. We examine two simple ways to gauge 'the degree of randomness' of the treatment assignment, where one compares the mean and SD of x across the two groups, and the other determines if d is explained by any observed variables.

Eberwien *et al.* (1997) assess the effects of classroom training on the employment histories of disadvantaged women in a randomized data ($N = 2600$). Part of their Table 1 for mean (SD) is

	age	schooling	black	never married	never worked for pay
Treatment	31.7 (0.2)	11.3 (0.04)	0.33 (0.01)	0.34 (0.01)	0.20 (0.01)
Control	31.6 (0.3)	11.3 (0.1)	0.33 (0.02)	0.39 (0.02)	0.21 (0.02)

Of course, instead of the mean and SD, we can look at other distributional aspects in detail. The table shows well balanced covariates, supporting randomization. If desired, one can test for whether the group averages are different or not for each covariate.

Krueger and Whitmore (2001) estimate the effect of class size in early grades on college tests using data Project Star ($N = 11600$) in Tennessee. The 79 elementary schools in the data were not randomly selected in Tennessee: schools meeting some criteria participated voluntarily (self-selection), and a state mandate resulted in a higher proportion of inner-city schools than the state average. Randomization, however, took place within each school when the students were assigned to the T group (small-size class) and the C group (regular-size class). Part of their Table 1 is

	% minority	% black	% poor	expenditure
Data	33.1	31.7	24.4	$3,423
Tennessee	23.5	22.6	20.7	$3,425
USA	31.0	16.1	18.0	$4,477

where 'expenditure' is the average current expenditure per student. This clearly shows that the sample is not representative of the population (Tennessee or the USA): the sample is close to Tennessee only in expenditure, and to the USA only in the % minority.

Krueger and Whitmore (2001) also present a table to show that the treatment assignment within each school was indeed randomized. They did LSE of d on some covariates x using the 'linear probability model':

$$d_i = x_i'\beta + \varepsilon_i, \qquad E(d|x) = x'\beta \implies V(\varepsilon|x) = x'\beta(1 - x'\beta);$$

after the initial LSE b_N was obtained, Generalized LSE (GLS) was done with $x'b_N(1 - x'b_N)$ for the weighting function. As is well known, the linear probability model has the shortcoming that $x'\beta$ for $E(d|x)$ may go out of the bound $[0, 1]$. Part of their Table 2 is ($R^2 = 0.08$)

Regressors	1	white/Asian	female	free lunch
estimate (SD)	0.278 (0.014)	−0.011 (0.016)	0.000 (0.008)	−0.016 (0.010)

where 'free lunch' is 1 if the student ever received free or reduced-price lunch during the kindergarten to grade 3; the difference across schools as well as the grade in which the student joined the experiment were controlled for with dummy variables. Despite the substantial differences in the two ethnic variables in their Table 1, white/Asian cannot explain d in their Table 2 due to the randomization within each school. The variables 'female' and 'free lunch' are also insignificant.

2.4 Overt bias, hidden (covert) bias, and selection problems

2.4.1 Overt and hidden biases

No two variables in the world work in isolation. In unraveling the treatment effect of d_i on y_i, one has to worry about the other variables x_i and ε_i affecting y_i and d_i. In cross-section context, if x_i or ε_i differs across i, then it is not clear to what extent the differences in y_i across i are due to the differences in d_i across i. In a time-series context, for a given individual, if x_i or ε_i changes over time as d_i does, again it is difficult to see to what extent the resulting change in y_i over time is due to the change in d_i over time. Ideally, if x_i and ε_i are the same for all i, and if both do not change over time while the causal mechanism is operating, it will be easy to identify the treatment effect. This, however, will hardly ever be the case, and how to control (or allow) for x_i and ε_i that are heterogenous across i or variant over time, is the main task in treatment effect analysis with observational data.

If the T group differs from the C group in x, then the difference in x, not in d, can be the real cause for $E(y|d = 1) \neq E(y|d = 0)$; more generally, $E(y|d = 1) \neq E(y|d = 0)$ can be due to differences in both d and x; whenever the difference in x contributes to $E(y|d = 1) \neq E(y|d = 0)$, we incur an *overt bias*. Analogously, if the T group differs from the C group in ε, then the difference in ε may contribute to $E(y|d = 1) \neq E(y|d = 0)$; in this case, we incur a *hidden (covert) bias*—terminologies taken from Rosenbaum (2002). In the two biases, *overt bias can be removed by controlling for x* (that is, by comparing the treated and untreated subjects with the same x), but hidden bias is harder to deal with.

It will be difficult to abstract from time-dimension when it comes to causality of any sort. Unless we can examine panel data where the same individuals are observed more than once, we will stick to cross-section type data, assuming that a variable is observed only once over time. Although (d, x', y) may be observed only once, they are in fact observed at different times. A treatment should precede the response, although we can think of exceptions, such as gravity, for simultaneous causality (simultaneous causality occurs also due to temporal aggregation: d and y affect each other sequentially over time, but when they are aggregated, they appear to affect each other simultaneously). With the temporal order given, the distinction between 'pre-treatment' and 'post-treatment' variables is important in controlling for x: which part of x and ε were realized before or after the treatment. In general, we control for observed pre-treatment variables, not post-treatment variables, to avoid overt biases; but there are exceptions. For pre-treatment variables, it is neither necessary nor possible to control for all of them. Deciding which variables to control for is not always a straightforward business.

As will be discussed in detail shortly, often we say that there is an overt bias if

$$E(y_j|d) \neq E(y_j) \quad \text{but} \quad E(y_j|d, x) = E(y_j|x).$$

In this case, we can get $E(y_0)$ and $E(y_1)$ for $E(y_1 - y_0)$ in two stages with

$$\int E(y|d = j, x) F_x(dx) = \int E(y_j|d = j, x) F_x(dx) = \int E(y_j|x) F_x(dx) = E(y_j):$$

first the x-conditioned mean is obtained and then x is integrated out using the population distribution F_x of x. If $F_{x|d=j}$ is used instead of F_x, then we get $E(y_j|d = j)$ from the integration.

Pearl (2000) shows graphical approaches to causality, which is in essence equivalent to counter-factual causality. We will also use simple graphs as visual aids. In the graphical approaches, one important way to find treatment effects is called 'back-door adjustment' (Pearl (2000, pp. 79–80)). This is nothing but the last display with the back-door referring to x. Another important way to find treatment effects in the graphical approaches, called 'front-door adjustment', will appear in Chapter 7.

2.4.2   Selection on observables and unobservables

In observational data, treatment is self-selected by the subjects, which can result in selection problems: 'selection-on-observables' and 'selection-on-unobservables'.

For y_j with density or probability f,

$$f(y_j|d) \neq f(y_j) \quad \text{but} \quad f(y_j|d, x) = f(y_j|x) \quad \textit{for the observables } x$$

is called *selection-on-observables*. The first part shows a selection problem (i.e., overt bias), but the second part shows that the selection problem is removed by controlling for x. For selection-on-observables to hold, d should be determined

- by the observed variables x,
- and possibly by some unobserved variables independent of y_j given x.

Hence, d becomes irrelevant for y_j once x is conditioned on (i.e., $y_j \amalg d|x$). An example where d is completely determined by x will appear in 'regression-discontinuity design' in Chapter 3; in most cases, however, d would be determined by x and some unobserved variables.

If

$$f(y_j|d, x) \neq f(y_j|x) \quad for \ the \ observables \ x,$$

but

$$f(y_j|d, x, \varepsilon) = f(y_j|x, \varepsilon) \quad for \ some \ unobservables \ \varepsilon,$$

then we have *selection-on-unobservables*. The first part shows a selection problem (i.e., hidden bias) despite controlling for x, and the second part states that the selection problem would disappear had ε been controlled for. For selection-on-unobservables to hold, d should be determined

- possibly by the observed variables x,
- by the unobserved variables ε related to y_j given x,
- and possibly by some unobserved variables independent of y_j given x and ε.

Hence, d becomes irrelevant for y_j only if both x and ε were conditioned on (i.e., $y_j \amalg d|(x, \varepsilon)$).

Since we focus on mean treatment effect, we will use the terms selection-on-observables and -unobservables mostly as

selection-on-observables: $E(y_j|d) \neq E(y_j)$ but $E(y_j|d, x) = E(y_j|x)$;

selection-on-unobservables: $E(y_j|d, x) \neq E(y_j|x)$ but $E(y_j|d, x, \varepsilon) = E(y_j|x, \varepsilon)$.

Defined this way, selection on observables is nothing but $y_j \perp d|x$.

Recall the example of college-education effect on lifetime earnings, and imagine a population of individuals characterized by $(d_i, x_i', y_{0i}, y_{1i})$ where $d_i = 1$ if person i chooses to take college education and 0 otherwise. Differently from a treatment that is randomly assigned in an experiment, d_i is a trait of individual i; e.g., people with $d_i = 1$ may be smarter or more disciplined. Thus, d_i is likely to be related to (y_{0i}, y_{1i}); e.g., $COR(y_1, d) > COR(y_0, d) > 0$. An often-used model for the dependence of d on (y_0, y_1) is $d_i = 1[y_{1i} > y_{0i}]$: subject i chooses treatment 1 if the gain $y_{1i} - y_{0i}$ is positive. In this case, selection-on-unobservables is likely and thus

$$E(y|d = 1, x) - E(y|d = 0, x) = E(y_1|d = 1, x) - E(y_0|d = 0, x)$$
$$= E(y_1|y_1 > y_0, x) - E(y_0|y_1 \leq y_0, x)$$
$$\neq E(y_1|x) - E(y_0|x) \text{ in general:}$$

the conditional group mean difference does not identify the desired conditional mean effect. Since the conditioning on $y_1 > y_0$ and $y_1 \leq y_0$ increases both terms, it is not clear whether the group mean difference is greater or smaller than $E(y_1 - y_0|x)$. While $E(y_1 - y_0|x)$ is the treatment intervention effect, $E(y|d = 1, x) - E(y|d = 0, x)$ is the treatment self-selection effect.

Regarding d as an individual characteristic, we can think of the *mean treatment effect on the treated*:

$$E(y_1 - y_0|d = 1),$$

much as we can think of the mean treatment effect for 'the disciplined', for instance. To identify $E(y_1 - y_0|d = 1)$, selection-on-observables for *only* y_0 is sufficient, because

$$E(y|d = 1, x) - E(y|d = 0, x) = E(y_1|d = 1, x) - E(y_0|d = 0, x)$$
$$= E(y_1|d = 1, x) - E(y_0|d = 1, x) = E(y_1 - y_0|d = 1, x)$$
$$\implies \int \{E(y|d = 1, x) - E(y|d = 0, x)\} F_{x|d=1}(dx) = E(y_1 - y_0|d = 1).$$

The fact that $E(y_1 - y_0|d = 1)$ requires selection-on-observables only for y_0, not for both y_0 and y_1, is a non-trivial advantage in view of the case $d = 1[y_1 - y_0 > 0]$, because d here depends on the increment $y_1 - y_0$ that can be independent of the baseline response y_0 (given x).

Analogously to $E(y_1 - y_0|d = 1)$, we define the mean treatment effect on the untreated (or 'the undisciplined') as

$$E(y_1 - y_0|d = 0),$$

for which selection-on-observables for *only* y_1 is sufficient. It goes without saying that both effects on the treated and untreated can be further conditioned on x.

For the example of job-training on wage, we may be more interested in $E(y_1 - y_0|d = 1)$ than in $E(y_1 - y_0)$, because most people other than the unemployed would not need job training; the former is for those who select to take the job training while the latter is for the public in general. In contrast, for the effects of exercise on blood pressure, we would be interested in $E(y_1 - y_0)$, for exercise and blood pressure are concerns for almost everybody, not just for people who exercise.

2.4.3 Linear models and biases

We mentioned above that, in general, the group mean difference is not the desired treatment effect if $E(y_j|d) \neq E(y_j)$. To see the problem better, suppose each potential response is generated by

$$y_{ji} = \alpha_j + x_i'\beta_j + u_{ji}, \quad j = 0, 1, \qquad E(u_{ji}) = 0, \qquad E(u_{ji}|x_i) = 0,$$

where x_i does not include the usual constant 1 (this is to emphasize the role of intercept here; otherwise, we typically use the same notation x_i that includes 1) and $d_i = 1[y_{1i} > y_{0i}]$. Then

$$d_i = 1[\alpha_1 - \alpha_0 + x_i'(\beta_1 - \beta_0) + \varepsilon_i > 0], \qquad \varepsilon_i \equiv u_{1i} - u_{0i}.$$

Without loss of generality, suppose all x_i and $\beta_1 - \beta_0$ are positive. Then $d_i = 1$ means either x_i or ε_i taking a big positive value, relative to the case $d_i = 0$: the T group differs from the C group in the observed covariates x_i or in the unobserved variable ε_i.

The individual effect is

$$y_{1i} - y_{0i} = \alpha_1 - \alpha_0 + x_i'(\beta_1 - \beta_0) + u_{1i} - u_{0i},$$

that is not a constant but varies across i. Whereas the desired mean treatment effect is

$$E(y_{1i} - y_{0i}) = \alpha_1 - \alpha_0 + E(x_i)'(\beta_1 - \beta_0) + E(u_{1i} - u_{0i}) = \alpha_1 - \alpha_0 + E(x_i')(\beta_1 - \beta_0),$$

the group mean difference can be written as

$$E(y|d=1) - E(y|d=0) = \alpha_1 - \alpha_0 + E(x'|d=1)\beta_1 - E(x'|d=0)\beta_0$$
$$+ E(u_1|d=1) - E(u_0|d=0)$$
$$= \alpha_1 - \alpha_0 + E(x')(\beta_1 - \beta_0) \quad \text{(desired effect)}$$
$$+ \{E(x|d=1) - E(x)\}'\beta_1 - \{E(x|d=0) - E(x)\}'\beta_0 \quad \text{(overt bias)}$$
$$+ E(u_1|d=1) - E(u_0|d=0) \quad \text{(hidden bias)}.$$

If the observed variables are balanced in the sense that $E(x|d) = E(x)$, then the overt bias disappears. If the unobserved are balanced in the sense that $E(u_1|d=1) = E(u_0|d=0)$, then the hidden bias disappears. Note that, for the hidden bias to be zero, $E(u_j|d=j) = 0$, $j = 0,1$, is sufficient but not necessary, because we need only

$$E(u_1|d=1) = E(u_0|d=0).$$

If we use the conditional group mean difference, then the overt bias is removed:

$$E(y|d = 1, x) - E(y|d = 0, x) = \alpha_1 - \alpha_0 + x'(\beta_1 - \beta_0) \quad \text{(desired effect)}$$
$$+ E(u_1|d = 1, x) - E(u_0|d = 0, x) \quad \text{(hidden bias)}.$$

The zero hidden bias condition is now

$$E(u_1|d = 1, x) = E(u_0|d = 0, x).$$

If the dimension of x is large, or if x takes too many different values, then estimating $E(y|d = 1, x)$ with the group mean is problematic, as only a few observations will fall in the subpopulation with x. One way to avoid the dimension problem in x is to use a parametric regression function. For instance, in the above linear model, we get

$$y_i = (1 - d_i)(\alpha_0 + x_i'\beta_0 + u_{0i}) + d_i(\alpha_1 + x_i'\beta_1 + u_{1i})$$
$$= \alpha_0 + (\alpha_1 - \alpha_0)d_i + x_i'\beta_0 + x_i'd_i(\beta_1 - \beta_0) + u_{0i} + (u_{1i} - u_{0i})d_i$$
$$= \gamma_1 + \gamma_d d_i + x_i'\gamma_x + x_i'd_i\gamma_{xd} + v_i, \quad \text{where}$$
$$\gamma_1 \equiv \alpha_0, \quad \gamma_d \equiv \alpha_1 - \alpha_0, \quad \gamma_x \equiv \beta_0, \quad \gamma_{xd} \equiv \beta_1 - \beta_0, \quad v_i \equiv u_{0i} + (u_{1i} - u_{0i})d_i.$$

The γ parameters can be estimated by the LSE of y_i on 1, d_i, x_i, and x_id_i under the assumption that v_i is uncorrelated with the regressors. The assumption includes

$$E(dv) = E[d\{du_1 + (1 - d)u_0\}] = E(du_1) = 0,$$

which may not be plausible. If this assumption cannot be made, but if there are enough instruments for d_i and x_id_i, then an instrumental variable estimator (IVE) may be applicable. Be aware, however, that both LSE and IVE run the risk of specification error when the linear models for the latent responses do not hold, whereas conditioning on x does not have this problem.

2.5   Estimation with group mean difference and LSE

2.5.1   Group-mean difference and LSE

If $y_j \perp d$, $j = 0, 1$, then the mean treatment effect is identified with the group mean difference $E(y|d = 1) - E(y|d = 0)$. This can be estimated consistently in two ways: sample group mean difference and LSE of y on $(1, d)$.

The sample group mean difference is

$$\frac{\sum_i d_i y_i}{\sum_i d_i} - \frac{\sum_i (1 - d_i)y_i}{\sum_i (1 - d_i)},$$

which is consistent for $E(y|d = 1) - E(y|d = 0)$ owing to a LLN; $\sum_i d_i$ is the number of subjects in the T group and $\sum_i (1 - d_i)$ is the number of subjects in the C group.

Define the sample size, sample mean and sample variance, respectively, as

$$\text{C group: } N_0, \ \bar{y}_0, \ s_0^2,$$
$$\text{T group: } N_1, \ \bar{y}_1, \ s_1^2.$$

It is well known that, as N_0 and N_1 tend to ∞,

$$\frac{(\bar{y}_1 - \bar{y}_0) - E(y_1 - y_0)}{(s_1^2/N_1 + s_0^2/N_0)^{1/2}} \rightsquigarrow N(0, 1).$$

If N_1 and N_0 are small, then under $y_j \sim N(\mu_j, \sigma^2)$, $j = 0, 1$ (note the same variance for both groups) and

$$s_p^2 \equiv \left(\frac{N_0 - 1}{N_0 + N_1 - 1} \right) s_0^2 + \left(\frac{N_1 - 1}{N_0 + N_1 - 1} \right) s_1^2,$$

it holds that

$$\frac{(\bar{y}_1 - \bar{y}_0) - E(y_1 - y_0)}{s_p(N_0^{-1} + N_1^{-1})^{1/2}} \quad \text{follows } t_{N_0 + N_1 - 2}.$$

For the small sample case, s_0^2 and s_1^2 should be computed with the denominator $N - 1$, not N.

As an example for the large sample case, the effect of working (d) on the number of visits to doctors per year (y) was estimated with a data set of $N = 8484$ for the year 1992 drawn from the Health and Retirement Study (University of Michigan). The following was obtained:

$$N_1 = 5884, \quad \bar{y}_1 = 2.975, \quad s_1 = 4.730, \quad N_0 = 2600, \quad \bar{y}_0 = 5.152, \quad s_0 = 8.001$$
$$\implies \frac{\bar{y}_1 - \bar{y}_0}{(s_1^2/N_1 + s_0^2/N_0)^{1/2}} = -12.92;$$

the hypothesis of no effect of working on doctor visits is easily rejected. Since, $\bar{y}_1 - \bar{y}_0 = -2.177$, as one starts working, the number of doctor visits changes by $\{(\bar{y}_1 - \bar{y}_0)/\bar{y}_0\}100 = (-2.177/5.152) \times 100 = -42\%$ on average. In this example, however, there are good reasons to suspect $E(y_j|d = 1) \neq E(y_j)$, $j = 0, 1$. For instance, health can influence both d and y_j: it is possible that the healthy work more and visit doctors less often than the unhealthy; health is the common factor driving both d and y_j. Then, the T and C groups differ in terms of health, and this difference, not d, may be the real cause for the difference in y. The treatment effect of d on y is confounded by a third variable health which is called a *confounder*.

Alternatively to the sample average difference, we can do LSE of y_i on 1 and d_i to estimate the treatment effect, because the slope parameter is the same as

$E(y_1 - y_0)$: with $\pi \equiv P(d = 1)$,

$$
\begin{aligned}
\frac{COV(y, d)}{V(d)} &= \frac{E(\{dy_1 + (1-d)y_0\}d) - E(\{dy_1 + (1-d)y_0\})\pi}{\pi(1-\pi)} \\
&= \frac{E(dy_1) - E(dy_1)\pi - E\{(1-d)y_0\}\pi}{\pi(1-\pi)} \\
&= \frac{E(dy_1)(1-\pi) - E\{(1-d)y_0\}\pi}{\pi(1-\pi)} \\
&= \frac{E(y_1|d=1) \cdot \pi(1-\pi) - E(y_0|d=0) \cdot \pi(1-\pi)}{\pi(1-\pi)} = E(y_1 - y_0).
\end{aligned}
$$

For the work effect on doctor visit example, the LSE result is: $R^2 = 0.028$, and

	1	d
estimate	5.152	−2.177
t-value	32.84	−12.92

The slope estimate and the t-value are the same as the mean difference and its t-value.

2.5.2   A job-training example

As another empirical example, we use female job-training data from the Department of Labor in South Korea, where the C group consists of the unemployed who chose to receive unemployment insurance benefit instead of a job-training. The women in the data became unemployed during the period January 1999 to the end of March 2000, and either took a job training to complete it or received unemployed insurance benefit instead. There are $N_1 = 973$ treated units and $N_0 = 9312$ control units. The response variable is ln(unemployment duration) where unemployment duration is the duration from the beginning of the job training (or of receiving unemployment insurance benefit) until the time the woman gets employed. There is a right-censoring problem with the duration in that some women remained unemployed when the study ended, which means that the recorded response in this case is not the actual duration but the censoring time. This censoring problem is, however, ignored here to simplify our presentation.

Although an unemployed woman can choose d to some extent, she has to meet some criteria to be eligible for unemployment-insurance benefit; for instance, paying for the insurance for at least half a year is required. Unemployment-insurance benefit does not last for more than six months in general, although there are exceptions depending on factors such as age and disability. Also, if she quits her job voluntarily, she is not eligible for unemployment-insurance benefit in principle. Due to these institutional constraints and the self-selection of d, the treatment and control groups differ in covariates: the T group is 7.4 years younger, worked 205 days less in the last workplace, and is more educated as the table below shows, where 'employment days at ex-firm' is the number of days the woman worked at her last workplace, and education has six completion levels (primary, middle, high, junior college, college, and graduate school).

	C group		T group	
Covariate mean and SD for job trainings				
	mean	SD	mean	SD
ln(unemployment days)	5.385	0.68	5.506	0.37
age in years	34.0	10.8	26.6	5.45
employment days at ex-firm	908	477	703	93.5
education level (1 to 6)	3.19	1.03	3.50	0.84

Ignoring the difference in x across the two groups for the moment, the group mean difference $\bar{y}_1 - \bar{y}_0$ is 0.121: the job training lengthens the unemployment duration by 12%. Using the large sample distribution result for $\bar{y}_1 - \bar{y}_0$, a 95% confidence interval for $E(y_1 - y_0)$ is

$$(0.094, 0.148).$$

$H_0: E(y_1 - y_0) = 0$ is easily rejected with the test statistic value 8.82. The LSE result is: $R^2 = 0.003$, $s = 0.659$, and

	1	d
estimate	5.385	0.121
t-value	762	8.82

The slope estimate and the t-value are the same as the group mean difference and its t-value.

The above table on the C and T groups indicates unbalanced covariates across the two groups. To check to what extent the covariates explain the treatment dummy, we did probit to obtain the following result where 'ed' stands for education:

	1	age	age^2/100	ex-firm	ed
estimate	0.611	-0.059	0.008	-0.069	-0.025
tv	1.673	-2.439	0.201	-13.549	-1.125

As the above table on the C and T groups indicates, age and ex-firm have significant negative effects on d in this table. Differently from the table, however, education effect here is negative but insignificant.

2.5.3   Linking counter-factuals to linear models

It is instructive to derive the linear model $y_i = \beta_0 + \beta_d d_i + u_i$ from $y_i = (1 - d_i)y_{0i} + d_i y_{1i}$. Observe

$$y_i = (1 - d_i)y_{0i} + d_i y_{1i} = y_{0i} + (y_{1i} - y_{0i}) \cdot d_i$$
$$= y_{0i} + \beta_i d_i, \quad where \ \beta_i \equiv y_{1i} - y_{0i};$$

β_i is nothing but the individual effect of d_i on y_i. Rewrite β_i and y_{0i} as

$$\beta_i = E(\beta_i) + \{\beta_i - E(\beta_i)\} = \beta_d + v_i, \quad where \ \beta_d \equiv E(\beta_i), \ \ v_i \equiv \beta_i - E(\beta_i),$$

$$y_{0i} = E(y_{0i}) + \{y_{0i} - E(y_{0i})\} = \beta_0 + \varepsilon_i, \quad where \ \beta_1 \equiv E(y_{0i}), \ \varepsilon_i \equiv y_{0i} - E(y_{0i}).$$

Then y_i can be written as a simple regression model

$$y_i = \beta_0 + \beta_d d_i + u_i, \quad where \ u_i \equiv \varepsilon_i + d_i v_i,$$

where β_0 is the intercept (the mean of the 'baseline' response), β_d is the slope (the mean treatment effect), and u_i is the error term consisting of two terms: the base line heterogeneity ε_i and the individual effect heterogeneity v_i (times d_i). Note that, in the simple regression model, the intercept may be better denoted as β_1 with the subscript referring to the 'regressor' 1, although we used β_0 as a reminder for $\beta_0 = E(y_0)$.

The LSE for the equation requires

$$E(du) = E(d\varepsilon) + E(dv) = 0.$$

The assumption $E(d\varepsilon) = 0$ that a treatment is uncorrelated with the baseline response error may not be so restrictive, but $E(dv) = 0$ is troublesome, because d is likely to depend on the gain $\beta_i = y_{1i} - y_{0i}$. The random (i.e., varying or heterogenous) effect with v_i poses a problem to the simple LSE approach.

Going one step further, we introduce covariates x_i and w_i into the model, which gives a multiple regression model. Suppose we have, instead of the above simple rewriting of β_i and y_{0i},

$$y_{0i} = x_i'\beta_{0x} + \varepsilon_i, \quad \beta_i = w_i'\beta_{dw} + v_i, \quad E(\varepsilon_i|x_i, w_i) = 0 \ \text{ and } \ E(v_i|x_i, w_i) = 0,$$

where w_i may overlap with x_i, β_{0x} and β_{dw} are unknown parameters, and both x_i and w_i include 1 as its first element. We have already specified a linear model for both y_{0i} and y_{1i} in Subsection 2.4.3. Here we are doing essentially the same thing, but this time for y_{0i} and $y_{1i} - y_{0i}$. The linear models yield

$$y_i = x_i'\beta_{0x} + (d_i w_i')\beta_{dw} + u_i, \qquad where \ u_i = \varepsilon_i + d_i v_i.$$

There are three types of regressors:

- First, those in only x_i (no interaction with d_i) in the y_i equation; since $\beta_i = y_{1i} - y_{0i}$, these regressors must appear both in y_{0i} and y_{1i} with the same coefficient, and are thus cancelled out in β_i.

- Second, those in only w_i (only interaction with d_i); these regressors appear in y_{1i}, but not in y_{0i}.

- Third, those in both x_i and w_i; these regressors must appear either only in y_{0i}, or in both y_{0i} and y_{1i} with different coefficients.

Four different cases for β_i can be thought of:

(i) *constant effect*: v_i and the slopes of β_{dw} are zero $\forall i$ ($\beta_i = \beta_d$),

(ii) varying effect with zero v_i $\forall i$: $\beta_i = w_i'\beta_{dw}$,

(iii) varying effect with independent v_i: v_i is independent of d_i given x_i, w_i,

(iv) varying effect with dependent v_i: v_i is dependent on d_i given x_i, w_i.

Assumption (i) is restrictive but is a reasonable starting point. Assumption (ii) allows the effect to depend only on observables. Assumption (iii) is more general than (ii), but its restrictive nature comes from the independence. For instance, we may have $d_i = 1[y_{1i} - y_{0i} > 0] = 1[w_i'\beta_{dw} + v_i > 0]$, in which case (iii) does not hold. Assumption (iv) is the most general. Assumption (iv) makes estimation of β_{0x} and β_{dw} troublesome, because the error term is related to d_i which is a regressor. See Heckman (2001) and the references therein for more on heterogenous effects.

The treatment effect $E(y_1 - y_0)$ is something of a 'blackbox', for it does now show what is going on in the causal mechanism running from the treatment to the response; $E(y_1 - y_0)$ does not show where a third variable may come within or outside the causal link. In contrast, regression models tend to specify fully how the treatment and response are generated and where the third variables may come, as the above linear models show. In this sense, regression analysis is 'structural' while treatment effect analysis is not. In principle, estimating $E(y_1 - y_0)$ or $E(y_1 - y_0|x)$ does not require regression models; recall that $E(y_1 - y_0)$ or $E(y_1 - y_0|x)$ can be estimated by the group mean difference in randomized data. In observational data with $E(y_j|x) \neq E(y_j|x,d)$, however, assumptions regarding unobservables are needed to identify $E(y_1 - y_0|x)$; here, regression models can motivate those assumptions or help demonstrate whether those assumptions are plausible or not.

For the job-training data, let $x_i = (1, age, age^2/100,$ *ex-firm, ed*$)'$. Doing
the LSE of y_i on x_i and $x_i d_i$, we get $R^2 = 0.056$, $s = 0.641$, and

	1	age	$\dfrac{age^2}{100}$	ex-firm	ed	d	age * d	$\dfrac{age^2}{100} * d$	ex-firm * d	ed * d
est.	4.19	0.055	−0.058	0.046	−0.017	0.899	−0.015	−0.001	−0.035	−0.051
tv	44.9	11.8	−9.97	8.71	−2.07	3.72	−0.93	−0.052	−5.30	−3.05

Judging from the t-values, age and $age^2/100$ seem to influence both y_{0i} and
y_{1i} with the same coefficients, whereas ex-firm employment days and education
influence both y_{0i} and y_{1i} with different coefficients. With the covariates considered, the effect of d on y looks quite different from when the covariates are
ignored; interaction terms should be taken into account now and perhaps more
extensively than usually done in practice.

In the discussion of varying effect $\beta_i = w_i'\beta_{dw} + v_i$, the error term v_i gets
attached to d_i in $\beta_i d_i$, and as a result, $v_i d_i$ becomes part of the error term u_i in
the model $y_i = x_i'\beta_{0x} + (d_i w_i')\beta_{dw} + u_i$. Because of this, $COR(d, u) \neq 0$ in general and LSE would be invalid. We already know also that d can be endogenous
given x, even when $v = 0$, if selection on observables does not hold. As a justification for selection-on-observables, we mentioned 'quasi experiments': if d is
a rule or law not subject to individual selection, then $d \amalg y_j$ or $d \amalg y_j|x$ may
hold for individual data. For state-level data, d may be decided by each state's
economic, demographic and political variables. These variables may also influence the response variable. In this case, rules or laws are no longer exogenous
and quasi experiments fail, as illustrated in Besley and Case (2004). Just as we
did for individually self-selected d, state-level covariates should be controlled
for in these cases to get at least $d \amalg y_j|x$.

2.6   Structural form equations and treatment effect

When d is randomized, there is no equation for d; d is just a random variable
unrelated to any other random variable. When d is self-selected, however, there
must be an equation for d (e.g., $d = 1[y_1 > y_0]$). In order to identify informative
parameters for the y_j equation, despite the change in d, we make a fundamental
assumption:

> *the y_j equation does not change when the d-equation does.*

Without this assumption, the parameters in the y_j equation are useless for
policy intervention on d. For instance, if y_j is drawn from a probability distribution A when $d = j$ is randomly assigned, but drawn from a probability
distribution B when $d = j$ is self-selected, then the y_j equation changes

when the d-generating mechanism does from self-selection to intervention. The fundamental assumption rules out these kind of cases.

Consider a 'structural form (SF)'equation for y_i along with an equation for d_i:

$$y_i = \beta_1 + \beta_2 d_i + \beta_3' x_i + u_i, \qquad d_i = \alpha_x' x_i + \alpha_c' c_i + \varepsilon_i,$$

where β_1, β_2, and β_3 are the SF parameters, c_i is an observed vector, and u_i and ε_i are error terms. Substitute the second equation into the first to get

$$y_i = \beta_1 + \beta_2 \alpha_c' c_i + (\beta_3' + \beta_2 \alpha_x') x_i + u_i + \beta_2 \varepsilon_i,$$

which is the y reduced form (RF) equation with the RF parameters β_1, $\beta_2 \alpha_c$, and $\beta_3 + \beta_2 \alpha_x$. The equation for d came only because of self-selection. *If we impose d on the subjects (intervention), then the d equation disappears* while the y equation still remains intact. Even if the selection mechanism changes in some other way, the SF for y will remain exactly the same owing to the fundamental assumption. The SF parameters are worth estimating for this reason. The causal effect of d changing from 0 to 1 by intervention is given by β_2 no matter how d is determined in reality.

Estimating the RF parameters would not make much sense if the mechanism generating d changes (the 'Lucas critique'), because the RF parameters involve the parameters α_x and α_c in the d-equation which are useless for intervention on d. Taking d as a policy, we can change the d-generating mechanism to achieve a goal, and we would want to know how people will react to this policy intervention. y-SF can show us this, while the y-RF cannot.

It is possible that d has its own SF. Imagine a product, and suppose that y is supply or demand (both to be equalized by the market equilibrium), while d is the price. We can imagine counter-factual demand equations of the consumers with respect to various potential prices (price being the treatment). We can also imagine counter-factual pricing equations of the producers with respect to various quantities supplied (quantity supplied being the treatment). Under demand = supply, this yields two SF's, say,

$$y_i = \beta_1 + \beta_2 d_i + \beta_3' x_i + u_i, \qquad d_i = \alpha_1 + \alpha_2 y_i + \alpha_3' z_i + \varepsilon_i.$$

For the government, it is sensible to ask: what will be the change in the demand if the government forces a price increase by one unit? The answer can be found from the y-SF: β_2. It is also sensible to ask: what will be the change in the price if the government forces the producers to increase production by one unit? The answer can be found from the d-SF: α_2. Another example for two SF's is a household with two people maximizing an objective function together. Each person has a choice variable, and this leads to the first-order condition with two equations; the one corresponding to person 1's choice variable shows how person 1 would react to person 2's *potential* choice.

One may argue that 'the y-SF can be solved for d, and in this case the meaning of the y-SF is no-longer clear', which is something that bothers many economists and econometricians. The only way to avoid this argument is to take the y-SF as something less than an equation. It is an equation, but with a causal meaning where d_i in $\beta_1 + \beta_2 d_i + \beta_3' x_i + u_i$ temporally precedes y_i. Here d_i is realized first, and then combined with x_i and u_i later to generate y_i. If one puts y_i on the right-hand side and d_i on the left, the temporal order, and consequently the causal meaning, are lost. Another way to answer the query of solving the y-SF for d is *assignment* (as in Pearl (2000)): in computer programming, 'x = x + 1' means adding 1 to x and storing the sum where x is currently stored; the equality in the SF may be taken as assignment. The point is that the equality in the SF is not the usual equality that can be manipulated anyway one desires; it is an equality with assignment meaning, and can be manipulated so long as the causal meaning of generating the left-hand side variable from the right-hand side variables is maintained. For instance, inserting the d-equation into the y-equation does not disturb the causal relation and is thus allowed, while putting y on the right-hand side is not.

In relation to intervention, an interesting question arises. Suppose

$$E(y_{ji}|x_i) = \beta_1 + \beta_2 j + \beta_3' x_i, \qquad j = 0, 1$$
$$\implies E(y_1 - y_0|x) = \beta_2 \implies E(y_1 - y_0) = \beta_2.$$

Since the two potential regression functions differ only by $\beta_2 j$, one may wonder whether it is all right to write

$$E(y_i|d_i, x_i) = \beta_1 + \beta_2 d_i + \beta_3' x_i.$$

Lee and Kobyashi (2001) show

$$E(y_i|d_i, x_i) = \beta_1 + \beta_2 d_i + \beta_3' x_i \iff E(y_{ji}|x_i, d_i) = E(y_{ji}|x_i).$$

That is, replacing j (intervention) on the right-hand side of $E(y_{ji}|x_i) = \beta_1 + \beta_2 j + \beta_3' x_i$ with d_i (self-selection) is not innocuous: it requires the mean independence (or selection-on-observables).

Showing the equivalence between the two equations, first '$\implies$':

$$E(y_{ji}|x_i, d_i = j) = E(y_i|x_i, d_i = j) \quad \text{because } y_i = (1 - d_i)y_{0i} + d_i y_{1i}$$
$$= \beta_1 + \beta_2 j + \beta_3' x_i \qquad \text{because } E(y_i|d_i, x_i) = \beta_1 + \beta_2 d_i + \beta_3' x_i$$
$$= E(y_{ji}|x_i).$$

Second, '$\impliedby$':

$$E(y_i|x_i, d_i) = (1 - d_i) \cdot E(y_i|x_i, d_i = 0) + d_i \cdot E(y_i|x_i, d_i = 1)$$
$$= (1 - d_i) \cdot E(y_{0i}|x_i, d_i = 0) + d_i \cdot E(y_{1i}|x_i, d_i = 1)$$
$$= (1 - d_i) \cdot E(y_{0i}|x_i) + d_i \cdot E(y_{1i}|x_i)$$
$$= (1 - d_i) \cdot (\beta_1 + \beta_3' x_i) + d_i \cdot (\beta_1 + \beta_2 + \beta_3' x_i) = \beta_1 + \beta_2 d_i + \beta_3' x_i.$$

2.7 On mean independence and independence*

Independence and conditional independence and their mean versions have appeared many times. In this section, three questions involving these concepts are addressed.

2.7.1 Independence and conditional independence

Does $y_j \amalg d|x$ imply $y_j \amalg d$? The answer is no, because x can be the only common factor linking y_j and d; i.e., y_j and d can be related only through x. In this case, when x is fixed, y_j and d are independent, but when x is not fixed, y_j and d are dependent.

The opposite question is: Does $y_j \amalg d$ imply $y_j \amalg d|x$? This is more difficult than the previous question, because one may think that, if two random variables are independent, it is impossible to create dependence using a third variable. The answer is, however, no again. To understand this, consider

$$d \longrightarrow x \longleftarrow y_j,$$

which is called a 'collider' (the common factor case $d \longleftarrow x \longrightarrow y_j$ is called a 'fork'). If y_j and d are independent but both affect x positively, then conditioning on x being high implies that y_j and d tend to take high values as well, which means a positive dependence between y_j and d.

As an example for collider, suppose d is a job-training, y_j is ability, and x is the post-training wage. Assume that the training d does not affect one's ability y_j but does affect the post-training wage x, because employers think the training must have done some good to the trainees. Also assume that ability y_j affects the post-training wage x. If we look at a high post-training wage group (i.e., if we condition on a high x), then the group will consist of people with high y_j who are likely to have taken the training and we will find a positive relation between y_j and d for the high x group. This is a sample selection (or selected sample) problem. A simpler but more drastic example is $x = y_j + d$ where $y_j \amalg d$: if x is fixed at 100, then $y_j = 100 - d$, implying $COR(y_j, d|x = 100) = -1$ despite $y_j \amalg d$ in the population!

Despite this discussion in the two preceding paragraphs, we do not have to worry about colliders in treatment effect analysis, because we almost always impose the temporal restriction, that x is a pre-treatment variable so that $d \rightarrow x$ cannot occur. Even when we allow x to be a post-treatment variable, we will always impose the restriction that x occurs at least before y_j so that $x \longleftarrow y_j$ cannot occur; for $d \rightarrow x \rightarrow y_j$, which is allowed, y_j and d are dependent so that the question: does $y_j \amalg d$ imply $y_j \amalg d|x$?, is meaningless. In short, in treatment effect analysis, we have

$y_j \amalg d|x$ does not necessarily imply $y_j \amalg d$, but $y_j \amalg d$ implies $y_j \amalg d|x$.

2.7.2   Symmetric and asymmetric mean-independence

The zero-correlation or mean-independence of y_j and d

$$COR(y_j, d) = 0 \iff E(y_j d) = E(y_j)E(d)$$

is symmetric in y_j and d. We use, however, the asymmetric version

$$E(y_j|d) = E(y_j)$$

as well, which can be called the 'mean-independence of y_j from d'. But this is not always equivalent to the symmetric version. How are the two versions related?

It is easy to see that the asymmetric version implies the symmetric version, because

$$E(y_j d) = E\{E(y_j d|d)\} = E\{E(y_j|d) \cdot d\} = E(y_j)E(d).$$

For the reverse, suppose the symmetric version holds with a binary d. Then,

$$E(y_j d) \ (= E(y_j|d = 1)P(d = 1)) = E(y_j)E(d).$$

From this,

$$E(y_j|d = 1) = E(y_j) \quad \text{under } P(d = 1) > 0.$$

Here $d = 1$; it remains to show that $E(y_j|d = 0) = E(y_j)$.

Observe

$$\begin{aligned}
E(y_j) &= E(y_j|d = 1)P(d = 1) + E(y_j|d = 0)P(d = 0) \\
&= E(y_j|d = 1)\{1 - P(d = 0)\} + E(y_j|d = 0)P(d = 0) \\
&= E(y_j|d = 1) + \{E(y_j|d = 0) - E(y_j|d = 1)\} \cdot P(d = 0).
\end{aligned}$$

If $P(d = 0) > 0 \iff P(d = 1) < 1$, then $E(y_j|d = 1) = E(y_j)$ implies that

$$E(y_j|d = 0) = E(y_j|d = 1) \ (= E(y_j)) \iff E(y_j|d) = E(y_j).$$

Therefore, *when d is binary* and $0 < P(d = 1) < 1$, the symmetric version of mean independence is equivalent to the asymmetric version.

In the preceding derivation, d being binary was critical. In general, unless y_j is binary with $0 < P(y_j = 1) < 1$, the mean independence $E(y_j d) = E(y_j)E(d)$ does not necessarily imply the other asymmetric mean-independence $E(d|y_j) = E(d)$, which can be called the 'mean-independence of d from y_j'.

Analogously with x conditioned on throughout, when d is binary and $0 < P(d = 1|x) < 1$, we have

$$\begin{aligned}
E(y_j d|x) &= E(y_j|x)E(d|x) \\
&\iff E(y_j|d, x) = E(y_j|x) \ \{\iff E(y_j|d = 1, x) = E(y_j|d = 0, x)\}.
\end{aligned}$$

Without the overlapping-x condition $(0 < P(d = 1|x) < 1)$, if $P(d = 1|x = x_o) = 1$, then those treated subjects with $x = x_o$ cannot find any comparable control subject with $x = x_o$.

2.7.3 Joint and marginal independence

As shown already, for the effect on the treated to be identified with the group mean difference, we need only $y_0 \perp d$. For the effect on the untreated, we need only $y_1 \perp d$. If both hold $(y_j \perp d, j = 0, 1)$, then the group mean difference is the effect on the population, $E(y_1 - y_0)$. For correlations and mean effects, no more than $y_j \perp d$, $j = 0, 1$, are needed. Suppose we strengthen the zero correlations to independence y_j II d, $j = 0, 1$. This may be needed, because $COR(y_j, d) = 0$ does not imply, e.g., $COR(\ln(y_j), d) = 0$—an unpleasant situation. With independence invoked, instead of zero correlation, we see joint independence

$$(y_0, y_1) \text{ II } d$$

as well. This is stronger than the two 'marginal' independences y_j II d, $j = 0, 1$. A question is then whether the two marginal independences imply the joint independence. The answer is no, as can be seen in the following.

Instead of the two marginal independences, if

$$y_1 \text{ II } d|y_0 \quad \text{and} \quad y_0 \text{ II } d, \quad \text{(or symmetrically if } y_0 \text{ II } d|y_1 \quad \text{and} \quad y_1 \text{ II } d),$$

then the joint independence holds. To see this, observe

$$
\begin{aligned}
f(y_0, y_1, d) &= f(d, y_1|y_0)f(y_0) \\
&= f(d|y_0)f(y_1|y_0)f(y_0) \quad \text{due to } y_1 \text{ II } d \,|y_0 \\
&= f(d)f(y_1|y_0)f(y_0) \quad\quad \text{due to } y_0 \text{ II } d \\
&= f(d)f(y_0, y_1),
\end{aligned}
$$

which is the joint independence.

The reverse also holds under $f(y_0) > 0$ so that the joint independence is equivalent to y_1 II $d|y_0$ and y_0 II d under $f(y_0) > 0$. To see this, integrate out y_1 from the joint independence

$$f(y_0, y_1, d) = f(d)f(y_0, y_1)$$

to get y_0 II d. Rewrite the last display as

$$
\begin{aligned}
f(y_1, d|y_0)f(y_0) &= f(d)f(y_1|y_0)f(y_0) \\
\implies f(y_1, d|y_0) &= f(d)f(y_1|y_0) \text{ after dividing both sides by } f(y_0) \\
\implies f(y_1, d|y_0) &= f(d|y_0)f(y_1|y_0) \text{ using } y_0 \text{ II } d,
\end{aligned}
$$

which is y_1 II $d|y_0$. These derivations all hold with x conditioned on.

Why not just assume the joint independence and forget about the marginal versions? For one good reason, recall that the mean effect on the treated is identified under $y_0 \amalg d$. The assumption $y_0 \amalg d$ allows for $y_1 - y_0$ to be related to d. This is important because a self-selected treatment d is likely to depend on the treatment gain $y_1 - y_0$ as in $d = 1[y_1 > y_0]$. In contrast, $(y_0, y_1) \amalg d$ rules out dependence between $y_1 - y_0$ and d.

2.8   Illustration of biases and Simpson's Paradox*

Although overt bias can be illustrated with observational data, hidden bias cannot. Here, we use simulated data to illustrate hidden as well as overt biases. Since these biases are of utmost importance in treatment effect analysis with observational data, seeing the biases (and getting seriously concerned about them) is not a waste of time. At least the 'Simpson's Paradox' that a positive (negative) effect for each sub population could become negative (positive) in the whole population, is striking if the reader has never seen it before.

2.8.1   Illustration of biases

First, a data set was simulated as:

$$y_{0i} = 70 + 10 \cdot x_i + u_{0i}, \quad y_{1i} = 70 + 10 \cdot x_i + u_{1i}, \quad i = 1, \ldots, 200,$$
$$x_i \sim B(1, 0.5), \quad u_{0i}, u_{1i} \sim U[-10, 10] \text{ independently of } x_i,$$
$$\text{and } d_i \text{ follows } B(1, 0.5) \text{ independently of } x_i, u_{0i}, u_{1i};$$

d_i is randomly assigned. This data illustrates the effect of being a vegetarian ($d = 1$) versus being a meat-eater ($d = 0$) on life span y_i where $x_i = 1$ for female and 0 for male. The model states that the mean life span for males is 70 years ($E(y_0|x = 0) = E(y_1|x = 0) = 70$), and for females is 80 ($E(y_0|x = 1) = E(y_1|x = 1) = 80$). Since the mean life span is the same across the two treatments for males and females, there is no effect of being a vegetarian on life span, although there is a biological gender effect (females live longer than males).

Using the population expressions instead of the sample expressions to simplify presentation, the data yield

$$E(y_1) - E(y_0) = 75.308 - 75.582 = -0.274;$$

note that both y_{1i} and y_{0i} are observed in the simulated data. The total number of the treated is 98, and the total number of females is 107; the number of females in the T and C group is (% in each group is in ($\cdot$)), respectively,

51 (52.0%) and 56 (54.9%). The group mean difference is almost zero, as it should be:

$$E(y|d = 1) - E(y|d = 0) = 75.253 - 75.267 = -0.014.$$

Second, we now change the model: we keep the same y_{0i}, y_{1i}, x_i but generate a new d_i with

d_i follows $B(1, 0.25(1 - x_i) + 0.75x_i)$ independently of u_{0i} and u_{1i},

which contains selection-on-observables (more women in the T group), and will thus cause an overt bias. Now the number of the treated is 103, and 107 females are unevenly assigned to the two groups: 80 in the treatment group and 27 in the control. As a result,

$$E(y|d = 1) - E(y|d = 0) = 78.707 - 72.620 = 6.087,$$

is much bigger than the preceding group mean difference. Hence, despite no treatment effect, this group mean difference shows a false positive effect of d simply because there are more females in the T group than in the C group. A way to avoid being misled by x is to find the mean effect for each gender separately, and then the weighted average:

Females : $E(y|x=1, d=1) - E(y|x=1, d=0) = 80.977 - 80.441 = 0.536$;
Males : $E(y|x=0, d=1) - E(y|x=0, d=0) = 70.350 - 69.756 = 0.594$;
weighted Avg. : $0.536 \cdot P(x = 1) + 0.594 \cdot P(x = 0)$
$$= 0.536 \times 0.535 + 0.594 \times 0.465 = 0.564.$$

The positive effect 6.087 has all but disappeared.

Third, we still keep the same y_{0i}, y_{1i}, x_i but generate a new d_i with

$$d_i = 1[x_i + e_i > 0], \quad \text{where } e_i \text{ is the standardized average of } u_{0i} \text{ and } u_{1i}$$
$$(\text{i.e., } SD(e) = 1)$$

which contains selection-on-unobservable, as d_i is related to (u_{0i}, u_{1i}) in (y_{0i}, y_{1i}) through e_i. Due to the dependence of d_i on x_i and e_i which influence y_{0i} and y_{1i}, there will be overt and covert biases. The number of the treated is 125, and 107 females are unevenly assigned to the two groups: 88 in the T group and 19 in the C group. The group mean difference is

$$E(y|d = 1) - E(y|d = 0) = 79.605 - 68.911 = 10.694,$$

which is even bigger than the preceding group mean difference. Despite no treatment effect, this group's mean difference shows a false positive effect due to overt and covert biases. Controlling for x,

$$\text{Females}: E(y|x=1,d=1) - E(y|x=1,d=0) = 82.242 - 74.092 = 8.150;$$
$$\text{Males}: E(y|x=0,d=1) - E(y|x=0,d=0) = 73.333 - 67.153 = 6.179;$$
$$\text{weighted Avg.}: 8.150 \cdot P(x=1) + 6.179 \cdot P(x=0)$$
$$= 8.150 \times 0.535 + 6.179 \times 0.465 = 7.411.$$

Although controlling for x mitigates the bias from 10.694 to 7.411, the hidden bias still shows a false positive effect.

2.8.2 Source of overt bias

It is instructive to formalize the preceding discussion on overt bias in the second data set: suppose

$$E(y_j|x,d) = E(y_j|x): \text{ mean-independence of } y_j; \text{ from } d \text{ given gender } x;$$
$$E(y_1|x=1) = E(y_0|x=1) > E(y_1|x=0) = E(y_0|x=0):$$
$$\text{females live longer than males;}$$
$$P(x=1|d=1) > P(x=1|d=0): \text{ more females in T than in C.}$$

Then,

$$E(y|d=1) - E(y|d=0) =$$
$$E(y_1|x=1,d=1)P(x=1|d=1) + E(y_1|x=0,d=1)P(x=0|d=1)$$
$$-E(y_0|x=1,d=0)P(x=1|d=0) - E(y_0|x=0,d=0)P(x=0|d=0).$$

Using the mean independence, this becomes

$$E(y_1|x=1)P(x=1|d=1) + E(y_1|x=0)P(x=0|d=1)$$
$$-E(y_0|x=1)P(x=1|d=0) - E(y_0|x=0)P(x=0|d=0).$$

Collecting the terms with $E(y_j|x=1)$ and $E(y_j|x=0)$, we get

$$E(y_j|x=1)\{P(x=1|d=1) - P(x=1|d=0)\}$$
$$+ E(y_j|x=0)\{P(x=0|d=1) - P(x=0|d=0)\}.$$

Rewrite $P(x=0|d=1) - P(x=0|d=0)$ as

$$1 - P(x=1|d=1) - (1 - P(x=1|d=0)) = P(x=1|d=0) - P(x=1|d=1)$$

to get the final desired expression

$$E(y|d=1) - E(y|d=0) = \{E(y_j|x=1) - E(y_j|x=0)\}\{P(x=1|d=1)$$
$$- P(x=1|d=0)\} > 0.$$

That is, despite no true effect of d, the group mean difference is positive because the two terms on the right-hand side are positive: females live longer, and more females in the T group than in the C group.

2.8.3   Simpson's Paradox

To a layman's eyes, the following *Simpson's Paradox* can be striking:

$$E(y|d = 1) - E(y|d = 0) > (<)0, \quad \text{while } E(y|x, d = 1) - E(y|x, d = 0) < (>)0$$
$$\text{for all } x.$$

In other words, for each subpopulation characterized by x, the effect of d on y takes one sign, while the effect takes the opposite sign for the whole population! To see how this can happen, recall the vegetarian example where $x = 1$ for females and $d = 1$ for vegetarians. Suppose

$$E(y|x = 0, d = 0) = 65, \quad E(y|x = 0, d = 1) = 60 \quad \text{(vegetarian effect for}$$
$$\text{males is } -5)$$
$$E(y|x = 1, d = 0) = 80, \quad E(y|x = 1, d = 1) = 75 \quad \text{(vegetarian effect for}$$
$$\text{females is } -5)$$
$$P(x = 1|d = 0) = 0.2, \quad E(x = 1|d = 1) = 0.7.$$

Comparing the four expected values vertically, the 'female effect' is 15 for both meat-eaters and vegetarians. Then,

$$E(y|d = 0) = E(y|x = 0, d = 0)P(x = 0|d = 0) + E(y|x = 1, d = 0)P(x = 1|d = 0)$$
$$= 65 \times 0.8 + 80 \times 0.2 = 52 + 16 = 68;$$
$$E(y|d = 1) = E(y|x = 0, d = 1)P(x = 0|d = 1) + E(y|x = 1, d = 1)P(x = 1|d = 1)$$
$$= 60 \times 0.3 + 75 \times 0.7 = 18 + 52.5 = 70.5.$$

Despite the vegetarian effect of -5 for both males and females, since the female effect is much bigger ($+15$ for both meat-eaters and vegetarians) and there are more females in the T group than in the C group, the female effect dominates the vegetarian effect, resulting in the misleading number $2.5 = E(y|d = 1) - E(y|d = 0)$ for the whole population.

To see what went wrong with the Simpson's Paradox, we compute the vegetarian effect for males and females separately, to get the gender-weighted sum:

$$E(y|x = 0, d = 1) - E(y|x = 0, d = 0) = 60 - 65 = -5,$$
$$E(y|x = 1, d = 1) - E(y|x = 1, d = 0) = 75 - 80 = -5$$
$$\Rightarrow -5 \cdot P(x = 0) - 5 \cdot P(x = 1) = -5.$$

Had we used $P(x)$ instead of $P(x|d)$ in computing $E(y|d = 0)$ and $E(y|d = 1)$ above, then the paradox would not have occurred. In other words, if gender x is independent of d so that $P(x|d) = P(x)$, then the paradox will not occur.

3

Controlling for covariates

In finding a treatment (d) effect on a response variable (y) with observational data, the control group with $d = 0$ (or C group) may be different from the treatment group with $d = 1$ (or T group) in observed variables x. This can cause an 'overt bias', where the difference between the two groups' responses may be due to the difference in x, rather than to the difference in d. Also, if the T group differs from the C group in unobserved variables ε, then this can cause a 'hidden (or covert) bias'. This and the following chapter deal with controlling for x in order to avoid overt bias. The basic way to control for x is by 'matching'. This topic is examined at length in the next chapter. All the other issues concerning overt bias are discussed here. No hidden bias will be assumed throughout. Controlling for x means we compare treated and control subjects that share the same value of x. This raises a number of issues: (i) which variables to control for, (ii) what is identified when x is controlled for, (iii) what if the C and T groups do not overlap in x, etc. In general, (i) pre-treatment variables should be controlled for; (ii) with x controlled for, the conditional effect $E(y_1 - y_0|x)$ is identified where y_j is the potential response when $d = j$; (iii) 'regression discontinuity design' may be useful if the values of x do not overlap. Instead of getting $E(y_1 - y_0)$ via $E(y_1 - y_0|x)$, we can also use a 'weighting' approach to find $E(y_1 - y_0)$.

3.1 Variables to control for

To avoid overt bias, x should be controlled for. But, before we embark on the task, we need to determine which variables to control for. A general answer is *control for the pre-treatment covariates*—the variables that matter for y_j and d but are not affected by d. But there are practical complications, and choosing the variables to control for is not as easy as it sounds. In this section, we show four broad categories where controlling for x is a must, no-no, yes/no (depending on what we want to know), and an option. More complicated cases than these will be discussed in Chapters 6 and 7. The first category where x must be controlled for is then further examined in case only a proxy x_p is observed instead of x.

3.1.1   Must cases

Consider a 'causal chain' with each arrow meaning 'causing' or 'affecting':

$$
\begin{array}{c}
\text{must (i)} \\
d \quad \longrightarrow \quad y \ . \\
\uparrow \quad \nearrow \\
x
\end{array}
$$

Here, x is a pre-treatment variable and x must be controlled for, because x can be unbalanced across the T and C groups. If x is not controlled for, the difference in x across the two groups can result in

$$E(y|d=1) \neq E(y|d=0) \quad \text{despite} \quad E(y|x,d=1) = E(y|x,d=0) \text{ for all } x.$$

This is the classic case of imbalance in x across the two groups—known as *confounding* by x where x is called a 'confounder'. If the arrow between d and y is removed, then there is no causal effect from d to y. Here, x is simply the 'common factor' for d and y, responsible for the *prima facie* causal relation between d and y. In the example of the work effect on a doctor's visits, health (x) may affect both the work decision and the doctor's visits.

A specific model for this case is

$$d_i = 1[\alpha_1 + \alpha_x x_i + \varepsilon_i > 0], \quad y_i = \beta_1 + \beta_d d_i + \beta_x x_i + u_i, \quad u_i \amalg \varepsilon_i | x_i.$$

Suppose $\beta_d = 0$ (no effect of d on y), which implies $E(y|x,d=1) = E(y|x,d=0) = \beta_1 + \beta_x x$; note $E(u|x,d) = 0$ owing to $u \amalg \varepsilon|x$. But, so long as $\alpha_x \neq 0$,

$$E(y|d=1) = \beta_1 + \beta_x E(x|d=1) \neq E(y|d=0) = \beta_1 + \beta_x E(x|d=0).$$

If the arrow $x \longrightarrow y$ in the diagonal is removed (i.e., if $\beta_x = 0$), then we get

$$x \rightarrow d \rightarrow y$$

and

$$E(y|x,d) = \beta_1 + \beta_d d :$$

x may be unbalanced across the two groups, but the imbalance has no consequence for the effect of d on y.

In the example of the work (d) effect on a doctor's visits (y), health (x) can affect d and y and be affected by y. A better description may, therefore, be where x exchanges effects with y: $x \longleftrightarrow y$. Hence this case could be expressed as

$$\text{must (ii)}$$

$$
\begin{array}{ccc}
d & \longrightarrow & y \\
\uparrow & \nearrow & \downarrow \\
x_{pre} & \longrightarrow & x_{post}
\end{array}
$$

where x_{pre} is the x before treatment and x_{post} is the x after treatment. This is the must case with x_{post} added. Here as well, x_{pre} should be controlled for. But x_{post} should not be controlled for as we will explain below.

3.1.2   No-no cases

Consider

$$\text{no-no (i)}$$

$$d \to y \to w.$$

In this case, w is a *post-response* variable and should not be controlled for, because fixing w will remove part (or all) of the effect of d on y. At the extreme, if w is a one-to-one function of y, then fixing w is the same as fixing y, which will always result in zero treatment effect, because subjects with the same y are being compared. For example, suppose that d is an education program in the first year of high school, y is GPA in the third year, and w is entering a college or not. Fixing w means we compare the third year of high school GPA of the subjects with the same w and the difference in y will be small across the T and C groups that share the same w.

In no-no (i), the difference in y across the T and C groups is weakened when a post-response variable w is controlled for. An opposite case to no-no (i) where a difference in d is weakened is

$$\text{no-no (ii)}$$

$$
\begin{array}{ccccc}
d & \longrightarrow & e_1 & \longrightarrow & y. \\
 & \searrow & & \nearrow & \\
 & & e_2 & &
\end{array}
$$

Here, d affects y in two ways, and controlling for a *post-treatment* variable e_1 weakens the treatment difference. For instance, suppose that d is living in a city or not, y is happiness, e_1 is access to theatres and e_2 is access to restaurants. We want to know the effect on happiness of exogenously relocating a person living in the countryside to a city. In this case, the T group is city dwellers, the C group is country dwellers, and the covariates influencing both d and y should be controlled for (such as marital status and the number of school-age children). Controlling for access to theatres is wrong however, since better access to theatres is part of city living. At the extreme, if we control for all aspects of city or country living, then there would be no difference between city and country living.

3.1.3   Yes/no cases

Consider a causal chain related to no-no (ii)

$$\text{yes-no (i)}$$
$$d \to w \to y.$$

Here, w is a post-treatment variable, because it is affected by d. If w is fixed, the effect of d on y will be zero. If we want to know the effect of d 'net of w' on y, then controlling for w is the right thing to do. Otherwise, if we want any effect of d on y, then w should not be controlled for.

For an education-program effect on earnings, suppose that the program $(d = 1)$ works only by making the students stay in school and get the diploma $(w = 1)$; that is, there is only a 'sheepskin effect'. In comparing students with and without the program, if w is fixed at 1, then we will not see any of the effect of d. Fixing w is all right if what we want is the effect from the actual accumulated knowledge due to the program other than from just getting the diploma—the effect is zero in this case. However, if we want to know any effect of the program on earnings, then any variable in the causal chain between the program and earnings should not be controlled for.

More generally, suppose that d affects y directly as well as indirectly through w (the program can affect both graduation and earnings). Then we get

$$\text{yes-no (ii)}$$
$$d \quad \longrightarrow \quad y.$$
$$\searrow \quad \uparrow$$
$$w$$

Controlling for w will show only the direct effect of d on y.

A specific model for this case is

$$w_i = \alpha_1 + \alpha_d d_i + \varepsilon_i, \qquad y_i = \beta_1 + \beta_d d_i + \beta_w w_i + u_i, \qquad (d, w) \amalg u,$$
$$\varepsilon \equiv w - E(w|d).$$

The latter equation is the structural form (SF) equation for y_i. Substitute the w-equation into the y-SF to get

$$y_i = \beta_1 + \beta_d d_i + \beta_w (\alpha_1 + \alpha_d d_i + \varepsilon_i) + u_i$$
$$= (\beta_1 + \beta_w \alpha_1) + (\beta_d + \beta_w \alpha_d) d_i + \beta_w \varepsilon_i + u_i,$$

which is the reduced form (RF) equation for y. We have the following effects of d on y :

$$\textit{total effect} : E(y|d = 1) - E(y|d = 0) = \beta_d + \beta_w \alpha_d \quad \text{(from the } y\text{-RF),}$$
$$\textit{direct effect} : E(y|d = 1, w) - E(y|d = 0, w) = \beta_d \quad \text{(from the } y\text{-SF),}$$
$$\textit{indirect effect} : \{E(w|d = 1) - E(w|d = 0)\} \cdot \{E(y|d, w = 1) - E(y|d, w = 0)\}$$
$$= \alpha_d \beta_w.$$

If $\beta_d = 0$ in the model, then we are back to the case $d \to w \to y$. In this case, the total effect equals the indirect effect $\alpha_d \beta_w$.

3.1.4   Option case

Consider

$$\begin{array}{c} \text{option} \\ d \to y \leftarrow z. \end{array}$$

In terms of a temporal sequence, z may be a pre-treatment or a post-treatment variable. Here z is balanced across the T and C groups, and controlling for z is optional. However, depending on whether this is done, we may identify different effects. Note that when d and z are not directly linked as in $d \to y \leftarrow z$, we assume $d \amalg z$.

With z controlled for, first we will have $E(y|d=1,z) - E(y|d=0,z)$ and then we can find its integrated version

$$\int \{E(y|d=1,z) - E(y|d=0,z)\} f_z(z) dz = E(y|d=1) - E(y|d=0).$$

In the first stage, we can see whether or not $E(y|d=1,z) - E(y|d=0,z)\ \forall z$, which is more informative than bypassing the first-stage just to check $E(y|d=1) - E(y|d=0)$. Instead of integrating z with f_z, we could use a weighting function $w(z)$ to get

$$M_\omega \equiv \int \{E(y|d=1,z) - E(y|d=0,z)\} w(z) dz.$$

A specific model for this case is

$$d_i = 1[\alpha_1 + \varepsilon_i > 0], \quad y_i = \beta_1 + \beta_d d_i + \beta_z z_i + \beta_{dz} d_i z_i + u_i, \quad \varepsilon_i \amalg (u_i, z_i).$$

We take two cases separately: $\beta_{dz} = 0$ or not (interaction or not between d and z). First, suppose $\beta_{dz} = 0$. Controlling for z, we get $E(y|d=1,z) - E(y|d=0,z) = \beta_d$, and $M_\omega = \beta_d$ for any $w(z)$. Without controlling for z, $\beta_z z_i$ becomes part of the error term, and we get

$$E(y|d=1) - E(y|d=0) = \beta_d + \beta_z \{E(z|d=1) - E(z|d=0)\}$$
$$= \beta_d \quad \text{due to } \varepsilon_i \amalg (u_i, z_i).$$

In this case, controlling for z makes no difference.

Second, suppose $\beta_{dz} \neq 0$. With z controlled for,

$$E(y|d=1,z) - E(y|d=0,z) = \beta_d + \beta_{dz} z \implies M_\omega = \beta_d + \beta_{dz} \int z\, w(z) dz.$$

With z not controlled for,

$$E(y|d=1) - E(y|d=0) = \beta_d + \beta_{dz}E(z),$$

which equals M_ω if $\omega(z) = f_z$. The term $\beta_d + \beta_{dz}z$ demonstrates that z is an important variable and separating β_d from β_{dz} is interesting. However, $\beta_d + \beta_{dz}E(z)$ shown by the group mean difference is just a single number that does not give any clue to whether z matters in the effect of d on y.

3.1.5 Proxy cases

What concerns us most is the must cases, because it may happen that the variable that should be controlled for may not be observed. Certainly, unobservability is not an issue for the no-no and option cases. The natural thing to do is to look for a proxy x_p for x. Then it matters where x_p stands in the causal link from d to y. For example, d is serving in the military, y is life-time earnings, x is ability, and x_p is schooling—ability is not observed but schooling is.

Because there are three arrows in must (i), we can think of x_p coming in as follows:

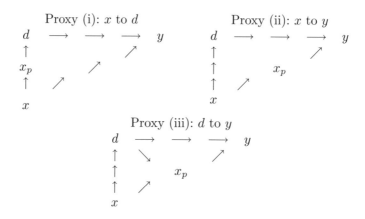

In Proxy (i), by controlling for x_p, we get the case option $(d \to y \longleftarrow x)$; no imbalance of x across groups C and T. In Proxy (ii), by controlling for x_p, we get the case $x \to d \to y$. As already mentioned, the imbalance in x does not pose any problem. In both Proxy (i) and (ii), controlling for x_p removes a bias that would otherwise be present.

In Proxy (iii), had x_p broken the direct link between d and y, then controlling for x_p would have wiped out the causal effect of d on y, which is why x_p enters the figure as it does in Proxy (iii). Proxy (iii) is a combination of must (i) and yes-no (ii), and thus we face a dilemma here: if x_p is not controlled for, we will incur a bias; if x_p is controlled for, we get yes-no (ii) where only the direct effect of d on y is identified. An interesting example in Rosenbaum (2002) for

Proxy (iii) is that

x is the ability or quality of some high school students,

d is a self-selected education program in the first year of high school,

x_p is a test score in the second year (thus, x_p is a post-treatment variable),

y is the test score in the third-year.

Not controlling for x_p implies a potential imbalance of x across the T and C groups. Controlling for x_p, however, will diminish the effect of d on y.

3.2   Comparison group and controlling for observed variables

3.2.1   Comparison group bias

We know that controlling for x removes overt bias. A natural question is: what is identified if overt bias is removed? This question has been answered in the previous chapter, but we will examine it again here so that we can introduce new terminologies and take a more detailed look at it. In short, we will show

(i) $y_0 \perp d \mid x$	$\implies E(y_1 - y_0 \mid d = 1, x)$	*effect on the treated*
(ii) $y_1 \perp d \mid x$	$\implies E(y_1 - y_0 \mid d = 0, x)$	*effect on the untreated*
(iii) $y_0 \perp d \mid x$ and $y_1 \perp d \mid x$	$\implies E(y_1 - y_0 \mid x)$	*effect on the population.*

For (i), observe

$$E(y \mid d = 1, x) - E(y \mid d = 0, x) = E(y_1 \mid d = 1, x) - E(y_0 \mid d = 0, x)$$
$$= E(y_1 \mid d = 1, x) - E(y_0 \mid d = 1, x) + \{E(y_0 \mid d = 1, x) - E(y_0 \mid d = 0, x)\}$$
$$= E(y_1 - y_0 \mid d = 1, x) + \text{`}y_0 \text{ comparison group bias'}$$

where

$$y_0 \text{ comparison group bias} \equiv E(y_0 \mid d = 1, x) - E(y_0 \mid d = 0, x).$$

Thus, the conditional mean difference identifies *the conditional treatment effect on the treated* $E(y_1 - y_0 \mid d = 1, x)$, if the y_0 comparison group bias is zero, which is nothing but $y_0 \perp d \mid x$ (i.e., selection-on-observables for y_0).

Suppose that we have a treated person from whom y_1 is observed. If we had a carbon copy of the treated person in the control group, then that person would yield the counter-factual y_0, and we could identify the individual treatment effect $y_1 - y_0$. Although this is not possible, if we can find some subjects in the control group with characteristics (age, gender, schooling, income, . . .)

similar to those of the treated person, they can then be used to construct the desired counter-factual y_0. We call them a 'comparison group'. For $E(y_1 - y_0 | d = 1, x)$, we do not need y_0 *per se* as it is enough to find $E(y_0 | d = 1, x)$ that is also a counter-factual. Owing to $y_0 \perp d | x$, $E(y_0 | d = 1, x)$ is equal to the identified $E(y_0 | d = 0, x)$.

Once $E(y_1 - y_0 | d = 1, x)$ is identified under $y_0 \perp d | x$, we can integrate x out to get a marginal effect: for a weighting function $w(x)$:

$$\int \{E(y_1 | d = 1, x) - E(y_0 | d = 0, x)\} w(x) dx = \int E(y_1 - y_0 | d = 1, x) w(x) dx.$$

Particularly, if $w(x) = f_{x|d=1}(x)$, then

$$\int \{E(y_1 | d = 1, x) - E(y_0 | d = 0, x)\} f_{x|d=1}(x) dx$$

$$= \int \{E(y_1 | d = 1, x) - E(y_0 | d = 1, x)\} f_{x|d=1}(x) dx$$

$$= E(y_1 | d = 1) - E(y_0 | d = 1) = E(y_1 - y_0 | d = 1).$$

Therefore, under $y_0 \perp d | x$, the (marginal) effect on the treated can be identified.

For (ii), one can also rewrite the conditional mean difference $E(y | d = 1, x) - E(y | d = 0, x)$ as

$$\{E(y_1 | d = 1, x) - E(y_1 | d = 0, x)\} + E(y_1 - y_0 | d = 0, x)$$

where the first term is the 'y_1 comparison group bias'. Thus, the conditional mean difference identifies *the conditional treatment effect on the untreated* $E(y_1 - y_0 | d = 0, x)$, if the y_1 comparison group bias is zero, which is $y_1 \perp d | x$ (i.e., selection-on-observables for y_1). Integrating out x in $E(y_1 - y_0 | d = 0, x)$ using $f_{x|d=0}$ gives the (marginal) effect on the untreated $E(y_1 - y_0 | d = 0)$.

For (iii), if both comparison group biases are zero (i.e., if $y_0 \perp d | x$ and $y_1 \perp d | x$), then the effect on the treated is the same as the effect on the untreated. Because

$$E(y_1 - y_0 | x) = E(y_1 - y_0 | x, d = 0) P(d = 0 | x) + E(y_1 - y_0 | x, d = 1) P(d = 1 | x),$$

this means that all three effects are the same and

$$E(y | d = 1, x) - E(y | d = 0, x) = E(y_1 - y_0 | x) :$$

the conditional mean difference identifies the conditional effect $E(y_1 - y_0 | x)$. Integrating out x with f_x gives $E(y_1 - y_0)$.

The main question is how plausible the zero comparison group bias assumptions are. Intuitively, if x is detailed enough, then the zero comparison group bias may well hold. However, one could argue that the very fact that two people with the same x picked different treatments may indicate that they differ in unobserved variables affecting y_j. To see the answer, consider the model

$$y_{ji} = x_i'\beta_j + u_{ji}, \quad j = 0, 1, \qquad d_i = 1[x_i'\alpha + \varepsilon_i > 0], \quad \varepsilon \amalg (u_0, u_1)|x.$$

For this model, since u_j *is independent of d given* x, the zero comparison group biases hold: for $j = 0, 1$,

$$\begin{aligned} E(y_j|d = 1, x) &= x'\beta_j + E(u_j|d = 1, x) = x'\beta_j \\ &= x'\beta_j + E(u_j|d = 0, x) = E(y_j|d = 0, x). \end{aligned}$$

In words, imagine two people with the same x but different ε: one person has a large positive ε and the other a large negative ε. As a result, one person has $d = 1$ and the other has $d = 0$. If ε is related to u_j, then a big difference in ε will have a serious implication on y_j (e.g., if the relationship is positive, then a large positive ε implies a large positive y_j, and a large negative ε implies a large negative y_j). This would result in a non-zero comparison group bias. However, so long as $\varepsilon \amalg (u_0, u_1)|x$, comparison group biases are zero. If $\varepsilon \amalg u_0|x$ while ε is dependent on u_1 given x, then the zero comparison group bias holds only for y_0, and only the effect on the treated can be identified. The assumption $\varepsilon \amalg (u_0, u_1)|x \iff d \amalg (y_0, y_1)|x$ can be called 'conditionally randomized treatment'—with x controlled for, the treatment assignment is determined by the 'pure' random error ε. There are several different expressions all meaning essentially the same thing in observational data: conditional independence, ignorable treatment, selection-on-observables, zero comparison-group bias, and conditional randomization.

3.2.2 Dimension and support problems in conditioning

Although x can be controlled for by conditioning on x, there are two problems associated with conditioning:

- First, a *dimension problem*. If the dimension of x is large, conditioning on exactly the same value of x can result in too few observations for each subpopulation characterized by x.
- Second, a *support problem*. The values of x observed for the T group may not overlap a great deal with those observed for the C group (e.g., most treated subjects have $x = x_1$, while most control subjects have $x = x_0$, with x_0 being far smaller than x_1).

There are ways to get around the dimension problem as we will show later, but there is no way of avoiding the support problem, because there are simply no comparable subjects across the two groups. For the support problem, we just have to restrict the conditional effect to the overlapping part of the two supports. Let X_T and X_C denote the support of x for the T and C groups, respectively: that is, X_T and X_C are the smallest closed set such that

$$P(x \in X_T | d = 1) = 1 \quad \text{and} \quad P(x \in X_C | d = 0) = 1.$$

Instead of $E(y|d = 1, x) - E(y|d = 0, x)$, consider the conditional mean for those x in the overlapping support:

$$E(y|d = 1, x) - E(y|d = 0, x), \quad \text{for } x \in X_{CT} \equiv X_C \cap X_T.$$

Once this is identified, the identified marginal version is

$$E(y_1 - y_0 | x \in X_{CT}) = \frac{\int_{x \in X_{CT}} \{E(y|d = 1, x) - E(y|d = 0, x)\} f_x(x) dx}{\int_{x \in X_{CT}} f_x(x) dx}$$

where f_x is density of x on the population. Cases of X_{CT} being almost a single point will appear in Section 3.3.

Related to the dimension problem is the problem of x taking too many values. For instance, suppose x is one-dimensional. If x takes many values, say, $1, \ldots, M$, then we can define dummy variables $1[x = 1], \ldots, 1[x = M]$ and consider this vector instead of x. In this case a dimension problem would occur. But, if x takes cardinal values, then this problem may be avoided by *bracketing* the data in the T and C groups, such that the observations within a bracket are similar in x. The same brackets should be created for both the T and C groups. For instance, the data may be bracketed according to education or income levels in both groups. Once this is done, *matching* is possible. For each treated subject in a bracket, one or more control subjects in the same bracket are selected to form a comparison group for the treated subject. The comparison group then renders the desired counter-factual $E(y_0|x, d = 1)$ for the effect on the treated. Matching can be also done for control subjects. For each control subject in a bracket, one or more treated subjects in the same bracket are selected to form a comparison group for the control subject.

The preceding use of the terminology 'matching' within the same bracket is narrow. In its broad sense, for a subject in one group, matching refers to all methods of finding one or more subjects in the other group similar in x and then constructing the desired counter-factual nonparametrically, as we explain briefly in the next paragraph. Matching will be studied in detail in the next chapter. See Imbens (2004) for a review on matching and controlling for x.

With a comparison group for a treated subject, we try to construct $E(y_0|d = 1, x)$ without specifying the functional form. The idea of getting a conditional mean using the similarity in neighboring (in terms of x) observations without specifying the functional form falls in the realm of nonparametrics, one well-known method of which—kernel nonparametric estimation—is reviewed in the appendix. The idea is as follows. Let x_o denote the observed characteristics of a treated subject. For the control group with N_0 subjects, let x_i denote their observed characteristics, $i = 1, \ldots, N_0$. We can use a distance $|x_i - x_o|$ to select controls close to the treated subject, say, those within one SD-distance from x_o: $|x_i - x_o| < SD(x)$. More generally, we can assign a weight to each control subject such that the weight is a decreasing function of $|x_i - x_o|$. The weight can take zero for some control subjects, which means that they are not included in the comparison group. The (weighted) average of y_i's in the comparison group is then taken as the counter-factual $E(y_0|d = 1, x_o)$.

3.2.3 Parametric models to avoid dimension and support problems

Parametric regression models avoid the dimension and support problems (associated with matching) with parametric restrictions and extrapolation. Of course, however, there is a risk of misspecification. Suppose

$$E(y_{ji}|x_i) = \rho(x_i, j; \beta)$$

where the functional form for ρ is known up to the parameter β. Further suppose

$$y_{ji} = \rho(x_i, j; \beta) + u_i, \quad j = 0, 1, \qquad E(u_i|x_i, d_i) = 0.$$

Note that, although we can define $u_{ji} \equiv y_{ji} - E(y_{ji}|x_i)$ to get $E(u_{ji}|x_i) = 0$ by construction, the assumption $E(u_i|x_i, d_i) = 0$ is not trivial, because it contains the selection-on-observable assumption $E(y_j|x, d) = E(y_j|x)$, $j = 0, 1$, owing to

$$E(y_j|x, d) = E\{\rho(x, j; \beta) + u|x, d\} = \rho(x, j; \beta) = E(y_j|x).$$

Also u_i is not indexed by j.

The conditional effect on x is

$$E(y_1|x, d = 1) - E(y_0|x, d = 0) = \rho(x, 1; \beta) - \rho(x, 0; \beta).$$

Integrating out x with its density f_x, we get the marginal effect

$$E(y_1 - y_0) = \int \{\rho(x, 1; \beta) - \rho(x, 0; \beta)\} f_x(x) dx.$$

Here, hidden bias is ruled out by the selection-on-observable assumption, overt bias is removed by controlling for x, and the dimension problem is avoided by parameterization. Also, the support problem is easily overcome in the parametric model, because any desired counter-factual can be constructed using the parametric regression function: for example,

$$E(y_0|d = 1, x_o) = E\{\rho(x_o, 0; \beta) + u|d = 1, x_o\} = \rho(x_o, 0; \beta).$$

The only thing needed for this counter-factual is β; it does not matter whether or not there are any control units with $x = x_o$. If there is no control unit with

$x = x_o$, then using $\rho(x_o, 0; \beta)$ is an extrapolation, for x_o is not in the support of $x|d = 0$.

To be specific on $\rho(x, j; \beta)$, suppose

$$\rho(x, j; \beta) = \beta_1 + \beta_x x + \beta_{x2} x^2 + \beta_d j + \beta_{xd} jx, \quad \beta \equiv (\beta_1, \beta_x, \beta_{x2}, \beta_d, \beta_{xd})'.$$

Then the conditional effect is $\beta_d + \beta_{xd} x$, and the marginal effect is $\beta_d + \beta_{xd} E(x)$. In this model, the hypothesis of no effect is $H_o : \beta_d = \beta_{xd} = 0$. If $\beta_{xd} = 0$, then the conditional effect is the constant β_d and no integrating out is necessary for x. Substitute the y_{0i}- and y_{1i}-model into $y_i = (1 - d_i)y_{0i} + d_i y_{1i}$ to get

$$y_i = \beta_1 + \beta_x x_i + \beta_{x2} x_i^2 + \beta_d d_i + \beta_{xd} d_i x_i + u_i.$$

Owing to the selection-on-observable assumption, this equation can be estimated with LSE.

3.2.4 Two-stage method for a semi-linear model*

In the preceding parametric approach, one may be wary of the linear specification. Robins *et al.* (1992) suggest a way to relax the parameterization with a semi-linear model

$$y_i = \beta d_i + g(x_i) + u_i, \qquad E(u|d, x) = 0$$

where $g(x)$ is an unknown function. In this model, the only substantial restriction other than $E(u|d, x) = 0$ is the lack of interaction between d and x.

From the equation, we get

$$E[\{y - \beta d\}\{d - E(d|x)\}] = E[\{g(x) + u\}\{d - E(d|x)\}] = E[g(x)\{d - E(d|x)\}]$$
$$= E[g(x) \cdot E[\{d - E(d|x)\}|x]] = 0.$$

Solve the moment condition $E[\{y - \beta d\}\{d - E(d|x)\}] = 0$ for β:

$$\beta = \frac{E[\{d - E(d|x)\}y]}{E[\{d - E(d|x)\}d]}.$$

Assuming for a while that $E(d|x)$ is known, a sample version for this is

$$b_{No} = \frac{N^{-1} \sum_i \{d_i - E(d|x_i)\} y_i}{N^{-1} \sum_i \{d_i - E(d|x_i)\} d_i} = \frac{N^{-1} \sum_i \{d_i - E(d|x_i)\}\{\beta d_i + g(x_i) + u_i\}}{N^{-1} \sum_i \{d_i - E(d|x_i)\} d_i}$$

$$= \beta + \frac{N^{-1} \sum_i \{d_i - E(d|x_i)\}\{g(x_i) + u_i\}}{N^{-1} \sum_i \{d_i - E(d|x_i)\} d_i}.$$

With this, doing analogously to deriving the asymptotic distribution of LSE, it follows that

$$\sqrt{N}(b_{No} - \beta) \rightsquigarrow N\left(0, \ \frac{E[\{d - E(d|x)\}^2 (y - \beta d)^2]}{E^2[\{d - E(d|x)\}d]}\right)$$

$$= N\left(0, \ \frac{C_o}{E^2[\{d - E(d|x)\}d]}\right),$$

where $C_o \equiv E[\{d - E(d|x)\}^2(y - \beta d)^2]$ and E^2 means $[E(\cdot)]^2$.

Since $E(d|x)$ has to be estimated in practice, suppose that the logit model holds for $E(d|x)$:

$$p_i(\alpha) \equiv P(d = 1|x_i) = \frac{\exp(x_i'\alpha)}{1 + \exp(x_i'\alpha)}.$$

Let a_N denote the logit estimator. Then a feasible version for b_{No} is

$$b_N \equiv \frac{N^{-1}\sum_i\{d_i - p_i(a_N)\}y_i}{N^{-1}\sum_i\{d_i - p_i(a_N)\}d_i} = \beta + \frac{N^{-1}\sum_i\{d_i - p_i(a_N)\}\{g(x_i) + u_i\}}{N^{-1}\sum_i\{d_i - p_i(a_N)\}d_i}$$

which is a two-stage estimator. Below, we describe another view on the estimator and then present the asymptotic distribution, whose derivation is in the appendix.

To view the idea from a different perspective, rewrite $y_i = \beta d_i + g(x_i) + u_i$ as

$$y_i = \beta\{d_i - E(d|x_i)\} + \beta E(d|x_i) + g(x_i) + u_i = \beta\{d_i - E(d|x_i)\} + v_i,$$

where $v_i \equiv \beta E(d|x_i) + g(x_i) + u_i$. Observe

$$E[\{d - E(d|x)\}v] = E[\{d - E(d|x)\}\{\beta E(d|x) + g(x) + u\}]$$

$$= E[E[\{d - E(d|x)\}\{\beta E(d|x) + g(x) + u\}|x]]$$

$$= E[\{\beta E(d|x) + g(x)\} \cdot E\{d - E(d|x)|x\}] = 0.$$

Hence, LSE can be applied to yield another estimator

$$\frac{N^{-1}\sum_i\{d_i - p_i(a_N)\}y_i}{N^{-1}\sum_i\{d_i - p_i(a_N)\}^2}.$$

It can be shown that this estimator's asymptotic distribution is the same as that of b_N.

The asymptotic distribution for b_N is

$$\sqrt{N}(b_N - \beta) \rightsquigarrow N(0,\ E^{-2}\{(d_i - p_i(\alpha))d_i\}(C_o - LI_f^{-1}L')).$$

The part $C_o - LI_f^{-1}L'$ can be estimated consistently with

$$N^{-1}\sum_i [\{(y_i - b_N d_i) - L_N I_{Nf}^{-1}x_i\}^2 (d_i - p_i(a_N))^2],\ \text{where}$$

$$L_N \equiv N^{-1}\sum_i p_i(a_N)(1 - p_i(a_N))(y_i - b_N d_i)x_i',$$

$$I_{Nf} \equiv N^{-1}\sum_i p_i(a_N)(1 - p_i(a_N))x_i x_i'.$$

Despite being a two-stage estimator affected by the first-stage estimation error, the asymptotic variance of b_N is smaller than that of b_{No} due to $-LI_f^{-1}L'$— a surprising result of the kind first discovered by Pierce (1982).

3.3 Regression discontinuity design (RDD) and before-after (BA)

Sometimes treatments are determined solely by the level of x. For instance, $d = 1[x > \tau]$, where τ is a known threshold. In this case there is no overlap in x values across the T and C groups. Suppose that x also affects the response variable directly, which means that x should be controlled for in assessing the effect of d on y. However, conditioning on the same x is not possible due to the support problem. Although the T and C groups are not comparable in most x values, they are comparable on a small neighborhood of $x = \tau$. This leads us to find the treatment effect for the subpopulation with $x \simeq \tau$, which is the topic of this section. Readers further interested in the material in this section can consult Battistin and Rettore (2002), van der Klaauw (2002), and their references.

In the usual treatment effect framework with observational data, the treatment is selected by the individuals. But in this section, it is imposed on the individuals by a law or rule depending on x (and other variables) such that d has a break at a known point $x = \tau$. In the following, first, we will deal with the case where the rule depends only on x and the size of the break is one. Second, where the rule depends on x and some error term ε, and the size of the break is unknown.

3.3.1 Parametric regression discontinuity

Suppose that the eligibility for a family aid program d is determined solely by the observed income x, say, $d = 1[x \le \$20,000]$, and we are interested in the program eligibility effect on children's health y. The C and T groups certainly differ in d, but they also differ in x: the C group is the low income group and the

T group is the high income group. If $d \perp y_j$ for $j = 0, 1$, then the usual group mean difference identifies $E(y_1 - y_0)$. For the aid example, however, $d \perp y_j$ is not plausible, because income affects d and is likely to affect y_j directly as well.

Rewrite the group mean difference as

$$
\begin{aligned}
E(y|x, d = 1) - E(y|x, d = 0) &= E(y_1|x, d = 1) - E(y_0|x, d = 0) \\
&= \{E(y_1|x, d = 1) - E(y_0|x, d = 1)\} \\
&\quad + \{E(y_0|x, d = 1) - E(y_0|x, d = 0)\} \\
&= (\text{effect for 'post-break'}) \\
&\quad + (y_0 \text{ comparison group bias}).
\end{aligned}
$$

If the y_0 comparison group bias is zero (i.e., if $y_0 \perp d|x$), then the *effect for post-break* is identified by the group mean difference. If $y_1 \perp d|x$ as well, then the effect for post-break becomes $E(y_1 - y_0|x)$.

If the two groups do not overlap in x, we have a support problem as already mentioned. This is the case in the aid example, where the law or rule applied to everybody with no exception, is the reason for there being no overlap in x. Until now, we have dealt mostly with cases where d is not completely determined by x—under selection-on-observable assumption, d is determined by x and an error term independent of y_j given x. In the aid example, however, d was fully determined by x and is monotonic in x, which separates the C and T groups in terms of x. Also notable in the aid example is that $P(d = 1|x)$ takes on either 0 or 1.

An answer to the support problem can be found in the parametric regression model

$$
y_i = \beta_1 + \beta_d d_i + \beta_x x_i + u_i, \qquad E(u) = 0, \quad E(u|x) = 0.
$$

Since d is determined solely by x, $E(u|x) = 0$ implies $E(u|d) = 0$. This regression model is familiar to economists. For example, y is earnings, x is schooling years and d is the dummy for a college diploma (e.g., $d = 1[x \geq 16]$). Here we can see if there is a 'sheepskin effect' in addition to schooling. The model states that, if $\beta_d \neq 0$, then there is a break or discontinuity in the earnings regression function as x increases, yielding the name *regression discontinuity design (RDD)*.

If we apply the linear regression model to the aid program example, the regression model helps to construct the counter-factual; for example,

$$
E(y|x = 30{,}000, d = 1) = \beta_1 + \beta_d + \beta_x 30{,}000,
$$

although nobody satisfies the condition $x = 30{,}000$ and $d = 1$. Subtracting $E(y|x = 30{,}000, d = 0) = \beta_1 + \beta_x 30{,}000$ from this, the treatment effect for the subpopulation $x = 30{,}000$ is β_d. In fact, the treatment effect for any x is still β_d. The critical assumption here is that the parametric regression function used for extrapolation (i.e., for the counter-factual) is correctly specified. The true model can be, say,

$$y_i = \beta_1 + \beta_x x_i + \beta_{x2} x_i^2 + \beta_{x3} x_i^3 + \beta_{x4} x_i^4 + u_i,$$

and a data plot generated from this nonlinear model could be mistaken for the one generated from the linear model with a break.

Is there any way to separate the linear model with d from this kind of smooth model nonlinear in x? The answer is a qualified yes. For instance, suppose $d = 1[x \leq \tau_0 \text{ or } x > \tau_1]$ where τ_0 and τ_1 are known thresholds with $\tau_0 < \tau_1$, and $\beta_1, \beta_x, \beta_{x2}, \beta_{x3}, \beta_{x4}$ and x are all positive. Then, the linear model with the dummy is nonmonotonic in x, whereas the nonlinear model is monotonic in x. It will not be difficult to tell one model from the other (by plotting the data at hand).

Berk and de Leeuw (1999) estimate the effect of inmate 'violence classification score' x, and prison security level d, on a binary in-prison misconduct variable y. Inmates are assigned to four different security level prisons based on their x determined solely by observed inmate covariates (age, marital status, work history, prior incarcerations and sentence length). They look only at $d = 1$ (the highest level security) versus $d = 0$ (the other three levels). Using California state data of about $N = 4{,}000$ with inmates admitted early in 1994 and then followed up for 18 months, they did a logit analysis to find that $\beta_d \simeq -0.761$ (0.138) and $\beta_x \simeq 0.025$ (0.003) with SD given in $(\cdot)$. Thus, the higher security reduces in-prison misconduct and the higher classification score leads to more misconduct. Although interesting, it is worrying that the findings may have come from a misspecified regression function that is highly nonlinear in x with zero effect from d. Hence, we turn to nonparametric RDD.

3.3.2 Sharp nonparametric regression discontinuity

RDD as just explained is heavily model-dependent, which is not very attractive. We would not want to derive false conclusions due to a model misspecification. In this and the following subsection, we relax the parametric assumptions under $d_i = 1[x_i \geq \tau]$ where τ is a known threshold. As we will see shortly, the essential nonparametric identification requirement in RDD is that the *direct effect of x on y be negligible relative to the effect of x on d when x is near the threshold τ.*

Consider

$$y_{ji} = \beta_d j + g(x_i) + u_{ji}, \qquad j = 0, 1,$$
$$\text{(i)} \lim_{x \to \tau} E(u_0|x) = \lim_{x \to \tau} E(u_1|x)$$
$$\text{(ii)} \ g(\cdot) \text{ is an unknown function continuous at } x = \tau.$$

Despite no randomization taking place, the assumptions (i) and (ii) are for *borderline (or threshold) randomization*: those subjects near the threshold are likely to be similar in all aspects except in the treatment; (i) is for the similarity in the unobservables and (ii) is for the similarity in the observables. From the model,

$$y_{1i} - y_{0i} = \beta_d + u_{1i} - u_{0i}$$
$$\implies \lim_{x \to \tau} E(y_1 - y_0 | x) = \beta_d + \lim_{x \to \tau} E(u_1 - u_0 | x) = \beta_d;$$

β_d is the treatment *effect for the subpopulation* $x \simeq \tau$.

Turning to identifying β_d, note that the observed response model is

$$y_i = \beta_d d_i + g(x_i) + u_i, \qquad u_i \equiv (1 - d_i)u_{0i} + d_i u_{1i}, \quad \text{where}$$
$$\lim_{x \downarrow \tau} E(u|x) = \lim_{x \downarrow \tau} E(u_1|x) \quad \text{and} \quad \lim_{x \uparrow \tau} E(u|x) = \lim_{x \uparrow \tau} E(u_0|x).$$

The *propensity score* $E(d_i | x_i)$ is either 0 or 1, depending on whether $x_i < \tau$ or $x_i \geq \tau$, and thus

$$\lim_{x \downarrow \tau} E(d|x) = 1, \qquad \lim_{x \uparrow \tau} E(d|x) = 0.$$

Observe

$$\lim_{x \downarrow \tau} E(y|x) = \beta_d + \lim_{x \downarrow \tau} g(x) + \lim_{x \downarrow \tau} E(u_1|x) \quad \text{and}$$
$$\lim_{x \uparrow \tau} E(y|x) = \lim_{x \uparrow \tau} g(x) + \lim_{x \uparrow \tau} E(u_0|x)$$
$$\implies \lim_{x \downarrow \tau} E(y|x) - \lim_{x \uparrow \tau} E(y|x) = \beta_d :$$

β_d is identified with the difference between the right and left limits of $E(y|x)$ at $x = \tau$. How to estimate the limits will be discussed in the next subsection.

The semi-linear model may look restrictive compared with the purely non-parametric model in that the former does not seem to allow interaction between d and x. But this is not the case. To see this, replace $y_{ji} = \beta_{dj} + g(x_i) + u_{ji}$ with $y_{ji} = \beta_{dj} + \gamma(x)j + g(x_i) + u_{ji}$ where the interacting term $\gamma(x)$ has the limit $\gamma(\tau)$ at $x = \tau$. Then,

$$y_{1i} - y_{0i} = \beta_d + \gamma(x) + u_{1i} - u_{0i}$$
$$\implies \lim_{x \to \tau} E(y_1 - y_0 | x) = \beta_d + \gamma(\tau) + \lim_{x \to \tau} E(u_1 - u_0 | x) = \beta_d + \gamma(\tau).$$

The effect for the subpopulation $x \simeq \tau$ is $\beta_d + \gamma(\tau)$. However, this case can be accommodated in $y_{ji} = \beta_{dj} + g(x_i) + u_{ji}$ by simply redefining β_d as $\beta_d + \gamma(\tau)$. That is, there is no loss of generality by considering the semi-linear model.

The treatment $d_i = 1[x_i \geq \tau]$ is asymmetric in that the threshold case $x_i = \tau$ gets treated. Instead, consider a symmetric version with a tie-breaking randomization

$$d_i = 1[x_i > \tau] + 1[x_i = \tau] \cdot 1[\varepsilon_i = 1],$$

where ε_i is a random variable independent of the other random variables with $P(\varepsilon_i = 1) = P(\varepsilon_i = 0) = 0.5$. In this case, $E(d_i | x_i) = 1$ if $x_i > \tau$, 0.5 if $x_i = \tau$, and 0 if $x_i < 0.5$. But we still get

$$\lim_{x \downarrow \tau} E(d|x) = 1, \ \lim_{x \uparrow \tau} E(d|x) = 0 \implies \beta_d = \lim_{x \downarrow \tau} E(y|x) - \lim_{x \uparrow \tau} E(y|x).$$

Now we present an empirical example in Black (1999) exploiting the pseudo borderline randomization idea. Black (1999) estimates how much parents are willing to pay for better education for their children. School quality can affect house prices because parents choose to live in a higher-quality school area. The usual way of estimating the effect of school quality on house prices is hedonic price modeling. ln(house price) is regressed on house characteristics, neighborhood characteristics, school-district characteristics and school quality. There can be, however, many omitted variables at the level of school district and neighborhood to bias these hedonic price model estimates. Black (1999) instead samples houses close to school attendance district boundaries: houses on the opposite side of a boundary, but close to it, are likely to differ only in terms of the school quality (the treatment) while sharing the same school district and neighborhood characteristics. Putting this in RDD framework, imagine one boundary, two schools (one good on the right-hand side of the boundary, the other poor on the left-hand side), $d = 1$[right-hand side of boundary], and house prices affected smoothly by distance from the boundary.

Using the full sample consisting of 22,679 single-family residences within 39 school districts and 181 attendance district boundaries, part of Table II in Black (1999) shows the estimates (and t-values in (·)):

	school quality	bedrooms	bathrooms	bathrooms^2	building age
Hedonic regression for willingness to pay for school quality					
All	.035	.033	.147	−.013	−.002
houses	(.004)	(.004)	(.014)	(.003)	(.0003)
Boundary	.016	.038	.143	−.017	−.002
houses	(.007)	(.005)	(.018)	(.004)	(.0002)

where the row for 'all houses' is for the usual hedonic regression using all house data, the row for 'boundary houses' is a hedonic regression using only the houses within 0.35 miles from the boundary, and school quality is measured by a standardized test for the fourth grade (the test score ranges from 0 to 16 with an average of about 13.8 and a SD of about 0.7). More covariates were used for the results, however, which have been omitted. The table shows that the results are similar for the house characteristics, but the key effect is halved in the boundary house case, which controls the school district and neighborhood characteristics better than the all-house case does.

Although attractive, borderline randomization is not fail-safe. In the family aid program example

$$y_i = \beta_1 + \beta_d 1[x_i \leq \$20,000] + \beta_x x_i + u_i,$$

it is possible for a family to lower their income to qualify for the program. Suppose $\beta_d, \beta_x > 0$ and the family's income m without the program is above \$20,000. The gain of lowering the initial income m to \$20,000 is β_d and the cost is $\beta_x(m - 20000)$. Hence the net gain is positive, if

$$\beta_d > \beta_x(m - 2000) \iff m < \frac{\beta_d}{\beta_x} + 20,000.$$

If β_d is large and β_x is small, then families with an initial income much greater than \$20,000 may lower their income to \$20,000. These families may have observed or unobserved characteristics very different from the families whose initial income is \$20,000 or slightly lower. Hence borderline randomization fails in this case. One way to check this possibility is to look at the income distribution around the threshold. A fairly symmetric distribution around the threshold would support the borderline randomization, whereas clustering on one side would suggest otherwise.

In the above school-quality and house-price example, it is possible that families with children would locate on the side of the boundary with higher-quality schools, whereas no-children families would locate on the other side. The two types of families may demand different types of houses. The houses around the borderline would then differ in observed or unobserved characteristics. This would also spell trouble for the borderline randomization.

3.3.3   Fuzzy nonparametric regression discontinuity

In the literature, a design with d completely determined by x_i is called a *sharp RDD*, whereas a design with d determined by x and some error term ε is called a *fuzzy RDD*. In practice, sharp RDD would be rare in observational studies, because treatment assignment typically involves multiple decisions. However, if selection-on-observable holds at $x \simeq \tau$, if the propensity score $E(d|x)$ has a break at τ, and if $\lim_{x \to \tau} E(u_j|x) = 0$, then fuzzy RDD can be dealt with as follows.

Recall the semi-linear model for sharp RDD. The main difference in fuzzy RDD is that $E(d|x)$ has a break at $x = \tau$ of an unknown magnitude:

$$\lim_{x \downarrow \tau} E(d|x) - \lim_{x \uparrow \tau} E(d|x) \neq 0.$$

This cannot hold for sharp RDD because $E(d|x) = d$. Since the characterization of β_d as the effect on the subpopulation $x \simeq \tau$ in the preceding subsection does not depend on the preceding display, the characterization of β_d still holds in fuzzy RDD.

For identification, observe, for the same semi-linear model,

$$\lim_{x\downarrow\tau} E(y|x) = \beta_d \lim_{x\downarrow\tau} E(d|x) + \lim_{x\downarrow\tau} g(x) + \lim_{x\downarrow\tau} E(u|x) \quad \text{and}$$

$$\lim_{x\uparrow\tau} E(y|x) = \beta_d \lim_{x\uparrow\tau} E(d|x) + \lim_{x\uparrow\tau} g(x) + \lim_{x\uparrow\tau} E(u|x)$$

$$\Longrightarrow \lim_{x\downarrow\tau} E(y|x) - \lim_{x\uparrow\tau} E(y|x) = \beta_d \{\lim_{x\downarrow\tau} E(d|x) - \lim_{x\uparrow\tau} E(d|x)\}$$

$$\Longrightarrow \frac{\lim_{x\downarrow\tau} E(y|x) - \lim_{x\uparrow\tau} E(y|x)}{\lim_{x\downarrow\tau} E(d|x) - \lim_{x\uparrow\tau} E(d|x)} = \beta_d;$$

note that $\lim_{x\to\tau} E(u|x) = 0$. Hence, β_d is identified by the ratio of the one-sided derivative difference, which includes the sharp RDD case as a special case when the denominator is one.

It is instructive to regard the ratio as

$$\frac{\text{total effect of } x \text{ on } y \text{ at } x = \tau}{\text{effect of } x \text{ on } d \text{ at } x = \tau}.$$

Suppose the *direct effect of x on y is negligible around* $x = \tau$, relative to the effect of x on d. The direct effect refers to $\lim_{x\downarrow\tau} g(x) - \lim_{x\uparrow\tau} g(x)$ that is zero by the continuity of $g(x)$ at $x = \tau$. Then the total effect becomes the indirect effect of x on y in $x \to d \to y$, which is the product of the effect of x on d and the effect of d on y—recall Subsection 3.1.3. Since the denominator removes the former, the above ratio becomes the effect of d on y. Later, when we study instrumental variable estimation (IVE), an analogous expression will appear under the name 'Wald estimator', and RDD will be accorded an IVE interpretation.

Turning to estimating the limits in the identification of β_d, in principle, nonparametric estimation can be done by replacing the limits of $E(y|x)$ with nonparametric estimators. In kernel nonparametric estimation, one can use a one-sided kernel: for $\lim_{x\downarrow\tau} E(y|x)$, a one-sided kernel at τ is $K((x_i - \tau)/h)1[x_i > \tau]$, and with this,

$$\frac{\sum_i K((x_i - \tau)/h)1[x_i > \tau]y_i}{\sum_i K((x_i - \tau)/h)1[x_i > \tau]} \to^p \lim_{x\downarrow\tau} E(y|x).$$

However, the one-sided kernel estimator's small sample behavior could be poor. Hahn *et al.* (2001) propose minimizing for a, b

$$\sum_i \{y_i - a - b(x_i - \tau)\}^2 K\left(\frac{x_i - \tau}{h}\right) 1[x_i > \tau],$$

in order to use the minimizer $\hat{a}$ as an estimator of $\lim_{x\downarrow\tau} E(y|x)$. As an alternative, Robinson's (1988) two-stage estimation method for semi-linear models can be used, as explained in the following two paragraphs. For further discussion and for an empirical example, see Battistin and Rettore (2002).

For the two-stage method, recall $y_{ji} = \beta_d j + g(x_i) + u_{ji}$ and, as invoked above

$$\lim_{x \to \tau} E\{(1 - d)u_0 + du_1 | x\} = 0$$

which is in essence a selection-on-observables near τ:

$$u_0 \perp d|x, \quad u_1 \perp d|x, \quad E(u_0|x) = 0 = E(u_1|x) \qquad \text{for } x \simeq \tau,$$

because these conditions imply

$$E\{(1 - d)u_0 + du_1 | x\} = E(1 - d|x)E(u_0|x) + E(d|x)E(u_1|x) = 0 \quad \text{for } x \simeq \tau.$$

Now take $E(\cdot|x_i)$ on $y_i = \beta_d d_i + g(x_i) + u_i$ for $x_i \simeq \tau$ to get

$$E(y|x_i) = \beta_d E(d|x_i) + g(x_i) \quad \text{for } x_i \simeq \tau.$$

Subtract this from $y_i = \beta_d d_i + g(x_i) + u_i$ to get

$$y_i - E(y|x_i) = \beta_d \{d_i - E(d|x_i)\} + u_i \quad \text{for } x_i \simeq \tau.$$

In the first stage, $E(y|x_i)$ and $E(d|x_i)$ are estimated nonparametrically, and in the second stage, LSE of $y_i - E(y|x_i)$ on $d_i - E(d|x_i)$ is done to estimate β_d. In both stages, only the observations with $x_i \in (\tau - c, \tau + c)$ are used where $c \to 0$ as $N \to \infty$. This two-stage idea does not work for sharp RDD because $d_i - E(d|x_i) = 0 \ \forall i$.

Due to the shrinking neighborhood $(\tau - c, \tau + c)$, the convergence rate of the LSE to β_d is slower than the usual $\sqrt{N}$ rate. In practice, however, this aspect may be ignored, which then makes the two-stage RDD estimation fairly straightforward. Ignoring this aspect means we assume, for some fixed neighbor X_τ of $x = \tau$,

$$u_0 \perp d|x, \quad u_1 \perp d|x, \quad E(u_0|x) = 0 = E(u_1|x) \quad \forall x \in X_\tau \quad \text{and}$$

$$g(x) \text{ is 'flat' on } x \in X_\tau.$$

These assumptions render $\beta_d = E(y_1 - y_0 | x \in X_\tau)$.

With $E_N(\cdot|x_i)$ denoting a nonparametric estimator for $E(\cdot|x_i)$ using all but observation i, an estimator for β_d is

$$b_d \equiv \frac{\sum_i \{d_i - E_N(d|x_i)\}\{y_i - E_N(y|x_i)\}1[x_i \in X_\tau]}{\sum_i \{d_i - E_N(d|x_i)\}^2 1[x_i \in X_\tau]}.$$

The asymptotic variance of $b_d - \beta_d$ can be estimated with

$$\frac{\sum_i \{d_i - E_N(d|x_i)\}^2 [y_i - E_N(y|x_i) - b_d\{d_i - E_N(d|x_i)\}]^2 1[x_i \in X_\tau]}{(\sum_i \{d_i - E_N(d|x_i)\}^2 1[x_i \in X_\tau])^2}.$$

An example for $1[x_i \in X_\tau]$ is $1[|x_i - \tau| < SD(x)]$, or for a given problem, one may have some idea of X_τ on which borderline randomization holds. This two-stage procedure would be easier to use in practice and behave better than the (local linear) kernel regression for $\lim_{x \downarrow \tau} E(y|x)$ and $\lim_{x \uparrow \tau} E(y|x)$.

Van der Klaauw (2002) describes an example of fuzzy RDD by estimating the effect of financial aid on college enrollment using data from an east coast college for the period 1989 to 1993. Let the college have an ability index x and offer, say, three levels of financial aid depending on

$$\gamma_1 1[x \geq \tau_1] + \gamma_2 1[x \geq \tau_2] + \gamma_3 1[x \geq \tau_3], \quad \text{where } \tau_1 < \tau_2 < \tau_3 \text{ are known.}$$

The actual amount of financial aid differs from this step function because the admission officers take other factors into account, such as extracurricular activities and recommendation letters, which makes the RDD fuzzy. Although there is an endogeneity issue, that financial aid from competing colleges is related to x but omitted, we will not discuss this here. In Van der Klaauw (2002), y is binary (enrollment or not) and d is the financial aid amount measured in the thousands of 1991 dollars.

In his Table 2, $\gamma_1, \gamma_2, \gamma_3$ are estimated to be $1280, 1392, 3145$, respectively. As the ability index goes over τ_3, the financial aid offered increases by \$3145 which is γ_3. In his Table 3, Van der Klaauw (2002) presents nonparametric estimates for the treatment effect (recall the ratio of two nonparametric estimate differences). Part of Table 3, for those who applied for federal financial aid, is shown in the table below where SD's are obtained with a 'bootstrap'.

RDD for financial aid effect on enrollment		
threshold 1	threshold 2	threshold 3
effect (SD) 0.010 (0.238)	0.040 (0.041)	0.067 (0.029)

Only the last estimate is significant. The effect of the financial aid offer on enrollment probability is 6.7% for those students with an ability index of about τ_3.

3.3.4   Before-after (BA)

Closely related to RDD is 'before-after (BA)' design ('interrupted time-series' design or 'pre-break and post-break design') where discontinuity takes place in time-dimension. Here, the control responses come from the era before the treatment, whereas the treated responses come from the era after the treatment. As in RDD, BA identifies the post-break effect $E(y_1 - y_0|d = 1)$ under $y_0 \perp d$ (given x). For example, if we want to know the effect of a speed limit law d that was introduced in 1995, on the number of accidents y per car, we can compare y before and after the speed limit law. With t denoting years, $d_t = 1[t \geq 1995]$. As in RDD, conditioning on t is problematic. Conditioning on t or variables that change monotonically as t increases, is troublesome because the periods before and after the treatment break are not comparable in terms of t and those monotonic variables.

As in RDD, counter-factuals such as $E(y|d = 0, t = 1996)$ can be provided by a parametric regression model involving d and t. A misspecified regression model may, however, give a false impression that d matters. For instance, suppose that the car registration fee w has been increasing steadily over the years to discourage driving, which means that y drops as w goes up. Suppose d has no effect. The relationship between w and y could be nonlinear with a steep decline in 1995, which may be mistaken for the effect owing to d. If w is not available, we could take $y_t = \beta_d d_t + g(t) + u_t$ as the true model, where $g(t)$ captures the omitted but smooth influence of w on y. The nonparametric method for RDD could be applied to this model.

For a BA design to be effective, the treatment (i.e., the break) should be defined clearly and take place fast, and the effect should be felt quickly before other covariates change (Marcantonio and Cook (1994)). This is analogous to the borderline randomization of RDD, where in a small temporal treatment neighborhood, the period just before the treatment should be comparable to the period just after the treatment, because other changes are unlikely to take place over the short term. If the treatment takes place gradually over time and if the effect diffuses slowly, then it is difficult to separate the treatment effect from the 'time effect' due to other factors that vary over the same period.

As we will show in the next chapter, 'difference-in-differences' (DD) design is a big improvement over RDD and BA, in that there is a control group which incurs the time effect but not the treatment effect. Using the control group, the treatment effect can be identified even if the treatment takes place gradually. In a DD, the treatment is given only to a certain group of individuals, and those left out constitute the control group. In contrast, in BA (and RDD), everybody gets the treatment without exception. Hence there is no 'contemporary' control group in BA. Only the treatment group's past before the treatment is available as a control group. In DD, if we focus (i.e., condition) on the treated group overtime, perhaps because the non-treated group does not constitute a good control group for some reason, then we get a BA.

3.4 Treatment effect estimator with weighting[*]

When selection-on-observables holds, it is possible to estimate the marginal effect $E(y_1 - y_0)$ or the effect on the (un)treated without estimating the conditional means $E(y_1 - y_0|x, d)$. We examine one approach in this section, and another in the following section.

When a sample is selected not from the whole population but from a subpopulation, we can correct for the difference with weighting. For instance, suppose that an income (y) data set is sampled from a region with income density $g(y)$, but we desire to know $E(y) = \int y f(y) dy$ where $f(y)$ is the income density for the whole population. Then, because

$$\int y f(y) dy = \int \frac{y}{r(y)} g(y) dy, \quad \text{where } r(y) \equiv \frac{g(y)}{f(y)},$$

$N^{-1} \sum_i y_i / r(y_i)$ is consistent for $E(y)$.

Weighting can be used to correct for the wrong density in treatment effect analysis, because the main problem in treatment effect analysis is that y_j is observed only for the subpopulation $d = j$, $j = 0, 1$, and subpopulations can differ in observed and unobserved variables. If we could create an artificial world, where both y_0 and y_1 are drawn from the same population, then the problem would disappear. As it is, weighting solves half of the problem by removing the imbalance in x. Thus, *weighting is an alternative to conditioning on x.* Compared to conditioning, in practice, weighting does not have a dimension problem, because only scalar weights are used. In theory though, the dimension problem still appears in estimating the weight. This dimension-reduction aspect will be looked at again in the following chapter when we examine 'propensity score matching'. It is possible to do both conditioning and weighting to control for x, although this combination will not be examined.

Under selection-on-observables and $\pi(x) \equiv E(d|x)$, observe $d \cdot y = d\{dy_1 + (1 - d)y_0\} = d \cdot y_1$, and

$$E\left\{\frac{d \cdot y}{\pi(x)}\right\} = E\left[E\left\{\frac{d \cdot y}{\pi(x)}\Big|x\right\}\right] = E\left[\frac{E\{d \cdot y_1|x\}}{\pi(x)}\right]$$

$$= E\left[\frac{E(d|x)E(y_1|x)}{\pi(x)}\right] = E[E(y_1|x)] = E(y_1).$$

Analogously,

$$E\left\{\frac{(1 - d)y}{1 - \pi(x)}\right\} = E(y_0).$$

We will examine the effect on the untreated first, followed by the effect on the treated and the effect on the population.

Weighting is useful not only to correct for the selection-on-observable problem, but also to raise the efficiency of an estimator. Hahn (1998) derives the efficiency bounds for $E(y_1 - y_0)$ and $E(y_1 - y_0|d = 1)$ and proposes efficient estimators that achieve these bounds. Hirano *et al.* (2003) propose simpler efficient estimators that are weighting-based. The bounds and estimators will be described in this section. Despite the attractiveness of the weighting idea, however, we will demonstrate an empirical example where the weighting estimators are unreliable. Here, the problem arises when the weight in the denominator is almost zero.

3.4.1   Effect on the untreated

For the effect on the untreated, observe

$$E\left\{\frac{d \cdot y}{\pi(x)}\right\} = E(y_1) = E(y_1|d=0)P(d=0) + E(y_1|d=1)P(d=1)$$

$$= E(y_1|d=0)P(d=0) + E(d \cdot y),$$

because $E(d \cdot y) = E(d \cdot y_1) = E(y_1|d=1)P(d=1)$. Solve the equation for $E(y_1|d=0)$:

$$E(y_1|d=0) = P(d=0)^{-1}\left[E\left(\frac{d \cdot y}{\pi(x)}\right) - E(d \cdot y)\right].$$

Hence, the effect on the untreated $E(y_1|d=0) - E(y|d=0)$ is

$$P(d=0)^{-1}\left[E\left(\frac{d \cdot y}{\pi(x)}\right) - E(d \cdot y)\right] - E(y|d=0)$$

$$= P(d=0)^{-1}\left[E\left(\frac{d \cdot y}{\pi(x)}\right) - E(d \cdot y)\right] - P(d=0)^{-1}E\{(1-d)y\}$$

$$= P(d=0)^{-1}\left[E\left(\frac{d \cdot y}{\pi(x)}\right) - E(dy) - E\{(1-d)y\}\right]$$

$$= P(d=0)^{-1}E\left\{\left(\frac{d}{\pi(x)}-1\right)y\right\} = P(d=0)^{-1}E\left\{\left(\frac{d-\pi(x)}{\pi(x)}\right)y\right\}.$$

With a consistent estimator $\pi_N(x)$ for $\pi(x)$, a consistent estimator for the effect on the untreated is

$$U_N \equiv \left(\frac{N_0}{N}\right)^{-1} \cdot N^{-1}\sum_i \left(\frac{d_i - \pi_N(x_i)}{\pi_N(x_i)}\right)y_i.$$

In the following, we assume $E(d|x) = \Phi(x'\alpha)$ where Φ is the $N(0,1)$ distribution function and estimate α with probit a_N. In this case, $\pi_N(x_i) = \Phi(x_i'a_N)$.

Let $\sqrt{N}(a_N - \alpha) = N^{-1/2}\sum_i \eta_i + o_p(1)$ where η_i is an influence function for probit. Denoting the probit score function as s_i, we have $\eta_i = E^{-1}(ss')s_i$ where $E^{-1}(\cdot)$ denotes the inverse of $E(\cdot)$. Denoting the $N(0,1)$ density function as ϕ, define

$$\lambda_i \equiv \frac{(d_i - \pi(x_i))y_i}{\pi(x_i)} - E\left\{\frac{(d-\pi(x))y}{\pi(x)}\right\} - E\left\{\frac{\phi(x'\alpha)x'y}{\pi(x)}\right\}\eta_i.$$

In the appendix we see that

$$\sqrt{N}\{U_N - E(y_1 - y_0|d=0)\} \rightsquigarrow N\left(0, \frac{E(\lambda^2)}{P(d=0)^2}\right).$$

A consistent estimator for $E(\lambda^2)$ is its sample analog $N^{-1}\sum_i \lambda_{Ni}^2$, where

$$\lambda_{Ni} \equiv \frac{(d_i - \pi_N(x_i))y_i}{\pi_N(x_i)} - U_N\frac{N_0}{N} - \left\{N^{-1}\sum_j \frac{\phi(x_j'a_N)x_j'y_j}{\pi_N(x_j)}\right\}\eta_{Ni},$$

$\eta_{Ni} \equiv (N^{-1}\sum_i s_{Ni}s_{Ni}')^{-1}s_{Ni}$, and s_{Ni} is the estimated probit score function:

$$s_{Ni} \equiv \frac{\{d_i - \Phi(x_i'a_N)\}\phi(x_i'a_N)x_i}{\Phi(x_i'a_N)\{1 - \Phi(x_i'a_N)\}}.$$

3.4.2   Effects on the treated and on the population

For the effect on the treated $E(y_1 - y_0|d = 1)$, observe

$$E\left\{\frac{(1-d)y}{1-\pi(x)}\right\} = E(y_0) = E(y_0|d=0)P(d=0) + E(y_0|d=1)P(d=1)$$
$$= E((1-d)y) + E(y_0|d=1)P(d=1).$$

Solve the equation for $E(y_0|d=1)$:

$$E(y_0|d=1) = P(d=1)^{-1}\left[E\left\{\frac{(1-d)y}{1-\pi(x)}\right\} - E((1-d)y)\right].$$

Hence, the effect on the treated $E(y|d=1) - E(y_0|d=1)$ is

$$E(y|d=1) - P(d=1)^{-1}E\left\{\frac{(1-d)y}{1-\pi(x)}\right\} + P(d=1)^{-1}E(y_0|d=0)P(d=0)$$
$$= P(d=1)^{-1}\left[E(dy) - E\left\{\frac{(1-d)y}{1-\pi(x)}\right\} + E\{(1-d)y\}\right]$$
$$= P(d=1)^{-1}E\left[\left\{1 - \frac{1-d}{1-\pi(x)}\right\}y\right] = P(d=1)^{-1}E\left[\left\{\frac{d-\pi(x)}{1-\pi(x)}\right\}y\right].$$

A consistent estimator for this is

$$T_N \equiv \left(\frac{N_1}{N}\right)^{-1}N^{-1}\sum_i\left\{1 - \frac{1-d_i}{1-\pi_N(x_i)}\right\}y_i$$
$$= \left(\frac{N_1}{N}\right)^{-1}N^{-1}\sum_i\left\{\frac{d_i - \pi_N(x_i)}{1-\pi_N(x_i)}\right\}y_i.$$

For the asymptotic distribution of T_N, we see in the appendix that

$$\sqrt{N}\{T_N - E(y_1 - y_0|d=1)\} \rightsquigarrow N\left(0, \frac{E(\zeta^2)}{P(d=1)^2}\right),$$
$$\text{where } \zeta_i \equiv -E\left(\frac{\phi(x'\alpha)x'y}{1-\pi(x)}\right)\eta_i - \frac{(\pi(x_i)-d_i)y_i}{1-\pi(x_i)} + E\left\{\frac{(\pi(x)-d)y}{1-\pi(x)}\right\}.$$

A consistent estimator for $E(\zeta^2)$ is its sample analog $N^{-1}\sum_i \zeta_{Ni}^2$, where

$$\zeta_{Ni} \equiv -\left\{ N^{-1}\sum_j \frac{\phi(x_j'a_N)x_j'y_j}{1-\pi_N(x_j)} \right\}\eta_{Ni} - \frac{(\pi_N(x_i)-d_i)y_i}{1-\pi_N(x_i)} + T_N\frac{N_1}{N}.$$

As for the effect on the population, observe

$$E(y_1 - y_0) = E\left\{ \frac{dy}{\pi(x)} - \frac{(1-d)y}{1-\pi(x)} \right\} \quad \left(= E\left[\frac{\{d-\pi(x)\}y}{\pi(x)(1-\pi(x))} \right] \right);$$

$$A_N \equiv U_N\frac{N_0}{N} + T_N\frac{N_1}{N} = N^{-1}\sum_i \left\{ \frac{d_i}{\pi_N(x_i)} - \frac{1-d_i}{1-\pi_N(x_i)} \right\}y_i$$

$$= N^{-1}\sum_i \left\{ \frac{d_i - \pi_N(x_i)}{\pi_N(x_i)(1-\pi_N(x_i))} \right\}y_i \longrightarrow^p E(y_1 - y_0).$$

From $A_N = U_N(N_0/N) + T_N(N_1/N)$, it follows that

$$\sqrt{N}\{A_N - E(y_1 - y_0)\} \rightsquigarrow N(0,\ E\{(\lambda + \zeta)^2\}),$$

and the asymptotic variance can be estimated consistently with $N^{-1}\sum_i(\lambda_{Ni} + \zeta_{Ni})^2$.

3.4.3 Efficiency bounds and efficient estimators

Define

$$p \equiv P(d=1), \qquad \sigma_j^2(x) \equiv V(y_j|x), \quad j = 0,1,$$
$$\tau(x) = E(y_1 - y_0|x), \qquad \tau \equiv E(y_1 - y_0), \qquad \tau_1 \equiv E(y_1 - y_0|d=1).$$

Under $(y_0, y_1) \amalg d|x$, Hahn (1998) demonstrates that the semiparametric efficiency bounds for τ and τ_1 are, respectively,

$$V \equiv E\left[\frac{\sigma_1^2(x)}{\pi(x)} + \frac{\sigma_0^2(x)}{1-\pi(x)} + \{\tau - \tau(x)\}^2 \right],$$

$$V_1 \equiv E\left[\frac{\pi(x)\sigma_1^2(x)}{p^2} + \frac{\pi(x)^2\sigma_0^2(x)}{p^2\{1-\pi(x)\}} + \frac{\{\tau_1 - \tau(x)\}^2\pi(x)}{p^2} \right].$$

Hahn (1998) also demonstrates that, when $\pi(x)$ is known, the efficiency bound V for τ does not change, whereas that for τ_1 becomes

$$V_{known\ \pi(x)} \equiv E\left[\frac{\pi(x)\sigma_1^2(x)}{p^2} + \frac{\pi(x)^2\sigma_0^2(x)}{p^2\{1-\pi(x)\}} + \frac{\{\tau_1 - \tau(x)\}^2\pi(x)^2}{p^2} \right]$$

which differs from V_1 only in that $\pi(x)^2$ instead of $\pi(x)$ appears in the last term. Since $\pi(x)^2 < \pi(x)$, $V_{known\ \pi(x)}$ is smaller than V_1. That is, knowing $\pi(x)$ is informative for estimating the effect on the treated τ_1, whereas it is not for the effect on the population τ. Imbens (2004) intuitively explains this with different weights used for τ and τ_1 as follows. $E(y_1 - y_0)$ is the $f(x)$-weighted average of $E(y_1 - y_0|x)$ but $E(y_1 - y_0|d = 1)$ is the $f(x|d = 1)$-weighted average of $E(y_1 - y_0|d = 1, x)$. Rewrite $f(x|d = 1)$ as

$$f(x|d = 1) = \frac{P(d = 1|x)f(x)}{P(d = 1)} = \frac{\pi(x)f(x)}{p}$$

to see that knowing $\pi(x)$ can help estimating $f(x|d = 1)$ whereas this is not the case for $f(x)$.

Let $E_N(\cdot|x)$ denote a nonparametric estimator (e.g., a kernel estimator) for $E(\cdot|x)$. Define

$$\tau_{1N}(x) \equiv \frac{E_N(d \cdot y|x)}{E_N(d|x)} \to^p E(y|d = 1, x),$$

$$\tau_{0N}(x) \equiv \frac{E_N((1 - d) \cdot y|x)}{1 - E_N(d|x)} \to^p E(y|d = 0, x).$$

Define

$$\hat{y}_{1i} \equiv d_i y_i + (1 - d_i)\tau_{1N}(x_i) \quad \text{and} \quad \hat{y}_{0i} \equiv (1 - d_i)y_i + d_i\tau_{0N}(x_i);$$

where $\hat{y}_{1i}$ shows that, when $d_i = 0$, $\tau_{1N}(x_i)$ is used for the unobserved y_{1i} ($\hat{y}_{0i}$ can be interpreted analogously). Proposition 4 in Hahn (1998) states that efficient estimators for τ and τ_1 are, respectively:

efficient estimators for τ: $\quad \hat{\tau} \equiv N^{-1} \sum_i (\hat{y}_{1i} - \hat{y}_{0i}),$

$$\tilde{\tau} \equiv N^{-1} \sum_i \{\tau_{1N}(x_i) - \tau_{0N}(x_i)\},$$

efficient estimators for τ_1: $\quad \hat{\tau}_1 \equiv \frac{N^{-1} \sum_i d_i(\hat{y}_{1i} - \hat{y}_{0i})}{N^{-1} \sum_i d_i},$

$$\tilde{\tau}_1 \equiv \frac{N^{-1} \sum_i d_i\{\tau_{1N}(x_i) - \tau_{0N}(x_i)\}}{N^{-1} \sum_i d_i}.$$

Hirano *et al.* (2003) provide weighting-based efficient estimators for τ and τ_1 that require nonparametric estimation only of $\pi(x)$, which are simpler than $\hat{\tau}$, $\tilde{\tau}$, $\hat{\tau}_1$ and $\tilde{\tau}_1$:

for τ: $\quad \tau^w \equiv N^{-1} \sum_i \left\{ \frac{d_i y_i}{\pi_N(x_i)} - \frac{(1 - d_i)y_i}{1 - \pi_N(x_i)} \right\},$

for τ_1: $\quad \tau_1^w \equiv \left(\frac{N_1}{N} \right)^{-1} N^{-1} \sum_i \left\{ d_i y_i - \frac{\pi_N(x_i)(1 - d_i)y_i}{1 - \pi_N(x_i)} \right\}$

$$= \left(\frac{N_1}{N} \right)^{-1} N^{-1} \sum_i \left\{ \frac{d_i - \pi_N(x_i)}{1 - \pi_N(x_i)} \right\} y_i.$$

Hirano *et al.* (2003) also show that the estimators using the true $\pi(x)$ for the weighting function are less efficient. This is not totally surprising because we have already seen an example in Subsection 3.2.4 where estimating nuisance parameters yields a more efficient estimator. In the preceding subsection, we saw A_N and T_N using probit for $\pi(x)$, and A_N and T_N differ from τ^w and τ_1^w, respectively, only in that τ^w and τ_1^w use a nonparametric estimator instead of the probit. Despite this, the asymptotic variances of A_N and T_N do not seem to be V and V_1, respectively, which is also surprising.

A possible shortcoming of τ^w and τ_1^w is that the weights do not necessarily sum to one; e.g., $N^{-1}\sum_i d_i/\pi_N(x_i) = 1$ may not hold. For this, modified versions of τ^w and τ_1^w in Imbens (2004) are

$$\hat{\tau}^w \equiv \sum_i \frac{d_i y_i}{\pi_N(x_i)} \bigg/ \sum_i \frac{d_i}{\pi_N(x_i)} - \sum_i \frac{(1-d_i)y_i}{1-\pi_N(x_i)} \bigg/ \sum_i \frac{(1-d_i)}{1-\pi_N(x_i)},$$

$$\hat{\tau}_1^w \equiv N_1^{-1}\sum_i d_i y_i - \sum_i \frac{\pi_N(x_i)(1-d_i)y_i}{1-\pi_N(x_i)} \bigg/ \sum_i \frac{\pi_N(x_i)(1-d_i)}{1-\pi_N(x_i)}.$$

3.4.4 An empirical example

Recall the example of the job-training effect on ln(unemployment duration) with $N_1 = 973$ and $N_0 = 9312$ that appeared in the preceding chapter. The covariates are age, tenure at the last workplace, and education in six levels. With only a small number of covariates, this example is for illustration only. Using probit for $\pi_N(x)$ (age^2 is used as well for the probit), we obtained the results in the table below, where two t-values are provided in $(\cdot)$: the first is the correct t-value and the second ignores the first-stage error with η replaced by zero.

Weighing estimators for training effects on unemployment duration		
	all observations	$0.001 < \pi_N(x) < 0.999$
effect on untreated U_N (tv)	8.102 (2.07; 2.00)	-0.006 (-0.011; -0.012)
effect on treated T_N (tv)	0.290 (15.79; 1.53)	0.264 (14.88; 1.39)
effect on population A_N (tv)	7.363 (2.07; 2.01)	0.019 (0.034; 0.038)

When all observations were used for the second column of the table, non-sensical results were obtained: a seven- to eight-fold increase in unemployment duration due to the treatment. This must have been because a few $\pi_N(x)$ had fallen near zero or one. Thus, we selected only the observations with $0.001 < \pi_N(x) < 0.999$ in the last column, losing 19 observations. Consequently, A_N and U_N changed dramatically, whereas T_N remained about the same. Hence, the problem must be $\pi_N(x) \simeq 0$, which appears as a denominator for A_N and U_N. In fact, all 19 dropped observations had $\pi_N(x) < 0.001$. As we will show in Subsection 4.3.3, the magnitude of T_N and its correct t-value are comparable to those obtained with propensity score matching methods.

Also notable in the above table is the huge changes in the t-values for T_N when the first-stage estimation error is ignored. Typically in two-stage estimators, ignoring the first-stage error makes little difference. Robins *et al.* (1992) show another such case when $P(d = 1|x)$ is estimated with logit. Here the variance with an accurate first-stage correction is more than 10 times smaller than the variance without.

The empirical example warns us that weighting estimators should be used with caution. A caution is also warranted for other treatment effect estimators with propensity score estimators in the denominators (e.g., Abadie *et al.* (2002) and Abadie (2003) for quantile and mean regression function estimation for 'compliers' which will be discussed in Chapter 5).

3.5   Complete pairing with double sums*

Suppose we want to estimate the treatment effect on the treated with matching. This is typically done in two stages. First, for treated subject i, a comparison group is selected. Second, the average of the comparison group is subtracted from the response of treated subject i, and the difference is averaged over the T group. These two stages, which are examined in detail in the next chapter, have three shortcomings. First, many decisions have to be made in the first matching stage. Second, by plugging in the sample average of the comparison group, the resulting estimator becomes a two-stage procedure whose asymptotic distribution is hard to derive. Third, one should be vigilant of the non-overlapping support problem.

In view of the first shortcoming, one may wonder why not use all possible pairs, i.e., N_0 pairs for each treated subject (thus, $N_0 N_1$ pairs in total), instead of trying to select only some of them and consequently making arbitrary decisions on the way. The idea is *complete pairing*, and this section examines one such idea, drawing on Lee (2003b). The resulting estimator is a one-, not two-, stage estimator whose asymptotic distribution is easy to derive. Also, as it turns out, the estimator is consistent for a particular weighted average of $E(y_1 - y_0|x)$, although $E(y_1 - y_0|x)$ is not directly estimated. Interestingly, the weighted average has a built-in feature taking care of the support problem. We will study discrete-x cases first, followed by continuous x, and then mixed (discrete/continuous) x. We provide an empirical example as well. As in the other sections of this chapter, selection-on-observable will be maintained.

3.5.1   Discrete covariates

Suppose x is discrete. A marginal (treatment) effect estimator using all possible pairs is

$$L_N \equiv \frac{(N_0 N_1)^{-1} \sum_{j \in T} \sum_{i \in C} 1[x_i = x_j](y_j - y_i)}{(N_0 N_1)^{-1} \sum_{j \in T} \sum_{i \in C} 1[x_i = x_j]}$$

where i indexes the C group and j indexes the T group. In L_N, each matched pair with the same x from the T and C groups is compared with their responses, and all possible pairing is considered with no need to select any particular pair.

Suppose

the T and C groups share the common support points $x_r, r = 1, \ldots, R$, for x.

Let $\pi_{1r} \equiv P(x = x_r | d = 1)$ and $\pi_{0r} = P(x = x_r | d = 0)$. The expected value of the denominator of L_N is

$$
\begin{aligned}
E\{1[x_i = x_j]\} &= \sum_{r=1}^{R} P(x_j = x_r | x_i = x_r) P(x_i = x_r) \\
&= \sum_r P(x_j = x_r) P(x_i = x_r) = \sum_r \pi_{1r} \pi_{0r}
\end{aligned}
$$

whereas the variance of the denominator converges to zero as $N \to \infty$. Thus, the denominator of L_N is consistent for $\sum_r \pi_{1r} \pi_{0r}$.

Doing analogously, the numerator of L_N is consistent for

$$
\begin{aligned}
\sum_r \{E(y_j | x_j = x_r) &- E(y_i | x_i = x_r)\} \pi_{1r} \pi_{0r} \\
&= \sum_r \{E(y | d = 1, x = x_r) - E(y | d = 0, x = x_r)\} \pi_{1r} \pi_{0r} \\
&= \sum_r \{E(y_1 | x = x_r) - E(y_0 | x = x_r)\} \pi_{1r} \pi_{0r} \\
&= \sum_r E(y_1 - y_0 | x = x_r) \pi_{1r} \pi_{0r}.
\end{aligned}
$$

Therefore,

$$
L_N \to^p \sum_r E(y_1 - y_0 | x_r) w(r) \quad \text{as } N \to \infty, \quad \text{where } w(r) \equiv \frac{\pi_{1r} \pi_{0r}}{\sum_r \pi_{1r} \pi_{0r}}.
$$

The probability limit is zero under the H_0: $E(y_1 | x) = E(y_0 | x) \; \forall x$. Otherwise, it is a weighted average of the conditional mean effects. L_N can be used to test the null hypothesis of no conditional effect. Furthermore, if we are willing to take the probability limit as a marginal effect of interest, then L_N is an estimator for the marginal effect.

Although we assumed the common support, it is in fact not necessary. What is required is only $\sum_r \pi_{1r} \pi_{0r} > 0$ and $\pi_{1r} \pi_{0r} \neq 0$ for a single r is enough.

To appreciate the benefit of the product $\pi_{1r}\pi_{0r}$ in $\sum_r \pi_{1r}\pi_{0r}$, consider $\pi_{1r}+\pi_{0r}$ as a weight leading to a marginal effect

$$\sum_r E(y_1 - y_0|x_r)\frac{\pi_{1r} + \pi_{0r}}{\sum_r(\pi_{1r} + \pi_{0r})}.$$

When $\pi_{0r} = 0 \neq \pi_{1r}$, we get $\pi_{1r} + \pi_{0r} > 0$ whereas $\pi_{1r}\pi_{0r} = 0$; the latter is preferable because the two groups are not comparable on $x = x_r$. The product $\pi_{1r}\pi_{0r}$ assures comparing $E(y_1 - y_0|x)$ only on the common support, taking care of the support problem.

Now we turn to the asymptotic distribution of L_N. Under the null hypothesis of no effect $E(y_1 - y_0|x)\ \forall x$, it holds that

$$N^{1/2}L_N \rightsquigarrow N\left\{0, \frac{\lambda^{-1}\psi_0 + (1-\lambda)^{-1}\psi_1}{(\sum_r \pi_{1r}\pi_{0r})^2}\right\}, \quad \text{where } \lambda \equiv \lim_{N\to\infty} N_0/N,$$
$$\psi_0 \equiv E[E\{1[x_i = x_j](y_j - y_i)|x_i, y_i\}^2],$$
$$\psi_1 \equiv E[E\{1[x_i = x_j](y_j - y_i)|x_j, y_j\}^2].$$

As for the consistent estimation of ψ_0 and ψ_1, sample analogs can be used:

$$\psi_{N0} \equiv N_0^{-1}\sum_{a\in C}\left\{N_1^{-1}\sum_{b\in T}1[x_b = x_a](y_b - y_a)\right\}^2,$$

$$\psi_{N1} \equiv N_1^{-1}\sum_{a\in T}\left\{N_0^{-1}\sum_{b\in C}1[x_a = x_b](y_a - y_b)\right\}^2.$$

Plug these into the asymptotic variance formula, and replace λ with N_0/N and $\sum_r \pi_{1r}\pi_{0r}$ with the denominator of L_N to get a consistent estimator for the asymptotic variance.

3.5.2 Continuous or mixed (continuous or discrete) covariates

If x is continuous with dimension $k \times 1$, then instead of L_N, use

$$M_N \equiv \frac{(N_0N_1)^{-1}\sum_{j\in T}\sum_{i\in C}h^{-k}K((x_i - x_j)/h)(y_j - y_i)}{(N_0N_1)^{-1}\sum_{j\in T}\sum_{i\in C}h^{-k}K((x_i - x_j)/h)}$$

where h is a bandwidth and K is a kernel. Let $g_1(x)$ and $g_0(x)$ be density of x for group T and C, respectively. Analogously to L_N,

$$M_N \to^p \int E(y_1 - y_0|x)w(x)\ \ as\ N\to\infty, \quad \text{where } w(x) = \frac{g_1(x)g_0(x)}{\int g_1(x)g_0(x)dx}.$$

The asymptotic distribution is

$$N^{1/2} M_N \rightsquigarrow N\left[0, \; \frac{\lambda^{-1}\phi_0 + (1-\lambda)^{-1}\phi_1}{\{\int g_1(x)g_0(x)dx\}^2}\right],$$

where the form of ϕ_0 and ϕ_1 is analogous to that of ψ_0 and ψ_1. For consistent estimation of the asymptotic variance, replace $\int g_1(x)g_0(x)dx$ with the denominator of M_N and replace ϕ_0 and ϕ_1 with

$$\phi_{N0} \equiv N_0^{-1} \sum_{i \in C} \left\{ N_1^{-1} \sum_{j \in T} h^{-k} K\left(\frac{x_i - x_j}{h}\right)(y_j - y_i)\right\}^2,$$

$$\phi_{N1} \equiv N_1^{-1} \sum_{j \in T} \left\{ N_0^{-1} \sum_{i \in C} h^{-k} K\left(\frac{x_i - x_j}{h}\right)(y_j - y_i)\right\}^2.$$

As for choosing the bandwidth h, there is no particularly good way to choose the bandwidth h in practice. Nevertheless, the following cross-validation idea looks reasonable, particularly when $N_0 \simeq N_1$. Let

$$N_c \equiv \min(N_0, N_1), \quad z_i \equiv y_{1i} - y_{0i}, \quad i = 1,\ldots, N_c, \quad \rho(x_0, x_1) \equiv E(z|x_0, x_1)$$

pretending that subject i in group T and C is the same person. We may choose h by minimizing $\sum_{i=1}^{N_c} \{z_i - \rho_N(x_{0i}, x_{1i}; h)\}^2$, where $\rho_N(x_{0i}, x_{1i}; h)$ is the 'leave-one-out' kernel estimator for $\rho(x_{0i}, x_{1i})$ that uses all but the ith observation. Alternatively, the often-used rule of thumb—$h \simeq 1$ when k is small with all regressors standardized—may be used.

Suppose $x = (x_c', x_d')'$ where x_c (x_d) is a continuous (discrete) regressor vector of dimension k_c (k_d), and $k = k_c + k_d$. Denote conditional density of $x_c|x_d$ as $g_j(x_c|x_d)$ and let π_{jr} denote $P(x_{jd} = x_r)$, $j = 0, 1$. Instead of M_N, use

$$M_N' \equiv \frac{(N_0 N_1)^{-1} \sum_{j \in T}\sum_{i \in C} 1[x_{id} = x_{jd}] \, h^{-k_c} K((x_{ic} - x_{jc})/h)(y_j - y_i)}{(N_0 N_1)^{-1} \sum_{j \in T}\sum_{i \in C} 1[x_{id} = x_{jd}] \, h^{-k_c} K((x_{ic} - x_{jc})/h)}.$$

M_N' is consistent for

$$\int E(y_1 - y_0|x)w'(x),$$

$$\text{where} \quad w'(x) \equiv \frac{g_1(x_c|x_d = x_r)g_0(x_c|x_d = x_r)\pi_{1r}\pi_{0r}}{\sum_r \int g_1(x_c|x_d = x_r)g_0(x_c|x_d = x_r)dx_c \pi_{1r}\pi_{0r}}.$$

$N^{1/2} M_N'$ is asymptotically normal with mean zero and variance

$$\frac{\lambda^{-1}\zeta_0 + (1-\lambda)^{-1}\zeta_1}{\{\sum_r \int g_1(x_c|x_d = x_r)g_0(x_c|x_d = x_r)dx_c \, \pi_{1r}\pi_{0r}\}^2}$$

where ζ_0 and ζ_1 can be estimated in the same way as ϕ_0 and ϕ_1 are estimated with $h^{-k} K((x_i - x_j)/h)$ replaced by $h^{-k_c} K((x_{ic} - x_{jc})/h)1[x_{id} = x_{jd}]$.

In practice, hardly any regressor is 'exactly continuous', and we need to consider whether a cardinal regressor should be taken as continuous or discrete. For any discrete regressor, using $1[x_{jd} = x_{id}]$ is asymptotically equivalent to using $K(0)^{-1}K((x_{jd} - x_{id})/h)$ because only the exactly matching observations will be picked up as $h \to 0$. If $K(0)$ for the discrete regressors and h^{k_c} for the continuous regressors in the numerator and denominator of M'_N cancel each other out, then smoothing can be applied indiscriminately to all regressors. This is indeed the case for M'_N. That is, in practice, one can apply smoothing indiscriminately to M'_N using a product kernel. Instead of matching on x, Lee (2003a) does matching on the propensity score $E(d|x)$ for L_N, M_N, and M'_N.

3.5.3   An empirical example

Lee (2003b) examines the job-training effect on female work hours to illustrate the above approach, using data from the Korean Labor Panel Data wave 1 for 1998, which is collected by the Korean Labor Research Institute; $N_0 = 3722$, $N_1 = 315$, and $N = 4037$. The treatment takes 1 if the subject receives any job training during the year surveyed and the response variable is work hours per week during the same year. The covariates are age, the number of children of age 0–3 years, 4–7 years, and 8–13 years, education in six levels (primary school, middle school, high school, junior college, college, and graduate school), household yearly income other than the female's own income in 10,000 Korean Won ($\simeq$\$10), and a marriage dummy.

Mean and SD of control and treatment group				
Variable	C group avg.	C group SD	T group avg.	T group SD
δ	0.364		0.460	
$y\|\delta = 1$	54.97		53.25	
y	20.00	28.80	24.51	29.17
age	36.57	13.27	32.87	11.18
# kids aged 0–3	0.096	0.310	0.127	0.343
# kids aged 4–7	0.102	0.311	0.102	0.303
# kids aged 8–13	0.186	0.460	0.159	0.459
education (0–5)	1.260	1.257	1.867	1.419
household income	1577	1273	1515	1100
married or not	0.743		0.648	

Descriptive statistics are shown in the table where δ is the dummy variable for working or not. The T group works 9.6% more, but the hours worked among the workers of the T group is 1.72 hours lower than the C group. The T group is 3.7 years younger with slightly more younger children and is close to high-school graduation, whereas the C group is close to middle-school graduation. The T group is 9.5% less likely to be married.

The covariates are mixed, with some continuous and some discrete. Smoothing was applied indiscriminately to all regressors, for which a product kernel was used with each marginal kernel being the bi-weight kernel. The benchmark bandwidth for the cross-validation scheme turned out to be $h = 0.96$ with all regressors standardized; this bandwidth is almost the same as the rule-of-thumb bandwidth. For the sake of comparison, we use two more bandwidths: twice smaller and greater. The results are

bandwidth	work-hour effect (tv)	participation effect (tv)
0.48	3.39 (1.35)	0.060 (1.46)
0.96	4.64 (1.91)	0.076 (1.98)
1.92	6.45 (2.54)	0.10 (2.57)

where the last column is for the participation effect that is obtained simply by replacing y_j and y_i with δ_j and δ_i. The results indicate some positive job-training effect on hours worked that is, however, not stable enough to make a firm conclusion. A similar result was found for the participation effect. The job-training seems to increase hours worked per week by between 3 to 6 hours and increase participation by 6% to 10%. Note that hours worked can increase without any participation increase if the existing workers work more. Also note that there is a sample-selection problem that hours worked is observed only for the workers ($\delta = 1$). This issue is discussed in Lee (2003b).

4

Matching

If the treatment (T) and control (C) groups are different in observed variables x, then the difference in outcome y cannot be attributed to the difference in the treatment. The obvious solution is to compare only those subjects with the same (or similar) value of x across the two groups. Selecting subjects similar in x across the T and C groups is *matching*. Treatment-effect estimators with matching (or simply 'matching estimators') are introduced first, assuming that the matching has been done already. We then discuss how to do matching in practice. If x is high-dimensional, it is hard to find matched subjects, but there is a simple way to avoid the dimension problem, called 'propensity score matching'. Matching can also be done to control for unobservables (e.g., using identical twin as controls for genes). Combining before-after design with matching yields the popular 'difference-in-differences' design, which can be generalized to 'difference-in-differences-in-differences'. These difference-based designs can deal with unobserved confounders to some extent. It is thus fitting that they are examined in the second half of this chapter, before we deal with hidden bias in the following chapters. A treated subject is called just a 'treated' and a control subject a 'control' in this chapter.

4.1   Estimators with matching

4.1.1   Effects on the treated

It was shown earlier that, if $E(y_0|d, x) = E(y_0|x)$, then we can identify the treatment *effect on the treated* $E(y_1 - y_0|d = 1)$ with

$$\int \{E(y|x, d = 1) - E(y|x, d = 0)\} f(x|d = 1) dx$$
$$= E(y|d = 1) - \int E(y|x, d = 0) f(x|d = 1) dx$$
$$= E\{y - E(y_0|x, d = 0)|d = 1\}$$
$$= E\{y_1 - E(y_0|x, d = 1)|d = 1\} = E(y_1 - y_0|d = 1).$$

Examine closely what went on in the derivation. In $E(y_1|d = 1) - E(y_0|d = 1)$, the second term is the counter-factual to be constructed. The way we construct it is to use $E(y_0|x_i, d = 0) = E(y_0|x_i, d = 1)$: for a treated i with x_i, we find a group of controls whose x is the same as x_i. The group, say C_i, is a 'comparison group' for treated i. They are similar to treated i in x, and presumably also similar in y_0. The comparison group average is $E(y_0|x_i, d = 0)$ that is equal to $E(y_0|x_i, d = 1)$, which is in turn equal to $E(y_0|x_i)$. This explains the second term in $E\{y_1 - E(y_0|x, d = 1)|d = 1\}$. Integrating out x in $E(y_0|x, d = 1)$ over the T group with $f(x|d = 1)$, we get $E(y_0|d = 1)$. *Matching in its narrow sense* is a process of finding C_i for each treated i; *matching in its wide sense* includes the next step of estimating the treatment effect.

For example, suppose there are three treated subjects $(T1, T2, T3)$ and four controls $(C1, C2, C3, C4)$ matched as follows where $|C_i|$ denotes the number of controls in C_i:

$$T1 : C1, C2, C3 \Rightarrow C_1 = \{C1, C2, C3\}, \quad |C_1| = 3;$$
$$T2 : C4 \Rightarrow C_2 = \{C4\}, \quad |C_2| = 1;$$
$$T3 : no\ matched\ control \Rightarrow C_3 = \emptyset, \quad |C_3| = 0.$$

If no good match is found, we may not want to force matching. $T3$ is passed over. The number of successfully matched treated subjects

$$N_{1u} \equiv \sum_{\iota \in T} 1[C_i \neq \emptyset]$$

is two. How to select C_i from the 'control reservoir' (i.e., the C group or a subset of the C group) will be discussed in detail in the next section.

With $|C_i|^{-1} \sum_{m \in C_i} y_{mi}$ being an estimator for $E(y_0|x_i, d = 0)$ where y_{mi} refers to a response variable in C_i, an estimator for the *effect on the treated*

$E\{y - E(y|x, d = 0)|d = 1\}$ is

$$T_N \equiv N_{1u}^{-1} \sum_{i \in T_u} \left(y_i \ - |C_i|^{-1} \sum_{m \in C_i} y_{mi} \right)$$

where T_u is the set of the used (i.e., successfully matched) treated subjects:

$$T_u \equiv \{i : \ |C_i| \neq \emptyset, \ i \in T\}.$$

Defining X_M as the values of x that are 'matchable' (i.e., X_M is the overlapping support of x across group C and T, or a 'slightly enlarged' version of it), the population version of T_N can be written as

$$\begin{aligned}
&E\{y - E(y_0|x, d = 0)|d = 1, x \in X_M\} \\
&= E\{y_1 - E(y_0|x, d = 1)|d = 1, x \in X_M\} \\
&= E(y_1|d = 1, x \in X_M) - E(y_0|d = 1, x \in X_M).
\end{aligned}$$

If $|C_i| = 1$ for all $i \in T$, we get a pair matching without passing over. If $|C_i| = 0, 1$ for all i, having $|C_i| = 0$ means that treated i is passed over. In the latter pair matching, which includes the former as a special case, T_N becomes just a sum of differences

$$T_{pN} \equiv N_{1u}^{-1} \sum_{i \in T_u} (y_i - y_{mi}).$$

This pair matching estimator is extremely simple. An opposite estimator is obtained when all controls are used with varying weights to construct $E(y_0|x_i, d = 1)$. Such an estimator can be written as

$$N_1^{-1} \sum_{i \in T} \left(y_i \ - \sum_{j \in C} w_{ij} y_j \right), \quad \sum_{j \in C} w_{ij} = 1 \ \forall i \quad \text{and} \quad w_{ij} > 0 \ \forall i, j;$$

note $C_i = C \ \forall i$. To be specific on w_{ij}, let

$$w_{ij} = \frac{K((x_j - x_i)/h)}{\sum_{j \in C} K((x_j - x_i)/h)},$$

where K is a 'kernel' (e.g., the $N(0, 1)$ density function) and h is a 'bandwidth' determining how the weights are concentrated or spread around x_i. A (kernel) nonparametric estimator is reviewed in the appendix. With this weight, denoting the size of group T as N_1, the matching estimator becomes

$$T_{wN} \equiv N_1^{-1} \sum_{i \in T} \left\{ y_i - \frac{\sum_{j \in C} K((x_j - x_i)/h) y_j}{\sum_{j \in C} K((x_j - x_i)/h)} \right\}.$$

If we allow $w_{ij} = 0$ for some j, then the controls with $w_{ij} = 0$ are not used for treated i. We can allow for $w_{ij} = 0$ by using a kernel with a bounded support.

Define a generic nonparametric matching estimator for the effect on the treated as

$$T_{gN} \equiv N_{1u}^{-1} \sum_{i \in T_u} \{y_i - E_N(y|x_i, d = 0)\}$$

where $E_N(y|x_i, d = 0)$ is a nonparametric estimator using C_i for $E(y|x_i, d = 0)$. There are many different estimators for $E_N(y|x_i, d = 0)$. Frölich (2003) recommends a version of local linear regression in Seifert and Gasser (1996, 2000). It will probably take some more time before we know which estimator works best in practice.

Abadie and Imbens (2002) examine a number of matching estimator. For the effect on the treated, the estimator considered is T_N with $|C_i| = M$ for all i where M is a chosen constant, and T_{gN} with a nonparametric 'series estimator' used for $E_N(y|x_i, d = 0)$; Abadie and Imbens (2002) consider only matchings that allow the same unit to be matched multiple times. They call the former a 'simple' matching estimator and the latter a 'covariance-adjustment' or 'regression imputation' matching estimator. They also consider a 'bias-corrected' matching estimator

$$T_{bN} \equiv N_1^{-1} \sum_{i \in T} \left[y_i - M^{-1} \sum_{m \in C_i} \{y_{mi} + E_N(y|x_i, d = 0) - E_N(y|x_{mi}, d = 0)\} \right].$$

The motivation for this estimator comes from the fact that matching is not exact (i.e., controls with $x_{mi} \neq x_i$ are used), which causes a bias. The last two terms in T_{bN} are to avoid this bias. Abadie and Imbens (2002) recommend a simplified version of T_{bN} where the nonparametric estimators in T_{bN} are replaced by linear regression estimators.

4.1.2   Effects on the population

So far in this chapter, we have discussed only estimators for the effect on the treated. For the effect on the untreated, define T_j as the matched treated subjects for control j, and

$$N_{0u} \equiv \sum_{j \in C} 1[T_j \neq \emptyset], \quad C_u \equiv \{j : |T_j| \neq \emptyset, \ j \in C\}.$$

An estimator for the *effect on the untreated* $E\{E(y|x, d = 1) - y|d = 0\}$ that is analogous to T_N is

$$U_N \equiv N_{0u}^{-1} \sum_{j \in C_u} \left(|T_j|^{-1} \sum_{m \in T_j} y_{mj} - y_j \right)$$

where y_{mj} is a response in T_j.

Define $N_u \equiv N_{0u} + N_{1u}$. Since

$$E(y_1 - y_0 | x \in X_M) = P(d = 1 | x \in X_M) \cdot E(y_1 - y_0 | x \in X_M, d = 1)$$
$$+ P(d = 0 | x \in X_M) \cdot E(y_1 - y_0 | x \in X_M, d = 0),$$

an estimator for the *effect (on the whole matchable sub-population)* $E(y_1 - y_0 | x \in X_M)$ is

$$TU_N \equiv \frac{N_{1u}}{N_u} \cdot T_N + \frac{N_{0u}}{N_u} \cdot U_N = \frac{N_{1u}}{N_u} N_{1u}^{-1} \sum_{i \in T_u} \left(y_i - |C_i|^{-1} \sum_{m \in C_i} y_{mi} \right)$$

$$+ \frac{N_{0u}}{N_u} N_{0u}^{-1} \sum_{j \in C_u} \left(|T_j|^{-1} \sum_{m \in T_j} y_{mj} - y_j \right)$$

$$= N_u^{-1} \sum_{i \in T_u} \left(y_i - |C_i|^{-1} \sum_{m \in C_i} y_{mi} \right) + N_u^{-1} \sum_{j \in C_u} \left(|T_j|^{-1} \sum_{m \in T_j} y_{mj} - y_j \right)$$

$$= N_u^{-1} \sum_{i=1}^{N} \left\{ \left(y_i - |C_i|^{-1} \sum_{m \in C_i} y_{mi} \right) 1[i \in T_u] \right.$$

$$\left. + \left(|T_i|^{-1} \sum_{m \in T_i} y_{mi} - y_i \right) 1[i \in C_u] \right\},$$

where i indexes all observations in the pooled sample $T \cup C$. If matching is done for all units so that no unit is passed over (i.e., if $N = N_u$), then $i \in T_u$ and $i \in C_u$ in the last display are replaced by $i \in T$ and $i \in C$, respectively, and the last display can be written as an average of differences:

$$\hat{\tau} = N^{-1} \sum_{i=1}^{N} \left[\left\{ y_i 1[i \in T] + |T_i|^{-1} \sum_{m \in T_i} y_{mi} 1[i \in C] \right\} \right.$$

$$\left. - \left\{ |C_i|^{-1} \sum_{m \in C_i} y_{mi} 1[i \in T] + y_i 1[i \in C] \right\} \right].$$

Observe, under $E(y_j | x, d) = E(y_j | x)$, $j = 0, 1$,

$$E(y_1 - y_0) = E\{E(y_1 | x) - E(y_0 | x)\} = E\{E(y | x, d = 1) - E(y | x, d = 0)\}.$$

In the first equality, the outer expectation is for x on the population, not on the C nor on the T group. This suggests yet another estimator for the effect:

$$\tilde{\tau} = N^{-1} \sum_{i=1}^{N} \{E_N(y | x_i, d = 1) - E_N(y | x_i, d = 0)\}.$$

This and the preceding estimator have already been described in Subsection 3.4.3.

4.1.3   Estimating asymptotic variance

It is hard to find the asymptotic distribution of a matching estimator, because selecting C_i involves all observations, which then implies dependence across observations in the sum for a matching estimator. This problem gets worse if matching is 'elaborate'. In the following, we show some practical ways to do asymptotic inference, and then turn to a matching estimator in Abadie and Imbens (2002) to present its asymptotic distribution. The asymptotic distribution of T_{wN} is provided in the appendix under the heading 'nonparametric matching'.

In pair matching, usually the matched pair differences, $y_i - y_{mi}$, $i = 1, \ldots, N_{1u}$, are taken as iid, and

$$V_{pN} \equiv N_{1u}^{-2} \sum_{i \in T_u} \left\{ (y_i - y_{mi}) - N_{1u}^{-1} \sum_{i \in T_u} (y_i - y_{mi}) \right\}^2$$

is used as an estimator for the asymptotic variance of $T_{pN} = N_{1u}^{-1} \sum_{i \in T_u} (y_i - y_{mi})$. $T_{pN}/V_{pN}^{1/2}$ is then the t-value. Other controls however, not just y_{mi}, are involved when y_{mi} is selected. This implies dependence across the pairs in the pair matching and the iid presumption is in fact false. For matching schemes where a control is matched at most to one treated, however, the iid assumption seems fairly harmless. Also, if the C group is much bigger than the T group so that the chance of a control being used multiple times is slim, then the iid assumption is not so far-fetched.

One rule of thumb to obtain asymptotic confidence intervals (CI's), or to do tests with matching estimators, is the following bootstrap. Draw randomly N_0 times with replacement from group C and N_1 times with replacement from group T to get a pseudo sample of size N, and apply the same matching procedure to the pseudo sample to get a pseudo effect estimate. Repeat this B times (e.g., $B = 500$) to get B-many pseudo estimates for the treatment effect. The 2.5% and 97.5% quantiles in these pseudo estimates can be used to construct a 95% CI for the treatment effect and to test for zero effect. Although bootstrap for matching has not been justified, it has been used, e.g., in Heckman *et al.* (1998), Dehejia and Wahba (2002), and Behrman *et al.* (2004). The sample variance of the B-many pseudo estimates may be used as a variance estimator. It is, however, more difficult to justify this practice than to justify bootstrap CI's.

For T_N with more than one control allowed per treated and each control used only once, Lee and Lee (2004a) propose to use, for the asymptotic variance of T_N,

$$V_N \equiv N_{1u}^{-2} \sum_{i \in T_u} \left\{ y_i^2 - 2y_i \left(|C_i|^{-1} \sum_{m \in C_i} y_{mi} \right) + |C_i|^{-2} \sum_{m \in C_i} y_{mi}^2 \right.$$

$$\left. + |C_i|^{-1}(|C_i| - 1) \left(|C_i|^{-1} \sum_{m \in C_i} y_{mi} \right)^2 \right\};$$

$T_N / V_N^{1/2}$ is then the t-value. A heuristic justification for this is provided in the appendix.

Abadie and Imbens (2002) derive the asymptotic distribution for their simple matching estimator (the bias-corrected version has the same asymptotic distribution). They show that the simple matching estimator may not be $\sqrt{N}$-consistent when more than one continuous regressor is used, because there is a bias term that may not banish at a rate faster than $\sqrt{N}$. Recall TU_N with no unit passed over and M matches used for each observation:

$$N^{-1} \sum_{i=1}^{N} \left[\left\{ y_i 1[i \in T] + M^{-1} \sum_{m \in T_i} y_{mi} 1[i \in C] \right\} \right.$$

$$\left. - \left\{ M^{-1} \sum_{m \in C_i} y_{mi} 1[i \in T] + y_i 1[i \in C] \right\} \right].$$

Abadie and Imbens demonstrate, when the bias term is negligible and all covariates are continuous,

$$\sqrt{N}\{TU_N - E(y_1 - y_0)\} \rightsquigarrow N(0, V_1 + V_2),$$

$$V_1 = N^{-1} \sum_i \{E_N(y|x_i, d = 1) - E_N(y|x_i, d = 0)\}^2 + o_p(1),$$

$$V_2 = N^{-1} \sum_i \left(1 + \frac{\# \text{ unit } i \text{ matched}}{M} \right)^2 \frac{\{y_i - y_{l(i)}\}^2}{2} + o_p(1),$$

where '# unit i matched' is the number of times the unit i is matched, and $l(i)$ is the closest unit to unit i in terms of x in the same group.

4.2 Implementing matching

4.2.1 Decisions to make in matching

We have seen many treatment effect estimators with matching in the preceding section. Now we turn to the question of how to do matching in practice. To simplify this discussion, we will consider matching controls only for each treated.

Once this is understood, then matching treated subjects to each control is straightforward.

The comparison group C_i for treated i should be chosen such that their x are as close as possible to x_i, if not exactly the same. If x takes many values or if the dimension of x is large, exact matching is difficult, and we have to allow for some leeway in matching: a small neighborhood of x_i is set up and any control with its x falling in the neighborhood is regarded as matched. There are two polar methods for selecting close controls. In the first method, a fixed neighborhood N_i is chosen for x_i and all controls whose x fall in N_i are included in the set C_i; $|C_i|$ are random. In the second method, a fixed number of nearest neighbor (NN) controls are selected regardless of their distances to treated i— $|C_i|$ is fixed. An example of the latter method is pair matching with $|C_i| = 1$ for all i. An example of the former method is given in the next paragraph.

For a given treated i, similarity of a control to treated i can be measured by a metric on x. For instance, we can use *Mahalanobis distance*

$$(x_i - x_m)'C_N^{-1}(x_i - x_m)$$

where m indexes the C group and C_N is a sample covariance matrix for x using either the T or C group. Instead of C_N, we could use only the diagonal of C_N. Using either C_N or its diagonal gives us a quadratic form (or distance) of $x_i - x_m$. For treated i, we could include in C_i only the controls with $(x_i - x_m)'C_N^{-1}(x_i - x_m)$ less than a threshold that is also called a 'caliper'.

If we want to avoid sensitivity to outliers or monotonic transformation of variables, we could use (Rosenbaum (1991)), instead of a quadratic distance,

$$\sum_{j=1}^{k} |q_{ij} - q_{mj}|$$

where q_{ij} is the rank of the jth component x_{ij} of x_i in the pooled sample, $j = 1, \ldots, k$, and q_{mj} is the rank of the jth component x_{mj} of x_m in the pooled sample. Denoting the SD of the jth component of x_i as SD_j, we could also use

$$\sum_{j=1}^{k} 1[|x_{ij} - x_{mj}| > cSD_j]$$

for some constant $c > 0$. Here, the distance is a sum of k sub-distances, and each sub-distance is zero if x_{mj} is within cSD_j from x_{ij} and otherwise it is one.

Sometimes, matching is done in two stages. Let $x = (x_1', x_2')'$, where x_1 is a vector of covariates that should be matched (almost) exactly. In the first stage, *stratification* is performed: the same strata (cells or clusters) are formed depending on x_1 in both the T and C groups. In the second stage, for treated i

in stratum s, matching controls are selected only from the same stratum s using x_2. For instance, for a job training program, the T and C group subjects may be classified by $x_1 = (\text{gender}, \text{age})'$. Then, for treated i in stratum s with, say, males in their 40's, one or more controls are chosen from the corresponding stratum s (males of age 40's) using $x_2 = (\text{schooling years}, \text{job experience})'$; the above quadratic distance is calculated only with x_2.

In practice, various matching schemes are used for computational convenience, ease of deriving the asymptotic variance of the ensuing matching estimator, and efficiency of the matching estimator. If the comparison group consists of only one nearest control for each treated, we have pair matching. If more than one control is allowed in the comparison group, then we have 'matching with multiple controls' or *multiple matching*. In multiple matching, the number of matched controls can be the same for all the treated as in NN or can be different across the treated. If each treated is matched to at least one control and each control is matched to at least one treated, then we have *full matching*. It is possible for a control to be matched to multiple treated subjects; if a control is matched to only one treated at most (to simplify the ensuing statistical analysis), then we have *greedy matching*.

Matching can be done sequentially or non-sequentially. In *non-greedy sequential matching*, which is computationally convenient, each unit is considered one by one. Once a treated is matched (or passed over), the treated is removed from further matching consideration for the other remaining treated subjects and the control reservoir stays the same. In *greedy sequential matching*, the matched controls to a treated are also removed from further matching considerations, and the control reservoir shrinks as the matching progresses. A problem with this is that a control matched to treated i may be more important to treated i', which would then have a hard time finding matched control. This is clearly inferior to *greedy non-sequential matching* where all controls and treated subjects are considered together. However, implementing non-sequential matching is more difficult because consideration of all possible pairs is computationally burdensome. See the appendix for examples of two non-sequential matching schemes. In the literature, sometimes sequential matching is called greedy matching, but we will use the term greedy matching with the definition above.

In summary, there are a number of key decisions to make when matching. First, we should choose the covariates to be used for (stratification and) matching. As we will show later, $P(d = 1|x)$ which is called 'propensity score' can be used instead of (or along with some components of) x. Second, if the number of controls that are to be matched within a fixed distance to a treated varies, then that distance must be chosen. Alternatively, if the same number of controls are to be matched to each treated as in NN, the number should be chosen as well. Third, we should select a distance to use for measuring similarity in x. Fourth, we should also determine the greedy/non-greedy and sequential/non-sequential aspects of the matching.

4.2.2   Evaluating matching success

Once (all) treated subjects are matched in a given matching scheme, we need to evaluate how successful the matching is. The after-matching T group is the same as the before-matching T group unless some treated subjects were passed over, whereas the after-matching C group differs from the before-matching C group. The after-matching C group will be much closer to the T group in terms of x than the before-matching C group.

There are essentially two ways to evaluate matching success:

- One is to see how close each comparison group is to its matched treated unit at the individual level in terms of x;

- The other is to see how balanced x is across the two groups at the aggregate level, regardless of the matching success at the individual level.

The former is microscopic and more stringent in its matching evaluation, whereas the latter is macroscopic and more lenient. Gu and Rosenbaum (1993) call the former 'distance' and the latter 'balance'. It can happen that, in the latter, each of treated i and i' may have a poor comparison group, but the comparison group biases may cancel each other out with x still well balanced across the two groups.

A microscopic evaluation criterion which penalizes poor matchings at individual level is the *average absolute imbalance after matching*: for the jth component of x_i:

$$M_{|j|} \equiv \frac{\sum_{\iota \in T} \left| x_{ij} - |C_i|^{-1} \sum_{m \in C_i} x_{mj} \right| \cdot 1[C_i \neq \emptyset]}{\sum_{\iota \in T} 1[C_i \neq \emptyset]}.$$

$M_{|j|}$, $j = 1, \ldots, k$, can be normalized and summed up for x_i. Recall the example in Subsection 4.1.1 with $N_1 = 3$, $N_0 = 4$, and

$$C_1 = \{C1, C2, C3\}, \qquad C_2 = \{C4\}, \quad C_3 = \emptyset.$$

In this example, setting $j = 1$ for a scalar x,

$$M_{|1|} = \frac{|x_{T1} - ((x_{C1} + x_{C2} + x_{C3})/3)| + |x_{T2} - x_{C4}|}{2}.$$

A macroscopic evaluation criterion which penalizes a poor matching only at the aggregate level is the *average imbalance after matching*: for the jth component of x_i,

$$M_{(j)} \equiv \frac{\sum_{\iota \in T} \left(x_{ij} - |C_i|^{-1} \sum_{m \in C_i} x_{mj} \right) \cdot 1[C_i \neq \emptyset]}{\sum_{\iota \in T} 1[C_i \neq \emptyset]};$$

this is $M_{|j|}$ with the absolute value replaced by $(\cdot)$. $M_{(j)}$, $j = 1, \ldots, k$, can be normalized and summed up for x_i. $M_{(j)}$ is relatively more favorable for full matching than $M_{|j|}$, because forcing matching, as in full matching, can result in many positive and negative imbalances of a big magnitude in x, which can still cancel one another out at the aggregate level.

Although criteria such as $M_{|\cdot|}$ and $M_{(\cdot)}$ are easily computable and thus can be used to compare different matching schemes, it should be borne in mind that the eventual goal of matching is to construct a good counter-factual estimator. Recall the estimator T_N for the effect on the treated in Subsection 4.1.1. If we force matching, $M_{(\cdot)}$ for the average balance of x may be small, but large positive values of comparison group bias may or may not be cancelled by large negative values.

There is a trade-off in retaining/discarding poorly matched treated units. If we are highly selective in matching, then $C_i = \emptyset$ for many i. This would reduce $M_{|\cdot|}$, but also lower the efficiency of the ensuing matching estimator due to the information (data) loss. N_u would get smaller, leading to a higher variance estimator. On the other hand, if we force matching on all subjects, then we would have to be generous in matching, and this would increase $M_{|\cdot|}$ but enhance the efficiency, as all available information would have been used. The effect on $M_{(\cdot)}$ of retaining/discarding poorly matched units is not clear.

In the classic trade-off of bias and variance, typically, bias weighs more heavily in large samples because the variance goes to zero in large samples, while the bias remains. This point favors $M_{|\cdot|}$ not using poorly matched subjects. On the other hand, not using poorly matched subjects makes comparing different matching schemes with $M_{|\cdot|}$ ambiguous, because one can make $M_{|\cdot|}$ small simply by using only a handful of highly well matched subjects. This concern—the bias criterion $M_{|\cdot|}$ is subject to manipulation by discarding many subjects while the efficiency loss is not easy to quantify—may prompt us to use $M_{(\cdot)}$ and full matching. Indeed, full matching under $M_{(\cdot)}$ has been advocated by Rosenbaum (1991).

In a given data set, matching success can be evaluated only in terms of how similar x is across groups C and T. However, as noted above, the ultimate goal of matching in observational data is to come up with a control group with zero comparison group bias (e.g., $E(y_0) = E(y_0|d = 0) = E(y_0|d = 1)$). In the literature, zero comparison group biases have been evaluated with randomized data. For instance, in a randomized study with C and T groups, $E(y_0)$ is estimated with the C group whereas $E(y_0|d = 1)$ is estimated with $\int E(y_0|x, d = 0) f(x|d = 1) dx$ using some outside 'generic' observational data. Findings on the performance of matching (and propensity matching in the following section) are mixed with both pessimistic and optimistic views. Overall, however, they tend to be more pessimistic than optimistic. See Lalonde (1986), Fraker and Maynard (1987), Heckman and Hotz (1989), Friedlander and Robins (1995), Heckman, Ichimura, and Todd (1997), Heckman *et al.* (1998), Dehejia and Wahba (1999, 2002), Agodini and Dynarski (2004), and Michalopoulos *et al.* (2004). The lessons from these studies may be summarized as: find a *control group as locally as possible* in terms of both space and time, and make the *baseline difference as little as possible*. This is in order to 'compare comparable subjects'.

4.2.3   Empirical examples

This subsection provides some empirical examples of sequential matchings. As we will see shortly, it is hard to draw any firm conclusion in order to recommend the use of any particular matching scheme. Although this is disappointing, since matching is a nonparametric procedure, there can be no single best matching scheme as there is no single best nonparametric estimator.

Recall the job-training example for Korean women. The data set with $N_1 = 973$ and $N_0 = 9312$ was in fact drawn from a much larger data set with $N_1 = 5031$ and $N_0 = 47060$, which is used in Lee and Lee (2005). Lee and Lee (2005) apply two sequential pair matchings, one greedy and the other not. As it turns out, since the control reservoir is so huge, the greediness aspect is not very important. In their table S5, that is reproduced below, the mean values of the covariates used for Mahalanobis distance are compared. The t-values are for the tests whether or not the covariate means are the same across the two groups.

	Balance of covariates with pair matching								
	After sequential pair matching						Before matching		
	Greedy			Non-greedy					
	T	C	t-value	T	C	t-value	T	C	t-value
age	27.7	28.4	−6.1	27.8	28.1	−2.9	27.8	34.9	−76.8
job experience (yrs)	1.8	1.9	−1.4	1.8	1.8	0.9	1.8	2.5	−21.4
last unemp. dur. (days)	65.1	53.3	11.0	65.0	58.1	7.1	65.1	33.6	41.1

In the table, 'last unemp. dur.' is the number of days an unemployed woman searched for a job before taking a training (T group) or starting to receive unemployment insurance benefit (C group). The non-greedy matching does slightly better than the greedy matching. Although there are still some differences left after matching between the two groups, the differences are much smaller than before and seem to have negligible economic significance.

We present another empirical example using part of the data in Vella and Verbeek (1998) that was originally drawn from the US National Longitudinal Survey. The data set is for 1987 with $N = 545$, $d = 1$ for labor union membership and 0 otherwise, and $y = \ln(wage)$; the data set is only for males working full-time with $N_1 = 143$ and $N_0 = 402$. The group mean difference for

$E(y|d = 1) = E(y|d = 0)$ is 0.087, suggesting that the effect of union membership on wage is 8.7%. Although many covariates are available in the data source, we use only the following: education in years (edu), job experience in years (exr), regional dummies (north central, north east, south), dummy for rural area, and 12 industry dummies.

The variables other than edu and exr are used for stratification (the first stage), while edu and exr are used for matching (the second stage) within the same stratum. For distance, Mahalanobis distance is used with the covariance matrix estimated using the whole sample. All controls within h-distance are selected for multiple matching whereas only the nearest is selected for pair matching. If there is no control within h-distance, then the treated subject is passed over. In the first row of the table four sequential matchings are compared: Multi-NG is non-greedy multiple matching (NG stands for Non-Greedy), Pair-NG is non-greedy pair matching, and Pair-G is greedy pair matching.

Comparison of sequential multiple and pair matchings				
	Multi-NG ($h = 1$)	Pair-NG ($h = 1$)	Pair-G ($h = 1$)	Pair-G ($h = \infty$)
mean effect (tv)	2.7%	4.7% (0.77)	5.8% (0.84)	6.7% (1.21)
mean abs. diff. (edu,exr)	0.283, 0.415	0.333, 0.390	0.443, 0.375	0.902, 0.870
mean diff. (edu,exr)	−0.130, 0.098	−0.124, 0.086	−0.193, 0.080	−0.252, 0.138
% treated used	73.4%	73.4%	61.5%	86.0%
avg. # controls per treated	4.30	1	1	1

The treatment effect varies somewhat across the four matchings. Multi-NG carries no t-value, because no practical formula is available to compute the standard error. In terms of the absolute difference in edu and exr, Pair-G with $h = \infty$ is the worst, but it is hard to rank the other three matching schemes. When we use the criterion without the absolute value, Pair-NG is the best and Pair-G with $h = \infty$ is the worst. In terms of the percentage of treated units used, Pair-G with $h = \infty$ uses the most. The average number of matched controls is 4.3 for Multi-NG. It is hard to say which is the best matching scheme, but Pair-NG seems to be the preferred in this example, because (i) relatively many treated units are used despite being a pair matching with $h = 1$ (73.4%), (ii) the covariate differences across the two groups are reasonably small, and (iii) there is a practical formula for the t-value.

To see the sensitivity of matching with respect to the bandwidth h, examine the following table 'Sensitivity of Multiple Matching to Bandwidth', where

No-Strata uses no stratification (i.e., all covariates are used for Mahalanobis distance), and the zeros in the fourth column are for the covariates other than edu and exr.

Sensitivity of multiple matching to bandwidth			
	Multi-NG $(h = 0.5)$	Multi-NG $(h \leq 0.4)$	No-Strata $(h = 0.5)$
mean treatment effect	2.8%	12.5%	4.1%
mean abs. diff.	0.437, 0.244	0.000, 0.000	$0.393, 0.393, 0, \ldots, 0$
mean diff. (edu, exr)	$-0.186, 0.109$	0.000, 0.000	$-0.126, 0.126, 0, \ldots, 0$
% of treated used	61.5%	37.1%	53.8%
avg. # controls per treated	3.58	2.04	2.64

Multi-NG with $h = 0.5$ is slightly different from Multi-NG with $h = 1$, but very different from Multi-NG with $h \leq 0.4$ where all covariates match perfectly. The reason for the same outcome for all $h \leq 0.4$ is that all covariates are discrete, and there is a threshold beyond which h makes no difference as h gets smaller. Multi-NG with $h = 1$ and $h = 0.5$ show that a smaller h does not always mean a smaller difference in x. Although not presented here, No-Strata with $h \leq 0.4$ yields exactly the same outcome as Multi-NG with $h \leq 0.4$. As Multi-NG with various h's shows, matching is sensitive to the bandwidth, and when we avoid the sensitivity with perfect matching ($h \leq 0.4$), a great deal of information is lost: only 37.1% of the treated are used in Multi-NG or No-Strata with $h \leq 0.4$. If there is a continuous component in x, perfect matching is impossible. Nonetheless, insisting on strict matching may give better estimates, as Dehejia and Wahba (2002) illustrate.

4.3 Propensity score matching

In the preceding section, we saw how to control for the observed variables x with matching. A major disadvantage for matching is the dimension problem: if the dimension of x is high, it takes a rather big sample size to do matching successfully. In this section, we introduce a way to get around this problem by matching on the propensity score $\pi(x) \equiv P(d = 1|x)$. The idea of avoiding the dimension problem by using $\pi(x)$ appeared already when weighting estimators were examined in the preceding chapter.

4.3.1 Balancing observables with propensity score

Suppose

$$0 < \pi(x) < 1 \quad \text{for all } x.$$

Take $E(\cdot|\pi(x))$ on $\pi(x) = E(d|x)$ to get

$$\pi(x) = E(d|\pi(x)).$$

Observe, for any $t \in R$,

$$
\begin{aligned}
P\{d = 1, \ x \le t|\pi(x)\} &= E\{d \cdot 1[x \le t]|\pi(x)\} = E\{E(d \cdot 1[x \le t]|x)|\pi(x)\} \\
&= E\{E(d|x)1[x \le t]|\pi(x)\} = E\{\pi(x)1[x \le t]|\pi(x)\} \\
&= \pi(x) \cdot P\{x \le t|\pi(x)\} = P\{d = 1|\pi(x)\} \cdot P\{x \le t|\pi(x)\}.
\end{aligned}
$$

Thus,

$$
\begin{aligned}
P\{x \ \le \ t|d = 1, \pi(x)\} &= P\{x \le t|\pi(x)\} \\
\Longleftrightarrow P\{x \le t|d = 1, \pi(x)\} &= P\{x \le t|d = 0, \pi(x)\} :
\end{aligned}
$$

given $\pi(x)$, the distribution of x is the same across the two groups.
  A function $\zeta(x)$ of x such that

$$P\{x \le t|d = 1, \zeta(x)\} = P\{x \le t|d = 0, \zeta(x)\}$$

is called a *balancing score*; trivially, x is a balancing score. Any balancing score is 'finer' than the propensity score in the sense that $\pi(x) = g(\zeta(x))$ for some function $g(\cdot)$. Thus, $\pi(x)$ is the most 'condensed' among all the balancing scores (see Rosenbaum and Rubin (1983a)).
  Matching on x makes x the same across the two groups, whereas randomization makes x and the unobserved variables ε balanced (i.e., the distribution of (x, ε) is identical) across the two groups. Matching on $\pi(x)$ goes half-way: it balances only x but not ε, suggesting we estimate the treatment effect conditioning only on $\pi(x)$, if there is no hidden bias. This is formalized in the following.

4.3.2 Removing overt bias with propensity-score

Suppose

$$d \amalg (y_0, y_1) \ |x$$

which rules out hidden bias. As already mentioned, this is also called 'selection-on-observables', 'no comparison-group bias', 'd is ignorable given x', or 'randomization of d given x'. Rosenbaum and Rubin (1983a) show that, if the conditional independence holds, then

$$d \text{ is independent of } (y_0, y_1) \text{ given just } \pi(x): \quad d \amalg (y_0, y_1) \, | \pi(x).$$

The proof follows simply by observing

$$E(d|y_0, y_1, \pi(x)) = E\{E(d|y_0, y_1, x)|y_0, y_1, \pi(x)\} = E\{E(d|x)|y_0, y_1, \pi(x)\}$$
$$= E\{\pi(x)|y_0, y_1, \pi(x)\} = \pi(x) = E(d|\pi(x));$$

since d is binary, the mean-independence is the same as the independence. With $d \amalg (y_0, y_1)|\pi(x)$, the mean effect conditional on $\pi(x)$ is identified:

$$E(y|\pi(x), d = 1) - E(y|\pi(x), d = 0) = E\{y_1 - y_0|\pi(x)\}.$$

Integrate out $\pi(x)$ with its density to get the marginal effect:

$$E[E\{y_1 - y_0|\pi(x)\}] = E(y_1 - y_0).$$

A caution is that, although $(y_0, y_1) \amalg d|x$ implies $(y_0, y_1) \amalg d|\pi(x)$, it does *not* imply

$$E(y_j|x, d) = E(y_j|\pi(x), d), \quad j = 0, 1.$$

As in other matchings, for propensity-score matching, the values of $\pi(x)$ should overlap across the C and T groups.

$\pi(x)$ instead of x in the conditioning, implies a considerable reduction of dimension because $\pi(x)$ is only one-dimensional. $\pi(x)$ is also convenient in presenting the outcome of the data analysis, for there is effectively only one regressor $\pi(x)$. One shortcoming of this is, however, estimating $\pi(x)$, say with $\pi_N(x)$, and then accounting for the effect of the estimation error $\pi_N(x) - \pi(x)$ on the asymptotic variance of the treatment effect estimator in use. In practice, often $\pi(x)$ is estimated with logit or probit, and the error $\pi_N(x) - \pi(x)$ is ignored for the asymptotic variance of the treatment effect estimator. Alternatively, bootstrap can be used, as was explained earlier. In the preceding chapter, however, we showed how to account for $\pi_N(x) - \pi(x)$ while reviewing the Robins et al. (1992) study, where using the estimated propensity score was found to be more beneficial than using the true propensity score, in terms of reducing the variance of the resulting treatment effect estimator. Lu et al. (2001, p. 1248) also state that 'theoretical results, practical experience, and simulation results all suggested that estimated propensity scores performed slightly better than true propensity scores' (in matching).

There are many studies using propensity score matching: see Smith (1997), Dehejia and Wahba (1999, 2002), Lechner (2000, 2002), Aakvik (2001), and Wagner (2002) among many others. Since matching is a nonparametric method, we tend to think of it as less efficient than parametric methods. But Smith (1997) gives an example where matching is more efficient than multiple regression when N_1 (39) is much smaller than N_0 (5053), although the theoretical underpinning is not demonstrated.

The ultimate goal of matching in observational data is to come up with a control group that has zero comparison group bias, not just a similar x across groups C and T. This was noted in the previous section, where many studies comparing a randomized control group to a matched control group based on outside observational data, were mentioned. An alternative to randomized data in evaluating matching schemes is simulation. Zhao (2004) compares propensity score matching to covariate matching with various distances. No clear winner was found in the study. Nonetheless, there is hardly any doubt that propensity matching is a useful practical tool.

4.3.3 Empirical examples

To see to what extent propensity score helps matching, we take an example in Rosenbaum and Rubin (1985). In a Danish study to assess the effects of prenatal exposure to an organic acid on the psychological development of children, the T group takes 221 exposed children and the C group 7027 unexposed children. Instead of computing the propensity score with logit, the linear regression function in the latent model was used in matching:

$$q(x) \equiv \ln \left\{ \frac{\pi(x)}{1 - \pi(x)} \right\} = x'\beta$$

instead of $\pi(x)$. Although $q(x)$ is a one-to-one function of $\pi(x)$, $q(x)$ and $\pi(x)$ can result in different comparison groups because the distances to the right and left from a given point are scaled differently when $\ln(\cdot)$ is used. Three sequential pair matchings were used in Rosenbaum and Rubin (1985):

1. Matching on $q(x)$.
2. Matching on $(x', q(x))$ with Mahalanobis distance for $(x', q(x))$.
3. For treated i with $q(x_i)$, controls are selected whose $q(x)$ satisfies $|q(x) - q(x_i)| < caliper$, and then the closest control is selected from the 'calipered' controls following 2.

Part of their tables 1 and 3 are given below and show standardized mean difference

$$100 * \frac{(treated\ mean) - (control\ mean)}{SD}$$

for each covariate across the two groups with no matching, and with the matching methods 1, 2, and 3. That is, the mean difference is computed across the T and C groups first before matching, and then across the T group and its newly matched C group under the scheme 1, 2, and 3.

		Propensity-score based matching schemes			
		no matching	1	2	3
child sex	male = 1, female = 0	−7	0	0	0
twin	yes = 1, no = 0	−10	−3	0	0
oldest child	yes = 1,no = 0	−16	−5	5	0
child age	months	3	7	6	−6
mother education	4 categories (1 to 4)	15	−17	−3	−7
mother single	yes = 1, no = 0	−43	−7	−3	−2
mother age	years	59	−8	5	−1

The table shows clearly that matching improves the balance in x, and matching 2 and 3 do much better than matching 1. Although matching 2 and 3 perform well, balance in the other covariates, not shown here, is better for matching 3.

Evaluating various matching schemes, Gu and Rosenbaum (1993) make a number of recommendations which include the following. First, if the goal is to increase the balance in x (i.e., if the macroscopic evaluation criterion is adopted) and if the dimension of x is large, then propensity score distance is better than Mahalanobis distance. Second, multiple matching with a fixed number of controls is inferior to multiple matching with a variable number of controls. Third, non-sequential matching often does much better with Mahalanobis distance than with sequential matching, but only modestly better with the propensity-score distance. Non-sequential matching does no better than sequential matching in balancing x, because both select more or less the same controls but assign them to different treated units. In the assignment, non-sequential matching does a better job in the microscopic evaluation criterion.

Recall the job-training example with $N_1 = 973$ and $N_0 = 9312$ as appeared in Subsection 3.4.4. There, the response variable is ln(unemployment days) and the covariates are age, tenure at the last workplace, and education at six levels. Doing greedy pair-matching with calipered propensity score (i.e., for each treated, the closest control in terms of propensity score is matched so long as the propensity score distance is smaller than the caliper; otherwise, the treated is not used), we obtained the results in the table below where 'ex-firm' is the tenure in years in the last workplace and 'edu' is education at six levels.

Greedy pair matching with calipered propensity score					
	Caliper: 0.00001			Caliper: 0.001		
effect on treated (tv)	0.248 (5.94)			0.326 (11.38)		
% used treated	39%			91%		
	age	ex-firm	edu	age	ex-firm	edu
$M_{(\cdot)}$	0.113	−0.106	0.016	0.104	−0.079	−0.024
$M_{|\cdot|}$	1.997	1.622	0.702	2.086	1.694	0.835

Despite the huge difference in the percentage of used treated units, the treatment effect is not much different and the two matching schemes perform comparably in terms on $M_{|\cdot|}$ and $M_{(\cdot)}$. In this example, the strict matching with the smaller caliper resulted in a loss of efficiency as reflected in the t-values, while little was gained in terms of $M_{|\cdot|}$ (and $M_{(\cdot)}$). The effect magnitudes are close to those from the weighting estimator T_N in subsection 3.4.4.

4.4 Matching for hidden bias

So far we have discussed only matching on the observables x. It is also possible, however, to use matching to control for some unobserved variables. For example, if we compare identical twins, one with $d = 1$ and the other with $d = 0$, there is no hidden bias from their genes; that is, *matching with twins* controls for genes. Another example is *matching with siblings*: since siblings share the same parents, matching with siblings controls for unobserved variables related to parental influence. Yet another example is matching with neighbors who share the same residential characteristics. Similarly, we can think of matching with best friends to control for unobserved peer pressure, matching with schoolmates to control for unobserved school effects, etc. In short, whenever two subjects that share some characteristics are compared, the same characteristics are controlled for, whether observed or not.

Note, however, that if we match subjects on covariates, then the effect from them cannot be assessed. For instance, in the effects of high school education on working (or not working) for females, matching with siblings compares two (or more) siblings, where one is high school-educated and the other is not. Because they share the same parental influence, the effect of parental influence on working (or not working) cannot be assessed, although this effect may not be of primary importance.

In the well known study of smoking and illness, it is argued that there might exist a genetic predisposition to smoking and illness. The suggestion here is that there is a common factor (genes) that affects both the susceptibility to smoke and illness, and thus even if the smoking habit is altered, it will have no effect on illness. To refute this, a twins study conducted in Finland found that, out of 22 identical twin pairs with each pair consisting of a smoker and a non-smoker, the smoker died first in 17 cases. If smoking had no effect whatsoever on any form of death, the chance of this happening would have been the same as tossing a fair coin 22 times to get 17 heads. Also, there were 9 cases in which one twin of the pair had died of heart disease, and 2 cases of lung cancer; those 9 and 2 cases were smokers. The key unobserved confounder (genes) was controlled for with pair matching, and the gene argument was refuted. This example of pair matching with identical twins is taken from Freedman (1999).

It is instructive to cast the pair matching for the twins study in a regression framework. Suppose

$$y_{si} = \beta d_{si} + \delta_s + u_{si}, \quad E(u_{si}) = 0, \quad s = 1, \ldots, S, \quad i = 1, 2,$$

where s indexes pairs (or strata), y_{si} is the life-span of subject i in stratum s, d_{si} is the treatment dummy, δ_s is the (random) effect of pair s genes on y_{si}, u_{si} is an error term, and β is the parameter of interest. We may try to do the LSE of y_{si} on d_{si} *and* S-many dummy variables for all pairs. This will not work, however, so long as S is large, because there are too many parameters: β and δ_s, $s = 1, \ldots, S$. If we ignore the dummies, then we could incur an omitted variable bias because the genes lurking in δ_s may be correlated to (d_{s1}, d_{s2}).

In the pair matching, we looked at the difference

$$y_{s2} - y_{s1} = \beta(d_{s2} - d_{s1}) + u_{s2} - u_{s1}, \quad s = 1, \ldots, S,$$

which is free of δ_s. Since *concordant pairs* (pairs with $d_{s2} = d_{s1}$) are irrelevant for this equation, we remove them, and for the remaining *discordant pairs* (pairs with $d_{s2} \neq d_{s1}$), order each pair such that $d_{s2} = 1$ and $d_{s1} = 0$. Then the equation becomes

$$y_{s2} - y_{s1} = \beta + (u_{s2} - u_{s1}), \quad \text{for all discordant pairs;}$$

β can be estimated by the sample average over the discordant pairs. In the difference, δ_s is removed. For the sibling-matching example of high-school education on working or not, parental influence drops out, for it is part of δ_s.

For a more general situation where there are more than two subjects in the stratum sharing the same unobserved characteristics (e.g., matching with siblings), the difference can be replaced by subtracting the stratum mean from each subject. For instance, let n_s denote the number of subjects in stratum s. Then δ_s in $y_{si} = \beta d_{si} + \delta_s + u_{si}$ can be removed by mean-differencing:

$$y_{si} - n_s^{-1} \sum_{m=1}^{n_s} y_{sm} = \beta \left(d_{si} - n_s^{-1} \sum_{m=1}^{n_s} d_{sm} \right) + \left(u_{si} - n_s^{-1} \sum_{m=1}^{n_s} u_{sm} \right).$$

Readers familiar with panel data will associate 'fixed-effect estimation' to this model. Unfortunately, this term has been also used for estimating both β and δ_s's in $y_{si} = \beta d_{si} + \delta_s + u_{si}$.

4.5 Difference in differences (DD)

4.5.1 Mixture of before-after and matching

In a before-after design (BA), we compare the same subjects' response variables before and after the treatment to infer the effect. If, however, the treatment takes a long time to implement or the effect takes a long time to manifest itself, then some variables may have changed during that time. In this case, apparent differences in the response variables before and after the treatment may be due to changes in those variables. If the variables are observed, then they can be controlled for in many different ways. Otherwise, they might be controlled for with matching for hidden bias, which is explored in this section.

In general, the idea is as follows. Consider the 'three-strike law' implemented in California (CA) some time ago. The law was designed to lower crime rates: if a person is convicted three times, then they are jailed for life or worse—the details of the law differ somewhat from this, but this outline is enough for our illustration purpose. We can see the effect of the law in CA by comparing the crime rates in CA one year before and after the law. Of course, if we are interested in the long-term effects, after-treatment responses can be taken several years after the law. In the study period, however, many other things can change. For instance, the CA economy may improve, which would lower crime rates. Another possibility is that laws controlling alcohol consumption could be toughened, which would also lower crime rates.

One way to remove the undesired 'economy effect' is matching. To do this we find another state, say Washington state, that did not have the treatment but experienced the same change in economic conditions. The crime rate difference in CA over the study period will contain both the economy effect and the three-strike-law effect, whereas that in Washington State will contain only the former. Hence, subtracting the Washington State crime rate difference from the CA crime rate difference will yield the desired treatment effect. This is the idea of *difference-in-differences (DD)*, which combines BA design with matching. If we are concerned only with the economy effect, we can use any other state that has a similar economic condition. But, by choosing Washington state, that is presumably similar to CA in some unobserved aspects as well, those unobserved variables as well as the economy effects are controlled for. In the following paragraph, we demonstrate another example of DD.

Immigration of cheap labor (d) is sometimes blamed for minority unemployment (y). Miami experienced an influx of cheap labor from Cuba between 1979 and 1981. During the period, the Miami unemployment rate has increased by 1.3%. This suggests a negative effect from the influx of cheap labor. The increase in unemployment, however, can be due to other factors as well (e.g., economic slowdown). Card (1990), who explains the influx in detail—the change in the U.S. government policy handling Cuban refugees, Castro releasing criminals and mental patients, and so on—selects four cities similar to Miami in their minority population proportion and unemployment trend before 1979, namely Atlanta, Houston, Los Angeles, and Tampa, which become a comparison group. Using the Current Population Survey, the following table shows the unemployment rates and their differences (these numbers are taken from Angrist and Krueger (1999)):

DD for immigration effect on unemployment			
	1979	1981	1981–1979 (SD)
Miami	8.3	9.6	$9.6 - 8.3 = 1.3$ (2.5)
Comparison Group Average	10.3	12.6	$12.6 - 10.3 = 2.3$ (1.2)
Treatment Effect			$1.3 - 2.3 = -1.0$ (2.8)

Despite no incoming cheap labor, the comparison group experienced an even higher increase in unemployment than Miami. The difference in the last row, -1.0, is taken as the treatment effect, which is not significantly different from zero. The logic is that the Miami difference contains the effect of (x, ε) as well as the effect of d, whereas the comparison group difference contains only the effect of (x, ε). Subtracting the latter from the former, the desired effect of d is found. See Friedberg and Hunt (1995) and the references therein for a further discussion of immigration and labor markets. They compare several papers and conclude that a 10% increase in the fraction of immigrants reduced the wage of natives by up to 1%—almost a zero effect.

DD is a popular and often convincing study design. For more examples of DD see Meyer (1995), Meyer $et\ al.$ (1995), Eissa and Liebman (1996), Corak (2001) and Donohue $et\ al.$ (2002), among many others. Besley and Case (2004) also provide many references for DD and warn of its misuse with a poor control group or an endogenous policy variable.

4.5.2 DD for post-treatment treated in no-mover panels

Suppose there are two regions, region 1 is exposed to a treatment over time, and region 0 is not. Let a, b with $a < b$ denote two time periods, and the treatment be given at some time between a and b. Assume for a while that we have balanced panel data where there is no moving in or out of each region. Also that each subject is observed twice in the same region. Thus being in region 1 at time b means being treated. Define

$$r_i \; = \; 1 \quad \text{if residing in region 1 and 0 otherwise (in region 0),}$$
$$\tau_t \; = \; 1 \quad \text{if } t = b, \text{ and 0 otherwise}$$
$$\Longrightarrow d_{it} = r_i \tau_t \quad \text{if being in region 1 at time } b \text{ means having received}$$
$$\text{the treatment.}$$

Let y_{jit} denote the potential response for person i at time t, $j = 0$ (not treated) and $j = 1$ (treated). The observed response y_{it} is

$$y_{it} = (1 - d_{it})y_{0it} + d_{it}y_{1it} = (1 - r_i\tau_t)y_{0it} + r_i\tau_t y_{1it}.$$

Omitting the subscript i, we have

$$DD = E(y_b - y_a|r = 1) - E(y_b - y_a|r = 0) \qquad \text{(in observed responses)}$$
$$= E(y_{1b} - y_{0a}|r = 1) - E(y_{0b} - y_{0a}|r = 0) \qquad \text{(in potential responses)}.$$

The above is hard to interpret because both the treatment and time change in the first term, whereas only time changes in the second.

Subtract and add the counter-factual $E(y_{0b} - y_{0a}|r = 1)$ to get

$$DD = \{E(y_{1b} - y_{0a}|r = 1) - E(y_{0b} - y_{0a}|r = 1)\}$$
$$+ \{E(y_{0b} - y_{0a}|r = 1) - E(y_{0b} - y_{0a}|r = 0)\}.$$

If the *same time-effect* condition (the mean-independence of $y_{0b} - y_{0a}$ from r)

$$E(y_{0b} - y_{0a}|r = 1) = E(y_{0b} - y_{0a}|r = 0)$$

holds, which means that the untreated response changes by the same magnitude on average for both regions, then

$$DD = E(y_{1b} - y_{0b}|r = 1):$$

DD identifies the treatment effect for region 1 at time b if the same time-effect condition holds. Since no parametric assumption is made, call the DD 'the nonparametric DD'. The treated are those in region 1 at time b. Thus, it is natural that DD identifies only the effect for region 1 at time b, not the effect that is applicable to all regions and at all times, unless some assumptions are imposed as in a simple linear model in Subsection 4.5.4. To make the same time-effect condition plausible, the above derivation can be conditioned on the observed covariates at the two periods $x \equiv (x'_a, x'_b)'$.

Rewrite the same time-effect condition as

$$E(y_{0b}|r = 1) - E(y_{0b}|r = 0) = E(y_{0a}|r = 1) - E(y_{0a}|r = 0).$$

If we assume $E(y_{0t}|r) = E(y_{0t})$, $t = a, b$, then both sides of this equation become zero. The same time-effect condition is weaker than $E(y_{0t}|r) = E(y_{0t})$, $t = a, b$, because both sides of the same time-effect condition have to be equal, but not necessarily zero. The two regions may be different systematically, but so long as the same time-effect condition holds, the difference will not matter. For instance, the two regions may differ in some unobserved variables affecting the 'baseline response' y_{0a}, but the same time-effect condition will involve only the change $y_{0b} - y_{0a}$. In this sense, *DD allows for unobserved confounders*.

The same time-effect condition

$$E(\text{untreated response change}|r=1) = E(\text{untreated response change}|r=0)$$

is analogous to $y_0 \perp d$, i.e.,

$$E(\text{untreated response}|d=1) = E(\text{untreated response}|d=0),$$

which is used for the effect on the treated $E(y_1 - y_0|d=1)$ in cross-section data. DD $E(y_{1b} - y_{0b}|r=1)$ is analogous to this effect on the treated. To see this analogy better, define

$$Y \equiv y_b - y_a, \qquad Y_1 \equiv y_{1b} - y_{0a}, \qquad Y_0 \equiv y_{0b} - y_{0a}$$

to get

$$\begin{aligned}
DD &= E(Y|r=1) - E(Y|r=0) = E(Y_1|r=1) - E(Y_0|r=0) \\
&= E(Y_1|r=1) - E(Y_0|r=1) + \{E(Y_0|r=1) - E(Y_0|r=0)\} \\
&= E(Y_1 - Y_0|r=1), \qquad \text{if } E(Y_0|r=1) = E(Y_0|r=0).
\end{aligned}$$

Written this way, it is clear that DD is analogous to the effect on the treated with the same time-effect condition written as $Y_0 \perp r$. With x conditioned on, $Y_0 \perp r|x$ is nothing but a selection-on-observables.

As shown already in Section 3.4, an alternative to conditioning is weighting: recall, for cross-section data with $\pi(x) = E(d|x)$,

$$E(y_1 - y_0|d=1) = P(d=1)^{-1}E\left\{\left(1 - \frac{1-d}{1-\pi(x)}\right)y\right\}.$$

Doing analogously for DD, define $p(x) \equiv E(r|x)$ and $p \equiv P(r=1)$ to get

$$E(Y_1 - Y_0|r=1) = p^{-1}E\left\{\left(1 - \frac{1-r}{1-p(x)}\right)Y\right\}.$$

As in Subsection 3.4.2, rewrite this as

$$E(Y_1 - Y_0|r=1) = p^{-1}E\left[\frac{r - p(x)}{1 - p(x)}Y\right].$$

Abadie (2005) uses this to propose a number of nonparametric estimators where $p(x)$ is nonparametrically estimated. In practice, we could use logit or probit for $p(x)$. The weighting estimator with probit was shown in Section 3.4.

Consider a change in a tax law that affects a high-income group far more than a low-income group. Applying DD to find the effect of the change in tax law on work hours, the high-income group is taken as the T group and the low income group as the C group. DD is done for the two groups' before-after differences (this example is taken from Triest (1998) who refers to Eissa (1995)).

As in other treatment effect analyses, the aim is to separate the effect of the change in law from the effects of the other changes. Here, the same time-effect condition is that the other changes in the economy will have an equal influence on the high-income and low-income groups in the absence of the change in tax law. Although DD is a better design than the BA which applies only to the T group under the assumption of no other changes in the economy, the same time-effect assumption is still questionable in this example, because the other changes in the economy are likely to influence the high-income and low-income groups differently.

4.5.3 DD with repeated cross-sections or panels with movers

Now consider independent cross-section data instead of panel data, where a person is observed only once. As in the preceding subsection, there are three potential responses: $y_{0ia}, y_{0ib}, y_{1ib}$. In addition to these, each subject has (r_{ia}, r_{ib}) indicating whether the subject resides in region 1 or not at time a and b. Let $\tau_i = 1$ if subject i is observed at $t = b$, and $\tau_i = 0$ otherwise. What is considered (even at time a) is

$$y_{0ia}, y_{0ib}, y_{1ib}, \qquad r_{ia}, r_{ib}, \tau_i,$$

whereas what is observed is (τ_i, r_i, y_i) where

$$r_i \equiv (1 - \tau_i)r_{ia} + \tau_i r_{ib}, \quad \text{and} \quad y_i = (1 - \tau_i)y_{0ia} + \tau_i(1 - r_i)y_{0ib} + r_i\tau_i y_{1ib}.$$

In this case,

$$
\begin{aligned}
DD &= E(y|r = 1, \tau = 1) - E(y|r = 1, \tau = 0) - \{E(y|r = 0, \tau = 1) \\
&\quad - E(y|r = 0, \tau = 0)\} \\
&= E(y_{1b}|r_b = 1, \tau = 1) - E(y_{0a}|r_a = 1, \tau = 0) - \{E(y_{0b}|r_b = 0, \tau = 1) \\
&\quad - E(y_{0a}|r_a = 0, \tau = 0)\}.
\end{aligned}
$$

The next two paragraphs for the identification of DD are partly drawn from Kang *et al.* (2005).

Assume

(i) τ is mean-independent of y_{0a}, y_{0b}, y_{1b} given r_a or r_b, and

(ii) $E(y_{0a}|r_a = c) = E(y_{0a}|r_b = c), c = 0, 1$, to get

$$
\begin{aligned}
DD &= E(y_{1b}|r_b = 1) - E(y_{0a}|r_a = 1) - \{E(y_{0b}|r_b = 0) - E(y_{0a}|r_a = 0)\} \\
&= E(y_{1b} - y_{0a}|r_b = 1) - E(y_{0b} - y_{0a}|r_b = 0) \\
&= E(y_{1b} - y_{0b}|r_b = 1) \qquad \text{if } E(y_{0b} - y_{0a}|r_b = 1) = E(y_{0b} - y_{0a}|r_b = 0).
\end{aligned}
$$

Again, the derivation and assumption can be conditioned on x.

Unlike the preceding subsection, however, we need the mean independence condition (i) and (ii). Without this there would be four different subpopulations in DD and the DD identification result would fail. The mean independence condition rules out systematic moves across regions. To appreciate this point, examine $E(y_{0a}|r_a = 1) = E(y_{0a}|r_b = 1)$. Noting that everybody has y_{0a} as a potential response even at time b, $E(y_{0a}|r_a = 1)$ is the y_{0a} average for those residing in region 1 at time a, whereas $E(y_{0a}|r_b = 1)$ is the y_{0a} average for those residing in region 1 at time b. Thus, those in region 1 at time a should be similar to those in region 1 at time b in terms of y_{0a}. This can be violated if some big event happens in region 1 between time a and b, which is big enough to change the composition of the subjects in region 1 over time. This problem never occurs in no-mover panels.

Although we assumed independent cross-sections, the preceding derivation works for other data as well so long as the mean independence holds (e.g., for panel data with movers between the two regions, where a subject may be observed only once or twice in the same or different regions). This is because we can always form four groups to get DD. To see this better, define

$$\delta_{it} = 1 \quad \text{if person } i \text{ is observed at time } t \text{ and 0 otherwise,}$$
$$r_{it} = 1 \quad \text{if person } i \text{ resides in region 1 at time } t \text{ and 0 otherwise.}$$

What is observed is

$$\delta_{ia}, \delta_{ib}, \; \delta_{ia}r_{ia}, \delta_{ib}r_{ib}, \; \delta_{ia}y_{0ia}, \delta_{ib}\{(1 - r_{ib})y_{0ib} + r_{ib}y_{1ib}\}.$$

From this, we can still form four groups from the data for DD. Having an unbalanced panel with movers across two regions does not matter for the mean independence condition nor for the identification result of DD. It only matters if we want the standard error for a DD estimator.

DD can be also used when we are interested in the interaction effect of two factors. The marginal effects of the two factors can be removed in sequence by differencing twice. For example, suppose we want to know the effect of interaction between diet and exercise on the percentage of body fat. The C group is exposed to no exercise at time $t = a$ and to a diet at time $t = b$, whereas the T group is exposed to exercise at $t = a$ and to both diet and exercise at $t = b$. In this case, the T group's temporal difference consists of the diet effect and the interaction effect of exercise and diet, whereas the C group's temporal difference consists only of the diet effect. DD is then the interaction effect of diet and exercise.

In assessing the effect of employer-provided health insurance on men's job mobility (Madrian (1994)), the effect would be felt only for those who have no other health insurance. That is, we would want to know the interaction effect of employer-provided health insurance (EPH) and the lack of other health insurance (OH). We take the former being 1 as time b and the latter being 1 as region 1. The DD in this case is

(mobility for EPH $=1$ and OH $=1$) $-$ (mobility for EPH $=0$ and OH $=1$)
$-\{$(mobility for EPH $=1$ and OH $=0$) $-$ (mobility for EPH $=0$ and OH $=0$)$\}$.

Instead of OH, Madrian (1994) also uses variables for whether the household uses health care heavily or not: family size (because large family size means more health care use) or wife being pregnant are used as a measure of health care usage. Madrian (1994) concludes that 'job-lock' due to EPH reduces job mobility from 16% to 12% per year. In this example, the counter-factual of being untreated despite EPH $=1$ and OH $=1$ (i.e., being at region 1 at time b) means zero interaction effect despite each of EPH $=1$ and OH $=1$ having some effect.

4.5.4 Linear models for DD

To enhance understanding of DD, we go back to the no-mover panel case and consider a linear potential response equation

$$y_{jit} = \beta_1 + \beta_r r_i + \beta_\tau \tau_t + \beta_d j + u_{jit}, \quad j = 0, 1, \quad i = 1, \ldots, N, \quad t = a, b,$$
$$E(u_{jit}) = 0.$$

From this, we get $y_{1it} - y_{0it} = \beta_d + u_{1it} - u_{0it}$, and thus

$$\beta_d = E(y_{1it} - y_{0it}),$$

which is the main parameter of interest. From $y_{it} = (1 - r_i \tau_t)y_{0it} + r_i \tau_t y_{1it}$, the observed response is

$$y_{it} = \beta_1 + \beta_r r_i + \beta_\tau \tau_t + \beta_d r_i \tau_t + (1 - r_i \tau_t)u_{0it} + r_i \tau_t u_{1it}.$$

This simple linear model embodies many restrictions as it will become clear shortly when more general equations are examined, and as a consequence, β_d is the treatment effect not just for region 1 at time b, but for all regions at all times.

Omitting the subscript i, the two differences in the DD are

$$
\begin{aligned}
E(y_{1b} - y_{0a}|r = 1) &= \beta_1 + \beta_r + \beta_\tau + \beta_d + E(u_{1b}|r = 1) \\
&\quad - \{\beta_1 + \beta_r + E(u_{0a}|r = 1)\} \\
&= \beta_\tau + \beta_d + E(u_{1b} - u_{0a}|r = 1), \\
E(y_{0b} - y_{0a}|r = 0) &= \beta_1 + \beta_\tau + E(u_{0b}|r = 0) - \{\beta_1 + E(u_{0a}|r = 0)\} \\
&= \beta_\tau + E(u_{0b} - u_{0a}|r = 0).
\end{aligned}
$$

Ignoring the error term's conditional means, the first difference in the DD has both the time and treatment effect, whereas the second difference has only the time effect. The DD then has only the desired treatment effect β_d.

Without ignoring the error term conditional means, we have, under the same time-effect condition,

$$DD = E(y_{1b} - y_{0b}|r = 1)$$
$$= \beta_1 + \beta_r + \beta_\tau + \beta_d + E(u_{1b}|r = 1) - \{\beta_1 + \beta_r + \beta_\tau + E(u_{0b}|r = 1)\}$$
$$= \beta_d + E(u_{1b} - u_{0b}|r = 1),$$

which is β_d if $E(u_{1b} - u_{0b}|r = 1) = 0$. That is, although the nonparametric DD is the treatment effect only for region 1 at time b, if $E(u_{1b} - u_{0b}|r = 1) = 0$ holds in the linear model, then the linear-model DD is β_d—the treatment effect for all regions at all times. Thus, the finding (β_d) in the DD is applicable to all regions at all times, i.e., is 'externally valid' if $E(u_{1b} - u_{0b}|r = 1) = 0$.

The same time-effect condition in the linear model is equivalent to

$$E(u_{0b} - u_{0a}|r = 1) = E(u_{0b} - u_{0a}|r = 0),$$

because

$$E(y_{0b} - y_{0a}|r = 1) = \beta_1 + \beta_r + \beta_\tau + E(u_{0b}|r = 1) - \{\beta_1 + \beta_r + E(u_{0a}|r = 1)\}$$
$$= \beta_\tau + E(u_{0b} - u_{0a}|r = 1),$$
$$E(y_{0b} - y_{0a}|r = 0) = \beta_1 + \beta_\tau + E(u_{0b}|r = 0) - \{\beta_1 + E(u_{0a}|r = 0)\}$$
$$= \beta_\tau + E(u_{0b} - u_{0a}|r = 0).$$

So far, covariates have been ignored. The DD identification condition is more likely to hold if the conditioning set includes covariates. Augment the linear potential response model with $\beta_x' x_{it}$:

$$y_{jit} = \beta_1 + \beta_r r_i + \beta_\tau \tau_t + \beta_d j + \beta_x' x_{it} + u_{jit}.$$

Observe

$$E(y_{0b} - y_{0a}|x_a, x_b, r = 1) = \beta_1 + \beta_r + \beta_\tau + \beta_x' x_b + E(u_{0b}|x_a, x_b, r = 1)$$
$$- \{\beta_1 + \beta_r + \beta_x' x_a + E(u_{0a}|x_a, x_b, r = 1)\}$$
$$= \beta_\tau + \beta_x'(x_b - x_a) + E(u_{0b} - u_{0a}|x_a, x_b, r = 1),$$
$$E(y_{0b} - y_{0a}|x_a, x_b, r = 0) = \beta_1 + \beta_\tau + \beta_x' x_b + E(u_{0b}|x_a, x_b, r = 0)$$
$$- \{\beta_1 + \beta_x' x_a + E(u_{0a}|x_a, x_b, r = 0)\}$$
$$= \beta_\tau + \beta_x'(x_b - x_a) + E(u_{0b} - u_{0a}|x_a, x_b, r = 0).$$

Hence, the 'conditional same time-effect condition' is

$$E(u_{0b} - u_{0a}|x_a, x_b, r = 1) = E(u_{0b} - u_{0a}|x_a, x_b, r = 0).$$

Under this, the 'conditional DD' is

$$E(y_{1b} - y_{0b}|x_a, x_b, r = 1) = \beta_d + E(u_{1b} - u_{0b}|x_a, x_b, r = 1).$$

If $E(u_{1b} - u_{0b}|x_a, x_b, r = 1) = 0$, then the conditional DD is just β_d. Otherwise, the covariates x_a and x_b can be integrated out to yield the marginal effect. It is straightforward to generalize the linear model for y_{jit} by allowing for the interaction term jx_{it}, which will then result in the observed response model

$$y_{it} = \beta_1 + \beta_r r_i + \beta_\tau \tau_t + \beta_d r_i \tau_t + \beta'_x x_{it} + \beta'_{dx} r_i \tau_t x_{it} + (1 - r_i \tau_t) u_{0it} + r_i \tau_t u_{1it}.$$

As we saw in Subsection 4.5.2 with the nonparametric DD, the conditional same time-effect condition is a 'weak form' of selection-on-observables. In the time and region example, we could not choose time but we could move across the regions to get (un)treated, which raised the usual selection problem issue. As in cross-section data, the choice variable (r) should be irrelevant for the potential response variables (or the error terms therein) when covariates are controlled for. The analog for the usual selection-on-observable condition for the effect on the treated would be

$$E(u_{0t}|x_a, x_b, r) = E(u_{0t}|x_a, x_b), \quad t = a, b$$

which is sufficient, but not necessary, for the above conditional same time-effect condition.

We saw that DD identifies the effect on the treated at post-treatment periods, but it identifies the effect applicable to all groups at all periods under certain assumptions. If the finding in a study is applicable only to the study subpopulation, then the finding has no 'external validity'. If it is applicable to other subpopulations as well, the finding has external validity. 'Internal validity' is when the finding is valid for the study subpopulation. The issue, internal/external validity, is relevant to all study designs, not just to DD, but since both time and space dimension appear in DD, we mention this issue here.

In the remainder of this subsection, which may be skipped, we explore two linear models. In the first model, it will be shown that only the *treatment effect at time b* is identified. In the second model, only the effect for region 1 at time b is identified, despite more assumptions than in the nonparametric DD. Hence, the following two linear models will illustrate that the extent of external validity depends on the assumptions, but that adding assumptions does not always lead to more external validity. The two linear models will also improve our understanding of the meaning of 'same time-effect'.

First, instead of the simple regression model for DD, allow $\beta_1, \beta_r, \beta_\tau, \beta_d$ to depend on t (allowing β_τ to depend on t is meaningful only when t takes more than two values) to get

$$y_{jit} = \beta_{1t} + \beta_{rt} r_i + \beta_{\tau t} \tau_t + \beta_{dt} j + u_{jit}.$$

Under the same time-effect condition,

$$
\begin{aligned}
DD &= E(y_{1b} - y_{0b}|r = 1) \\
&= \beta_{1b} + \beta_{rb} + \beta_{\tau b} + \beta_{db} + E(u_{1b}|r = 1) - \{\beta_{1b} + \beta_{rb} + \beta_{\tau b} + E(u_{0b}|r = 1)\} \\
&= \beta_{db} + E(u_{1b} - u_{0b}|r = 1),
\end{aligned}
$$

which is β_{db}, the effect at time b, if $E(u_{1b} - u_{0b}|r = 1) = 0$. To see the same time-effect condition, observe

$$
\begin{aligned}
E(y_{0b} - y_{0a}|r = 1) &= \beta_{1b} + \beta_{rb} + \beta_{\tau b} + E(u_{0b}|r = 1) \\
&\quad - \{\beta_{1a} + \beta_{ra} + E(u_{0a}|r = 1)\} \\
&= \beta_{1b} - \beta_{1a} + \beta_{rb} - \beta_{ra} + \beta_{\tau b} + E(u_{0b} - u_{0a}|r = 1), \\
E(y_{0b} - y_{0a}|r = 0) &= \beta_{1b} + \beta_{\tau b} + E(u_{0b}|r = 0) - \{\beta_{1a} + E(u_{0a}|r = 0)\} \\
&= \beta_{1b} - \beta_{1a} + \beta_{\tau b} + E(u_{0b} - u_{0a}|r = 0).
\end{aligned}
$$

Hence the same time-effect condition holds if

$$
\beta_{rb} = \beta_{ra} \quad \text{and} \quad E(u_{0b} - u_{0a}|r = 1) = E(u_{0b} - u_{0a}|r = 0).
$$

The first condition is the *time-invariance of region effect*, and the second condition appeared already for the simple linear model.

Second, further allow β_{dt} to depend on r:

$$
y_{jit} = \beta_{1t} + \beta_{rt}r_i + \beta_{\tau t}\tau_t + \beta_{drt}j + u_{jit}.
$$

Again, under the same time-effect condition,

$$
\begin{aligned}
DD &= \beta_{1b} + \beta_{rb} + \beta_{\tau b} + \beta_{d1b} + E(u_{1b}|r = 1) - \{\beta_{1b} + \beta_{rb} + \beta_{\tau b} + E(u_{0b}|r=1)\} \\
&= \beta_{d1b} + E(u_{1b} - u_{0b}|r = 1),
\end{aligned}
$$

which is β_{d1b}, the effect for region 1 at time b, if $E(u_{1b} - u_{0b}|r = 1) = 0$. Despite the refined structure, compared to the nonparametric DD, only the effect for region 1 at time b is identified. The same time-effect condition is the same as that in the preceding linear model.

Unlike the nonparametric DD, the linear models include different restrictions, which makes it possible to identify different parameters (β_d, β_{db}, or β_{d1b}), depending on the generality of the model. Under the same time-effect, which includes time-invariance of the region effect, DD identifies at least the treatment effect for region 1 at time b.

4.5.5   Estimation of DD

Recall $DD = E(y_{1b} - y_{0a}|r = 1) - E(y_{0b} - y_{0a}|r = 0)$. Estimation of DD differs depending on the type of the data at hand. Suppose we have a no-mover panel, i.e., panel data with nobody moving between the two regions during the period

$[a, b]$. Then, as already noted, DD is equal to

$$E(Y|r = 1) - E(Y|r = 0), \quad \text{where } Y \equiv y_b - y_a.$$

This can be estimated with the group mean difference

$$N_1^{-1} \sum_{i \in T} Y_i - N_0^{-1} \sum_{i \in C} Y_i,$$

where the C and T groups are region 0 and 1, respectively. Alternatively, the LSE of $Y_i (= \Delta y_i)$ on $(1, r_i)$ can be done, and the slope estimator is DD.

If we want to control for some covariates x to get the conditional version

$$E(Y|r = 1, x) - E(Y|r = 0, x),$$

we can then use any of the techniques studied so far to control for x (e.g., matching). In selecting covariates x, since $Y = y_b - y_a$ is to be explained, fewer covariates are needed, in contrast to when y_b is to be explained. The baseline response y_a may be included in x to explain Y. In short, no-mover panel data turns DD estimation into a cross-section treatment effect problem, which we now know how to handle.

Panel data often suffer from attrition problems. Related to this in DD is movers' problem, where subjects may move across region 0 and 1. If movers are removed from the panel data, then this could cause a selection problem, because movers can be systematically different from non-movers. If the number of movers is small, this would not matter much, but if the number is large, then it would be better to treat the panel data as repeated cross-sections and proceed as follows.

When Y is not observed for every subject, we can form four groups to get

$$DD = E(y|r=1, t=b) - E(y|r=1, t = a) - \{E(y|r=0, t = b) - E(y|r=0, t = a)\}.$$

Let G_{rt} denote the group at region $r = 0, 1$ and time $t = a, b$. With n_{rt} denoting the number of observations at region r and time t, a natural estimator for DD is,

$$DD_N \equiv n_{1b}^{-1} \sum_{i \in G_{1b}} y_i - n_{1a}^{-1} \sum_{i \in G_{1a}} y_i - \left(n_{0b}^{-1} \sum_{i \in G_{0b}} y_i - n_{0a}^{-1} \sum_{i \in G_{0a}} y_i \right).$$

Finding the asymptotic distribution for DD_N is possible, but somewhat complicated. Instead, we can use the linear model

$$y_i = \beta_1 + \beta_r r_i + \beta_\tau \tau_i + \beta_d r_i \tau_i + u_i, \quad E(u_i|r_i, \tau_i) = 0$$

where $\tau_i = 1$ if subject i is observed at $t = b$ and $\tau_i = 0$ otherwise. The slope for $r_i \tau_i$ is the desired DD and its significance can be tested with the t-value. A caution is that, if unbalanced panel data with movers are used for the LSE, there may be dependence across the observations, and ignoring it would lead to incorrect (under-estimated) standard errors, unless the proportion of the data overlap is small across the two periods.

A simple solution would be to use a linear panel data model (the presence of x_{it} is explicit now)

$$y_{it} = \beta_1 + \beta_r r_{it} + \beta_\tau \tau_t + \beta_d r_{it}\tau_t + \beta'_x x_{it} + \beta'_{dx} r_{it}\tau_t x_{it} + u_{it}, \quad \text{where } u_{it} = \zeta_i + v_{it}.$$

Here, ζ_i is the 'individual-specific' time-invariant error, and u_{ia} and u_{ib} are dependent at least through δ_i. u_{ia} and u_{ib} can be also dependent through autocorrelations of v_{it} over time. The so-called 'random effect' estimator would be an easy estimator to use for this model, but there are also many other estimators even allowing for endogeneity of regressors; see Lee (2002). The sample selection issue about r_{it} may make r_{it} and $r_{it}\tau_t x_{it}$ endogenous in this model.

Bertrand *et al.* (2004) examine standard error estimation in DD and find that ignoring autocorrelations in u_{it} results in serious under-estimation of the standard errors. In their simulations using CPS data and 'placebo' policy changes, the null hypothesis of no effect is rejected more than 50% of the time in some designs despite a 5% nominal level. They found 92 papers using DD in six economic journals over 1990–2000 and, of these, two-thirds dealt with the autocorrelation problem inadequately. They suggest a couple of solutions to the problem, and the easiest to use is 'block bootstrap' resampling where the entire time-series of subject i is resampled. That is, if there are N subjects and subject i has T_i observations, then they make a pseudo-sample of size N by resampling from the original sample with replacement. If subject i is sampled in this process, all T_i time-series data of subject i are sampled together. Denoting the original sample estimate and its t-value as b_N and $t_N = b_N/SD(b_N)$, obtain b^*_{Nj} and $t^*_{Nj} = (b^*_{Nj} - b_N)/SD(b^*_{Nj})$, $j = 1, \ldots, B$ where B is the bootstrap replication number. Then $B^{-1}\sum_j 1[|t^*_{Nj}| > |t_N|]$ is the bootstrap p-value; reject the null if the bootstrap p-value is less than, say, 5%.

As an example of DD, we use data for the years 2000 and 2001 from the Korea Labor and Income Panel Study to assess the interaction effect of region ($r = 1$ for Seoul) and time (year 2001) on working or not for Korean women. The data used here, which are purely for illustration, are balanced panel data consisting of women aged 15–65 and $N = 3134$. Among the 3134 women, some moved during 2000 and 2001:

	Regional transition matrix		
	$r = 0, t = b$	$r = 1, t = b$	sum
$r = 0, t = a$	2341	132	2473
$r = 1, t = a$	146	515	661
sum	2487	647	3134

Let $y = 1$ for working and 0 for not working and the percentage of the women working was 46%. We have the following results with t–values in $(\cdot)$:

$$\text{LSE of } y_{ib} - y_{ia} \text{ on } (1, r_i) : \underset{(-1.13)}{-0.015} \underset{(-1.57)}{-0.049\, r_i}, \quad R^2 = 0.001,$$

with non-movers only;

$$DD_N : \underset{(-1.90)}{-0.058};$$

$$\text{LSE of } y_i \text{ on } (1, r_i, \tau_i, r_i\tau_i) : \underset{(45.6)}{0.457} + \underset{(0.43)}{0.009 r_i} \underset{(-0.84)}{-0.012\, \tau_i} \underset{(-1.90)}{-0.058\, r_i\tau_i}, \quad R^2 = 0.001.$$

There seems to be some interaction effect, and the magnitudes $(-0.049, -0.058, -0.058)$ are similar when using the panel data of non-movers versus using all observations. The last LSE result shows that, although the main effect of being in Seoul is insignificantly positive (0.009), its interaction effect with τ_i for year 2001 is almost significantly negative (-0.058). It seems that the Seoul job market in $t = b$ deteriorated more than the national job market.

The p-values from the t-values in the last LSE and their bootstrap p-value with $B = 400$ are

asymptotic (*bootstrap*) p-values: $0.00(0.00), 0.67(0.67), 0.40(0.90),$
$0.057(0.16).$

According to the last bootstrap p-value 0.16, the null hypothesis of no inter-action effect is not rejected, and the asymptotic p-value, not accounting for the error term autocorrelation in the panel data, seems to under-estimate the standard error.

4.6 Triple differences (TD)*

Generalizing DD, we can think of difference in differences in differences, 'triple differences (TD)'. This may be further generalized to quadruple differences and so on. In this section, we review TD and present an empirical example in Gruber (1994). In the preceding section for DD, we assumed that all people in region 1 at time b were treated. TD is relevant if only some qualified people ($g = 1$, because of, say, age) in region 1 at time b are treated. For our exposition, we will assume no-mover panel data across groups and regions. For other types of data, the extra assumption of the mean-independence of τ from the potential responses, given r *and* g (and covariates), would be necessary analogously to Subsection 4.5.3.

4.6.1 TD for qualified post-treatment treated

Define

$g_i = 1$ if 'treatment qualified' (i.e., in group 1), and 0 in group 0,

$r_i = 1$ if living in region 1, and 0 in region 0,

$\tau_t = 1$ if $t = b$, and 0 otherwise if $t = a$

$\Rightarrow \quad d_{it} = g_i r_i \tau_t$: being in group 1 of region 1 at time b means qualifying

for treatment.

Since the treated response is observed only for group 1 of region 1 at time b, unless some assumptions are imposed, we can only identify the effect for group 1 of region 1 at time b.

With y_{jit} being the potential response for individual i at time t, $j = 0, 1$, we consider four over-time differences: omitting i,

$$E(y_{1b} - y_{0a}|g = 1, r = 1), \quad E(y_{0b} - y_{0a}|g = 1, r = 0),$$
$$E(y_{0b} - y_{0a}|g = 0, r = 1), \quad E(y_{0b} - y_{0a}|g = 0, r = 0).$$

The first two will be used for one DD, and the second two for the other DD. The difference between the two DD's is the TD:

$$E(y_{1b} - y_{0a}|g = 1, r = 1) - E(y_{0b} - y_{0a}|g = 1, r = 0)$$
$$-\{E(y_{0b} - y_{0a}|g = 0, r = 1) - E(y_{0b} - y_{0a}|g = 0, r = 0)\}.$$

To see what the TD identifies, rewrite this as

$$E(y_{1b} - y_{0a}|g = 1, r = 1) - E(y_{0b} - y_{0a}|g = 1, r = 1)$$
$$+\{E(y_{0b} - y_{0a}|g = 1, r = 1) - E(y_{0b} - y_{0a}|g = 1, r = 0)\}$$
$$-[E(y_{0b} - y_{0a}|g = 0, r = 1) - E(y_{0b} - y_{0a}|g = 0, r = 0)].$$

Suppose *the difference between group-1 region-1 time effect and group-1 region-0 time effect is the same as the difference between group-0 region-1 time effect and group-0 and region-0 time effect.* Then the last two expressions in $\{\cdot\}$ and $[\cdot]$ cancel each other to yield

$$TD = E(y_{1b} - y_{0b}|g = 1, r = 1),$$

which is the treatment effect for group 1 of region 1 at time b.

If we regard DD of the preceding section as conditioned on $g = 1$, then the DD identification condition (the same time-effect) is

$$E(y_{0b} - y_{0a}|g = 1, r = 1) - E(y_{0b} - y_{0a}|g = 1, r = 0) = 0.$$

The TD identification condition is weaker than this DD identification condition, because the display in $\{\cdot\}$ does not have to be zero, but stronger than it because the display in $[\cdot]$ has to equal the display in $\{\cdot\}$. Thus if the DD identification condition is plausible, we can just use the DD for the sub-population $g = 1$. Using TD in this case would require the extra restriction $[\cdot] = 0$.

To see other TD identification conditions that lead to $TD = E(y_{1b} - y_{0b}|g = 1, r = 1)$, rewrite the TD as

$$E(y_{1b} - y_{0a}|g = 1, r = 1) - E(y_{0b} - y_{0a}|g = 1, r = 1)$$

$$+\{E(y_{0b} - y_{0a}|g = 1, r = 1) - E(y_{0b} - y_{0a}|g = 1, r = 0)\}$$

$$+\{E(y_{0b} - y_{0a}|g = 1, r = 1) - E(y_{0b} - y_{0a}|g = 0, r = 1)\}$$

$$-\{E(y_{0b} - y_{0a}|g = 1, r = 1) - E(y_{0b} - y_{0a}|g = 0, r = 0)\}.$$

If each of the last three lines is zero, then the first line is $E(y_{1b} - y_{0b}|g = 1, r = 1)$. Even if this does not hold, if the second and third lines cancel the fourth line, which can happen because the fourth line includes two changes in g and r whereas the second and third include only one change each, then the first line is still $E(y_{1b} - y_{0b}|g = 1, r = 1)$.

4.6.2 Linear models for TD

To see the essence of TD better, consider a simple linear model for TD:

$$y_{jit} = \beta_1 + \beta_g g_i + \beta_r r_i + \beta_\tau \tau_t$$
$$+ \beta_{r\tau} r_i \tau_t + \beta_d j + u_{jit}, \quad j = 0, 1, \ \ i = 1, \ldots, N, \ \ t = a, b, \ \ E(u_{jit}) = 0.$$

To simplify the exposition, suppose $E(u_{jit}|g, r) = 0$ for all g and r. The four differences in the TD are:

$$E(y_{1b} - y_{0a}|g = 1, r = 1) = \beta_1 + \beta_g + \beta_r + \beta_\tau + \beta_{r\tau} + \beta_d - (\beta_1 + \beta_g + \beta_r)$$
$$= \beta_\tau + \beta_{r\tau} + \beta_d \quad \text{(time, region} \times \text{time, treatment)};$$

$$E(y_{0b} - y_{0a}|g = 1, r = 0) = \beta_1 + \beta_g + \beta_\tau - (\beta_1 + \beta_g) = \beta_\tau \quad \text{(time)};$$

$$E(y_{0b} - y_{0a}|g = 0, r = 1) = \beta_1 + \beta_r + \beta_\tau + \beta_{r\tau} - (\beta_1 + \beta_r)$$
$$= \beta_\tau + \beta_{r\tau} \quad \text{(time, region} \times \text{time)};$$

$$E(y_{0b} - y_{0a}|g = 0, r = 0) = \beta_1 + \beta_\tau - \beta_1 = \beta_\tau \quad \text{(time)}.$$

The DD for the first two differences is $\beta_{r\tau} + \beta_d$, which is the *region* $\times$ *time* effect plus the treatment effect. The DD for the second two differences is $\beta_{r\tau}$ which is the *region* $\times$ *time* effect. Therefore, the TD is β_d. In each of the four differences, time and its interacting effects remain, because all the differences are in time.

In each of the two DD's, the interaction between time and the region remains because r changes in each DD. Finally, the interaction term between time and the region is removed in the TD, to result only in the desired treatment effect corresponding to the triple interaction term $g_i r_i \tau_t$.

Now we turn to a more general regression model that is used for the empirical example below:

$$y_{jit} = \beta_1 + \beta_g g_i + \beta_r r_i + \beta_\tau \tau_t + \beta_{gr} g_i r_i + \beta_{g\tau} g_i \tau_t + \beta_{r\tau} r_i \tau_t + \beta_d j + u_{jit}.$$

For this model, the four differences in TD are

$$E(y_{1b} - y_{0a} | g = 1, r = 1) = \beta_1 + \beta_g + \beta_r + \beta_\tau + \beta_{gr} + \beta_{g\tau} + \beta_{r\tau} + \beta_d$$
$$+ E(u_{1b} | g = 1, r = 1) - \{\beta_1 + \beta_g + \beta_r + \beta_{gr}$$
$$+ E(u_{0b} | g = 1, r = 1)\}$$
$$= \beta_\tau + \beta_{g\tau} + \beta_{r\tau} + \beta_d + E(u_{1b} - u_{0a} | g = 1, r = 1);$$

$$E(y_{0b} - y_{0a} | g = 1, r = 0) = \beta_1 + \beta_g + \beta_\tau + \beta_{g\tau} + E(u_{0b} | g = 1, r = 0)$$
$$- \{\beta_1 + \beta_g + E(u_{0a} | g = 1, r = 0)\}$$
$$= \beta_\tau + \beta_{g\tau} + E(u_{0b} - u_{0a} | g = 1, r = 0);$$

$$E(y_{0b} - y_{0a} | g = 0, r = 1) = \beta_1 + \beta_r + \beta_\tau + \beta_{r\tau} + E(u_{0b} | g = 0, r = 1)$$
$$- \{\beta_1 + \beta_r + E(u_{0a} | g = 0, r = 1)\}$$
$$= \beta_\tau + \beta_{r\tau} + E(u_{0b} - u_{0a} | g = 0, r = 1);$$

$$E(y_{0b} - y_{0a} | g = 0, r = 0) = \beta_1 + \beta_\tau + E(u_{0b} | g = 0, r = 0)$$
$$- \{\beta_1 + E(u_{0a} | g = 0, r = 0)\}$$
$$= \beta_\tau + E(u_{0b} - u_{0a} | g = 0, r = 0).$$

The DD of the first two differences is

$$\beta_{r\tau} + \beta_d + E(u_{1b} - u_{0a} | g = 1, r = 1) - E(u_{0b} - u_{0a} | g = 1, r = 0),$$

whereas the DD of the second two differences is

$$\beta_{r\tau} + E(u_{0b} - u_{0a} | g = 0, r = 1) - E(u_{0b} - u_{0a} | g = 0, r = 0).$$

Hence the TD is

$$\beta_d + E(u_{1b} - u_{0a} | g = 1, r = 1) - E(u_{0b} - u_{0a} | g = 1, r = 0)$$
$$- \{E(u_{0b} - u_{0a} | g = 0, r = 1) - E(u_{0b} - u_{0a} | g = 0, r = 0)\}.$$

If the expected values for the error terms are zero, then the TD identifies the desired effect β_d that is externally valid for all groups, regions, and times. Otherwise, DD identifies at least the treatment effect for group 1 of region 1 at time b.

4.6.3   An empirical example

Gruber (1994) estimates the effect of mandated maternity benefits on ln(real hourly wage). The main issue of interest is whether the cost to the employers of implementing the mandate is passed over to employees. Since it is costly to hire women of child-bearing age, or anybody whose health insurance covers the women group, the mandate may lower the wage of those people. Among the states which passed such laws, Gruber (1994) looks at three 'treatment-adopted' states ($r = 1$): Illinois, New Jersey, and New York. Some comparison group states ($r = 0$) are also picked: Ohio and Indiana for Illinois, and Connecticut, Massachusetts, and North Carolina for New Jersey and New York. In each treatment-adopted state, group 1 consists of married women of child-bearing age, while group 0 consists of males over 40 or single males aged 20–40. From the Current Population Survey, observations on individuals are taken for two years before the legislation (1974, 1975; $t = a$) and after (1977, 1978; $t = b$). The sample size varies depending on the year and state, but it is around 1,500 for the treatment-adopted states and 5,000 for the comparison states. The following is part of his Table 3 (some covariates such as education, experience, sex, marital status, race and industry are controlled for by adding $\beta_x' x_{it}$ to the regression model above): with SD in ($\cdot$),

TD for effect of mandated maternity benefits on wage			
	before ($t = a$)	after ($t = b$)	time-difference
group 1			
treatment-adopted ($r = 1$)	1.547	1.513	−0.034 (0.017)
comparison states ($r = 0$)	1.369	1.397	0.028 (0.014)
region difference	0.178 (0.016)	1.116 (0.015)	
DD for group 1			−0.062 (0.022)
group 0			
treatment-adopted ($r = 1$)	1.759	1.748	−0.011 (0.010)
comparison states ($r = 0$)	1.630	1.627	−0.003 (0.010)
region difference	0.129 (0.010)	0.121 (0.010)	
DD for group 0			−0.008 (0.014)
TD			−0.054 (0.026)

The treatment-adopted states have higher wage rates for both group 1 and 0 compared with the comparison states. While the comparison states experienced almost no change or a rise in the wage over time, the treatment-adopted states experienced a decline in wages. The TD shows a significant drop in the wage rate by 5.4% (for the treatment-qualified group in the treatment-adopted state at the post-treatment era), which constitutes a substantial shift in the cost of health insurance from employers to employees.

5

Design and instrument for hidden bias

If the treatment (T) and control (C) groups are different in unobserved variables ε as well as in observed variables x and if ε affects both the treatment and response, then the difference in outcome y cannot be attributed to the difference in the treatment d. The difference in x that causes overt bias can be removed with one of the methods discussed in the preceding chapters, but the difference in ε that causes hidden bias is harder to deal with. In this and the following chapter, we look at hidden bias due to the difference in ε. An econometrician's first reaction to hidden bias (or the endogeneity problem) is to use an instrument. But good instruments are hard to come by. An easier approach, but less conclusive, is to explore ways to detect only the presence of hidden bias by checking 'coherence' (or 'consistency'): whether or not the main scenario of the treatment effect is coherent with other auxiliary findings. This task can be done with multiple treatment groups, multiple responses, or multiple control groups, which are easier to find than instruments, and checking coherence emphasizes *study design* rather than estimation techniques. The treatment-effect literature sheds new light on instrumental variables. For example an instrumental variable estimator demonstrates the effect on those whose treatment selection is affected by the instrument.

5.1 Conditions for zero hidden bias

With y_j being the potential response for treatment $d = j$, we stated earlier that if

$$f(y_j|d, x) \neq f(y_j|x) \quad for\ the\ observables\ x,$$
$$but\ f(y_j|d, x, \varepsilon) = f(y_j|x, \varepsilon) \quad for\ some\ unobservables\ \varepsilon,$$

then we have *selection-on-unobservables* (or *hidden bias*). When focusing on the mean effect, instead of these conditions involving densities/probabilities, we also used the term selection-on-unobservables as

$$E(y_j|d, x) \neq E(y_j|x) \quad \text{for the observables } x,$$

$$\text{but } E(y_j|d, x, \varepsilon) = E(y_j|x, \varepsilon) \quad \text{for some unobservables } \varepsilon.$$

There are conditions under which hidden bias will disappear. One frequently invoked condition, mentioned already, is that d *is determined by x and an error term, say ε, that is mean-independent of y_0 and y_1 given x.* Let $d_i = g(x_i, \varepsilon_i)$ for some function $g(\cdot, \cdot)$. Then, y_j is mean-independent of d given x:

$$E(y_j|x, d) = E(y_j|x, g(x, \varepsilon)) = E\{E(y_j|x, \varepsilon)|x, g(x, \varepsilon)\}$$
$$= E\{E(y_j|x)|x, g(x, \varepsilon)\} = E(y_j|x), \qquad j = 0, 1,$$

resulting in zero hidden bias.

The mean-independence assumption does not hold in general, if people choose the treatment comparing y_{1i} and y_{0i}; for example,

$$d_i = 1[y_{1i} > y_{0i}].$$

With $y_{ji} = x_i'\beta_j + u_{ji}$, we get $d_i = 1[x_i'(\beta_1 - \beta_0) + u_{1i} - u_{0i} > 0]$ and $u_{1i} - u_{0i}$ is related to u_{ji} (thus to y_{ji}) given x_i in general.

In reality, d and x precede the response, which means that it may be more plausible to assume, instead of $d_i = 1[y_{1i} > y_{0i}]$,

$$d_i = 1[E(y_{1i}|x_i, v_{1i}) > E(y_{0i}|x_i, v_{0i})]$$

where v_{ji} consists of part of u_{ji} that is observed to person i at the time of choosing d_i, but not observed to econometricians. Suppose a linear model holds such that $E(y_{ji}|x_i, v_{ji}) = x_i'\beta_j + v_{ji}$, $j = 0, 1$. Then, $d_i = 1[x_i(\beta_1 - \beta_0) + v_{1i} - v_{0i} > 0]$. Since only $v_{1i} - v_{0i}$ appears as the error term instead of $u_{1i} - u_{0i}$, the (mean) independence condition of $v_{1i} - v_{0i}$ from (y_{0i}, y_{1i}), that is, from (u_{0i}, u_{1i}), given x is less stringent than that of $u_{1i} - u_{0i}$ from (y_{0i}, y_{1i}) given x.

At the extreme, v_{ji} may not appear at all in the d-equation because v_{ji} is not known to person i at the time of the decision; in this case,

$$d_i = 1[E(y_{1i}|x_i) > E(y_{0i}|x_i)] :$$

d_i is determined only by x_i. The condition that d is determined by x and ε that is mean-independent of (y_0, y_1) given x, may be taken as a generalization of this display.

In observational data, d is often a product of multiple decisions. For example, for a job-training program, we have to take into account applying to the program (decision by the applicant), being accepted in the program (decision by the program administrator), and completing the program (decision by the applicant). These decisions take place over time, and some of them (e.g., completing the program) may be affected by interim outcomes of the program. Since y is likely to be related to the interim outcomes, zero hidden bias in this case requires conditioning on the interim outcomes, which are however not observed for the C group. If the subjects with poor interim outcomes have the same chance of completing the program as the subjects with good interim outcomes, then d is not influenced by the interim outcomes and there will be no hidden bias due to the interim outcomes.

5.2 Multiple ordered treatment groups

Typically, a causal analysis for effects of d on y starts with finding an association between d and y. Then, we control for observed variables (or confounders) x to see whether the association still stands firm when x is taken out of the picture. In a sense, we try to negate the causal claim using x. For unobserved variables ε, we cannot do this. Instead, we try to prop up the *prima facie* causal finding by showing that the finding is 'coherent', i.e., consistent with other auxiliary findings. Sometimes we have an idea of the variables lurking in ε, and sometimes we do not. In either case, there are a number of ways to show coherence, which is the topic of this and the following two sections.

So far, we have looked only at a binary treatment d, where the treatment is either zero or full. Suppose that a positive effect has been found initially. One would expect that, if the treatment level is increased, say to double the dose, then the effect will become stronger. Likewise, if the treatment is reduced, say to half the dose, then the effect will become weaker. Furthermore, if the treatment is reversed, a negative effect will occur. Of course, the true relation between d and y can be highly nonlinear, either negative or positive depending on the level of d. If we ignore such cases and confirm the expectations, the initial causal finding is supported. If the expectations are not confirmed, then the initial causal finding is suspect and might have been due to some unobserved confounders.

5.2.1 Partial treatment

Suppose we examine the job-training effects on re-employment within certain days (e.g., reemployment within 100 days). The T group get the job training and the C group do not. Suppose there is a drop-out group, D group, who receive only part of the required training. The three groups are ordered in terms of treatment dose: C group with no training, D group with partial training, and

T group with full training. If there is no hidden bias, controlling for x, we expect to have

$$C > D > T \quad \text{(bad treatment)} \quad \text{or} \quad C < D < T \quad \text{(good treatment)}$$

where $C > D$ means that the reemployment probability is greater for the C group than for the D group.

Suppose that the observed finding is D > C > T. There are many possible scenarios for D > C > T. One scenario is that the training is harmful, but smart trainees see this and thus drop out. The D group finds jobs sooner than the C group for the D group is smarter, resulting in D > C > T. In this scenario, the unobserved confounder ε is how smart the person is. Another scenario is that the training is harmful but the D group drops out because they find a job due to a lower 'reservation' wage, resulting in D > C > T. In this scenario, the unobserved confounder ε is the reservation wage. There are many more scenarios, possibly based on different unobserved confounders. One may say that a goal in causal analysis with observational data is to negate those scenarios one by one to come up with non-negated (that is, coherent) scenarios.

In short, there is a coherence problem in the above job-training example with D > C > T, which needs to be explained before declaring the treatment good or bad. If the D group had been ignored, only C > T would have been considered in order to conclude a bad job training. The partial treatment group, which is an extra treatment group using an extra dose, casts doubt on the causal finding using only the full versus no treatment groups.

In another example, Ludwig *et al.* (2001) examine the effects on crime rates of moving into a lower poverty area. In observational data, people have some control over where they live, and living in a high or low poverty area includes an element of self-selection, which Ludwig *et al.* (2001) avoid by using experimental data. Since 1994, 638 families from a high-poverty area in Baltimore were randomly assigned to three groups: the T group receiving various helps to move to an area with poverty rate under 10%, the D group receiving helps to move without constraints on poverty rate, and the C group receiving no help. Low income families with children who lived in public housing were eligible, but participation in this experiment was voluntary, which means a selection problem. The D group was partially treated, because they could (and some did) move into an area with a poverty rate higher than 10%. The outcome was measured by juvenile-arrest records. A total of 279 teenagers were arrested 998 times in the pre- and post-program periods. The crimes were classified into three categories: violent crimes (assault, robbery, etc.), property crimes, and other crimes (drug offenses, disorderly conduct, etc.).

Part of their Table III for juveniles of ages 11–16 is shown below (some covariates are controlled for the table). The second column shows the mean number of arrests for 100 teenagers in the C group per quarter. The third column shows the treatment effect of the T versus the C group, whereas the fourth column shows the treatment effect of the D versus the C group. The two entries with one star are significant at a 10% level, and the entry with double stars is significant at 5%.

Effects of moving into low poverty area on crimes			
	Mean arrests for C	T versus C (SD)	D versus C (SD)
Violent crimes	3.0	−1.6 (0.8)**	−1.4 (0.8)*
Property crimes	2.0	1.3 (0.8)	−0.5 (0.8)
The other crimes	3.3	−0.7 (1.0)	−1.3 (1.0)
All crimes	8.3	−0.9 (1.8)	−3.1 (1.8)*

The treatment indeed seems to lower crime rates. Note that the increase in property crimes is likely to be related to the higher opportunity for such crimes present in higher-income areas. But, in terms of all crime rates, we have the ranking C > T > D, which is strange, for one would expect C > D > T. One explanation is that crime rates are over-estimated in the T group areas relative to the D group areas because there are likely to be more crimes undefected in the D group areas. In this case, the probability of crime detection is an unobserved confounder.

In the first job-training example, our conjecture on unobserved confounders was weak. In the second crime example, we had a better idea of the unobserved confounder (the probability of crime detection). Using multiple ordered treatment groups (from multiple doses) can either weaken or strengthen the initial causal finding, but at least it prevents us from being misled, which is good.

Sometimes, the ordering of the treatment levels is problematic. For instance, if we consider various types of smokers (non-smoker, passive smoker, non-inhaling smoker, light smoker, etc.), it is not clear how to order them in terms of the treatment doses. Hsu (1996) refers to White and Froeb (1980) for the following example where the SD of breathing capacity is about 0.5:

Smoker type:	non	passive	non-inhaling	light	moderate	heavy
Breathing capacity:	3.35	3.23	3.19	3.15	2.80	2.55

The result is coherent only partially, because we do not know *a priori* where to put passive or non-inhaling smokers in ordering the smoker types. If this was a randomized study, which it is not, the outcome (breathing capacity) would order the treatments without ambiguity: e.g., passive smoking is less harmful than light smoking despite the worry that passive smokers are exposed to smoke without filters.

5.2.2   Reverse treatment

If a change in treatment from 0 to 1 has a positive effect, then a change from 1 to 0 should have a negative effect, which is another way of being coherent. This can be checked with two similar groups where one group experiences a change from 0 to 1 and the other group experiences a change from 1 to 0. For each group, a before-after design is implemented. Contrast this to difference-in-differences (DD) where one group experiences a change from 0 to 1 and the other group experience no change (0 to 0). The reverse treatment design is stronger than DD, because the distinction between the two groups are clearer if indeed the treatment has had an effect.

It is also possible to try reverse treatment design on a single group. The treatment change is from 0 to 1 to see the effect, and then it is reversed back to 0 to see the reverse effect. If the treatment is effective, y will take level A, B, and back to A as the treatment changes from 0 to 1, and back to 0. Comparing this one-group three-point design with the preceding two-group two-point design (here, 'point' refers to time points), in the former we do not have to worry about the difference between the two groups, but we do have to be concerned more about the time effect because three time points are involved.

For time-series or panel data, suppose we use a before-after design to find a positive effect of d (water fluoridation) on y (tooth decay) over five years. In the beginning of the period, fluoridation started (treatment changing from 0 to 1) and lasted for five years. Comparing tooth decay at the beginning and end of the five-year period, the proportion had fallen. However, during this period, other things could have changed to affect y. For instance, a more healthy life style could have been adopted (a lower fat and lower-sugar diet improving oral health), and this could have been the reason for the lower tooth decay. To refute this possibility, suppose fluoridation stopped (the treatment changing from 1 to 0) and stayed that way for another five years. Suppose tooth decay increased during this second five year period. If an unhealthy life style was adopted during this period, then again this might explain the higher tooth decay, which is unlikely, however. Hence, the reverse treatment corroborates the initial finding. This example is a modified version of actual studies on fluoridation referred to in Gordis (2000, pp. 7–9).

In another example, Allison and Long (1990) examine the effects of department quality on faculty productivity. With $N = 177$ individual job moves from one university to another between 1961 and 1975, they compared the quality of the departments and classified the job moves into four categories: big upward move, upward move, downward move, and big downward move (these category names are different from those in Allison and Long (1990)). Productivity is compared in two ways: the number of publications in the five years before and after the change, and the number of citations in the year of the move and five years later; citations are to the articles published in the immediately preceding three-year interval. Part of their Table 3 where no covariates are controlled for is

Effect of department quality on productivity			
	Sample size	% Change in publications	% Change in citations
Big upward move	43	25	38
Upward move	30	−5	29
Downward move	64	−7	−16
Big downward move	40	−22	−57

Allison and Long (1990) could have compared the upward-move groups to a no-change group. Using the downward-move group instead of a no-change group makes the effect more salient and provides a coherence check as can be seen in the table.

5.3 Multiple responses

It is possible to check coherence with multiple responses. Suppose we found a positive effect of stress (d) on a mental disease (y) using data on some people. Over time, it was found that increasing stress levels raised the incidence of mental disease. Suppose also that the same people reported an increased number of injuries due to accidents. Since stress *per se* is unlikely to have affected the number of injuries due to accidents, this suggests the presence of an unobserved confounder. With the extra response variable (the number of injuries), coherence can be explored.

In an interesting example, there have been claims on the beneficial effects of moderate alcohol intake—particularly red wine—on heart disease. Since there are potential risks from drinking, it is difficult to conduct an experiment, and studies on a causal link are observational where people self-select their drinking level. Thun *et al.* (1997) examine a large data set on elderly U.S. adults with $N = 490,000$. In 1982, the subjects reported their drinking (and smoking) habits, and 46,000 died during the nine year follow-up. In the study, drinking habits were measured separately for beer, wine, and spirits and the sum was recorded as the total number of drinks per day. It was found that moderate drinking reduced death rates from cardiovascular diseases. Part of their Table 4 for women is

Deaths (SD) per 100,000 and number of drinks per day					
Cause of death	0	Less than 1	1	2–3	4 or more
cirrhosis, alcoholism	5.0 (0.9)	4.3 (0.9)	7.7 (1.9)	10.4 (1.9)	23.9 (4.5)
cardiovascular diseases	335 (7.8)	230 (7.5)	213 (10.2)	228(9.8)	251(16)
breast cancer	30.3(2.1)	33.3 (2.4)	37.6(4.1)	45.8(4.2)	29.1(5.3)
injuries, external causes	22.7 (1.9)	25.5 (2.2)	17.7 (2.8)	18.9 (2.7)	17.1 (4.0)

Examining the cirrhosis and alcoholism rows, clearly the death rate increases as more alcohol is consumed. The decrease to 4.3 from 5.0, as the number of drinks goes from 0 to less than 1, is within the margin of error judging from the SD's. The death rate from cardiovascular diseases decreases for moderate drinking but increases as the number of drinks increases. The death rate from breast cancer increases substantially, but then drops when four drinks or more per day are consumed, which casts some doubt on the study. The most problematic result is the death rate from injuries and external causes, which decreases when one drink or more is consumed.

If we do a randomized study, we would expect drinkers to have more, not less, accidents (thus have a higher death rate from injuries and external causes). Being otherwise suggests that drinkers may be systematically different from non-drinkers. Drinkers may be more careful to avoid accidents and attentive to their health and lifestyle, and this aspect, not the alcohol intake itself, may be the real reason for the lower death rate from cardiovascular disease. Wine drinkers are sometimes reported to have a healthy lifestyle in the U.S. This may be due to the fact that wine is more expensive than beer and that better educated people with more money tend to drink wine. Therefore, being better educated could be the common factor for wine drinking and a healthy life style in the U.S. In Thun *et al.* (1997), their subjects varied greatly in their level of education. Part of their Table 2 is

Demographic characteristics for women			
	current drinkers	lifelong non-drinkers	no info. on alcohol
Grade 13 or higher (%)	69	55	47
Employed (%)	51	47	41

Drinkers were found to be better educated and more likely to be employed. The women excluded from the study due to no information on alcohol consumption, also seemed to differ substantially from the women in the study. Although the above death rates were supposedly adjusted for these covariates, controlling for education might not have been enough to control lifestyle or carefulness.

The main point is that, by looking at the extra response variable (death rate due to injuries and external causes), we can detect hidden bias due to the unobserved variable consisting of alertness and carefulness. What is probably needed in order to make the claim that moderate drinking is beneficial is a convincing biological explanation that would bridge the gap between moderate drinking and better health.

In the drinking example, the extra response variable is expected to be affected by the treatment in a known direction. There are cases where an extra response variable is not supposed to be affected at all. For example, consider

the effect of a lower speed limit on the number of traffic accidents. One unobserved confounder could be degree of police patrol. It is possible that police
patrol is intensified to enforce the lower speed limit, which would then reduce
the number of traffic accidents, whereas the real effect of the lower speed limit
per se is nil. In this example, an extra response variable could be the crime rate,
that is not supposed to be affected by the speed limit. If the crime rate does
not change following the change in the speed limit, then we can rule out the
possibility that the intensified patrol efforts affected traffic accidents. Of course,
the best thing to do would be to find a variable that represented patrol efforts
and see if it really changed or not when the speed limit changed. If this is not
done, the next best thing would be to use the extra response variable (crime
rate) to detect the changes in the police patrol efforts.

Examining an extra response variable that is not supposed to be affected by
the treatment to rule out hidden bias, is similar to comparing $E(x|d = 1)$ with
$E(x|d = 0)$ where x is a pretreatment variable vector, because pretreatment
variables cannot be affected by the treatment. If y_b is the response variable
after the treatment that takes place at some time point between a and b, then
examining the pre-treatment response difference $E(y_a|d = 1) - E(y_a|d = 0)$
can be helpful as well, for y_a is similar to y_b but should not be affected by the
treatment. If $E(y_a|d = 1) \neq E(y_a|d = 0)$, one should suspect an unobserved
confounder is affecting the treatment, y_a, and y_b. Controlling for y_a (i.e., including y_a in x) may eliminate the hidden bias due to the unobserved confounder
to some extent.

For example, in assessing the effect of an education program on academic
achievements, suppose y is a test to measure academic achievements and we find

$$E(y_b|d = 1) > E(y_b|d = 0) \quad \text{and} \quad E(y_a|d = 1) > E(y_a|d = 0).$$

The former suggests effectiveness of the program, but the latter shows that
there is an unobserved confounder because y_a is a pre-treatment variable that
should not be affected by d. The unobserved confounder would be the different
quality (ability or IQ) of the students. One way to deal with quality difference
is to measure it, say, with an IQ test and control for IQ. Another way, either
because IQ tests are not available or because IQ itself is an imperfect measure
of quality, is to use y_a as a control variable.

5.4 Multiple control groups

Zero is an intriguing number, and *no treatment can mean many different things.*
With drinking as the treatment, it may mean the real non-drinkers, but it
may also mean the people who used to drink heavily a long time ago and
then stopped for health reasons (ex-drinkers). With a job-training program
as the treatment, no treatment could mean people who never applied to the
program, but it could also mean people who had applied but were then rejected

for some reason. Much as the real non-drinkers differ from the ex-drinkers, non-applicants can differ from the rejected. In the job-training example, there are two control groups: the non-applicants and the rejected. Both groups did not receive the treatment, but they could still differ in terms of unobserved confounders.

It is possible to detect the presence of unobserved confounders using multiple control groups. Let C denote non-applicants and C_r the rejected. Suppose $E(y|x, C) \neq E(y|x, C_r)$ for some x. Then C and C_r are systematically different other than in x. This must be due to an unobserved variable ε, which raises the suspicion that the T group might be also different from C and C_r in terms of ε. Specifically, the program administrators may have creamed-off applicants with higher values of ε, that could be quality or ability, to ensure success of the program. Hence C_r would comprise people with low ε. In this example, comparing the C group with the extra control group C_r helps us to see the presence of an unobserved confounder.

Card and Krueger (1994, 2000) analyze the effects of an increase in the minimum wage on employment. In 1992, New Jersey (NJ) increased its minimum wage from $4.25 to $5.05 per hour. From NJ and eastern Pennsylvania (PA), 410 fast food restaurants were sampled before and after the change in the minimum wage (treatment) for DD analysis. That is, fast food restaurants in PA were used as a comparison group. Since the NJ economy was going into recession when the treatment took place, a comparison group was needed to separate the economy effect from the treatment effect. Also, NJ fast food restaurants with starting wage higher than $5 were used as another control group. The idea is that those NJ restaurants are less likely to be affected by the treatment.

Part of Table 3 in Card and Krueger (1994) is presented in the table below showing the average (SD), where FTE (full-time equivalent) is the number of full-time workers plus 0.5 times the number of part-time workers, NJ ($4.25) represents NJ restaurants with a pre-treatment starting wage of $4.25 (the most vulnerable to the treatment), and NJ ($5) represents NJ restaurants with a pre-treatment starting wage of $5 or above (the least vulnerable to the treatment).

DD with two control groups for minimum wage effect on employment						
	NJ	PA	NJ − PA	NJ ($4.25)	NJ ($5)	NJ ($4.25) − NJ ($5)
FTE before	20.44	23.33	−2.89	19.56	22.25	−2.69
FTE after	21.03	21.17	−0.14	20.88	20.21	0.67
difference	0.59	−2.16	2.75 (1.36)	1.32	−2.04	3.36 (1.48)

From the left four columns, despite the minimum wage increase, NJ FTE increased whereas PA FTE decreased. The DD estimate is significantly positive, showing no negative effect from the minimum wage increase. From the right three columns using NJ ($5) as a second control group, almost the same finding is demonstrated. The second control group renders a coherent story, behaving similarly to the first control group. In the DD, no covariates were controlled for. Card and Krueger (1994) tried many regression models, only to conclude that there was no evidence of a reduction in employment due to the minimum wage increase.

Before we present another example, we introduce a *case-control study*, which is popular in clinical medicine, but not in econometrics. Usually in econometrics, we deal with a random sample (d and y are sampled (i.e., observed) jointly) or an exogenous sample (d is sampled first and then y). If y is sampled first and then d, we get an *endogenous sample*. Studies with endogenously sampled data are called 'case-control study', or *case-referent study* where $P(d|y)$ is identified, but not $P(y|d)$. For example, $y = 1$ is death from lung cancer and $d = 1$ is smoking. 50 people who died of lung cancer are sampled and another 50 people who died of a cause other than lung cancer are sampled to compare their smoking habits d. If the $y = 1$ group have more $d = 1$ people than the $y = 0$ group have, then this suggests an association between smoking and lung cancer. 'case' refers to the $y = 1$ group, and 'control' the $y = 0$ group. Since 'control' here is not the $d = 0$ group, the term 'case-referent' is better than 'case-control'.

Suppose both d and y are binary. With an endogenous sample, identifying $P(y = 1|d = 1) - P(y = 1|d = 0)$ or

$$relative\ risk \quad P(y = 1|d = 1)/P(y = 1|d = 0)$$

is impossible unless some assumptions are imposed. Instead, we can identify

$$odds\ ratio\ for\ response \quad \frac{\text{odds of } y = 1 \text{ for } d = 1}{\text{odds of } y = 1 \text{ for } d = 0}$$

$$= \frac{P(y = 1|d = 1)/P(y = 0|d = 1)}{P(y = 1|d = 0)/P(y = 0|d = 0)}$$

which is yet another measure of the treatment effect. If odds ratio is not one, then this means non-zero treatment effect.

To see how the odds ratio for response is identified with an endogenous sample, observe that

$$odds\ ratio\ for\ treatment \quad \frac{\text{odds of } d = 1 \text{ for } y = 1}{\text{odds of } d = 1 \text{ for } y = 0}$$

$$= \frac{P(d = 1|y = 1)/P(d = 0|y = 1)}{P(d = 1|y = 0)/P(d = 0|y = 0)}$$

is identified with endogenous sample, because this can be rewritten as

$$\frac{\{P(y = 1|d = 1)P(d = 1)/P(y = 1)\}/\{P(y = 1|d = 0)P(d = 0)/P(y = 1)\}}{\{P(y = 0|d = 1)P(d = 1)/P(y = 0)\}/\{P(y = 0|d = 0)P(d = 0)/P(y = 0)\}}$$

$$= \frac{P(y = 1|d = 1)/P(y = 0|d = 1)}{P(y = 1|d = 0)/P(y = 0|d = 0)}$$

cancelling $P(d = 0)$, $P(d = 1)$, $P(y = 0)$, and $P(y = 1)$. Hence the odds ratio for treatment equals the odds ratio for response.

Consider the effect of prenatal exposure (d) to some substance on an infant disease (y) to be analyzed in a case-referent study. The mothers of infants with the disease are asked to recall their prenatal exposure. However it can happen that mothers with diseased infants are more able to recall than mothers with healthy infants, because the former search more intensely for the cause of the disease. This causes *recall bias*. To check for recall bias, we form two referent ($y = 0$) groups. One referent group represents healthy infants, and the other referent group represents infants with some disease known to be unrelated to the substance in question. If $P(d = 1|y = 0)$ is the same across the two referent groups, then this indicates a lack of recall bias. If there were a recall bias, it would be present in the second referent group, resulting in a higher $P(d = 1|y = 0)$ for the second referent group than for the first referent group. In this example, we have a good idea of the unobserved confounder, which is the recall (or memory search) intensity of mothers.

As another example for multiple control groups, in assessing the effect of disability insurance benefit (d) on working or not working (y), the T group is those receiving disability insurance benefit, and the C group is those not receiving the disability insurance benefit. The eligibility depends on the level of health ε. If ε were observed and if there were a known threshold ε_o for ε such that $d = 1[\varepsilon < \varepsilon_o]$, then this would be a case of regression discontinuity design where d is determined by health, and health affects y directly as well as indirectly via d. One could then identify $E(y_1 - y_0|\varepsilon = \varepsilon_o)$. Since health ε is usually not observed, health becomes an unobserved confounder in finding $E(y_1 - y_0)$. Clearly, the T group is systematically different from the C group in terms of health. Consider an extra control group C_r who applied for disability insurance benefit but were rejected. Using data for 1978 that oversampled the disabled, part of Table 2 in Bound (1989) is

$$y = 1 \text{ in C: } 69.3\% \text{ out of } 1272 \text{ subjects,}$$

$$y = 1 \text{ in } C_r\text{: } 28.7\% \text{ out of } 136 \text{ subjects,}$$

$$y = 1 \text{ in T: } 2.3\% \text{ out of } 1722 \text{ subjects.}$$

First, comparing C and C_r, clearly health matters for y. Second, for the counter-factual question: what would be the probability $E(y_0|d=1)$ of working if a person receiving disability insurance had been denied the insurance? Certainly 0.693 for $E(y_0|d = 0)$ is not the correct answer. A better answer would be that the probability is lower than 0.287. In this example, the second control group serves two purposes. First, it shows that the unobserved confounder matters (when C_r is compared with C). Second, it provides a better counter-factual estimate—an upper bound in this example.

5.5   Instrumental variable estimator (IVE)

5.5.1   Potential treatments

Imagine a health program where half the subjects are randomly selected and given an education (z) on the benefits of exercise, and the other half are not. Suppose we are interested in the effects of exercise (d) on health (y), not the effects of education (z) on health. We have a situation where

$$z \to d \to y,$$

ruling out the direct effect of z on y, for the education itself is unlikely to affect health directly. This diagram can be viewed as a combination of two causal relations $z \to d$ and $d \to y$. The variable z, which affects d but not y directly, is called an *instrument*. Since we can think of potential responses y_0 and y_1 depending on d, we can also think of potential treatments d_1 and d_0 depending on z.

Suppose

$$d_{ji} = \alpha_1 + \alpha_2 j + \varepsilon_i, \qquad y_{ji} = \beta_1 + \beta_2 j + u_i, \quad j = 0, 1,$$
$$d_i \equiv (1 - z_i)d_{0i} + z_i d_{1i}, \qquad y_i = (1 - d_i)y_{0i} + d_i y_{1i};$$

d_{1i} is a constant-shifted version of d_{0i} and y_{1i} is a constant-shifted version of y_{0i} $\forall i$, which means a *constant effect*. From this, we get

$$d_i = \alpha_1 + \alpha_2 z_i + \varepsilon_i, \qquad y_i = \beta_1 + \beta_2 d_i + u_i.$$

Only $\{(z_i, d_i, y_i)\}_{i=1}^N$ is observed, although $\{(z_i, d_{0i}, d_{1i}, y_{0i}, y_{1i})\}_{i=1}^N$ is considered.

The potential responses were used to define the individual treatment effect $y_{1i} - y_{0i}$. Is there use for d_{0i} and d_{1i}? The answer is yes for two reasons: one is that $d_{1i} - d_{0i}$ is the individual effect of the instrument z on d, and the other is that, since each individual has $(z_i, d_{0i}, d_{1i}, y_{0i}, y_{1i})$, d_{0i} and d_{1i} characterize the person. Observe, following Angrist *et al.* (1996),

$d_{0i} = 0, d_{1i} = 0$: *never takers* (of the treatment, no matter what z_i is);

$d_{0i} = 0, d_{1i} = 1$: *compliers* (taking the treatment only when offered);

$d_{0i} = 1, d_{1i} = 0$: *defiers* (taking the treatment only when not offered);

$d_{0i} = 1, d_{1i} = 1$: *always takers* (no matter what z_i is).

For the exercise (d) example, never-takers never exercise regardless of their education z on the benefits of exercise—'the losers'. Compliers exercise only thanks to their education z—'the normal'. Defiers are hard to imagine—'the weird'. Always-takers always exercise regardless of their education—'the determined'. We need to observe both d_0 and d_1 to know, for instance, who is a complier and who is not, but only one of d_0 and d_1 is observed. Hence, we cannot categorize a given individual. Nevertheless, the four types characterize the subjects—the losers, normal, weird, and determined—and it is possible to identify the proportion of each type under some assumptions.

Substituting the d-equation into the y-structural form (SF), we get the y-reduced form (RF):

$$y_i = \beta_1 + \beta_2(\alpha_1 + \alpha_2 z_i + \varepsilon_i) + u_i = (\beta_1 + \alpha_1\beta_2) + \alpha_2\beta_2 z_i + (u_i + \beta_2\varepsilon_i).$$

Under $E(z\varepsilon) = 0$ and $E(zu) = 0$, the LSE of y_i on $(1, z_i)$ is consistent for $(\beta_1 + \alpha_1\beta_2, \alpha_2\beta_2)$. The slope for z_i is $\gamma_2 \equiv \alpha_2\beta_2$ that is the product of the two effects: α_2 for z_i on d_i, and β_2 for d_i on y_i. If we do the LSE of d on $(1, z)$ to estimate α_2 and divide the LSE for γ_2 with this, we can then estimate the main parameter of interest β_2 consistently. However there is a simpler one step procedure to get β_2, which is examined in the following.

Define

$$Z_i = (1, z_i)', \qquad D_i = (1, d_i)', \qquad \alpha \equiv (\alpha_1, \alpha_2)', \qquad \beta \equiv (\beta_1, \beta_2)',$$

to get

$$d_i = Z_i'\alpha + \varepsilon_i, \qquad y_i = D_i'\beta + u_i.$$

Suppose $COR(d_i, u_i) \neq 0$ (due to $COR(\varepsilon_i, u_i) \neq 0$) so that the LSE of y on D is inconsistent for β. Under $COR(z_i, u_i) = 0$ and $\alpha_2 \neq 0$, however, the instrumental variable estimator (IVE) is consistent for β:

$$\left\{(1/N)\sum_i Z_i D_i'\right\}^{-1}(1/N)\sum_i Z_i y_i \xrightarrow{p} \{E(ZD')\}^{-1}E(Zy)$$
$$= \{E(ZD')\}^{-1}E\{Z(D'\beta + u)\}$$
$$= \beta + \{E(ZD')\}^{-1}E(Zu) = \beta.$$

If we are interested only in testing H_0: $\beta_2 = 0$, then we can do the LSE of y on Z to test the H_0 with the slope estimator for z, because it is consistent for $\alpha_2\beta_2$ as shown above.

As can be seen in the last equation, an instrument z_i has to meet two necessary conditions:

$$COR(z_i, d_i) \neq 0 \quad and \quad COR(z_i, u_i) = 0;$$

the former is the *inclusion restriction* $\alpha_2 \neq 0$, where the education is effective in inducing the subjects to exercise, and the latter holds due to the randomization of z. An additional requirement should hold that z does not enter the y-equation directly, which is an *exclusion restriction*, where z should influence y only indirectly though d. If a covariate vector x with $COR(x, u) = 0$ appears in the d and y equations, we may replace $COR(z_i, d_i) \neq 0$ with $COR(z_i, d_i|x) \neq 0$.

The following two interesting facts regarding IVE will be shown in Section 5.6. First, the population version of the slope IVE—that is, β_2—can be written as

$$\frac{E(y|z=1) - E(y|z=0)}{E(d|z=1) - E(d|z=0)} = \frac{\text{effect of } z \text{ on } y}{\text{effect of } z \text{ on } d},$$

the sample version of which is called the 'Wald estimator'. If z takes two close values, say 0 and $0+h$ with $h \simeq 0$, then this becomes (see Heckman (1997))

$$\beta_2 = \frac{\partial E(y|z)/\partial z \mid_{z=0}}{\partial E(d|z)/\partial z \mid_{z=0}}.$$

Second, although we use a constant effect model above, the Wald estimator can be interpreted as $E(y_1 - y_0|\text{compliers})$ even when the treatment effect varies across i.

5.5.2 Sources for instruments

The concept of IVE is fundamental and IVE is widely used in econometrics. Hence IVE needs no more explanation. In practice, however, plausible instruments are hard to come by. The main problem with IVE is not what to do with the instruments, but where to find them. In the following, we explore the sources for instruments.

Recall the health program example where we were interested in the effects of exercise (d) on health (y) and the subjects randomized to the T group were given some education (z) on the benefits of exercises and the C group were not given any education. We have

$$d_i = \alpha_1 + \alpha_2 z_i + \varepsilon_i, \quad \alpha_2 \neq 0, \qquad y_i = \beta_1 + \beta_2 d_i + u_i,$$
$$COR(\varepsilon_i, u_i) \neq 0, \qquad COR(z_i, u_i) = 0,$$

and the randomization dummy z becomes an instrument for the endogenous treatment d. One may view d as a *compliance* to the randomization. Compliance, which often appears in clinical trials, is self-selection. So long as the randomization dummy z influences d, z can be used as an instrument.

One caution, however, is that randomization does not always provide an instrument. Angrist (1990) examine the effect of serving in the military for the Vietnam war (d) on lifetime earnings (y), where draft lottery (z) serves as an instrument for d (depending on the lottery number, a person is more (or less) likely to be drafted). However, as pointed out by Heckman (1996), potential employers may not hire those more likely to be drafted, which means that z can enter directly into the y-equation:

$$y_i = \beta_1 + \beta_2 d_i + \beta_z z_i + u_i.$$

In this case, randomization fails to deliver a legitimate instrument. Since z enters the y-equation along with d, we need a new instrument for d. Another problem occurs when d takes more than two values and a function of d along with d itself appear in the y-equation: e.g.,

$$y_i = \beta_1 + \beta_2 d_i + \beta_3 d_i^2 + u_i.$$

We need two instruments, for which a single randomization dummy is inadequate.

Next to randomized experiments, there are natural experiments where no deliberate randomization takes place, but the nature does a sort of randomization. One example is date of birth (z). In the literature of returns to schooling, typically ln(wage) is regressed on schooling (d) and some demographic variables, but the exogeneity of d is suspect due to 'ability' lurking in d and the y-equation error term. Angrist and Krueger (1991) use date of birth as an instrument for d. Normally, date of birth would not qualify as an instrument for d. In the U.S., however, there is a compulsory schooling law that requires school attendance until a certain age is reached, which means that one may quit school with less (or more) education than the average depending on the birth date. Angrist and Krueger (1991) find that, for example, those born in the first quarter received about 0.1 year less education than those born in the other three quarters.

Finding an instrument is looking for *a variation in d exogenous to the response variable* (conditional on some covariates). In the example just above, the variation in schooling due to date of birth is exogenous to y. Another example of natural experiment is the occurrence of a twin birth in the first pregnancy (Rosenzweig and Wolpin (1980)). In the effect of the number of children (d) on female labor supply (y), the number of children is likely to be endogenous to y, because d and y may be determined jointly. In searching for an exogenous variation for d, twin birth (z) provides an exogenous increase for d, because even though one can plan to have children, one cannot plan to have twins. Rosenzweig and Wolpin (1980) looked at only twin births in the first pregnancy, for if twin births at any pregnancy had been included, women that had multiple births would have been over-represented in the data leading to an endogeneity problem, as multiple births would have become a choice. Rosenzweig and Wolpin found that the labor participation rate decreased in the first few years following the twin birth and then increased in the later years. Hence the negative effect of an exogenous increase in the number of children due to a twin birth in the first pregnancy is only temporary.

Another example of a natural experiment can be seen in Hotz *et al.* (1997). They looked at the effects of teenage first-child-birth age on educational attainment and labor market performance. They use miscarriage as a 'contaminated instrument', because only random miscarriage qualified as an instrument. A miscarriage due to alcohol or drug abuse did not qualify as an instrument, because (self-selected) alcohol or drug abuse may have been related to the response variables.

Yet another example of natural experiments is sex composition in children (Angrist and Evans (1998)), which can give an exogenous variation to the number of children. If the couple preferred mixed sex children, then having only girls or boys in the first two births resulted in more children than the couple had otherwise planned. In other words, the random event (gender) for the first two children gives an exogenous variation to the number of children (fertility). Part of Table 8, using 1990 Census data, in Angrist and Evans (1998) is (SD is in $(\cdot)$)

	Effects of fertility on labor market outcomes			
	worked or not	weeks worked	hours per week	labor income
LSE	−0.155 (0.002)	−8.71 (0.08)	−6.80 (0.07)	−3984 (44.2)
2SLS (same sex)	−0.092 (0.024)	−5.66 (1.16)	−4.08 (0.98)	−2100 (664.0)
2SLS (boys, girls)	−0.092 (0.024)	−5.64 (1.16)	−4.10 (0.98)	−2096 (663.8)

where four different response variables are listed column-wise, 2SLS is 'two-stage LSE' that is equivalent to IVE, d is the dummy for more than two children or not, and the 'same sex' dummy is used as an instrument for d in the row '2SLS (same sex)' whereas two dummies (all boys and all girls) are used as instruments for d in the row '2SLS (boys, girls)'. The table shows almost identical results for the two 2SLS's, which are about 50–100% smaller than the LSE's results in magnitude. See Rosenzweig and Wolpin (2000), Angrist and Krueger (2001), and the references therein for more on natural experiments.

In the above examples, natural experiments are done at micro (individual) level. A natural experiment at macro level provides an opportunity for before-after design. For instance, consider the effect of an earthquake d on stress y. We may compare y before and after the earthquake. But the key aspect of randomization—balancing both observed and unobserved variables across the C and T groups—may not hold unless we focus on the immediate period preceding and following the earthquake. If something else changes over time (say, a spell of very high temperatures right after the earthquake), then the T and C groups are incomparable in this case confounded by temperature change. If the earthquake affects only some region, then we can apply DD. One advantage of a macro-level natural experiment like this is that the selection problem of the treatment being self-selected—earthquake (and region as well for DD in the short run)—can be ruled out.

As mentioned already, other than randomization and natural experiment, a quasi experiment owing to a law or regulation change can also provide an exogenous variation to d. For example, a tax law change may give an exogenous variation to the after-tax wage, and this fact may be exploited in identifying the effect of wage on work hours.

5.5.3   Relation to regression discontinuity design

Recall that, in the fuzzy regression discontinuity design (RDD) with $y_i = \beta_2 d_i + g(x_i) + u_i$ where d has discontinuity at $x = \tau$ and $g(x)$ is continuous in x, the effect of d on y at $x = \tau$ is identified with

$$\frac{\lim_{x \downarrow \tau} E(y|x) - \lim_{x \uparrow \tau} E(y|x)}{\lim_{x \downarrow \tau} E(d|x) - \lim_{x \uparrow \tau} E(d|x)} = \frac{\text{effect of } x \text{ on } y \text{ locally at } x = \tau}{\text{effect of } x \text{ on } d \text{ locally at } x = \tau}$$

that takes the same form as the Wald estimator. Here, x *is an instrument for* d *locally around* $x = \tau$, because the direct effect of x on y locally at $x = \tau$ can be ignored owing to no jump in $g(x)$ while there is a jump in $E(d|x)$. In other words x is as good as excluded from the y equation locally at $x = \tau$. In this sense, RDD is an IVE.

For the reverse, consider an equation

$$y_i = \beta_1 + \beta_2 d_i + \beta_x x_i + u_i, \quad x_i > 0 \quad \text{for all } i, \quad COR(d, u) \neq 0, \quad COR(x, u) = 0.$$

Suppose that x appears in the d-equation as well and that there is no instrument for d. In this rather hopeless situation, one may try to use x^2 as an instrument for d, which will work if x^2 appears only in the d-equation. Unfortunately this is not very convincing, for it is difficult to rule out *a priori* such a smooth function of x from the y equation. There are cases, however, where a non-smooth function of x with jumps, say $h(x)$, appears only in the d-equation. In such cases, $h(x)$ can be used as an instrument for d. This IVE can be written as a fuzzy RDD by substituting the d equation into the y equation. In the following, we present an example.

In estimating the effect of class-size on scholastic achievement, Angrist and Lavy (1999) adopt this approach. In their model, d is class size, x is enrollment (there are other covariates used in their study, which are omitted here), and

$$d_i = \frac{x_i}{int\{(x_i - 1)/40\} + 1} + \alpha_x x_i + \varepsilon_i, \quad \text{where } int \text{ is the integer function.}$$

The 'compulsory' class size (the first term on the right-hand side) is set such that the maximum class size is 40. If there are 41 students, there will be two classes of (almost) equal size. Examine the first term on the right-hand side of the d-equation closely:

x		...40	41	...80	81	...120	121	...
$h(x) = \dfrac{x}{int\{(x-1)/40\} + 1}$		...40	41/2	...40	81/3	...40	121/4	...
Drop magnitude			$40 - \frac{41}{2} = 19.5$		$40 - \frac{81}{3} = 13$		$40 - \frac{121}{4} = 9.75$	...

The term increases steadily as x goes up but drops by 19.5, 13, and 9.75, at $x = 41$, 81, and 121, respectively. This rule, called 'Maimonides' rule', has been used in Israel public schools since 1969. The actual class size d is determined by a rule which is the highly nonlinear function $h(x)$, enrollment x, (other covariates,) and error term ε.

With $h(x)$ excluded from the y-equation although x may be still in the y-equation, if the graph of (x, y) reveals discontinuity at the same points $(41, 81, 121, \ldots)$ as the graph of (x, d) does, then this means that d has some effect on y, because $h(x)$ should be irrelevant for y if d has zero coefficient in the y-equation. The magnitude of the discontinuities in (x, y) differs from that in (x, d), because the former is mediated by the effects of d on y. Angrist and Lavy (1999) find significant effects of class size on academic achievements for some grades; if further interested in the topic of class size effect, see the second volume of *Economic Journal* in 2003 that is special issue on this topic.

Substitute the d-equation into the y-equation to get

$$y_i = \beta_1 + \beta_2 \left(\frac{x_i}{int\{(x_i - 1)/40\} + 1} + \alpha_x x_i + \varepsilon_i \right) + \beta_x x_i + u_i$$

$$= \beta_2 \frac{x_i}{int\{(x_i - 1)/40\} + 1} + \beta_1 + (\alpha_x \beta_2 + \beta_x) x_i + (\beta_2 \varepsilon_i + u_i).$$

Taking the first term on the right-hand side as $\beta_2 d_i$, the equation takes the form of the RDD response equation $y_i = \beta_2 d_i + g(x_i) + u_i$ where $g(x) = \beta_1 + (\alpha_x \beta_2 + \beta_x) x$.

To identify β_2 in the RDD framework, take the upper limit of $x = 41$ and the lower limit of $x = 40$ to get

$$\lim_{x \downarrow 41} E(y|x = 41) = \beta_2 20.5 + \beta_1 + (\alpha_x \beta_2 + \beta_x) 41,$$

$$\lim_{x \uparrow 40} E(y|x = 40) = \beta_2 40 + \beta_1 + (\alpha_x \beta_2 + \beta_x) 40.$$

Subtracting the latter from the former yields

$$\lim_{x \downarrow 41} E(y|x = 41) - \lim_{x \uparrow 40} E(y|x = 40) = -\beta_2 19.5 + (\alpha_x \beta_2 + \beta_x).$$

In this display, -19.5 corresponds to $\lim_{x \downarrow \tau} E(d|x) - \lim_{x \uparrow \tau} E(d|x)$ in RDD, and the part $\alpha_x \beta_2 + \beta_x$ corresponding to $g(x)$, appears only because the two different points 40 and 41 are used for the limits instead of a single point. To get rid of $\alpha_x \beta_2 + \beta_x$, take the upper limit of $x = 81$ and the lower limit of $x = 80$

to get

$$\lim_{x \downarrow 81} E(y|x = 81) = \beta_2 27 + \beta_1 + (\alpha_x \beta_2 + \beta_x)81,$$

$$\lim_{x \uparrow 80} E(y|x = 80) = \beta_2 40 + \beta_1 + (\alpha_x \beta_2 + \beta_x)80.$$

Subtracting the latter from the former yields

$$\lim_{x \downarrow 81} E(y|x = 81) - \lim_{x \uparrow 80} E(y|x = 80) = -\beta_2 13 + (\alpha_x \beta_2 + \beta_x).$$

Finally, from the two limit differences about 40 and 80, we obtain

$$\beta_2 = 6.5^{-1} \cdot [\lim_{x \downarrow 81} E(y|x = 81) - \lim_{x \uparrow 80} E(y|x = 80)$$
$$- \{\lim_{x \downarrow 41} E(y|x = 41) - \lim_{x \uparrow 40} E(y|x = 40)\}].$$

The linearity of $g(x)$ plays no particular role. As long as $g(x)$ satisfies $g(41) - g(40) = g(81) - g(80)$, then β_2 is identified in the same way.

5.6   Wald estimator, IVE, and compliers

5.6.1   Wald estimator under constant effects

When the LSE of y on $(1, d)$ is consistent for β, the slope LSE is equivalent to the group mean difference. Although the consistency of the IVE for β was shown easily, there is an illuminating interpretation of the IVE when the instrument z is binary, linking the IVE to group mean differences $E(y|z = 1) - E(y|z = 0)$ and $E(d|z = 1) - E(d|z = 0)$. This has been shown to some extent already, but we will now take a closer look at it.

Recall the model

$$d_i = \alpha_1 + \alpha_2 z_i + \varepsilon_i, \qquad y_i = \beta_1 + \beta_2 d_i + u_i$$
$$\Longrightarrow y_i = (\beta_1 + \alpha_1 \beta_2) + \alpha_2 \beta_2 z_i + (u_i + \beta_2 \varepsilon_i)$$

and $Z_i = (1, z_i)'$, $D_i = (1, d_i)'$, $\beta \equiv (\beta_1, \beta_2)'$. In IVE, the slope part β_2 in $\beta = \{E(ZD')\}^{-1} E(Zy)$ can be written as

$$\frac{COV(y, z)}{COV(d, z)} = \frac{E(yz) - E(y)E(z)}{E(dz) - E(d)E(z)}.$$

With $E(dz) = E(d|z = 1)P(z = 1)$ and $d = d\{z + (1 - z)\}$, rewrite the denominator as

$$E(d|z = 1)P(z = 1) - E\{d(z + (1 - z))\}P(z = 1)$$
$$= E(d|z = 1)P(z = 1) - E(dz)P(z = 1) + E\{d(1 - z)\}P(z = 1)$$
$$= E(d|z = 1)P(z = 1) - E(d|z = 1)P(z = 1)^2 + E\{d(1 - z)\}P(z = 1)$$
$$= E(d|z = 1)P(z = 1)\{1 - P(z = 1)\} + E\{d(1 - z)\}P(z = 1)$$
$$= E(d|z = 1)P(z = 0)P(z = 1) - E(d|z = 0)P(z = 0)P(z = 1).$$

Doing analogously, the numerator is

$$E(y|z = 1)P(z = 0)P(z = 1) - E(y|z = 0)P(z = 0)P(z = 1).$$

Cancelling $P(z = 0)P(z = 1)$ that appears in all terms, we get

$$\frac{COV(y, z)}{COV(d, z)} = \frac{E(y|z = 1) - E(y|z = 0)}{E(d|z = 1) - E(d|z = 0)} = \frac{\alpha_2\beta_2}{\alpha_2} = \beta_2;$$

the equality '$= \alpha_2\beta_2/\alpha_2$' can be understood from the LSE of y on $(1, z)$ and the LSE of d on $(1, z)$. The sample version for this is the *Wald estimator*

$$\left(\frac{\sum_i y_i z_i}{\sum_i z_i} - \frac{\sum_i y_i(1 - z_i)}{\sum_i(1 - z_i)}\right) \cdot \left(\frac{\sum_i d_i z_i}{\sum_i z_i} - \frac{\sum_i d_i(1 - z_i)}{\sum_i(1 - z_i)}\right)^{-1},$$

whereas the sample version for $COV(y, z)/COV(d, z)$ is the IVE. In the causal route $z \to d \to y$, the numerator of the Wald estimator is for the indirect effect of z on y, and the denominator is for the effect of z on d. By doing the division, the direct effect of d on y is recovered.

In a clinical trial where z is a random assignment and d is 'compliance' if $d = z$ and 'non-compliance' if $d \neq z$, $E(y|z = 1) - E(y|z = 0)$ is called 'intent-to-treat effect', because it shows the effect of treatment intention (or assignment), not of the actual treatment received. Non-compliance to treatment dilutes the true effect and the Wald estimator blows up the diluted effect with the factor $\{E(d|z = 1) - E(d|z = 0)\}^{-1}$.

If z is an instrument for d, then z^2 or other functions of z may also be instruments for d. This brings up the question of the 'optimal' instrument, and in a sense $E(d|z)$ is an optimal instrument (see, e.g., Lee (1996, pp. 214–15)). If $\pi(z) \equiv E(d|z)$ takes many values, a version of the Wald estimator that is conditioned on $\pi(z) = p_1, p$ is

$$\frac{E(y|\pi(z) = p_1) - E(y|\pi(z) = p)}{p_1 - p}.$$

Heckman and Vytlacil (1999) call the limiting version $p_1 \rightarrow p$ a *local instrumental variable (LIV)* parameter:

$$\partial E(y|\pi(z) = p)/\partial p.$$

Assuming $d = 1[\mu(z) + \varepsilon > 0]$ for a function μ, Heckman and Vytlacil (1999) show that the mean effect, the mean effect on the treated, and the mean effect on the compliers can be all written as integrals of the LIV parameter.

5.6.2   IVE for heterogenous effects

So far, constant effect has been assumed for the IVE. If treatment effect is heterogenous and varies across individuals, the consistency of the IVE and the Wald estimator requires implausible conditions. To see this, recall $y_i = y_{0i} + (y_{1i} - y_{0i})d_i$ and suppose (x_i in this subsection does not include 1)

$$y_{1i} - y_{0i} = \beta_d + x_i'\gamma + v_i, \quad E(v) = 0 \Longrightarrow y_i = \beta_d d_i + x_i'd_i\gamma + (y_{0i} + v_i d_i)$$
$$[\Longrightarrow y_i = E(y_0 + vd) + \beta_d d_i + x_i'd_i\gamma + \{y_{0i} + v_i d_i - E(y_0 + vd)\}];$$

the treatment effect is heterogenous due to $x_i'\gamma$ and v_i. For the equation in $[\cdot]$, we may use the usual IVE $\{(1/N)\sum_i Z_i X_i'\}^{-1}(1/N)\sum_i Z_i y_i$ where $Z_i \equiv (1, z_i, x_i'z_i)'$ and $X_i \equiv (1, d_i, x_i'd_i)'$. The IVE is consistent for $(E(y_0 + vd), \beta_d, \gamma')'$ if

$$COR(z, y_0 + vd) = 0 \quad \text{and} \quad COR(xz, y_0 + vd) = 0.$$

However this is unlikely, at least because z is related to d.

To see the problem from the viewpoint of the Wald estimator which does not use x_i, take $E(\cdot|z = 1)$ and $E(\cdot|z = 0)$ on $y_i = \beta_2 d_i + x_i'd_i\gamma + (y_{0i} + v_i d_i)$ to get

$$E(y|z = 1) = \beta_2 E(d|z = 1) + E(x'd|z = 1)\gamma + E(y_0 + vd|z = 1),$$
$$E(y|z = 0) = \beta_2 E(d|z = 0) + E(x'd|z = 0)\gamma + E(y_0 + vd|z = 0).$$

Subtract the latter from the former to get

$$\{E(d|z = 1) - E(d|z = 0)\}\beta_2 = E(y|z = 1) - E(y|z = 0)$$
$$-\{E(x'd|z = 1) - E(x'd|z = 0)\}\gamma - \{E(y_0 + vd|z = 1) - E(y_0 + vd|z = 0)\}.$$

If the last two terms in this display are zero, that is, if

$$COR(xd, z) = 0 \quad \text{and} \quad COR(y_0 + vd, z) = 0,$$

then

$$\beta_2 = \frac{E(y|z = 1) - E(y|z = 0)}{E(d|z = 1) - E(d|z = 0)}.$$

Again, the conditions are unlikely to hold due to the relation between z and d.

If we further assume (x_0 in the following includes 1)

$$y_{0i} = x'_{0i}\beta_0 + v_{0i} \quad \text{with} \quad COR(x_0, v_0) = 0 \quad \text{and} \quad COR(x_0, vd) = 0,$$

then the observed response model becomes

$$y_i = x'_{0i}\beta_0 + \beta_d d_i + x'_i d_i \gamma + (v_{0i} + v_i d_i).$$

Applying IVE to this with $Z_i \equiv (x'_{0i}, z_i, x'_i z_i)'$ and $X_i \equiv (x'_{0i}, d_i, x'_i d_i)$, this IVE is consistent for $(\beta'_0, \beta_d, \gamma')'$ if

$$COR(z, v_0 + vd) = 0 \quad \text{and} \quad COR(xz, v_0 + vd) = 0.$$

These are still unlikely to hold at least because z is related to d. This shows that modeling y_{0i} does not help, because the source of the problem is the presence of vd and the relationship between z and d.

If we take away v_i, that is if $y_{1i} - y_{0i} = \beta_d + x'_i \gamma$, then the observed response model is

$$y_i = \beta_d d_i + x'_i d_i \gamma + y_{0i}$$

where y_{0i} (i.e., $y_{0i} - E(y_0)$) is the error term, and the troubling vd is absent. So long as d and dx are not correlated to the baseline response y_0, LSE can be applied. If desired, IVE can be applied with $(z, x'z)'$ as the instrument, in which case no correlation between xz and y_0 is necessary. Furthermore, we may assume $y_0 = x'_{0i}\beta_0 + v_{0i}$ to get

$$y_i = x'_{0i}\beta_0 + \beta_d d_i + x'_i d_i \gamma + v_{0i}$$

where x is less likely to be related to v_0 than to y_0 because part of y_0 is accounted for by $x'_0 \beta_0$.

From what has been shown so far in this subsection, it is the unobserved heterogenous treatment effect (v_i), not the part attributed to the observed covariates (x_i) that creates the difficulty for the IVE. In the following subsection, we show that, under the heterogenous effect $y_{1i} - y_{0i} = \beta_d + v_i$, the Wald estimator is consistent for the treatment effect on compliers without any functional form assumption. The difference $y_{1i} - y_{0i}$ may also depend on x_i, but as just noted, this is not the source of the IVE's trouble. For simplification, x will be omitted in the following subsection (or regarded as conditioned on if necessary).

5.6.3 Wald estimator as effect on compliers

Suppose

    (a) $P(d = 1|z)$ is a non-constant function of z,
    (b) $(y_{0i}, y_{1i}, d_{0i}, d_{1i})$ is independent of z_i, and
    (c)   for all i, either $d_{1i} \geq d_{0i}$ or $d_{1i} \leq d_{0i}$.

Condition (a) is just the inclusion restriction that z is in the d-equation. Condition (b) includes the exclusion restriction that z is not in the y_j-equation,

$j = 0, 1$. As the example in the following paragraph shows, (b) in fact includes more restrictions than this. Condition (c) is a *monotonicity* assumption.

One example in which the three conditions hold is

$$y_{ji} = \beta_j + u_{ji}, \quad j = 0, 1, \qquad d_i = 1[\alpha_0 + \alpha_1 z_i + \varepsilon_i > 0],$$
$$\alpha_1 \neq 0, \quad z_i \text{ is independent of } (\varepsilon_i, u_{0i}, u_{1i}), \varepsilon_i \text{ has unbounded support}$$

where α_j and β_j, $j = 0, 1$, are unknown parameters. In this example, $y_{1i} - y_{0i} = \beta_1 - \beta_0 + u_{1i} - u_{0i}$: the effects are heterogenous. Condition (a) holds due to $\alpha_1 \neq 0$ and the support of ε. Condition (b) holds because

$$(y_{0i}, y_{1i}, d_{0i}, d_{1i}) = (\beta_0 + u_{0i}, \ \beta_1 + u_{1i}, \ 1[\alpha_0 + \varepsilon_i > 0], \ 1[\alpha_0 + \alpha_1 + \varepsilon_i > 0]),$$

and z_i is independent of $(\varepsilon_i, u_{0i}, u_{1i})$. Condition (c) holds with $\geq$ ($\leq$) depending on $\alpha_1 > (<)0$. Surprisingly, Vytlacil (2002) shows the reverse, where allowing z to be a vector but restricting z to be discrete, (a)–(c) implies that $d_i = 1[\mu(z_i) + \varepsilon_i > 0]$ for some function μ and that $z \amalg (\varepsilon, y_0, y_1)$.

Without loss of generality, from now on assume $d_{1i} \geq d_{0i}$. This implies *no defiers* (i.e., nobody with $d_{1i} = 0$ and $d_{0i} = 1$). Also, owing to (a), it holds that

$$P(d = 1|z = 1) = P(d_1 = 1|z = 1) > P(d_0 = 1|z = 0) = P(d = 1|z = 0).$$

Observe

$$
\begin{aligned}
E(y|z = 1) - E(y|z = 0) &= E\{dy_1 + (1 - d)y_0|z = 1\} - E\{dy_1 + (1 - d)y_0|z = 0\} \\
&= E\{d_1 y_1 + (1 - d_1)y_0|z = 1\} - E\{d_0 y_1 + (1 - d_0)y_0|z = 0\} \\
&= E\{d_1 y_1 + (1 - d_1)y_0\} - E\{d_0 y_1 + (1 - d_0)y_0\} \quad \text{owing to (b)} \\
&= E\{(d_1 - d_0) \cdot (y_1 - y_0)\}.
\end{aligned}
$$

Consider the two cases of $d_1 - d_0$ being ± 1 to get

$$
\begin{aligned}
E\{(d_1 - d_0) \cdot (y_1 - y_0)\} &= E(y_1 - y_0|d_1 - d_0 = 1) \cdot P(d_1 - d_0 = 1) \\
&\quad - E(y_1 - y_0|d_1 - d_0 = -1) \cdot P(d_1 - d_0 = -1) \\
&= E(y_1 - y_0|d_1 - d_0 = 1) \cdot P(d_1 - d_0 = 1) \\
&\quad \text{because } P(d_1 - d_0 = -1) = 0 \text{ from no defiers.}
\end{aligned}
$$

Hence,

$$
\begin{aligned}
E(y|z = 1) - E(y|z = 0) &= E(y_1 - y_0|d_1 - d_0 = 1) \cdot P(d_1 - d_0 = 1) \\
\Longrightarrow E(y_1 - y_0|d_1 = 1, d_0 = 0) &= \frac{E(y|z = 1) - E(y|z = 0)}{P(d_1 = 1, d_0 = 0)}.
\end{aligned}
$$

The left-hand side is the *local average treatment effect (LATE)* of Imbens and Angrist (1994). It is the average treatment effect for the compliers $d_1 = 1$ and $d_0 = 0$. The 'local' qualifier in LATE seems to refer to the fact that LATE is specific to the instrument at hand. Written this way, it is not clear whether LATE is identified, for the right-hand side denominator involves both d_1 and d_0 which are not jointly observed.

To see that LATE is identified, observe

$$P(d_1 = 1) = P(d_1 = 1, d_0 = 1) + P(d_1 = 1, d_0 = 0),$$

$$P(d_0 = 1) = P(d_1 = 1, d_0 = 1) + P(d_1 = 0, d_0 = 1).$$

Take the difference to get

$$P(d_1 = 1) - P(d_0 = 1) = P(d_1 = 1, d_0 = 0)$$

for $P(d_1 = 0, d_0 = 1) = 0$ owing to the monotonicity. Then

$$E(d|z = 1) - E(d|z = 0) = E(d_1|z = 1) - E(d_0|z = 0)$$
$$= P(d_1 = 1) - P(d_0 = 1) = P(d_1 = 1, d_0 = 0);$$

the second equality follows because d_1 and d_0 are independent of z. In words,

$$P(d = 1|z = 1) = P(\text{always-taker or - complier}),$$
$$P(d = 1|z = 0) = P(\text{always-taker});$$

the difference is $P(\text{complier})$.

Thus, LATE is written in an identified ratio form

$$E(y_1 - y_0|d_1 = 1, d_0 = 0) = \frac{E(y|z = 1) - E(y|z = 0)}{E(d|z = 1) - E(d|z = 0)},$$

which is nothing but the Wald estimator. This is the LATE interpretation of IVE in Angrist *et al.* (1996) under the three conditions (a), (b), and (c) above. It is important to bear in mind that LATE can change as the instrument in use changes. If IVE changes as the instrument changes, then this is an indication of heterogenous treatment effects. The fact that IVE identifies the effect on those who change their behavior depending on the instrument value looks natural. Some further remarks on LATE are given in the appendix.

Abadie (2002) shows that the effect on complier can be written also as

$$\frac{E(yd|z=1) - E(yd|z=0)}{E(d|z=1) - E(d|z=0)} - \frac{E(y(1-d)|z=1) - E(y(1-d)|z=0)}{E(1-d|z=1) - E(1-d|z=0)}.$$

The derivation for this is essentially the same as that for $E\{(d_1 - d_0) \cdot (y_1 - y_0)\}$ above. That is, observe

$$\begin{aligned} E(yd|z=1) - E(yd|z=0) &= E(y_1 d_1|z=1) - E(y_1 d_0|z=0) \\ &= E(y_1 d_1) - E(y_1 d_0) \quad \text{owing to (b)} \\ &= E\{y_1(d_1 - d_0)\} \\ &= E(y_1|d_1 - d_0 = 1) \cdot P(d_1 - d_0 - 1); \end{aligned}$$

$E(y_1 d_0)$, not $E(y_0 d_0)$, appears for the second equality because $d_0 = 1$ means being treated. Hence, divide through by $P(d_1 - d_0 = 1) = E(d|z = 1) - E(d|z = 0)$ to get

$$E(y_1|\text{complier}) = \frac{E(yd|z=1) - E(yd|z=0)}{E(d|z=1) - E(d|z=0)}, \quad \text{and doing analogously,}$$

$$E(y_0|\text{complier}) = \frac{E(y(1-d)|z=1) - E(y(1-d)|z=0)}{E(1-d|z=1) - E(1-d|z=0)}.$$

The difference is $E(y_1 - y_0|\text{complier})$.

In the appendix, not just the mean effect, but the marginal distribution of y_0 and y_1 for the compliers are identified. Also tests for the equality of the two distributions are reviewed.

5.6.4   Weighting estimators for complier effects[*]

The previous subsection showed two formulas to identify $E(y_1 - y_0|\text{complier})$. In principle, covariates x can be allowed for by conditioning on x: for LATE,

$$E(y_1 - y_0|x, \text{complier}) = \frac{E(y|x, z=1) - E(y|x, z=0)}{E(d|x, z=1) - E(d|x, z=0)}.$$

However this can be cumbersome in practice if x takes too many values. An alternative is to parameterize the four conditional means as functions of x—e.g., linear functions of x—but this leads to a complicated nonlinear function of x for $E(y_1 - y_0|x, \text{complier})$. What would be ideal is to have a simple function $m(d, x)$—possibly linear—such that

$$m(1, x) - m(0, x) = E(y_1 - y_0|x, \text{complier}).$$

This subsection reviews a weighting-based approach in Abadie (2003) for this goal of finding $m(d, x)$. Also, a related approach in Abadie *et al.* (2002) is examined. Assume (a), (b), and (c) of the preceding subsection holds conditioned on x.

Define a 'local average response function' as a function $m(d, x)$ of d and x such that

$$m(0, x) = E(y_0|x, \text{complier}) \quad \text{and} \quad m(1, x) = E(y_1|x, \text{complier})$$
$$\Longrightarrow m(1, x) - m(0, x) = E(y_1 - y_0|x, \text{complier}),$$

which is the x-conditional mean effect for the compliers. For instance, if $m(d, x) = \beta_d d + x'\beta_x$, then $\beta_d = m(1, x) - m(0, x)$ has a causal interpretation because $\beta_d = E(y_1 - y_0|x,\text{complier})$. *The complier conditional mean $E(y|x, d,$ complier) is a local average response function,* because

$$E(y|x, d = 1, \text{complier}) = E(y_1|x, d = 1, \text{complier})$$
$$= E(y_1|x, z = 1, \text{complier}) \quad (\text{because } z = d \text{ for compliers})$$
$$= E(y_1|x, \text{complier}) \quad (\text{owing to } z \text{ II } (d_0, d_1, y_0, y_1)|x);$$
$$E(y|x, d = 0, \text{complier}) = E(y_0|x, d = 0, \text{complier})$$
$$= E(y_0|x, z = 0, \text{complier}) = E(y_0|x, \text{complier}).$$

Thus it is interesting to find $E(y|x, d,\text{complier})$, but it is not clear how this can be identified, for the compliers are not identified. In comparison, $E(y|x, d)$ is easy to identify, but has no causal interpretation when d is endogenous.

Define

$$\omega_0 \equiv (1 - d)\frac{1 - z - P(z = 0|x)}{P(z = 0|x) \cdot P(z = 1|x)}, \qquad \omega_1 \equiv d\frac{z - P(z = 1|x)}{P(z = 0|x) \cdot P(z = 1|x)},$$
$$\omega \equiv \omega_0 P(z = 0|x) + \omega_1 P(z = 1|x)$$
$$= (1 - d)\frac{1 - z - P(z = 0|x)}{P(z = 1|x)} + d\frac{z - P(z = 1|x)}{P(z = 0|x)}$$
$$= (1 - d)\left(1 - \frac{z}{P(z = 1|x)}\right) + d\left(\frac{z - 1}{P(z = 0|x)} + 1\right)$$
$$= 1 - \frac{(1 - d)z}{P(z = 1|x)} - \frac{d(1 - z)}{P(z = 0|x)}.$$

For any integrable function $g(y, d, x)$, Abadie (2003) shows that

$$E\{g(y, d, x)|\text{complier}\} = \frac{E\{\omega \cdot g(y, d, x)\}}{E(d|z = 1) - E(d|z = 0)}.$$

This expression means that the apparently non-identified left-hand is identified by the right-hand side which is free of '|complier'. In the following paragraph, we prove this display.

Since w has three terms, $E\{w \cdot g(y, d, x)\}$ consists of three terms:

$$E\{g(y, d, x)\} - E\left\{\frac{(1 - d)z \cdot g(y, d, x)}{P(z = 1|x)}\right\} - E\left\{\frac{d(1 - z) \cdot g(y, d, x)}{P(z = 0|x)}\right\}.$$

The third term's conditional mean given y, d, x has its numerator

$$
\begin{aligned}
g(y, d, x) \cdot E\{d(1 - z)|y, d, x\} &= g(y, d, x)E[\{(1 - z)d_0 + zd_1\}(1 - z)|y, d, x] \\
&= g(y, d, x)E\{(1 - z)d_0|y, d, x\} \\
&= g(y, d, x)P(d_0 = 1, z = 0|y, d, x).
\end{aligned}
$$

In the last paragraph of this subsection, it is shown that

$$P(d_0 = 1, z = 0|y, d, x) = P(z = 0|x) \cdot P(d_0 = d_1 = 1|y, d, x),$$

which can be understood in view of (b) and (c). Owing to $P(z = 0|x)$ here, the third term of $E\{w \cdot g(y, d, x)\}$ becomes

$$E\{g(y, d, x) \cdot P(d_0 = d_1 = 1|y, d, x)\}.$$

Doing analogously, the second term of $E\{w \cdot g(y, d, x)\}$ is

$$E\{g(y, d, x) \cdot P(d_0 = d_1 = 0|y, d, x)\}.$$

Since

$$1 = P(d_0 = d_1 = 0|y, d, x) + P(d_0 = d_1 = 1|y, d, x) + P(d_1 = 1, d_0 = 0|y, d, x),$$

we get

$$
\begin{aligned}
\frac{E\{w \cdot g(y, d, x)\}}{E(d|z = 1) - E(d|z = 0)} &= \frac{E\{g(y, d, x) \cdot P(d_1 = 1, d_0 = 0|y, d, x)\}}{P(\text{complier})} \\
&= \frac{E[E\{g(y, d, x) \cdot (1 - d_0)d_1|y, d, x\}]}{P(\text{complier})} \\
&= \frac{E[g(y, d, x) \cdot (1 - d_0)d_1]}{P(\text{complier})} = E\{g(y, d, x)|\text{complier}\}.
\end{aligned}
$$

To get $m(d, x) = E(y|x, d, \text{complier})$, suppose we parameterize $m(d, x)$ as $\beta_d d + x'\beta_x$. Setting $g(y, d, x) = (y - \beta_d d - x'\beta_x)^2$, the above display becomes

$$E\{(y - \beta_d d - x'\beta_x)^2|\text{complier}\} = \frac{E\{w \cdot (y - \beta_d d - x'\beta_x)^2\}}{E(d|z = 1) - E(d|z = 0)}.$$

To estimate β_d and β_x, suppose $P(z = 1|x) = \Phi(x'\alpha)$. Denoting the probit estimator as a_N, β_d and β_x for $E(y|x, d, \text{complier})$ can be estimated—despite the endogeneity of d—by minimizing

$$N^{-1}\sum_i \left\{1 - \frac{(1-d_i)z_i}{\Phi(x_i'a_N)} - \frac{d_i(1-z_i)}{1-\Phi(x_i'a_N)}\right\} \cdot (y_i - \beta_d d_i - x_i'\beta_x)^2;$$

$E(d|z=1) - E(d|z=0)$ is irrelevant for this minimization. In essence, the term in $\{\cdot\}$ makes the LSE applied only to the compliers.

Instead of $E(y|x, d, \text{complier}) = \beta_d d + x'\beta_x$, Abadie *et al.* (2002) postulate that the θth quantile function of $y|(x, d, \text{complier})$ is $\beta_d d + x'\beta_x$:

$$Q_\theta(y|x, d, \text{complier}) = \beta_d d + x'\beta_x.$$

Doing analogously as for the mean function, we get

$$\beta_d = Q_\theta(y_1|x, \text{complier}) - Q_\theta(y_0|x_0, \text{complier}).$$

However this does not go far enough, because the analogous expression for β_d should be, not the right-hand side of this equation, but $Q_\theta(y_1 - y_0|x, \text{complier})$. In general, quantile functions are not linear. Drawing on Lee (2000), the appendix shows what can be learned for $Q_\theta(y_1 - y_0|\cdot)$ from $Q_\theta(y_1|\cdot)$ and $Q_\theta(y_0|\cdot)$. However the result is useful essentially only for $\theta = 0.5$.

The θth quantile parameters β_d and β_x can be estimated by minimizing

$$N^{-1}\sum_i \left\{1 - \frac{(1-d_i)z_i}{\Phi(x_i'a_N)} - \frac{d_i(1-z_i)}{1-\Phi(x_i'a_N)}\right\} \cdot (\theta - 1[y_i - \beta_d d_i - x_i'\beta_x < 0])$$
$$\times (y_i - \beta_d d_i - x_i'\beta_x).$$

To understand the last two terms, observe

$$E[\{\theta - 1[y - h(x) < 0]\}\{y - h(x)\}]$$
$$= E[|y - h(x)| \cdot \{\theta\, 1[y > h(x)] + (1-\theta)\, 1[y < h(x)]\}] :$$

differently from $(y - h(x))^2$, this 'loss function' penalizes $y \neq h(x)$ asymmetrically by $|y - h(x)|\theta$ when $y > h(x)$ and by $|y - h(x)|(1-\theta)$ when $y < h(x)$. As is well known, the loss function is minimized when $h(x) = Q_\theta(y|x)$.

In the above minimization, ω plays the role of a weighting function. But ω is negative when $z \neq d$ which can make the minimum non-convex. For this, observe

$$E\{\omega \cdot g(y, d, x)\} = E[E\{\omega \cdot g(y, d, x)|y, d, x\}] = E[E\{\omega|y, d, x\} \cdot g(y, d, x)]$$
$$= E[\omega_c g(y, d, x)] \quad \text{where } \omega_c \equiv 1 - \frac{(1-d)E(z|y, d, x)}{P(z=1|x)} - \frac{d(1-E(z|y, d, x))}{P(z=0|x)}.$$

Further observe that the numerator of the last term of w_c can be written as

$$
\begin{aligned}
E\{d(1-z)|y,d,x\} &= E[\{(1-z)d_0 + zd_1\}(1-z)|y,d,x] = E[(1-z)d_0|y,d,x] \\
&= P(d_0 = 1, z = 0|y,d,x) = P(d_0 = d_1 = 1, z = 0|y,d,x) \\
&\qquad \text{(due to } d_1 \geq d_0|x) \\
&= P(z = 0|d_0 = d_1 = 1, y, d = 1, x) \cdot P(d_0 = d_1 = 1|y,d,x) \\
&\qquad \text{(considering the cases } d = 0 \text{ and } d = 1 \text{ separately)} \\
&= P(z = 0|d_0 = d_1 = 1, y_1, x) \cdot P(d_0 = d_1 = 1|y,d,x) \\
&\qquad \text{(due to } d_0 = d_1 = 1 \Rightarrow d = 1) \\
&= P(z = 0|x) \cdot P(d_0 - d_1 - 1|y,d,x) \\
&\qquad \text{(owing to } z \amalg (d_0, d_1, y_0, y_1)|x).
\end{aligned}
$$

It holds analogously for the second term of w_c that

$$
(1-d)E(z|y,d,x) = E\{(1-d)z|y,d,x\} = P(z = 1|x) \cdot P(d_0 = d_1 = 0|y,d,x).
$$

Hence

$$
w_c = 1 - P(d_0 = d_1 = 0|y,d,x) - P(d_0 = d_1 = 1|y,d,x) = P(d_1 > d_0|y,d,x) \geq 0.
$$

Empirical examples appear in Abadie *et al.* (2002) and Angrist (2001).

6

Other approaches for hidden bias*

This chapter continues the discussion of the preceding chapter on how to deal with hidden bias caused by unobserved differences between the treatment (T) and control (C) groups. The preceding chapter presented practical and basic approaches and this chapter demonstrates other approaches to hidden bias. Sensitivity analysis examines how a finding obtained under an assumption of no hidden bias changes as hidden bias is allowed for. Sensitivity analysis is informative but stops short of giving us a definite solution to the problem of hidden bias. A more conventional approach would be parametric 'selection-correction' or 'control-function' methods. These are relatively straightforward to implement, but possibly too restrictive. Perhaps too unrestrictive would be nonparametric 'bounding' approaches, where bounds on the treatment effect of interest are provided. The bounds are, however, typically too wide to be useful. An approach that avoids hidden bias by controlling for post-treatment covariates is available as well in some special circumstances.

6.1 Sensitivity analysis

Economists almost always use assumptions. One way to justify an assumption is to argue directly that it is plausible. Another way is to use a sensitivity analysis: first derive a result, say R, as a 'function' of an assumption, say $\mu = \mu_o$ (i.e., $R(\mu_o)$ is derived), and then see how $R(\mu)$ changes as μ moves around μ_o. If $R(\mu)$ changes a lot in response to just slight changes in μ around μ_o, then the finding $R(\mu_o)$ is regarded as sensitive to the assumption $\mu = \mu_o$. This kind of sensitivity analysis can be done for hidden bias. First derive the treatment effect under the assumption of no unobserved confounder ($\mu = \mu_o$), and then

see how the treatment effect changes as unobserved confounders are allowed for
with $\mu \neq \mu_o$.

Sensitivity analysis is different from avoiding hidden bias using instruments.
Here one tries to see how large the hidden bias needs to be in order to overturn
the findings derived under a no hidden bias (i.e., no unobserved confounder)
assumption. If only an excessively big hidden bias can overturn the findings,
then the findings are robust against hidden bias. In gauging the size of the
hidden bias, typically we do not have a good idea of its absolute magnitude,
but we may have some idea of its magnitude relative to a 'reference magnitude'.
For this, the 'sensitivity parameter' (μ in $R(\mu)$) will take a ratio form.

There are many types of response variables and treatment effects, and
there are many ways to choose μ and a neighborhood of μ_o, which means
that there are many ways to conduct sensitivity analysis. We will show some
of them in this section. First, one approach in Rosenbaum (1987) is introduced for matched pairs with a binary response and a binary treatment.
Second, a generalization in Gastwirth *et al.* (1998) of the sensitivity analysis in Rosenbaum (1987) is examined. Whereas Rosenbaum (1987) considers
unobservables that affect the treatment, Gastwirth *et al.* (1998) consider the
unobservables that affect the response variable as well as the treatment. Imbens
(2003) also shows a sensitivity analysis of this type. Third, Lee's (2004) sensitivity analysis is examined where the ratio of a selection-biased mean and the
true mean is used as the sensitivity parameter.

All approaches, except Lee's (2004) analysis, are 'of structural form' in
the sense that they are explicit on how the unobserved variables may cause
a bias (by influencing the treatment probability or the response variable). In
comparison, Lee's (2004) approach is 'of reduced form' in the sense that such
routes for hidden bias are not explicit. This is one of the disadvantages of the
RF approach, but it is easier to implement than the SF approaches. The SF
approaches can be simple in special cases, say binary responses or binary unobserved confounders. In general, however, SF approaches are more difficult to
implement. See Rosenbaum (2002) and the references therein for more on SF
sensitivity analyses.

6.1.1   Unobserved confounder affecting treatment

Consider

$$d_i = 1[x_i'\alpha + \gamma v_i + \varepsilon_i > 0], \qquad \gamma \geq 0,$$
$$y_{ji} = x_i'\beta_j + \beta_v j \cdot v_i + u_{ji}, \qquad \beta_v \geq 0, \quad j = 0, 1,$$

where $v_i, \varepsilon_i, u_{ji}$ are unobserved variables unrelated to x_i, and α, γ, β_j, and β_v
are unknown parameters. Assume that v is the only unobserved confounder
in the sense that

$$(y_0, y_1) \amalg d | (x, v) \iff (u_0, u_1) \amalg \varepsilon | (x, v).$$

For v to cause hidden bias, it is necessary (but not sufficient) for v to affect d. Hence, regardless of whether v affects (y_0, y_1) or not through β_v, it is possible to conduct a sensitivity analysis using only γ in the d-equation. Rosenbaum (1987) presents such a sensitivity analysis where the y_j-equation does not feature. Readers not interested in the derivation may want to turn to the last paragraph of this subsection.

Suppose that the distribution F_ε of ε is logistic and independent of x and v to get the *odds of receiving the treatment*

$$\frac{P(d = 1 | x, v)}{P(d = 0 | x, v)} = \frac{\exp(x'\alpha + \gamma v)/\{1 + \exp(x'\alpha + \gamma v)\}}{1/\{1 + \exp(x'\alpha + \gamma v)\}} = \exp(x'\alpha + \gamma v).$$

The odds *ratio* of receiving the treatment for two subjects with the same x but different v (v_1 and v_2) is

$$\frac{P(d = 1 | x, v_1)/P(d = 0 | x, v_1)}{P(d = 1 | x, v_2)/P(d = 0 | x, v_2)} = \frac{\exp(x'\alpha + \gamma v_1)}{\exp(x'\alpha + \gamma v_2)} = \exp\{\gamma(v_1 - v_2)\}.$$

If $\gamma \neq 0$, then the odds ratio is not equal to one and the two subjects have different chances of getting the treatment. If $v_1 = v_2$, then the odds ratio is one regardless of γ. We are interested in the former, not in the latter, as we allow $v_1 \neq v_2$.

Although the logistic distribution looks restrictive, as can be seen in Rosenbaum (2002),

$$0 \leq v \leq 1 \quad \text{and} \quad F_\varepsilon \text{ being logistic}$$
$$\Longleftrightarrow \Gamma^{-1} \leq \frac{P(d = 1 | x, v_1)/P(d = 0 | x, v_1)}{P(d = 1 | x, v_2)/P(d = 0 | x, v_2)} \leq \Gamma, \qquad \text{where } \Gamma \equiv \exp(\gamma) \geq 1.$$

That is, if we are willing to take the assumption that the odds ratio is bounded by the constants Γ^{-1} and Γ, then we should be as willing to take the logistic distribution assumption with $0 \leq v \leq 1$ and $\gamma = \ln(\Gamma) \geq 0$. Hence sensitivity analysis is done in the following with

$$\Gamma^{-1} \leq \exp\{\gamma(v_1 - v_2)\} \leq \Gamma, \qquad \text{where } \Gamma \geq 1 \Longleftrightarrow \gamma \geq 0.$$

Consider a matched-pair sample where there are n pairs matched, and in pair s matched on the value x_s of x, one subject is treated and the other is not, $s = 1, \ldots, n$. Let $d_{s1} = 1$ if the first subject in pair s is treated and 0 otherwise, and define d_{s2} analogously for the second subject. By construction, $d_{s1} \neq d_{s2} \Longleftrightarrow d_{s1} + d_{s2} = 1$. For a matched pair, $(x_{s1} = x_s, \ x_{s2} = x_s, v_{s1}, v_{s2}$

which should be in the conditioning set are omitted in the following display), observe

$$P(d_{s1}=1,d_{s2}=0|d_{s1}\neq d_{s2})=\frac{P(d_{s1}=1,d_{s2}=0)}{P(d_{s1}=1,d_{s2}=0)+P(d_{s1}=0,d_{s2}=1)}$$

$$=\frac{P(d_{s1}=1)P(d_{s2}=0)}{P(d_{s1}=1)P(d_{s2}=0)+P(d_{s1}=0)P(d_{s2}=1)}=\frac{\exp(\gamma v_{s1})}{\exp(\gamma v_{s1})+\exp(\gamma v_{s2})};$$

$$P(d_{s1}=0,d_{s2}=1|d_{s1}\neq d_{s2})=\frac{P(d_{s1}=0,d_{s2}=1)}{P(d_{s1}=1,d_{s2}=0)+P(d_{s1}=0,d_{s2}=1)}$$

$$=\frac{P(d_{s1}=0)P(d_{s2}=1)}{P(d_{s1}=1)P(d_{s2}=0)+P(d_{s1}=0)P(d_{s2}=1)}=\frac{\exp(\gamma v_{s2})}{\exp(\gamma v_{s1})+\exp(\gamma v_{s2})}.$$

In the ratio $P(d_{s1}=1,d_{s2}=0|d_{s1}\neq d_{s2})$ over $P(d_{s1}=0,d_{s2}=1|d_{s1}\neq d_{s2})$, the long denominators are cancelled to yield

$$\frac{P(d_{s1}=1,d_{s2}=0|d_{s1}\neq d_{s2},x_{s1}=x_s,x_{s2}=x_s,v_{s1},v_{s2})}{P(d_{s1}=0,d_{s2}=1|d_{s1}\neq d_{s2},x_{s1}=x_s,x_{s2}=x_s,v_{s1},v_{s2})}$$

$$=\frac{P(d_{s1}=1|x_{s1}=x_s,v_{s1})/P(d_{s1}=0|x_{s1}=x_s,v_{s1})}{P(d_{s2}=1|x_{s2}=x_s,v_{s2})/P(d_{s2}=0|x_{s2}=x_s,v_{s2})}=\exp\{\gamma(v_{s1}-v_{s2})\}.$$

In the preceding paragraph, no response variable appeared. Since concordant pairs are not informative, assume that the pairs are all discordant (i.e., $y_{s1}\neq y_{s2}\iff y_{s1}+y_{s2}=1$ for all s), to remove all concordant pairs (but we will use the same notation n for the number of discordant pairs). With a binary response variable, *McNemar's statistic M* is the number of treated subjects with $y=1$ among n-many discordant pairs:

$$M\equiv\sum_{s=1}^{n}z_s,\qquad\text{where }z_s\equiv d_{s1}y_{s1}+d_{s2}y_{s2}.$$

This is the main statistic for this and the following subsection.

Consider the distribution of M conditioned on

$$C\equiv\{x_{s1}=x_s,x_{s2}=x_s,v_{s1},v_{s2},d_{s1}\neq d_{s2},y_{s1},y_{s2},y_{s1}\neq y_{s2},\qquad s=1,\ldots,n\}.$$

On this set, only d_{s1} and d_{s2}, $s=1,\ldots,n$, are variable. For instance, if x and v are gender and ability, we can think of a group of pairs where pair s has $x_s=male$, $v_{s1}=low$, $v_{s2}=high$, $y_{s1}=0$, $y_{s2}=1$, and $d_{s1}\neq d_{s2}$. In this group, the only thing that is random is whether $d_{s1}=0$, $d_{s2}=1$ or $d_{s1}=1,d_{s2}=0$ for pair s. Under the strongest null hypothesis of no effect that the two potential responses are the same, d_{s1} is independent of y_{s1} and d_{s2} is independent of y_{s2}. Note that this independence between the choice and the *observed* response does not hold in general; the selection-on-observable assumption is for d and the *potential* responses. Under the null hypothesis,

$$P\{z_s = 1|C\} = y_{s1}P\{d_{s1} = 1, d_{s2} = 0|C\} + y_{s2}P\{d_{s1} = 0, d_{s2} = 1|C\}$$

$$= \frac{y_{s1}\exp(\gamma v_{s1}) + y_{s2}\exp(\gamma v_{s2})}{\exp(\gamma v_{s1}) + \exp(\gamma v_{s2})} = \frac{y_{s1}\exp(\gamma(v_{s1} - v_{s2})) + y_{s2}}{\exp(\gamma(v_{s1} - v_{s2})) + 1}$$

$$= \frac{\exp(\gamma(v_{s1} - v_{s2}))}{\exp(\gamma(v_{s1} - v_{s2})) + 1} \quad \text{if } y_{s1} = 1, \ y_{s2} = 0,$$

$$\text{or} \quad \frac{1}{\exp(\gamma(v_{s1} - v_{s2})) + 1} \quad \text{if } y_{s1} = 0, \ y_{s2} = 1.$$

Observe

$$\frac{a}{a+b}, \ a, b > 0, \ \text{is increasing in } a \text{ and decreasing in } b.$$

Using this fact and the bounds $\Gamma^{-1} \le \exp\{\gamma(v_{s1} - v_{s2})\} \le \Gamma$ yields

$$\frac{1}{\Gamma + 1} \le P(z_s = 1|C) \le \frac{\Gamma}{\Gamma + 1}.$$

If there is no difference in the treatment probabilities between the two subjects in pair s because $\gamma = 0$, then $P\{z_s = 1|C\} = 0.5$. If this holds for all s, then M conditioned on C follows $B(n, 0.5)$. Suppose that the realized value m of M is greater than $0.5n$ so that the null-rejecting interval is on the upper tail. This is achieved without loss of generality, for we can redefine y as $1 - y$. The p-value is then $P(M \ge m|\gamma = 0) = \sum_{a=m}^{n} \binom{n}{a} 0.5^n$. The notation '$|\gamma = 0$' is just to denote that γ is set at 0.

If $\gamma > 0$ (and of course $v_{s1} \ne v_{s2}$ for some s), then M no longer follows $B(n, 0.5)$ because z_s's are independent but follow different binary distributions due to $v_{s1} - v_{s2}$ varying across s. In this case, the bound in the above display yields

$$P(M \ge m|\gamma > 0) \le \sum_{a=m}^{n} \binom{n}{a}(p^+)^a(1 - p^+)^{n-a}, \quad \text{where } p^+ \equiv \frac{\Gamma}{1 + \Gamma} \ge 0.5.$$

With $m/n > 0.5$, this provides an informative upper bound only when $p^+ < m/n$. For instance, if $n = 100$, $m = 70$, and $p^+ = 0.7$, then the upper bound is the probability of 70 or more successes in 100 trials when the success probability is 0.7, which is about 0.5—a trivial non-informative bound. That is, for sensitivity analysis, we have to evaluate $\sum_{a=m}^{n} \binom{n}{a}(p^+)^a(1 - p^+)^{n-a}$ over

$$0.5 \le p^+ < m/n,$$

and see at which values of p^+ (i.e., Γ) the upper bound crosses the nominal level, say 5%. Since the upper bound does not depend on the conditioned variables in C, it is also a valid unconditional upper bound.

The question is then how to interpret the sensitivity parameter Γ. Suppose the upper bound of the p-value is 0.024 with $\Gamma = 2$ (for $\Gamma < 2$, the upper bound is even smaller) and 0.10 with $\Gamma = 3$. Here, rejecting or not the null hypothesis at 5% in the one-sided test is reversed as Γ changes from 2 to 3. The key question is whether $\Gamma = 3$ is a plausible value or not. The unobserved confounder v should be able to produce a three-fold increase in the probability ratio of getting treated between the two subjects in the same pair. If most of the relevant variables for a treatment decision have already been controlled for, and if it is difficult to think of a variable that results in a three-fold change in the probability ratio, then $\Gamma = 3$ is an implausible value. In this sense, three is too big a number, and the fact that it takes such a big number to reverse the initial conclusion makes the initial conclusion of rejecting the null hypothesis insensitive to the hidden bias.

Consider a study on smoking and lung cancer with 122 discordant pairs, and among the 122, there are 110 pairs where the smoker died of lung cancer, (the realized value for M is 110 and is taken from an example in Rosenbaum (2002)). If smoking has no effect, then it is like flipping a fair coin 122 times to get 110 heads. Ignoring hidden bias, the p-value of the test for no effect is $P(M \geq 110) < 0.0001$, which is computed using $B(0.5, 122)$. Here zero effect of smoking on lung cancer death is rejected easily. Now with $p^+ \equiv \Gamma/(1 + \Gamma)$, the upper bound on the p-value derived above allowing for hidden bias is

$$P(M \geq 110) \leq \sum_{a=110}^{122} \binom{122}{a} (p^+)^a (1 - p^+)^{122-a}.$$

If $\Gamma = 5$, then $p^+ = 5/6$ and the upper bound becomes 0.0238 (for $\Gamma < 5$, the upper bound is even smaller). If $\Gamma = 6$, then the upper bound becomes 0.0969, which raises doubt about the action of rejecting the null hypothesis under $\Gamma = 1$. The key question is whether $\Gamma = 6$ is a plausible value or not. The unobserved confounder should be able to produce a six-fold increase in the odds ratio of smoking across two subjects in the same pair. Presumably, most of the relevant variables for smoking that one can think of would have already been controlled for with matching. Even if this is not the case, it would be difficult to think of a variable that caused a six-fold difference in the odds ratio (one possibility may be a dummy for rough/tough jobs as people with those jobs tend to smoke more). In this sense, six is too big a number, and the fact that it takes such a big number to reverse the initial conclusion makes the initial conclusion insensitive to hidden bias.

6.1.2   Unobserved confounder affecting treatment and response

The preceding sensitivity analysis is relatively straightforward, but it is too conservative, because there should be no hidden bias if the unobserved confounder v does not affect the response variable, even when v affects the treatment. Ignoring this leads to a bound on the p-value even when the bound is in fact unwarranted. Gastwirth *et al.* (1998) generalize the sensitivity analysis of Rosenbaum (1987) and allow v to affect both the treatment and the response at the price of one additional sensitivity parameter. Rosenbaum and Rubin (1983b) considered the effect of v on both the treatment and the response for the first time, but their approach contained too many sensitivity parameters. Imbens (2003) also attempts to allow v to affect both the treatment and response. This subsection reviews Gastwirth *et al.* (1998) for the same matched discordant pairs and McNemar's statistic M as in the preceding subsection. Imbens' (2003) study will also be reviewed. Since x plays no role once matched pairs are found, omit x in this subsection.

Assume

$$P(d_{si} = 1 | v_{si}) = \frac{\exp(\alpha_s + \gamma v_{si})}{1 + \exp(\alpha_s + \gamma v_{si})},$$

$$P(y_{si} = 1 | v_{si}) = \frac{\exp(\kappa_s + \delta v_{si})}{1 + \exp(\kappa_s + \delta v_{si})}, \qquad i = 1, 2,$$

for some constants α_s and κ_s and for $0 \leq v_{si} \leq 1$. If $\gamma\delta \neq 0$, then v_{si} affects both the treatment and the response, causing a hidden bias. Otherwise, there is no hidden bias. The logistic functional forms and $0 \leq v_{si} \leq 1$ are assumptions, differently from the previous subsection; they do not follow from the bounds on the odds ratio.

From the logit form for $P(d_{si} = 1 | v_{si})$, we get

$$P(d_{s1} = 1, d_{s2} = 0 | v_{s1}, v_{s2}, d_{s1} \neq d_{s2}) = \frac{\exp(\gamma v_{s1})}{\exp(\gamma v_{s1}) + \exp(\gamma v_{s2})} \equiv \pi_s;$$

$$P(y_{s1} = 1, y_{s2} = 0 | v_{s1}, v_{s2}, y_{s1} \neq y_{s2}) = \frac{\exp(\delta v_{s1})}{\exp(\delta v_{s1}) + \exp(\delta v_{s2})} \equiv \theta_s.$$

It holds also

$$\frac{P(d_{s1} = 1, d_{s2} = 0 | v_{s1}, v_{s2}, d_{s1} \neq d_{s2})}{P(d_{s1} = 0, d_{s2} = 1 | v_{s1}, v_{s2}, d_{s1} \neq d_{s2})} = \exp\{\gamma(v_{s1} - v_{s2})\}$$

as in the preceding subsection. As opposed to the preceding subsection, however, y_{s1} and y_{s2} will not be in the conditioning set, for the sensitivity analysis in this subsection considers the effect of v_s on y_s, as clear in $P(y_{si} = 1 | v_{si})$ above.

The event that the treated has the greater response given v_{s1}, v_{s2}, $d_{s1} \neq d_{s2}$, $y_{s1} \neq y_{s2}$ is

$$d_{s1} = 1, \ d_{s2} = 0, \ y_{s1} = 1, \ y_{s2} = 0 \quad \text{or} \quad d_{s1} = 0, \ d_{s2} = 1, \ y_{s1} = 0, \ y_{s2} = 1.$$

Under the strongest null hypothesis of no effect that the two potential responses are the same, d_{si} is independent of y_{si} and the probability that the treated has the greater response is

$$p_s \equiv \pi_s \theta_s + (1 - \pi_s)(1 - \theta_s) \qquad (= 0.5 \text{ if } \gamma \delta = 0).$$

Under the no effect and no hidden bias ($\gamma \delta = 0$), the distribution of M is $B(n, 0.5)$ as in the previous subsection. To find the null distribution of M allowing for $\gamma \delta \neq 0$, define $q \equiv (q_1, \ldots, q_n)'$ as a vector of n-many 0's and 1's, and Q as the collection of all such q's (there are 2^n elements in Q). Then the p-value is, with m denoting the realized value of M such that $m > 0.5n$ as in the previous subsection,

$$P(M \geq m | \gamma \delta \neq 0) = \sum_{q \in Q} \left\{ 1 \left[\sum_{s=1}^{n} q_s \geq m \right] \cdot \prod_{s=1}^{n} p_s^{q_s} (1 - p_s)^{1-q_s} \right\}.$$

To bound this from the above, define

$$\Gamma \equiv \frac{\exp(|\gamma|)}{1 + \exp(|\gamma|)} \geq 0.5, \qquad \Delta \equiv \frac{\exp(|\delta|)}{1 + \exp(|\delta|)} \geq 0.5,$$

$$\zeta \equiv \Gamma \Delta + (1 - \Gamma)(1 - \Delta) = 1 - \Gamma - \Delta + 2\Gamma \Delta$$

$$= 2(\Gamma - 0.5)(\Delta - 0.5) + 0.5 \geq 0.5.$$

Since γ in the preceding subsection is restricted to being non-negative, the definition of Γ in this display is essentially the same as that in the preceding subsection. Proposition 1 in Gastwirth *et al.* (1998) shows that

$$P(M \geq m | \gamma \delta \neq 0) \leq \max \left\{ \sum_{a=m}^{n} \binom{n}{a} \zeta^a (1 - \zeta)^{n-a}, \quad \sum_{a=m}^{n} \binom{n}{a} 0.5^n \right\}.$$

But the second term on the right-hand side is $P(M \geq m | \gamma \delta = 0)$. Thus, we have only to evaluate the first term on the right-hand side over $0.5 \leq \zeta < m/n$. This is analogous to the previous subsection. The only difference is that ζ replaces p^+, and Δ as well as Γ are used in this subsection. Since the bound does not depend on the conditioned random variables, it also holds unconditionally.

As an example, an association was found between a type of tampon and toxic shock syndrome. An endogenous sample was available from a case-referent study where friend-matching was done: 50 cases were matched to 50 controls (each matched control was a friend of the case) and all 50 cases and 43 controls used the tampon. Recall the definition of 'case' and 'control' in Section 5.4. Also recall that the above bounds are not applicable to the endogenous samples where the responses are fixed, which is ignored here for the sake of illustration. There are seven discordant pairs, and the realized value m of McNemar's statistic M is seven. Under no hidden bias and no effect, from $B(7, 0.5)$, the p-value of the McNemar's test is $0.0078 = 0.5^7$, thereby rejecting the null hypothesis of no effect. Part of Table 1 in Gastwirth *et al.* (1998), shown below with some changes, presents the upper bound for the p-value for various combinations of Δ and Γ:

Upper bound for p-value with matched pairs and binary response		
$\Delta = 1$	$\Delta = 2$	$\Delta = 3$
$\Gamma = 1$ $\zeta = 0.500;\ 0.0078$	$\zeta = 0.500;\ 0.0078$	$\zeta = 0.500;\ 0.0078$
$\Gamma = 2$ $\zeta = 0.500;\ 0.0078$	$\zeta = 0.556;\ 0.0163$	$\zeta = 0.583;\ 0.0230$
$\Gamma = 3$ $\zeta = 0.500;\ 0.0078$	$\zeta = 0.583;\ 0.0230$	$\zeta = 0.625;\ 0.0373$

When either $\Delta = 1$ or $\Gamma = 1$, the upper bound is the same as the p-value, as can be seen in the first row and first column in the lower right 3×3 sub-table. As Δ or Γ goes up, the bound increases. The table is symmetric along the diagonal. Although not shown here, when Δ and Γ are four, the upper bound becomes 0.067, which sheds doubt on the initial rejection of no effect. Interpretation of the number four is the same as in the previous subsection: the unobserved confounder increases the odds ratio of the treatment (or response) by a multiple of four.

Turning to Imbens (2003), assume

$$(y_{0i}, y_{1i}) \amalg d_i | (x_i, v_i), \quad v_i \text{ is binary and independent of } x_i$$

$$\text{with success probability } 0.5,$$

$$P(d = 1 | x, v) = \frac{\exp(x'\alpha + \gamma v)}{1 + \exp(x'\alpha + \gamma v)},$$

$$y_j | (x, v) \sim N(j\tau + x'\beta + \delta v,\ \sigma^2) \quad \text{for parameters } \beta,\ \delta, \text{ and } \sigma,\ j = 0, 1.$$

The parameter τ is the treatment effect, which is constant in this model. Compared with the preceding sensitivity analyses, the last normality part is restrictive; also note that y_j is continuous, not binary. Ruling out hidden bias implies estimating $(\alpha', \beta', \tau, \sigma)$ under the assumption $\gamma = \delta = 0$ where v is the sole unobserved confounder. Imbens (2003) proposes to estimate $(\alpha', \beta', \tau, \sigma)$ while fixing (γ, δ) by maximizing the following likelihood function

$$\sum_i \ln \left[\frac{1}{2} \cdot \frac{1}{\sqrt{2\pi\sigma^2}} \exp\left\{ -\frac{1}{2\sigma^2}(y_i - d_i\tau - x_i'\beta)^2 \right\} \frac{\{\exp(x'\alpha)\}^{d_i}}{1 + \exp(x'\alpha)} \right.$$

$$\left. + \frac{1}{2} \cdot \frac{1}{\sqrt{2\pi\sigma^2}} \exp\left\{ -\frac{1}{2\sigma^2}(y_i - d_i\tau - x_i'\beta - \delta)^2 \right\} \frac{\{\exp(x'\alpha + \gamma)\}^{d_i}}{1 + \exp(x'\alpha + \gamma)} \right].$$

This conditional MLE yields estimates $(\hat{\alpha}', \hat{\beta}', \hat{\tau}, \hat{\sigma})$ as a function of (γ, δ). As γ and δ change, we can gauge the sensitivity of $(\hat{\alpha}', \hat{\beta}', \hat{\tau}, \hat{\sigma})$ as a function of γ and δ. However it is hard to see what values are plausible for γ and δ. To overcome this difficulty, define a R^2 at a fixed value for γ and δ:

$$R_y^2(\gamma, \delta) \equiv 1 - \frac{\hat{\sigma}^2(\gamma, \delta)}{N^{-1} \sum_i (y_i - \bar{y})^2}.$$

Also define a partial R^2 due to v with coefficients γ and δ:

$$R_{y,par}^2(\gamma, \delta) \equiv \frac{R_y^2(\gamma, \delta) - R_y^2(0,0)}{1 - R_y^2(0,0)} \left(= \frac{\hat{\sigma}^2(0,0) - \hat{\sigma}^2(\gamma, \delta)}{\hat{\sigma}^2(0,0)} \right)$$

which shows the relative proportion of the R^2 increase (or the relative proportion of the $\hat{\sigma}^2$ decrease) due to v.

For the binary treatment equation, define a pseudo logit R^2:

$$R_d^2 \equiv \frac{\hat{\alpha}(\gamma, \delta)' \sum_i (x_i - \bar{x})(x_i - \bar{x})' \hat{\alpha}(\gamma, \delta)}{\hat{\alpha}(\gamma, \delta)' \sum_i (x_i - \bar{x})(x_i - \bar{x})' \hat{\alpha}(\gamma, \delta) + (\gamma^2/4) + (\pi^2/3)}.$$

In the denominator, $\gamma^2/4$ comes from the variance of γv (recall that v is binary), and $\pi^2/3$ is the variance of the logistic error term. From R_d^2, define a partial R^2 due to v with coefficients γ and δ:

$$R_{d,par}^2(\gamma, \delta) \equiv \frac{R_d^2(\gamma, \delta) - R_d^2(0,0)}{1 - R_d^2(0,0)}.$$

Imbens (2003) proposes to look at values of $R_{d,par}^2(\gamma, \delta)$ and $R_{y,par}^2(\gamma, \delta)$ that will induce $|\hat{\tau}(\gamma, \delta) - \hat{\tau}(0,0)|$ to equal a certain amount or $\hat{\tau}(\gamma, \delta)$ to cross zero. The ratio for the partial R^2 in the two equations may be used to judge the plausibility of the hidden bias. That is, suppose the ratios

$$\frac{R_{d,par}^2(\gamma, \delta) \text{ for the required effect change}}{\text{the usual } R_{par}^2 \text{ for important covariates in } d\text{-eq.}}$$

and

$$\frac{R_{y,par}^2(\gamma, \delta) \text{ for the required effect change}}{\text{the usual } R_{par}^2 \text{ for important covariates in } y\text{-eq.}}$$

are small. Then a relatively unimportant unobserved confounder in view of the small ratios can result in a big change in the effect, implying that the initial finding is sensitive.

For instance, in an empirical application for the effect of a job training on earnings, consider $(R_{y,par}^2(\gamma, \delta), R_{d,par}^2(\gamma, \delta))$ that will induce the treatment effect to change by \$1000 where the treatment effect itself is \$1672 under $\gamma = 0$ and $\delta = 0$. It is found that $R_{d,par}^2(\gamma, \delta) = 0.20$ and $R_{y,par}^2(\gamma, \delta) = 0.02$ whereas the usual partial R-squared R_{par}^2 due to some important covariates is 0.013 and 0.011, respectively, for the treatment and outcome equation. The ratios are $0.20/0.013$ and $0.02/0.011$, respectively. The ratio for the treatment equation is big, and thus the initial effect \$1672 is deemed to be robust against hidden bias.

6.1.3 Average of ratios of biased to true effects

Lee and Kobayashi (2001) introduce conditional *proportional treatment effect*:

$$\frac{E(y_1 - y_0|x)}{E(y_0|x)} = \frac{E(y_1|x)}{E(y_0|x)} - 1,$$

and propose the following geometric-average-based marginal treatment effect:

$$\left\{ \prod_i \frac{E(y_1|x_i)}{E(y_0|x_i)} \right\}^{1/N} - 1.$$

Although the proportional effect is motivated by exponential regression functions, it is convenient for other regression functions as well, for it gives the proportional effect relative to the baseline $E(y_0|x)$. In this subsection, we present the nonparametric sensitivity analysis found in Lee (2004) using the proportional effect. While Lee (2004) deals with ordered treatments, we will use a binary treatment to simplify the exposition.

Rewrite the conditional proportional effect as

$$\frac{E(y_1|x)}{E(y_0|x)} - 1 = \frac{E(y|x, d = 1)}{E(y|x, d = 0)} A(x) - 1$$

$$\text{where } A(x) \equiv \frac{E(y|x, d = 0)}{E(y_0|x)} \cdot \left\{ \frac{E(y|x, d = 1)}{E(y_1|x)} \right\}^{-1}.$$

$A(x)$ is not identified and the conditional effect is identified only if $A(x) = 1$. Further rewrite the conditional proportional effect as

$$\exp\left[\ln\left\{ \frac{E(y|x, d = 1)}{E(y|x, d = 0)} \right\} + \ln A(x) \right] - 1.$$

The geometric-average-based marginal effect is

$$\exp\left[N^{-1} \sum_i \ln\left\{ \frac{E(y|x_i, d = 1)}{E(y|x_i, d = 0)} \right\} + N^{-1} \sum_i \ln A(x_i) \right] - 1$$

$$= B \cdot \exp\left\{ N^{-1} \sum_i \ln R(x_i) \right\} - 1$$

where

$$R(x_i) \equiv \frac{E(y|x_i, d = 1)}{E(y|x_i, d = 0)} \quad \text{and} \quad B \equiv \exp\left\{ N^{-1} \sum_i \ln A(x_i) \right\}.$$

$E(y|x_i, d = j)$ can be estimated with a nonparametric estimator, say $E_N(y|x_i, d = j)$, and the marginal effect is identified if $B = 1$. B is the geometric average of $A(x_i)$'s, $i = 1, \ldots, N$. For a given range of B, we can get the corresponding range for the marginal effect, which leads to a sensitivity analysis. In other words B is a sensitivity parameter.

Examining $A(x)$ closely, $A(x)$ consists of two ratios. The first ratio of $A(x)$ is, *with x controlled for*,

$$\frac{\text{mean response when zero treatment is self-selected}}{\text{mean response when zero treatment is exogenously given}},$$

whereas the second ratio of $A(x)$ is

$$\frac{\text{mean response when treatment is self-selected}}{\text{mean response when treatment is exogenously given}}.$$

These can certainly deviate from one. Nonetheless, there are reasons to believe that B is close to one:

1. If both ratios in $A(x_i)$ are one (i.e., if selection-on-observables holds), then $A(x_i)$ is one.

2. Even if the ratios differ from one (i.e., even if there are hidden biases), so long as they are equal (i.e., so long as the bias magnitudes are the same in the two ratios), then $A(x_i)$ is still one.

3. Even if $A(x_i) \neq 1$ for some i, B can still be one, for B is an average of $A(x_i)$.

In short, there are reasons to believe that B would differ little from one. If desired, one may use only a subset of x to bring B even closer to one.

Specifically, a nonparametric sensitivity analysis can be done as follows. First, estimate $R(x_i)$ with

$$R_N(x_i) \equiv \frac{\sum_{j,j\neq i} K((x_j - x_i)/h)d_j y_j}{\sum_{j,j\neq i} K((x_j - x_i)/h)d_j} \cdot \left\{ \frac{\sum_{j,j\neq i} K((x_j - x_i)/h)(1 - d_j)y_j}{\sum_{j,j\neq i} K((x_j - x_i)/h)(1 - d_j)} \right\}^{-1}.$$

Second, obtain the marginal effect

$$\exp\left\{ N^{-1} \sum_i \ln R_N(x_i) \right\} - 1.$$

Third, change B around 1 and see how

$$B \cdot \exp\left\{ N^{-1} \sum_i \ln R_N(x_i) \right\} - 1$$

changes. If this changes substantially (e.g., going from $+$ to $-$ as B changes only slightly), then the proportional treatment effect is sensitive to the assumption of no hidden bias.

If the dimension of x is high, then one may use the propensity score $P(d = 1|x)$ instead of x in the nonparametric estimation. In practice, $P(d = 1|x)$ can be estimated by probit or logit. The sensitivity analyses in the preceding two subsections are 'of a structural form' in the sense that they are explicit on how the unobserved confounder may cause a bias (by influencing the treatment or the response), whereas the one in Lee (2004) is 'of a reduced form' in the sense that such a route for hidden bias is not explicit. Lee's approach is consequently less informative on how the unobserved confounder operates. However the advantages are that there is no restriction on the number of unobserved confounders and that it is easy to implement.

The implementation of the third step with B can be modified to allow for a sampling error. Suppose a confidence interval (CI) for $\exp\{N^{-1}\sum_i \ln R_N(x_i)\}$ is $[G_L, G_U]$. Lee (2004) uses a bootstrap resampling from the original sample to get G_L and G_U. We would conclude a significant proportional effect under no hidden bias when

$$[G_L - 1, G_U - 1] \text{ that is a CI for } \exp\left\{ N^{-1}\sum_i \ln R_N(x_i) \right\} - 1 \text{ excludes } 0$$

$$\Longleftrightarrow [G_L, G_U] \text{ excludes } 1 \iff [G_U^{-1}, G_L^{-1}] \text{ excludes } 1.$$

Now, consider $B\exp\{N^{-1}\sum_i \ln R_N(x_i)\} - 1$ which can be greater (if $B > 1$) or smaller (if $B < 1$) than $\exp\{N^{-1}\sum_i \ln R_N(x_i)\} - 1$. For insensitivity to hidden bias, we want to have $[G_U^{-1}, G_L^{-1}]$ to exclude 1 by some margin. In other words

$$[G_U^{-1}, G_L^{-1}] \notin [1 - c, 1 + c] \quad \text{for a small constant } c > 0.$$

Here, c is the sensitivity parameter. For the three reasons cited already, B is likely to be close to 1, (i.e., c can be set at a small number, say, in $[0.05, 0.1]$). In the empirical example of Lee and Lee (2004b), setting $c = 0.08$ yields results comparable to those obtained from applying the sensitivity analysis of Gastwirth *et al.* (1998).

In the preceding paragraph, the focal point of the sensitivity analysis was $[G_U^{-1}, G_L^{-1}]$, for which there is an easy interpretation as follows. If we set $B\exp\{N^{-1}\sum_i \ln R_N(x_i)\} - 1$ at zero and solve the equation for B, then we get the value B_0 of B *making the effect cross zero*:

$$B_0 = \left[\exp\left\{ N^{-1}\sum_i \ln R_N(x_i) \right\} \right]^{-1}.$$

$[G_U^{-1}, G_L^{-1}]$ is nothing but the bounds for B_0. This shows that the sensitivity analysis is for the 'qualitative conclusion'—the effect being positive or negative.

Lee and Lee (2004c) apply the three sensitivity analyses explained in this section, except that of Imbens (2003), to the job-training data used in Lee and Lee (2004). The response variable is binary: reemployment or not by the study-ending date. Their conclusions are essentially what one would expect from sensitivity analysis. First, allowing for unobserved confounders by sensitivity analysis weakened the findings obtained under no hidden bias assumption in Lee and Lee (2004). Second, different sensitivity analyses led to different findings, but strong effects survived in different sensitivity analyses. Although the sensitivity analyses have arbitrary sensitivity parameters, the degree of the arbitrariness differs little from that in choosing the significance level in a test.

6.2 Selection correction methods

One way to handle hidden bias, under some restrictive parametric assumptions, is to avoid it by using an extra regressor in the response variable equation. The extra regressor is a function of the covariates, the functional form of which is known up to a parameter vector. It is called a 'selection-correction term' or a 'control function'.

Assume a parametric model where w_i denotes a covariate vector including x_i,

$$d_i = 1[w_i'\alpha + \varepsilon_i > 0], \qquad y_{ji} = x_i'\beta_j + u_{ji}, \quad j = 0, 1,$$

ε_i follows $N(0, \sigma_\varepsilon^2)$ where $\sigma_\varepsilon^2 \equiv V(\varepsilon)$, and ε_i is independent of w_i,

$$E(u_{ji}|w_i, \varepsilon_i) = \frac{\sigma_{\varepsilon j}}{\sigma_\varepsilon^2}\varepsilon_i, \qquad \sigma_{\varepsilon j} \equiv E(\varepsilon u_j), \quad j = 0, 1.$$

This model includes the exclusion restriction that the components of w other than x are excluded from the response equation. The exclusion restriction is not necessary, but without it, it is difficult to separate the selection bias from the regression function nonlinear components. From the model,

$$E(y_1 - y_0) = E(x') \cdot (\beta_1 - \beta_0),$$
$$E(y_1 - y_0|d = j) = E(x'|d = j)(\beta_1 - \beta_0) + E(u_1|d = j) - E(u_0|d = j), \quad j = 0, 1.$$

The treatment effect is identified once $\beta_1 - \beta_0$ is so, while the treatment effect on the treated or the untreated requires in addition $E(u_1|d = j) - E(u_0|d = j)$.

Owing to $E(u_{ji}|w_i, \varepsilon_i) = (\sigma_{\varepsilon j}/\sigma_\varepsilon^2)\varepsilon_i$, defining $V(u_j) \equiv \sigma_j^2$ and $COR(u_j, \varepsilon) \equiv \rho_{\varepsilon j}$, we get

$$E(u_j|w, d = 1) = E(u_j|w, \varepsilon > -w'\alpha) = \frac{\sigma_{\varepsilon j}}{\sigma_\varepsilon^2} \cdot E(\varepsilon|w, \varepsilon > -w'\alpha)$$

$$= \frac{\sigma_{\varepsilon j}}{\sigma_\varepsilon} \cdot E\left(\frac{\varepsilon}{\sigma_\varepsilon}|w, \frac{\varepsilon}{\sigma_\varepsilon} > \frac{-w'\alpha}{\sigma_\varepsilon}\right)$$

$$= \frac{\sigma_{\varepsilon j}}{\sigma_\varepsilon} \frac{\phi(-w'\alpha/\sigma_\varepsilon)}{1 - \Phi(-w'\alpha/\sigma_\varepsilon)} = \rho_{\varepsilon j}\sigma_j \frac{\phi(w'\alpha/\sigma_\varepsilon)}{\Phi(w'\alpha/\sigma_\varepsilon)},$$

where ϕ and Φ are, respectively, the $N(0,1)$ density and the distribution function. Doing analogously,

$$E(u_j|w, d = 0) = -\frac{\sigma_{\varepsilon j}}{\sigma_\varepsilon} \frac{\phi(-w'\alpha/\sigma_\varepsilon)}{\Phi(-w'\alpha/\sigma_\varepsilon)} = -\rho_{\varepsilon j}\sigma_j \frac{\phi(-w'\alpha/\sigma_\varepsilon)}{\Phi(-w'\alpha/\sigma_\varepsilon)}.$$

Using these results, we get

$$E(u_1|d = 1) - E(u_0|d = 1) = E\left\{\frac{\phi(w'\alpha/\sigma_\varepsilon)}{\Phi(w'\alpha/\sigma_\varepsilon)}\bigg| d = 1\right\} \cdot (\rho_{\varepsilon 1}\sigma_1 - \rho_{\varepsilon_0}\sigma_0);$$

$$E(u_1|d = 0) - E(u_0|d = 0) = E\left\{\frac{\phi(-w'\alpha/\sigma_\varepsilon)}{\Phi(-w'\alpha/\sigma_\varepsilon)}\bigg| d = 0\right\} \cdot (-\rho_{\varepsilon 1}\sigma_1 + \rho_{\varepsilon_0}\sigma_0).$$

Hence the treatment effect on the treated and the untreated are, respectively,

$$E(x'|d = 1)(\beta_1 - \beta_0) + E\left\{\frac{\phi(w'\alpha/\sigma_\varepsilon)}{\Phi(w'\alpha/\sigma_\varepsilon)}\bigg| d = 1\right\} \cdot (\rho_{\varepsilon 1}\sigma_1 - \rho_{\varepsilon_0}\sigma_0),$$

and

$$E(x'|d = 0)(\beta_1 - \beta_0) + E\left\{\frac{\phi(-w'\alpha/\sigma_\varepsilon)}{\Phi(-w'\alpha/\sigma_\varepsilon)}\bigg| d = 0\right\} \cdot (-\rho_{\varepsilon 1}\sigma_1 + \rho_{\varepsilon_0}\sigma_0).$$

The treatment effects can be estimated applying 'Heckman's (1979) two-stage estimator' separately to the subsample with $d = 0$ and $d = 1$. First, $\alpha/\sigma_\varepsilon$ is estimated by probit a_N, and then

$$\text{the LSE of } (1 - d_i)y_i \text{ on } \left((1 - d_i)x_i', (1 - d_i)\frac{\phi(-w_i'a_N)}{\Phi(-w_i'a_N)}\right)$$

yields estimates for $\gamma_0 \equiv (\beta_0', -\rho_{\varepsilon_0}\sigma_0)'$, whereas

$$\text{the LSE of } d_iy_i \text{ on } \left(d_ix_i', d_i\frac{\phi(w_i'a_N)}{\Phi(w_i'a_N)}\right)$$

yields estimates for $\gamma_1 \equiv (\beta_1', \rho_{\varepsilon 1}\sigma_1)'$. Let g_{Nj} denote the LSE for γ_j, $j = 0, 1$, and let the asymptotic variance for $\sqrt{N}(g_{Nj} - \gamma_j)$ be C_j, $j = 0, 1$, which is consistently estimated by, say, C_{Nj}. Stack the two estimates and parameters: $g_N \equiv (g_{N0}', g_{N1}')'$ and $\gamma \equiv (\gamma_0', \gamma_1')'$. $\sqrt{N}(g_N - \gamma)$'s asymptotic-variance matrix is $C \equiv diag(C_0, C_1)$ that is consistently estimated with $C_N \equiv diag(C_{N0}, C_{N1})$. Suppose x has the dimension $k_x \times 1$. Define

$$Q \equiv (-I_{k_x}, 0_{k_x}, I_{k_x}, 0_{k_x}),$$

where 0_{k_x} is the $k_x \times 1$ zero vector. Then an estimate for the treatment effect $E(x')(\beta_0 - \beta_1)$ and its asymptotic-variance estimate is

$$\bar{x}'Qg_N \quad and \quad (\bar{x}'Q)C_N(Q'\bar{x})/N.$$

For the treatment effect on the treated, let $\bar{x}_j$ be the mean of x for the subsample $d = j$, $j = 0, 1$. Define

$$\bar{z}_1 \equiv \left(\bar{x}'_1, N_1^{-1} \sum_i d_i \frac{\phi(w'_i a_N)}{\Phi(w'_i a_N)} \right)'.$$

Then an estimate for the treatment effect on the treated and its asymptotic-variance estimate are

$$\bar{z}'_1 Q_1 g_N \quad and \quad (\bar{z}'_1 Q_1)C_N(Q'_1 \bar{z}_1)/N,$$

where

$$Q_1 \equiv \begin{bmatrix} -I_{k_x} & 0_{k_x} & I_{k_x} & 0_{k_x} \\ 0'_{k_x} & 1 & 0'_{k_x} & 1 \end{bmatrix}.$$

For the treatment effect on the untreated, define

$$\bar{z}_0 \equiv \left(\bar{x}'_0, N_0^{-1} \sum_i (1 - d_i) \frac{\phi(-w'_i a_N)}{\Phi(-w'_i a_N)} \right)'.$$

An estimate for the treatment effect on the untreated and its asymptotic-variance estimate are

$$\bar{z}'_0 Q_0 g_N \quad and \quad (\bar{z}'_0 Q_0)C_N(Q'_0 \bar{z}_0)/N,$$

where

$$Q_0 \equiv \begin{bmatrix} -I_{k_x} & 0_{k_x} & I_{k_x} & 0_{k_x} \\ 0'_{k_x} & -1 & 0'_{k_x} & -1 \end{bmatrix}.$$

See Heckman *et al.* (2003) and the references therein for more on parametric selection correction approaches.

For an example, recall the example of job effect on doctor visits in subsection 2.5.1. In the preceding discussion we allowed $w \neq x$, but in the data set we could not find any variable to exclude from the potential response equations. Hence, $w = x$. With

$$x = (1, age, schooling, male, married, phy, psy)',$$

where *male* and *married* are dummy variables, and *phy* (*psy*) is self-assessed physical (psychological) condition in five categories (the lower the better). The following is the result (t-value in $(\cdot)$):

$$\text{effect on the population}: \quad E(y_1 - y_0) \simeq 3.151 \ (0.616),$$
$$\text{effect on the treated}: \quad E(y_1 - y_0|d = 1) \simeq 5.617 \ (1.420),$$
$$\text{effect on the untreated}: \quad E(y_1 - y_0|d = 0) \simeq -2.428 \ (-0.291).$$

With $E(d) \simeq 0.694$, we can easily verify that these numbers satisfy

$$E(y_1 - y_0) = E(y_1 - y_0|d = 1)P(d = 1) + E(y_1 - y_0|d = 0)P(d = 0).$$

None of the effects is significant, which is however not to say that there is no significant conditional effect, (e.g., for some x_o, $E(y_1 - y_0|x_o, d = 1)$ may be significantly different from zero). As one starts working, one can afford to visit doctors more often. However, the time spent on visiting doctors gradually becomes more costly. The above numbers suggest that the former weighs more heavily.

6.3   Nonparametric bounding approaches

The selection correction approach of the previous section is heavily parametric. There are, however, methods that need hardly any assumptions, and we will discuss one such idea in this section. The consequence of being assumption-free, is that what can be learned from a given data is rather limited.

Suppose y is binary, and we are interested in the treatment effect

$$E(y_1 - y_0|x) = P(y_1 = 1|x) - P(y_0 = 1|x).$$

Observe

$$P(y_1 = 1|x) = P(y_1 = 1|x, d = 0)P(d = 0|x) + P(y_1 = 1|x, d = 1)P(d = 1|x),$$

where $P(y_1 = 1|x, d = 0)$ is not identified while the other three terms are. Since $0 \leq P(y_1 = 1|x, d = 0) \leq 1$, substituting these bounds into the equation $P(y_1 = 1|x)$, we get

$$P(y_1 = 1|x, d = 1)P(d = 1|x) \leq P(y_1 = 1|x)$$
$$\leq P(d = 0|x) + P(y_1 = 1|x, d = 1)P(d = 1|x).$$

The width of these bounds is $P(d = 0|x)$. Doing analogously for y_0, it holds that

$$P(y_0 = 1|x, d = 0)P(d = 0|x) \leq P(y_0 = 1|x)$$
$$\leq P(d = 1|x) + P(y_0 = 1|x, d = 0)P(d = 0|x).$$

Applying the bounds for $P(y_1 = 1|x)$ and $P(y_0 = 1|x)$ to $P(y_1 = 1|x) - P(y_0 = 1|x)$, we get the following bounds on the treatment effect (e.g., the lower bound is the lower bound for $P(y_1 = 1|x)$ minus the upper bound for $P(y_0 = 1|x)$):

$$P(y_1 = 1|x, d = 1)P(d = 1|x) - P(d = 1|x) - P(y_0 = 1|x, d = 0)P(d = 0|x)$$
$$\leq P(y_1 = 1|x) - P(y_0 = 1|x)$$
$$\leq P(d = 0|x) + P(y_1 = 1|x, d = 1)P(d = 1|x)$$
$$- P(y_0 = 1|x, d = 0)P(d = 0|x).$$

This is the 'bottom line': without any assumption, what can be learned about the treatment effect is this; anything more should come from some assumptions. The 'bottom line' bounds are called the 'worst-case' bounds in the sense that they are the most conservative. Subtracting the lower bound from the upper bound, the width of the bounds is $P(d = 0|x) + P(d = 1|x) = 1$. In contrast, if the bounds for $P(y_1 = 1|x)$ and $P(y_0 = 1|x)$ are ignored, then $P(y_1 = 1|x) - P(y_0 = 1|x)$ falls in $[-1, 1]$ with the width at 2.

Manski *et al.* (1992) study the effect on high-school graduation y of family status d at age 14. Let $d = 1$ if the family is 'intact' (the parents, either biological or adoptive, are present) and $d = 0$ if the family is 'non-intact'. The treatment d in Manski *et al.* (1992) is defined in reverse. We use the preceding definition as we are interested in the effect of the policy intervention on making the family intact, not the other way around.

Manski *et al.* (1992) estimate the above bounds nonparametrically using a survey data taken in 1985 with $N = 2792$, and part of their Table 6 for white males is

Effect of family status on graduation						
	L−	L	NPR	U	U+	MLE
F < 12, M < 12	−.44	−.39	.15	.61	.67	.14
F < 12, M > 12	−.26	−.19	.45	.81	.87	.10
F > 12, M < 12	−.31	−.27	.05	.73	.84	.08
F > 12, M > 12	−.18	−.14	.05	.86	.89	.03

where 'F < 12 and M < 12' represents a father's and mother's schooling of less than 12 years (the cases with schooling being exactly 12 are omitted here); NPR is a nonparametric estimate for $P(y = 1|x, d = 0) - P(y = 1|x, d = 1)$ which is $P(y_0 = 1|x) - P(y_1 = 1|x)$ under the assumption of no-hidden-bias; L and U are nonparametric estimates for the lower and upper bounds derived above, respectively; L− and U+ are 90% confidence lower and upper bounds for L and U, respectively; and, MLE is the MLE for the treatment effect under a joint normality assumption.

It is important to note that, first, the major portion of the bound is due to U − L, while only a small fraction is due to the sampling errors (the differences between L− and L, and U and U+). Second, in three out of the four cases, the MLE is close to the nonparametric estimate, and even when they differ, the MLE still falls in $[L-, U+]$. If the MLE had fallen outside $[L-, U+]$, then this would have indicated that some assumption(s) in the MLE were false. Third, as the NPR and MLE columns show, the effect of making a family intact seems to increase the probability of graduating from the high school, although the confidence intervals include zero. Fourth, one should not have the 'illusion' that the true value falls near the middle of $[L, U]$.

As the above empirical example shows, the bounding approach can provide some information, but not much. As in other approaches, we can impose assumptions to get better results. One such assumption is a *monotonicity* (or 'ordered outcome') in d:

$$(0 \leq) P(y_1 = 1|x, d = 0) \leq P(y_1 = 1|x, d = 1).$$

To understand this, imagine an unobserved confounder, say, a conformist trait that is hereditary. A child with the trait is more likely to have $y_1 = 1$ than a child without it and parents with the trait are also more likely to have $d = 1$ than parents without it. Since the trait is hereditary, it affects both y_1 and d positively, resulting in the monotonicity inequality.

Substituting the monotonicity bounds instead of $0 \leq P(y_1 = 1|x, d = 0) \leq 1$ into the decomposition of $P(y_1 = 1|x)$, we get the following improved bounds for $P(y_1 = 1|x)$:

$$P(y_1 = 1|x, d = 1) P(d = 1|x) \leq P(y_1 = 1|x) \leq P(y_1 = 1|x, d = 1).$$

The width of these bounds is

$$P(y_1 = 1|x, d = 1) - P(y_1 = 1|x, d = 1) P(d = 1|x)$$
$$= P(d = 0|x) \cdot P(y_1 = 1|x, d = 1)$$

which is smaller than the width $P(d = 0|x)$ from the worst-case bounds.

Doing analogously, suppose

$$P(y_0 = 1|x, d = 0) \le P(y_0 = 1|x, d = 1) \ (\le 1).$$

The conformist trait example still applies here, for having the trait makes $y_0 = 1$ (as well as $y_1 = 1$) more likely. From this, we get the following bounds for $P(y_0 = 1|x)$:

$$P(y_0 = 1|x, d = 0) \le P(y_0 = 1|x) \le P(d = 1|x) + P(y_0 = 1|x, d = 0)P(d = 0|x).$$

Combining the bounds for $P(y_1 = 1|x)$ and $P(y_0 = 1|x)$, we get

$$P(y_1 = 1|x, d = 1)P(d = 1|x) - P(d = 1|x) - P(y_0 = 1|x, d = 0)P(d = 0|x)$$
$$\le P(y_1 = 1|x) - P(y_0 = 1|x)$$
$$\le P(y_1 = 1|x, d = 1) - P(y_0 = 1|x, d = 0).$$

In contrast to the worst-case bounds, call these 'monotonicity bounds'. Roughly speaking, the monotonicities cut down the uncertainty associated with the counter-factuals by 'half'.

Monotonicity in d is not the only way to tighten the bounds. Another way is to use an exclusion restriction. Let $w \equiv (x', c')'$ and suppose w is relevant for d while only x is relevant for y_j. That is, c does not influence y_j directly other than through d; instruments satisfy this condition. Recall the worst-case bound for $P(y_1 = 1|x)$. Replace x in $P(d|x)$ with $(x', c')'$. Take $\sup_c$ on the lower bound and $\inf_c$ on the upper bound to get

$$\sup_c\{P(y_1 = 1|x, d = 1)P(d = 1|x, c)\}$$
$$\le P(y_1 = 1|x)$$
$$\le \inf_c\{P(d = 0|x, c) + P(y_1 = 1|x, d = 1)P(d = 1|x, c)\}.$$

Because of the supremum and infimum, the bounds here are tighter than the worst-case bounds for $P(y_1 = 1|x)$. We call this kind of bounds 'exclusion-restriction bounds'.

Doing analogously, exclusion restriction bounds can be derived for $P(y_0 = 1|x)$. The exclusion bounds for $P(y_1 = 1|x)$ and $P(y_0 = 1|x)$ can be combined to render exclusion bounds for $P(y_1 = 1|x) - P(y_0 = 1|x)$. Furthermore, the monotonicity bounds can be tightened using exclusion restrictions additionally.

Lechner (1999) provides an example of nonparametric bounding approach on job training effects. Pepper (2000) also shows an example of the effects of growing up in a family on welfare on future welfare participation of the children. Pepper uses the aforementioned monotonicity. For more on nonparametric bounding approaches, see Manski (1995, 2003) and the references therein. While it is useful to know what can be done without the need of many assumptions, the bounding approaches shown in this section may not go far enough to be useful in most applications.

6.4   Controlling for post-treatment variables to avoid confounder

In controlling for covariates, in general, post-treatment covariates affected by the treatment d should not be controlled for. This was shown briefly earlier in Chapter 3 and it is also shown in detail in the appendix to this chapter. This section shows an exception, where an unobserved confounder ε is avoided by controlling for a post-treatment covariate m affected by d. The effect of d on y is confounded by ε, but when the effect is decomposed into two (d on m and m on y), the confounding problem disappears. This surprising and exceptional case is called 'front-door adjustment' in Pearl (2000), where 'front door' refers to the fact that m is a post-treatment variable, relative to 'back-door adjustment' where pre-treatment covariates are controlled for.

Suppose we are worried about selection-on-unobservables

$$E(y_j|d,x,\varepsilon) = E(y_j|x,\varepsilon) \quad \text{for all } x,\varepsilon$$
$$\text{but} \quad E(y_j|d,x) \neq E(y_j|x) \quad \text{for some } x, \qquad j = 0,1,$$

and there is a post-treatment variable m which stands in the causal path between d and y. Consider the following x-omitted causal diagram:

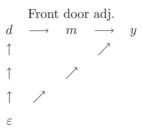

In this case, it is possible to identify the causal effect of d on y by controlling for the affected post-treatment covariate m despite the presence of the unobserved confounder ε. Specifically, first the effect of d on m is identified, for which ε is not a common factor. Second, the effect of m on y is identified, for which ε is not a common factor either. The idea is that, by breaking the effect of d on y into d on m and m on y, for each of which ε is not a confounder, one can identify the effect of d on y.

To see the idea better, define m_0 and m_1 as the two potential variables for the effect of d on m, just as y_0 and y_1 are the two potential variables for the effect of d on y. Consider simple 'parallel-shift' (i.e., constant effect) linear models:

$$d_i = \alpha_1 + x_i'\alpha_x + \varepsilon_i, \qquad E(\varepsilon|x) = 0,$$

$$m_{0i} = \gamma_1 + x_i'\gamma_x + e_i, \qquad m_{1i} = \gamma_1 + \gamma_d + x_i'\gamma_x + e_i \qquad E(e|x) = 0,$$

$$y_0 \text{ SF}: y_{0i} = \beta_1 + \beta_m m_{0i} + x_i'\beta_x + u_i,$$

$$y_1 \text{ SF}: y_{1i} = \beta_1 + \beta_m m_{1i} + x_i'\beta_x + u_i, \qquad E(u|x) = 0,$$

$$(u, \varepsilon) \amalg e|x, \quad \text{but} \quad u \text{ and } \varepsilon \text{ are related given } x,$$

where α, β, γ are parameters and ε, e, u are mean-zero error terms. We use a linear (probability) model for the binary d_i, which is inconsequential for the following analysis. Here, ε is an unobserved confounder, because ε is part of d while related to u that is part of y_0 and y_1. Other than through ε, d affects y_0 and y_1 only through m_0 and m_1. Thus this model satisfies the above causal diagram. If d were to affect y directly, we would have β_d added to the y_1 equation. In the model, the effect $E(m_1 - m_0)$ of d on m is γ_d, and the effect of d on y is

$$E(y_1 - y_0) = \beta_m E(m_1 - m_0) = \beta_m \gamma_d.$$

Thus β_m can be construed as the effect of m on y.

Turning to identifying the effect $\beta_m \gamma_d$ of d on y, the observed equations for m and y are

$$m_i = (1 - d_i)m_{0i} + d_i m_{1i} = \gamma_1 + \gamma_d d_i + x_i'\gamma_x + e_i,$$

$$y_i = (1 - m_i)y_{0i} + m_i y_{1i} = \beta_1 + \beta_m m_i + x_i'\beta_x + u_i.$$

From this, the y RF for d is

$$y_i = \beta_1 + \beta_m(\gamma_1 + \gamma_d d_i + x_i'\gamma_x + e_i) + x_i'\beta_x + u_i$$
$$= \beta_1 + \beta_m \gamma_1 + \beta_m \gamma_d d_i + x_i'(\beta_x + \beta_m \gamma_x) + \beta_m e_i + u_i.$$

Then,

$$E(y|d=1,x) - E(y|d=0,x) = \beta_m\gamma_d + E(\beta_m e + u|d=1,x) - E(\beta_m e + u|d=0,x),$$

where the error term conditional mean difference is the bias due to not controlling for m. The bias is not zero in general due to the relation between ε and u (i.e., d and u). This shows that not controlling for m leads to a bias, because ε is an unobserved confounder in this case.

Observe now, invoking $E(e|d,x) = E(e|x)$ and $E(u|m,x) = E(u|x)$,

$$E(m|d=1,x) - E(m|d=0,x) = \gamma_d + E(e|d=1,x) - E(e|d=0,x) = \gamma_d,$$

$$E(y|m=1,x) - E(y|m=0,x) = \beta_m + E(u|m=1,x) - E(u|m=0,x) = \beta_m.$$

Hence we can identify γ_d as the effect of d on m, and β_m as the effect of m on y. Therefore, splitting the effect of d on y into d on m and m on y can work. It is also possible, however, to identify $\beta_m \gamma_d$ in a single step, as in the following.

Pearl's (2000, p. 83) front-door adjustment shows that $E(y_j|x)$ is identified nonparametrically: omitting x to simplify notations, the front-door adjustment is

$$E(y_1) = \int f(m|d = 1)\{E(y|d = 1, m)P(d = 1) + E(y|d = 0, m)P(d = 0)\}dm,$$

$$E(y_0) = \int f(m|d = 0)\{E(y|d = 1, m)P(d = 1) + E(y|d = 0, m)P(d = 0)\}dm.$$

To see that the difference between these two becomes $\beta_m\gamma_d$ for the linear model, we only have to replace $E(y|d = j, m)$ with the parametric models: using $y_i = \beta_1 + \beta_m m_i + u_i$, $E(y_1)$ is

$$\int f(m|d = 1)\{(\beta_1 + \beta_m m + E(u|m, d = 1))P(d = 1)$$
$$+ (\beta_1 + \beta_m m + E(u|m, d = 0))P(d = 0)\}dm$$
$$= \int f(m|d = 1)\{\beta_1 + \beta_m m + E(u|d = 1)P(d = 1)$$
$$+ E(u|d = 0)P(d = 0)\}dm$$
$$= \int f(m|d = 1)(\beta_1 + \beta_m m)dm$$
$$= \beta_1 + \beta_m E(m|d = 1) = \beta_1 + \beta_m(\gamma_1 + \gamma_d).$$

The first equality results from (u, ε) II e yielding $E(u|m, d) = E(u|d)$ and the last equality uses $m_i = \gamma_1 + \gamma_d d_i + e_i$ and ε II e yielding $E(e|d) = E(e) = 0$. Doing analogously, we get

$$E(y_0) = \beta_1 + \beta_m\gamma_1.$$

Thus, $E(y_1 - y_0) = \beta_m\gamma_d$ is identified.

In the front-door adjustment, the outer parts $f(m|d = 1)$ and $f(m|d = 0)$ are for the effect of d on m whereas the inner part

$$E(y|d = 1, m)P(d = 1) + E(y|d = 0, m)P(d = 0)$$

is the *back-door adjustment* for the effect on m on y. To understand the latter better, consider the effect of ζ on y with x controlled for under selection-on-observables: first, we identify the conditional mean

$$E(y|x, \zeta = 1) = E(y_1|x, \zeta = 1) = E(y_1|x),$$

and then remove x with

$$\int E(y|x, \zeta = 1)f(x)dx = E(y_1).$$

On the left-hand side, $\zeta = 1$ is fixed and integration is over x. In the back-door adjustment, m is fixed and the integration is over d, showing that the back-door adjustment is for the effect of m on y.

In the above linear-model, front-door adjustment needs the two critical conditions (now putting x back in)

$$E(u|x,m,d) = E(u|x,d) \quad \text{and} \quad E(e|x,d) = E(e|x) = 0$$

which are satisfied when $(u, \varepsilon) \amalg e|x$. In observational studies, these conditions may be restrictive. No application of front-door adjustment seems to have appeared in econometrics.

To show an example where front-door adjustment is applicable, suppose that ε is ability, d is job-training and y is finding a job or not. Assume that people with high ability are more likely to take the job training and also to find a job more easily. Suppose that m is the certificate of the training conferred if the trainee attends the training sessions well, that m affects y positively, that job training has only the 'sheepskin' effect, and that e is related only to the weather. In this scenario, $(u, \varepsilon) \amalg e$ is plausible.

7

Multiple and dynamic treatments*

Treatments can be more than binary. This chapter generalizes binary treatments into multiple treatments, which can occur at a given time, if there are many comparable treatments. Multiple treatments can occur over time as well as at a given point in time. This aspect leads to dynamic treatment effect, which is an important and still evolving area of research. When a binary treatment is given consecutively over time, its duration can be handled as a single 'cross-section' cardinal treatment if the covariates are time-constant. Otherwise, if some covariates are time-variant, a 'hazard-based' causal framework may be used. The most difficult case in dynamic-treatment effect arises when interim responses are controlled for that are affected by the earlier treatments and affect the future treatments. A 'G algorithm' is introduced for this case.

7.1 Multiple treatments

Binary treatments are simple to handle, but in real life, there are plenty of examples of more than binary treatments:

- unemployment treatments: classroom-type teaching, simple assistance in job-search (such as helping CV-writing and interviewing), subsidy to employers, and no treatment.
- disease treatments: a surgery, a drug, and no treatment.
- tax effects on expenditure on durable goods: five levels of tax rates including zero.

171

In the first, there are four *unordered* (i.e., categorical or multinomial) treatments. In the second, there are three *ordered* treatments (no treatment, drug, and surgery) if we know *a priori* that the surgery is the stronger treatment than the drug. In the third, there are five *cardinal* treatments. In this section, we examine multiple treatments. Since multinomial treatment is the most general, we discuss mainly this treatment and then point out what can be done additionally for ordinal or cardinal treatments.

7.1.1 Parameters of interest

Suppose there are $J + 1$ mutually exclusive treatments $0, 1, \ldots, J$. The treatments may be cardinal, ordinal, or multinomial. Define

$$d_{ji} = 1 \quad \text{if subject } i \text{ gets treatment } j, \text{ and } 0 \text{ otherwise,}$$

where only one of d_{ji}, $j = 0, 1, \ldots, J$, is one and all the other treatment dummies are zero. Thus

$$\sum_{j=0}^{J} d_{ji} = 1 \quad \text{for all } i.$$

Let the observed treatment be

$$d_i = 1 \cdot d_{1i} +, \ldots, + J \cdot d_{Ji}.$$

Let the potential response of subject i with treatment j be y_{ji}. For subject i, the following variables are *considered*:

$$x_i, d_{ji}, y_{ji}, \qquad j = 0, 1, \ldots, J,$$

But what is *observed* is

$$x_i, d_{ji}, d_{ji}y_{ji}, \qquad j = 0, 1, \ldots, J,$$

where the product $d_{ji}y_{ji}$ means that y_{ji} is observed only when $d_{ji} = 1$. It does not mean that $d_{ji}y_{ji}$ is taken as the response variable. The observed response y_i can be written as

$$y_i = \sum_{j=0}^{J} d_{ji}y_{ji}$$

including $y_i = (1 - d_i)y_{0i} + d_i y_{1i}$ as a special case with $J = 1$, $d_i = d_{1i}$ and $1 - d_i = d_{0i}$.

Rewrite y_{ji} as

$$y_{ji} = \mu_j + u_{ji} \quad \text{where } \mu_j \equiv E(y_{ji}) \quad (\Longleftrightarrow E(u_{ji}) = 0)$$

$$\Longrightarrow y_i = \sum_{j=0}^{J} d_{ji}\mu_j + \sum_{j=0}^{J} d_{ji}u_{ji}.$$

If we replace μ_j with $\mu_{ji} \equiv x'_{ji}\beta_j$, then $y_{ji} = x'_{ji}\beta_j + u_{ji}$ and

$$y_i = \sum_{j=0}^{J} d_{ji}x'_{ji}\beta_j + \sum_{j=0}^{J} d_{ji}u_{ji}$$

which is a linear model where the parameters have causal meaning. For example, with $x_{ji} = x_i \; \forall j$,

$$E(\mu_{ji} - \mu_{0i}) = E(x')(\beta_j - \beta_0).$$

Turning back to $y_{ji} = \mu_j + u_{ji}$, multiple treatments raise the issue of what are the parameters of interest. Hsu (1996) lists a number of possibilities:

1. Pair-wise comparisons: $\mu_m - \mu_j \; \forall j \neq m$.
2. Comparisons with the control: $\mu_j - \mu_0 \; \forall j$ when treatment 0 is the control.
3. Comparisons with the best: $\mu_j - \max_{m \neq j} \mu_m$.
4. Contrasts: $\sum_j a_j \mu_j$ subject to $\sum_j a_j = 0$ (e.g., $\mu_3 - 0.5\mu_2 - 0.5\mu_1$).

Among these, we will focus on *comparisons with the control*, assuming that treatment 0 is the control (standard or base). If the treatment is ordinal, then $\mu_j - \mu_0$, $j = 0, 1, \ldots, J$, can be viewed as a 'dose-response' showing the varying effect as the treatment level changes. Furthermore, if the treatment is cardinal, then we can say how much a higher treatment results in a higher (or lower) effect.

Even when we focus on comparisons with the control, there still remains the difficulty of multiple comparisons, as there is, in general, no optimal way for making inferences. For instance, if we want to construct a $(1 - \alpha)100\%$ confidence region jointly for $\mu_1 - \mu_0$ and $\mu_2 - \mu_0$ with $\bar{y}_1 - \bar{y}_0$ and $\bar{y}_2 - \bar{y}_0$, then there are many ways to do this because there are many different τ_{1N} and τ_{2N} satisfying

$$P(\mu_1 - \mu_0 \in \bar{y}_1 - \bar{y}_0 \pm \tau_{1N}, \; \mu_2 - \mu_0 \in \bar{y}_2 - \bar{y}_0 \pm \tau_{2N}) \geq 1 - \alpha.$$

Here, we are using a rectangle on the plane for $\mu_1 - \mu_0$ and $\mu_2 - \mu_0$, but other figures (a circle or ellipse) can be used as well. See Hsu (1996) for more detail on multiple comparisons.

If we consider subpopulations, then more treatment effects can be thought of:

marginal and x-conditional effect: $\tau_{j0} \equiv E(y_j - y_0),\ \tau_{j0}(x) \equiv E(y_j - y_0|x)$,

effect on the 'compared': $\tau_{j0}(j,0) \equiv E(y_j - y_0|d = j, 0)$,

effect on the treated: $\tau_{j0}(j) \equiv E(y_j - y_0|d = j)$.

It goes without saying that many more treatment effects are conceivable as well; e.g.,

$$\tau_{j0}(x, j, 0) \equiv E(y_j - y_0|x, d = j, 0).$$

The effect on the compared $\tau_{j0}(j, 0)$ can be written as a weighted average of $\tau_{j0}(j)$ and $\tau_{j0}(0)$ (Lechner (2001)):

$$\begin{aligned}
\tau_{j0}(j,0) &= E\{(y_j - y_0)(d_j + d_0)|d_j = 1 \text{ or } d_0 = 1\}\\
&= E\{(y_j - y_0)d_j|d_j = 1 \text{ or } d_0 = 1\} + E\{(y_j - y_0)d_0|d_j = 1 \text{ or } d_0 = 1\}\\
&= E(y_j - y_0|d_j = 1)P(d_j = 1|d = j, 0)\\
&\quad + E(y_j - y_0|d_0 = 1)P(d_0 = 1|d = j, 0)\\
&= \tau_{j0}(j)\frac{P(d = j)}{P(d = j) + P(d = 0)} + \tau_{j0}(0)\frac{P(d = 0)}{P(d = j) + P(d = 0)}.
\end{aligned}$$

Hence, $\tau_{j0}(j, 0)$ is identified once $\tau_{j0}(j)$ and $\tau_{j0}(0)$ are identified. Also

$$\tau_{j0} = E(y_j - y_0) = \sum_j E(y_j - y_0|d = m)P(d = m) = \sum_j \tau_{j0}(m)P(d = m):$$

τ_{j0} can be identified once $\tau_{j0}(m)\ \forall m$ are identified. Thus one may 'declare' $\tau_{j0}(m)$, $m = 0, \ldots, J$, as the main parameters of interest in comparison with the control.

7.1.2   Balancing score and propensity score matching

Assume a weak selection-on-observables that

$$y_j \perp (d = j)|x \iff y_j \perp d_j|x.$$

This can be strengthened to

$$(y_0, \ldots, y_J) \amalg d|x \iff (y_0, \ldots, y_J) \amalg (d_1, \ldots, d_J)|x$$

which is stronger than the preceding orthogonality in three aspects: all potential responses appear jointly, all treatment dummies (except d_0) appear jointly, and $\amalg$ is assumed instead of $\perp$. Clearly, there are many intermediate versions between the weak and strong versions.

Identifying $\tau_{j0}(m)$ with matching is straightforward under the strong version of selection-on-observables: with ∂x used for integrals instead of dx to prevent confusion,

$$
\begin{aligned}
E(y|x, d &= j) = E(y_j|x) = E(y_j|x, d = m), \\
& E(y|x, d = 0) = E(y_0|x) = E(y_0|x, d = m) \\
\Longrightarrow & \int \{ E(y|x, d = j) - E(y|x, d = 0) \} F(\partial x|d = m) \\
= & \int \{ E(y_j|x, d = m) - E(y_0|x, d = m) \} F(\partial x|d = m) \\
= & \ E(y_j - y_0|d = m)
\end{aligned}
$$

where $F(x|d = m)$ is the conditional distribution for $x|d = m$. Note that we do not need the full force of the selection-on-observables, for we used only

$$
y_j \text{ II } (d_j, d_m)| \ x \quad \text{and} \quad y_0 \text{ II } (d_0, d_m)|x.
$$

As is well known, the above matching can have a dimension problem, for which propensity score matching provides an answer. For this, suppose

$$
0 < \pi_j(x) \equiv P(d = j|x) < 1 \quad \text{for all } j, x.
$$

Take $E(\cdot|\pi_j(x))$ on $\pi_j(x) = E(d_j|x)$ to get

$$
\pi_j(x) = E(d_j|\pi_j(x));
$$

note also $\pi_0(x) = 1 - \sum_{j=1}^{J} \pi_j(x)$. Define

$$
\pi(x) \equiv (\pi_1(x), \ldots, \pi_J(x))'.
$$

Doing as we did for binary treatments, for any $t \in R$, it holds that

$$
P\{x \le t|d = j, \pi_j(x)\} = P\{x \le t|\pi_j(x)\}.
$$

From this,

$$
P\{x \le t|d, \pi(x)\} = \sum_{j=0}^{J} P\{x \le t|d = j, \pi(x)\} d_j
$$

$$
= \sum_{j=0}^{J} P\{x \le t|\pi(x)\} d_j = P\{x \le t|\pi(x)\} \sum_{j=0}^{J} d_j = P\{x \le t|\pi(x)\} :
$$

given $\pi(x)$, the distribution of x is the same across all groups; $\pi(x)$ is a balancing score.

If we condition on two groups j and 0, then we have $d_j + d_0 = 1$, and defining

$$\pi_{j|j0} \equiv \frac{\pi_j(x)}{\pi_j(x) + \pi_0(x)},$$

we get

$$P\{x \le t | d, d_j + d_0 = 1, \pi_{j|j0}(x)\} = P\{x \le t | d_j + d_0 = 1, \pi_{j|j0}(x)\}.$$

For the sub-population $d = j, 0$ (i.e., $d_j + d_1 = 1$), $\pi_{j|j0}(x)$ is a balancing score. Turning to propensity score matching, we have, as in binary treatments,

$$y_j \perp d_j | x \implies y_j \perp d_j | \pi_j(x).$$

From this,

$$E\{y | \pi_j(x), d = j\} - E\{y | \pi_0(x), d = 0\} = E\{y_j | \pi_j(x), d = j\} - E\{y_0 | \pi_0(x), d = 0\}$$
$$= E\{y_j | \pi_j(x)\} - E\{y_0 | \pi_0(x)\}.$$

Here, $\pi_j(x)$ and $\pi_0(x)$ are set at the same value, say,

$$\pi_j(x) = a = \pi_0(x).$$

However this matching does not make sense, because the conditioning sets are different. Below, we will show four ways of avoiding this problem.

The first is conditioning on $d_j + d_0 = 1$ to use only $\pi_{j|j0}$ for propensity score matching:

$$E\{y | \pi_{j|j0}(x), d = j, d_j + d_0 = 1\} - E\{y | \pi_{j|j0}(x), d = 0, d_j + d_0 = 1\}$$
$$= E\{y_j - y_0 | \pi_{j|j0}(x), d_j + d_0 = 1\}.$$

The disadvantage of this approach is that only the effect on the subpopulation $d_j + d_0 = 1$ is identified.

The second is two-dimensional propensity score matching:

$$E\{y | \pi_0(x) = a, \pi_j(x) = b, \ d = j\} - E\{y | \pi_0(x) = a, \pi_j(x) = b, \ d = 0\}$$
$$= E\{y_j | \pi_0(x) = a, \pi_j(x) = b\} - E\{y_0 | \pi_0(x) = a, \pi_j(x) = b\},$$

where the conditioning sets are now the same, but the disadvantage is, however, a two-dimensional conditioning instead of one.

The third (Imbens (2000)) is to integrate out the different propensity scores:

$$\int E\{y | \pi_j(x) = a, d = j\} f_{\pi_j(x)}(a) \partial a - \int E\{y | \pi_0(x) = a, d = 0\} f_{\pi_0(x)}(a) \partial a = \tau_{j0},$$

where $f_{\pi_j(x)}$ denotes the population density of $\pi_j(x)$. Here, only τ_{j0} can be identified.

The fourth is weighting: since $d_j y = d_j y_j$,

$$E\left(\frac{d_j y}{\pi_j(x)}\right) = E\left\{E\left(\frac{d_j y_j}{\pi_j(x)}\middle| x\right)\right\} = E\{\pi_j(x)^{-1}E(d_j|x)E(y_j|x)\} = E(y_j)$$

$$\implies E\left(\frac{d_j y}{\pi_j(x)}\right) - E\left(\frac{d_0 y}{\pi_0(x)}\right) = E(y_j - y_0) = \tau_{j0}.$$

A disadvantage is, as already noted, the instability of the weighting estimators.

Suppose the treatments are ordinal and we want to examine $\mu_j - \mu_0$, $j = 1, \ldots, J$ at the same time. Then the dimension problem of the second approach above becomes severe because we need to condition on J propensity scores. Lee (2004) shows a way to reduce the dimension to one. Suppose a 'single index' assumption holds that, for some parameter vector α,

$$E(y_j|d_j, x'\alpha) = E(y_j|x'\alpha) \quad \forall j \qquad \text{under } E(d_j|x'\alpha) > 0.$$

Under the single-index assumption, we just have to condition only on the scalar $x'\alpha$, not on all $\pi_j(x)$'s. To see when the single index assumption may hold, suppose there is a latent variable $d_i^* = x_i'\alpha + \varepsilon_i$ for d_i and

$$d_i = j \quad \text{if } \gamma_j \leq x_i'\alpha + \varepsilon_i < \gamma_{j+1},$$
$$j = 0, \ldots, J, \quad \gamma_0 = -\infty, \ \gamma_1 = 0, \ \gamma_{J+1} = \infty,$$
$$\varepsilon_i \text{ is an error term that is mean-independent of } y_{ji} \text{ given } x_i'\alpha \ \forall j,$$

γ_j's are (un)known thresholds such that $0 < \gamma_2 <, \ldots, < \gamma_J$. In this model, given $x'\alpha$, d becomes mean-independent y_j's.

7.2 Treatment duration effects with time-varying covariates

Suppose a binary treatment is given consecutively over time. Once stopped, the treatment never resumes. If time t is continuous and the treatments are given consecutively over fixed equally-spaced grid points $(0 <)t_1 < t_2 <, \ldots, < t_J$, then J is the treatment frequency. If time t is discrete taking $t_1, t_2, \ldots, t_J$, then J is the treatment duration. For simplicity we will call J 'treatment duration' in both cases. In this section, drawing on Lee and Lee (2004a), we set up a counter-factual causal framework for the treatment-duration effect on a response variable y that is also a duration. For instance, one may be interested in the effect of the duration of a job training on unemployment duration. By fixing $t_1, \ldots, t_J$, we eschew the issue of choosing treatment timings. Also, by ruling out treatments that have been stopped and then resumed, we avoid the multiple treatment-spell issue.

If all covariates are time-constant, then the treatment duration may be taken as a 'cross-section' cardinal treatment, and its effect on the response duration can be analysed in a static framework. The cardinal treatment can be used as a regressor in a regression model, or it may be grouped into a number of treatment levels and matching may be done across the groups as in Behrman *et al.* (2004). Also applicable is 'complete pairing' in Lee (2003c), which allows for censored responses (this is shown in the appendix).

If the time-varying covariates are time-variant only in a limited fashion, then these static approaches can handle the time-variant covariates by creating dummy variables. For example, if a binary covariate w can change at a known time point t_w, then there are four possibilities (0 to 0, 0 to 1, 1 to 0, and 1 to 1) of w variation over time, for which three dummy variables can be created. This will reduce the time-varying covariate w to a number of time-constant covariates. But, if there are many covariates that take many different values and can change at unknown time points, then this way of turning a dynamic problem into a static one no longer works. For these cases, we establish a 'hazard-based' causal framework.

For ease of exposition, suppose time t is continuous. Let $z(t)$ denote the covariate vector at time t including time-variant and time-constant (i.e., time 0) covariates. Also let $Z(t)$ be the history of $z(t)$ up to just before t:

$$Z(t) \equiv \{z(a), 0 \leq a < t\}.$$

'Hazard' $\lambda\{t|Z(t)\}$ of leaving a state (or failing) at time t given $Z(t)$ is defined as

$$\lambda\{t|Z(t)\} \equiv \frac{f\{t|Z(t)\}}{S\{t|Z(t)\}},$$

where $f\{\cdot|Z(t)\}$ is a density function for $y|Z(t)$ and $S\{\cdot|Z(t)\} \equiv P\{y > \cdot|Z(t)\}$.

Ignore $Z(t)$ for a while. Analogously to the static treatment effect framework, consider a binary treatment at a fixed time t_1 and two potential responses at time $t > t_1$: $y_1^{(t_1,t)}$ and $y_0^{(t_1,t)}$, that indicate whether the person is reemployed or not by time t. The mean effect would be then $E(y_1^{(t_1,t)} - y_0^{(t_1,t)})$. But giving a treatment at t_1 makes sense only when the person remains unemployed at t_1. The static treatment effect framework cannot handle this dynamic aspect. Therefore, modify the mean effect to

$$E(y_1^{(t_1,t)} - y_0^{(t_1,t)}|\text{unemployed at } t_1)$$
$$= P(t_1 \leq T_1^{(t_1)} < t|\text{unemployed at } t_1) - P(t_1 \leq T_0^{(t_1)} < t|\text{unemployed at } t_1)$$

where $T_1^{(t_1)}$ and $T_0^{(t_1)}$ denote the potential unemployment duration with and without treatment at t_1, respectively. The potential durations are indexed not just by the treatment or not (in the subscript), but also by the timing of the treatment (in the superscript). $T_1^{(t_1)}$ and $T_0^{(t_1)}$ are not defined if they are shorter than t_1, but this is inconsequential for the above display owing to the condition of being unemployed at t_1 $\iff$ $T_1^{(t_1)}, T_0^{(t_1)} \geq t_1$. Now, to avoid the arbitrariness of t, let t approach t_1 to get

$$\lim_{t \to t_1} E(y_1^{(t_1,t)} - y_0^{(t_1,t)} | \text{unemployed at } t_1) = \lambda_1(t_1) - \lambda_0(t_1)$$

where $\lambda_0(t_1)$ and $\lambda_1(t_1)$ denote the (potential) hazard due to the treatment 0 and 1 at t_1, respectively. This shows that the treatment effect for duration can be assessed with hazards.

In a job training, usually the training is given repeatedly over time. Given that a training is given at t_1, consider another training at a fixed time t_2. We can assess the effect of additional training at t_2 with

$$\lambda_{11}(t_2) - \lambda_{10}(t_2)$$

where $\lambda_{11}(t_2)$ is the hazard with training at t_1 and t_2 and $\lambda_{10}(t_2)$ is the hazard with training at t_1 and no training at t_2. Defining $\lambda_{00}(t_2)$ as the hazard with no training at t_1 and t_2,

$$\lambda_{11}(t_2) - \lambda_{00}(t_2)$$

shows the effect of cumulative training at t_1 and t_2 relative to no training at t_1 and t_2. Going further,

$$\lambda_{11...1}(t_J) - \lambda_{00...0}(t_J), \qquad \text{with the subscripts being}$$
$$\textit{J-many 1's and 0's respectively,}$$

shows the effect of training at $t_1, \ldots, t_J$ versus no training at all.

Let τ denote the training duration; e.g., $\tau = 2$ means getting treated at t_1 and t_2. For the *hazard effect of treatment duration* τ (the ordering of words here follows that in 'mean effect of treatment d'), the selection-on-observable condition for 'treated hazards' is (now $Z(t)$ is explicitly considered)

$$\lambda_1\{t_1|Z(t_1), \tau = 1\} = \lambda_1\{t_1|Z(t_1)\},$$
$$\lambda_{11}\{t_2|Z(t_2), \tau = 2\} = \lambda_{11}\{t_2|Z(t_2)\}, \ldots,$$
$$\lambda_{11...1}\{t_J|Z(t_J), \tau = J\} = \lambda_{11...1}\{t_J|Z(t_J)\}.$$

To understand this, observe that $\lambda_{11}\{t_2|Z(t_2), \tau = 2\}$ in the second equation can be identified only by those failing over $[t_2, t)$ having received the training at t_1 and t_2:

$$P(t_2 \leq T < t|Z(t_2), \text{ unemployed at } t_2, \tau = 2)$$
$$= P(t_2 \leq T_{11}^{(t_1,t_2)} < t|Z(t_2), \text{ unemployed at } t_2, \tau = 2)$$
$$\to \lambda_{11}\{t_2|Z(t_2), \tau = 2\} \quad \text{as} \quad t \to t_2.$$

The second equation in the above selection-on-observables states that the same hazard should hold for those with $\tau \neq 2$ as well (conditioning on $Z(t_2)$), had they had $\tau = 2$ contrary to the fact. Those with $\tau = 1$ did not get the training at t_2, and those with $\tau = 3$ did not fail over $[t_2, t)$.

To understand the selection-on-observables better, write $\lambda_{11}\{t_2|Z(t_2)\}$ as

$$\lim_{t \to t_2} \sum_{j=0}^{J} P(t_2 \le T_{11}^{(t_1,t_2)} < t|Z(t_2), \text{unemployed at } t_2, \tau = j)$$
$$\times\, P(\tau = j|Z(t_2), \text{unemployed at } t_2).$$

The selection-on-observables applies to the first term. For those with $\tau = 0$ or 1, had the training been continued up to t_2 while remaining unemployed, then their $\lambda_{11}\{t_2|\ldots\}$ should be the same as the $\lambda_{11}\{t_2|\ldots\}$ of those with $\tau = 2$. For those $\tau = 3$ or higher, had the training been stopped after t_2, their $\lambda_{11}\{t_2|\ldots\}$ should be the same as the $\lambda_{11}\{t_2|\ldots\}$ of those with $\tau = 2$. Note that $P(\tau = j|Z(t_2), \text{unemployed at } t_2)$ is allowed to differ across j. Imagine a person with $\tau = 1$ because he found a job right after t_1. If the person found a job because of higher ability, then $\lambda_{11}\{t_2|\ldots\}$ would be still higher even if the subject had remained unemployed up to t_2, violating the selection-on-observables. An analogous (but opposite) scenario holds for a person with $\tau = 3$ and low ability.

Under the selection-on-observables, $\lambda_1\{t_1|Z(t_1)\}, \ldots, \lambda_{11\ldots1}\{t_J|Z(t_J)\}$ are identified. But for hazard effects, we also need '(partly) untreated hazards' such as $\lambda_0\{t_1|Z(t_1)\}$, $\lambda_{00}\{t_2|Z(t_2)\}$, $\lambda_{00\ldots0}\{t_J|Z(t_J)\}$, or $\lambda_{10}\{t_2|Z(t_2)\}$. For these, considering which group they can be identified with, the selection-on-observable conditions are

$$\lambda_0\{t_1|Z(t_1), \tau = 0\} = \lambda_0\{t_1|Z(t_1)\},$$
$$\lambda_{00}\{t_2|Z(t_2), \tau = 0\} = \lambda_{00}\{t_2|Z(t_2)\}, \ldots,$$
$$\lambda_{00\ldots0}\{t_J|Z(t_J), \tau = 0\} = \lambda_{00\ldots0}\{t_J|Z(t_J)\},$$
$$\lambda_{10}\{t_2|Z(t_2), \tau = 1\} = \lambda_{10}\{t_2|Z(t_2)\}.$$

The selection-on-observables for both treated and untreated hazards can be written succinctly as

$$\lambda_{11\ldots100\ldots0}\{t_{\dim(\tau)}|Z(t_{\dim(\tau)}), \tau = \text{number of 1's in } \lambda \text{ subscript}\}$$
$$= \lambda_{11\ldots100\ldots0}\{t_{\dim(\tau)}|Z(t_{\dim(\tau)})\}.$$

In the static counter-factual causality, we use $E(y|x, d = 1) - E(y|x, d = 0)$ to identify the conditional mean effect $E(y_1 - y_0|x)$. If the dimension of x is large, then the usual regression analysis may be used which embodies parametric assumptions. In duration analysis, 'proportional hazard' models with

$$\lambda\{t|Z(t)\} = \lambda_o(t) \cdot \psi\{Z(t), \beta\}$$

is a popular way of imposing parametric assumptions where $\lambda_o(t)$ is the 'base-line hazard' and the role of $\psi\{Z(t), \beta\}$ is to adjust $\lambda_o(t)$ proportionately. Among the proportional hazard models, the 'partial likelihood estimator' of Cox (1972) with

$$\psi\{Z(t), \beta\} = \exp\{z(t)'\beta\}$$

is particularly popular. Note that using only $z(t)$ in $\exp\{z(t)'\beta\}$ is not really a restriction (e.g., if $z(t-1)$ matters for $\psi\{t, Z(t)\}$, then $z(t)$ can be augmented with $s(t) \equiv z(t-1)$).

7.3 Dynamic treatment effects with interim outcomes

Suppose we have two periods with binary treatments d_1 and d_2 and a response variable y observed after period 2. Denoting the observed covariates as $x = (x_1', x_2')'$, where x_1 and x_2 are for period 1 and 2, assessing the effects of the treatment 'profile',

$$d \equiv (d_1, d_2)'$$

can be done as a special case of multiple treatments which were examined in Section 7.1, and there is no problem generalizing this into three or more periods in principle. However when multiple treatments are given over time, some later treatments are often adjusted depending on the progress measured by interim outcomes or related 'prognosis' variables. How to define the treatment effect of interest and how to identify it is not an easy task in this case, to say the least.

For example, consider a supposedly harmless vitamin treatment over time. There is no problem in randomly assigning the treatment each period, which requires no need to monitor any interim progress. The response variable is measured simply at the end. Now consider a costly treatment (with side-effects) for some illness. It may not be a good idea to continue giving the treatment to those that show a large improvement. In this case, even if we randomize at period 2, we would have to randomize only for those showing not much improvement. That is, it would be necessary to adjust d_2 depending on the interim response. This poses difficulty in finding the treatment profile effect, because d_2 is affected by the interim response and then affects the final response y.

In this section, first, failure of the usual regression analysis in dealing with this problem is shown using simple two-period linear models and, as usual, instruments provide a solution if they are available. Second, 'G algorithm' which does not need any instrument is introduced for two-period cases. G algorithm requires a dynamic version of selection-on-observables where the observables include the interim progress variable(s). Third, G algorithm is generalized for three periods and beyond.

7.3.1 Motivation with two-period linear models

Define the potential responses

y_{jk}: potential response when $d_1 = j$ and $d_2 = k$ are exogenously set,
$j, k = 0, 1$.

Here 'exogenously set' means $y_{jk} \amalg (d_1, d_2)$ or its weaker version $E(y_{jk}|d_1, d_2) = E(y_{jk})$. Suppose we want to know $E(y_{11} - y_{00})$—all treatments versus no treatment at all—but the observed data is d_1 that is self-selected initially, d_2 that is self-selected after observing an interim response m_2 (m_2 can be a lagged y or a variable closely related to y), and y. The situation is shown in the diagram that omits covariates x:

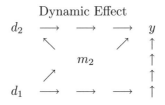

In this diagram, m_2 is a common factor for d_2 and y, and m_2 should be controlled for. However if m_2 is controlled for, then the indirect effect of d_1 on y through m_2 is not accounted for. The subscript 2 in m_2 is not necessary, but we use it here to be coherent with the generalization for more than two periods, which will be discussed in Subsection 7.3.3.

To understand the situation better, define m_{02} and m_{12} as the potential m-variables corresponding to $d_1 = 0$ and $d_1 = 1$, respectively, and consider a latent linear model

$$d_{1i} = \alpha_{11} + x_i'\alpha_{1x} + \varepsilon_{1i}, \quad E(\varepsilon_1|x) = 0,$$
$$m_{02i} = \gamma_1 + x_i'\gamma_x + e_i, \quad m_{12i} = \gamma_1 + \gamma_{d1} + x_i'\gamma_x + e_i \quad E(e|x) = 0,$$
$$d_{02i} = \alpha_{21} + x_i'\alpha_{2x} + \alpha_{2m}m_{02i} + \varepsilon_{2i},$$
$$d_{12i} = \alpha_{21} + x_i'\alpha_{2x} + \alpha_{2m}m_{12i} + \varepsilon_{2i}, \quad E(\varepsilon_2|x) = 0,$$

where d_{02} is the latent treatment at period 2 when $d_0 = 0$, d_{12} is the latent treatment at period 2 when $d_0 = 1$, and

y_{00} SF: $y_{00i} = \beta_1 + \beta_m m_{02i} + x_i'\beta_x + u_i,$
y_{10} SF: $y_{10i} = \beta_1 + \beta_{d1} + \beta_m m_{12i} + x_i'\beta_x + u_i,$
y_{01} SF: $y_{01i} = \beta_1 + \beta_{d2} + \beta_m m_{02i} + x_i'\beta_x + u_i,$
y_{11} SF: $y_{11i} = \beta_1 + \beta_{d1} + \beta_{d2} + \beta_m m_{12i} + x_i'\beta_x + u_i, \quad E(u|x) = 0.$

One has to imagine each individual with

$$x, \quad d_1, \quad m_{02}, m_{12}, \quad d_{02}, d_{12}, \quad y_{00}, y_{10}, y_{01}, y_{11},$$

of which only some are observed.

We allow e to be related to u given x, which is necessary to allow m_2 to be a lagged y. Assume

$$(u, e) \amalg \varepsilon_1|x \quad \text{and} \quad u \amalg \varepsilon_2|(x, \varepsilon_1, e);$$

these are needed for 'G algorithm' to appear in the next subsection. Although the second condition allows u to be related to ε_2 through ε_1 and e (and x), in fact u can be related to ε_2 only through e, because the first condition specifies that u be unrelated to ε_1 (given x). Applying the rule

$$(a, b) \amalg c \iff a \amalg c | b \quad \text{and} \quad b \amalg c,$$

the condition $(u, e) \amalg \varepsilon_1 | x$ can be written as $u \amalg \varepsilon_1 | (e, x)$ and $e \amalg \varepsilon_1 | x$. In essence, given x, the only dependence among the error terms $\varepsilon_1, e, \varepsilon_2, u$ is the common factor e affecting both ε_2 and u.

Because $\varepsilon_1, \varepsilon_2, e, u$ are the error terms in d_1, d_2, m_{j2}, y_{jk}, respectively, the above two conditions can be written as

$$(y_{jk}, m_{j2}) \amalg (d_1 = j) | x \quad \text{and} \quad y_{jk} \amalg (d_2 = k) | (x, d_1 = j, m_{j2}) \qquad \forall j, k = 0, 1.$$

These two conditions can be further written as

$$y_{jk} \amalg (d_1 = j) | (m_{j2}, x), \qquad m_{j2} \amalg (d_1 = j) | x,$$
$$\text{and} \quad y_{jk} \amalg (d_2 = k) | (x, d_1 = j, m_{j2}) \qquad \forall j, k = 0, 1.$$

The first and third conditions are selection-on-observables, for they state the independence of the treatments from the potential response given the observables including m_{j2}.

We can see that

$$E(m_{12} - m_{02} | x) = \gamma_{d1}.$$

Also substitute the m_{02} equation into the y_{00} equation and the m_{12} equation to the y_{11} equation to get

$$
\begin{aligned}
y_{00} &= \beta_1 + \beta_m (\gamma_1 + x' \gamma_x + e) + x' \beta_x + u \\
&= \beta_1 + \beta_m \gamma_1 + x' \gamma_x \beta_m + x' \beta_x + \beta_m e + u, \\
y_{11} &= \beta_1 + \beta_{d1} + \beta_{d2} + \beta_m (\gamma_1 + \gamma_{d1} + x' \gamma_x + e) + x' \beta_x + u \\
&= \beta_1 + \beta_{d1} + \beta_{d2} + \beta_m \gamma_1 + \beta_m \gamma_{d1} + x' \gamma_x \beta_m + x' \beta_x + \beta_m e + u.
\end{aligned}
$$

From these, we get

$$E(y_{11} - y_{00} | x) = \beta_{d1} + \beta_m \gamma_{d1} + \beta_{d2},$$

which is the total effect of d_1 and d_2 on y consisting of the direct effect β_{d1} of d_1, indirect effect $\beta_m \gamma_{d1}$ through m_2 of d_1, and the direct effect β_{d2} of d_2.
Doing analogously,

$$
\begin{aligned}
y_{10} &= \beta_1 + \beta_{d1} + \beta_m (\gamma_1 + \gamma_{d1} + x' \gamma_x + e) + x' \beta_x + u \\
&= \beta_1 + \beta_{d1} + \beta_m \gamma_1 + \beta_m \gamma_{d1} + x' \gamma_x \beta_m + x' \beta_x + \beta_m e + u, \\
y_{01} &= \beta_1 + \beta_{d2} + \beta_m (\gamma_1 + x' \gamma_x + e) + x' \beta_x + u \\
&= \beta_1 + \beta_{d2} + \beta_m \gamma_1 + x' \gamma_x \beta_m + x' \beta_x + \beta_m e + u.
\end{aligned}
$$

Observe

$$E(y_{10} - y_{00}|x) = \beta_{d1} + \beta_m \gamma_{d1} \quad \text{and} \quad E(y_{11} - y_{10}|x) = \beta_{d2} = E(y_{01} - y_{00}|x).$$

With these, $E(y_{11} - y_{00}|x)$ can be rewritten as

$$E(y_{11} - y_{00}|x) = \underbrace{E(y_{10} - y_{00}|x)}_{\text{effect of } d_1 \text{ on } y} + \underbrace{E(y_{11} - y_{10}|x)}_{\text{remaining effect}}$$

$$= \underbrace{E(y_{10} - y_{00}|x)}_{\text{effect of } d_1 \text{ on } y} + \underbrace{E(y_{01} - y_{00}|x)}_{\text{effect of } d_2 \text{ on } y}.$$

Observe

$$E(y_{11}|m_{12} = m, x) - E(y_{00}|m_{02} = m, x) = \beta_{d1} + \beta_{d2}.$$

Compared with $E(y_{11} - y_{00}|x)$, the indirect effect $\beta_m \gamma_{d1}$ of d_1 on y is lost in this mean difference controlling for m as well as x.

In the remainder of this subsection, which the reader may skip, the usual conditional mean difference approach (thus the regression approach as well) is shown to fail to identify $E(y_{11} - y_{00}|x)$. A completely different approach is needed as in the following subsection. When we showed that treatment effect analysis can be done with the usual regression analysis for a static 'one-shot' treatment, the question 'why one needs the treatment effect approach after all' might have occurred. One answer given already is that treatment effect analysis makes it possible to interpret the regression parameters as causal parameters. But this is not all: by showing cases which regression analysis cannot handle, dynamic treatment effect analysis, as shown in the next subsection, demonstrates a *raison-d'être* for the counter-factual treatment effect approach.

From the latent model, we get the model for the observed variables d_1, d_2, m_2, y:

$$d_1 = \alpha_{11} + x'\alpha_{1x} + \varepsilon_1,$$
$$m_2 = (1 - d_1)m_{02} + d_1 m_{12} = \gamma_1 + \gamma_{d1}d_1 + x'\gamma_x + e$$
$$\{= \gamma_1 + \gamma_{d1}(\alpha_{11} + x'\alpha_{1x} + \varepsilon_1) + x'\gamma_x + e\},$$
$$d_2 = (1 - d_1)d_{02} + d_1 d_{12} = \alpha_{21} + x'\alpha_{2x} + \alpha_{2m}m_2 + \varepsilon_2$$
$$[= \alpha_{21} + x'\alpha_{2x} + \alpha_{2m}(\gamma_1 + \gamma_{d1}\alpha_{11} + x'(\gamma_x + \alpha_{1x}\gamma_{d1}) + \gamma_{d1}\varepsilon_1 + e) + \varepsilon_2],$$
$$y = (1 - d_1)(1 - d_2)y_{00} + d_1(1 - d_2)y_{10} + (1 - d_1)d_2 y_{01} + d_1 d_2 y_{11}$$
$$= \beta_1 + \beta_{d1}d_1 + \beta_{d2}d_2 + \beta_m m_2 + x'\beta_x + u.$$

Substitute the m_2 equation into the y equation to get

'y *RF for* d_1, d_2': $y = \beta_1 + \beta_{d1}d_1 + \beta_{d2}d_2 + \beta_m(\gamma_1 + \gamma_{d1}d_1 + x'\gamma_x + e)$
$$+ x'\beta_x + u$$
$$= \beta_1 + \beta_m \gamma_1 + (\beta_{d1} + \beta_m \gamma_{d1})d_1 + \beta_{d2}d_2 + x'(\beta_x + \beta_m \gamma_x)$$
$$+ \beta_m e + u.$$

Observe

$$\tau_x \equiv E(y|d_1 = 1, d_2 = 1, x) - E(y|d_1 = 0, d_2 = 0, x)$$
$$= \beta_{d1} + \beta_m \gamma_{d1} + \beta_{d2} + E(\beta_m e + u|d = 1, x) - E(\beta_m e + u|d = 0, x).$$

In general, the error term conditional mean difference is not zero because $d = 1$ involves e as well as ε_1 and ε_2 as can be seen from the equations in $[\cdot]$ of the preceding paragraph. Hence,

$$E(y|d_1 = 1, d_2 = 1, x) - E(y|d_1 = 0, d_2 = 0, x) \neq E(y_{11} - y_{00}|x),$$

and thus $E(\tau_x) \neq \beta_{d1} + \beta_m \gamma_{d1} + \beta_{d2}$ in general.

Suppose

$$E(y_{jk}|d_1 = j, d_{j2} = k, m_{j2}, x) = E(y_{jk}|m_{j2}, x),$$

which holds in the linear model because

$$f(u|\varepsilon_1, \varepsilon_2, e, x) = f(u|\varepsilon_1, e, x) \qquad \text{(owing to } u \amalg \varepsilon_2|(x, \varepsilon_1, e))$$
$$= f(u|e, x) \qquad \text{(owing to } u \amalg \varepsilon_1|(e, x)).$$

Then

$$\tau_{mx} \equiv E(y|d_1 = 1, d_2 = 1, m = m_o, x) - E(y|d_1 = 0, d_2 = 0, m = m_o, x)$$
$$= E(y_{11}|m_{12} = m_o, x) - E(y_{00}|m_{02} = m_o, x) = \beta_{d1} + \beta_{d2}.$$

$E(\tau_{mx}) = \beta_{d1} + \beta_{d2}$ consists of the direct effect of d_1 and d_2 on y.

Therefore, the sum of the direct effects are identified using the mean differ-ence controlling for m as well as for x. However the indirect effect of d_1 through m_2 is missed and the mean difference controlling only for x does not identify the desired total effect $\beta_{d1} + \beta_m \gamma_{d1} + \beta_{d2}$. Hence, the conditional mean approach (i.e., the regression approach) fails.

If instruments for d_1 and d_2 are available, then the total effect is identified as the sum of the slopes for d_1 and d_2 in the IVE for the above 'y RF for d_1, d_2'. Differently from the static 'one-shot' treatment case, however, even if d_1 is randomized, d_2 is not because the subpopulation with $d_2 = 1$ is not representative of the population. For instance, if y is the progress of a disease, then $d_2 = 1$ only for patients with poor prognosis based on m_2—a kind of the problem discussed in Ham and Lalonde (1996). If z_1 is an instrument for d_1, then for z_2 to be an instrument for d_2, z_t should be time-variant for a reason related to d_2 yet unrelated to y given x. If z_t is time-constant, d_2 needs a fresh new source for an instrument. Thus, it will not be easy to find instruments for both d_1 and d_2. The next subsection shows what can be done to identify the total effect under a selection-on-observable assumption.

7.3.2   G algorithm under no unobserved confounder

To ense exposition, omit x (by considering the following as conditioned on x). As in Robins (1999), but changing the terminology somewhat, define

interim exogeneity of treatment: $m_{j2} \amalg d_{j2}|(d_1 = j)$ $\qquad \forall j$

outcome exogeneity of treatment: $y_{jk} \amalg d_{j2}|(d_1 = j)$, $y_{jk} \amalg d_1$ $\qquad \forall j, k$

no unobserved confounder (NUC): $y_{jk} \amalg d_{j2}|(d_1 = j, m_{j2})$, $y_{jk} \amalg d_1$ $\qquad \forall j, k.$

Note that these conditions are defined with latent, not observed, variables. NUC is also called 'sequential ignorability' or 'randomness given past'. *Assume NUC for dynamic treatment effects*, which is the key selection-on-observable assumption.

Outcome exogeneity is equivalent to $y_{jk} \amalg (d_{j2}, d_1 = j)$, which means y_{jk} is independent of the whole treatment profile $d = (d_1, d_2)'$, because

$$f(y_{jk}|d_{j2}, d_1 = j) = f(y_{jk}|d_1 = j) \quad \text{owing to } y_{jk} \amalg d_{j2}|(d_1 = j)$$
$$= f(y_{jk}) \quad \text{owing to } y_{jk} \amalg d_1.$$

In this case, $E(y_{jk})$ can be easily identified with $E(y|d_1 = j, d_2 = k)$.

In the linear model of the preceding subsection, interim exogeneity does not hold if e is related to ε_2 given ε_1, which is allowed by the assumptions of the model. Also, outcome exogeneity does not hold because m_{j2} is a common factor for d_{j2} and y_{jk}, which, however, allows NUC. Comparing outcome exogeneity to NUC, outcome exogeneity may be called 'no unobserved and observed confounder' where the observed confounder refers to m_{j2}. As for NUC, examine them in the linear model of the preceding subsection:

$$y_{jk} \amalg d_1 \iff u \amalg \varepsilon_1$$
$$y_{jk} \amalg d_{j2}|(d_1 = j, m_{j2}) \; (\iff u \amalg \varepsilon_2|(d_1 = j, m_{j2})) \; \impliedby u \amalg \varepsilon_2|(\varepsilon_1, e).$$

The first part, which is the outcome exogeneity of d_1 for y_{jk}, holds if ε_1 is unrelated to the error term u in the y_{jk} equation. The second part allows y_{jk} to be related to d_{j2} through m_{j2}.

Interim exogeneity is testable with the given data. *If interim exogeneity holds, then outcome exogeneity holds under NUC.* This follows because NUC means that m_{j2} is the only possible common factor relating y_{jk} to d_{j2} given $d_1 = j$, but interim exogeneity means d_{j2} is independent of m_{j2}. Thus, y_{jk} should be independent of d_{j2} given $d_1 = j$. In this case, as just mentioned, we can identify $E(y_{jk})$ easily. With $E(y_{jk})$, $E(y_{11}) - E(y_{00})$ can be identified and, if desired, $E(y_{10}) - E(y_{00})$ and $E(y_{01}) - E(y_{00})$ can be identified as well. What if interim exogeneity is rejected while NUC is still assumed? An answer is provided in the following.

The 'G algorithm' under NUC by Robins is

$$E(y_{jk}) = \int E(y|d_1 = j, d_2 = k, m_2) f(m_2|d_1 = j) \partial m_2, \qquad j, k = 0, 1,$$

where ∂ is used instead of d for integration to prevent confusion, and the right-hand side is identified (see Robins (1998, 1999) for a review and the original references). The equality holds because the right-hand side is

$$\int E(y_{jk}|d_1 = j, d_{j2} = k, \ m_{j2}) f(m_{j2}|d_1 = j) \partial m_{j2}$$

$$= \int E(y_{jk}|d_1 = j, \ m_{j2}) f(m_{j2}|d_1 = j) \partial m_{j2}$$

$$(\text{due to } y_{jk} \amalg d_{j2}|(d_1 = j, m_{j2}))$$

$$= E(y_{jk}|d_1 = j) = E(y_{jk}) \quad (m_2 \text{ integrated out and } y_{jk} \amalg d_1 \text{ used}).$$

If m_2 is binary, then the G algorithm becomes just

$$E(y_{jk}) = E(y|d_1 = j, d_2 = k, \ m_2 = 0) P(m_2 = 0|d_1 = j)$$
$$+ E(y|d_1 = j, d_2 = k, \ m_2 = 1) P(m_2 = 1|d_1 = j).$$

If d_1 is non-existent, then NUC becomes $y_k \amalg d_2|m_2$ where

$$
\begin{array}{ccc}
d_2 & \longrightarrow & y \\
\uparrow & \nearrow & \\
m_2 & &
\end{array}
$$

This is nothing but the static common factor model with m_2 as an observed confounder that has to be controlled for. The G algorithm gets reduced to

$$E(y_k) = \int E(y|d_2 = k, m_2) f(m_2) \partial m_2 = \int E(y_k|m_2) f(m_2) \partial m_2,$$

which is the usual static way of identifying $E(y_k)$ under selection-on-observable m_2. This shows that the *G algorithm is a dynamic generalization of the static covariate-conditioning approach*.

To appreciate the G algorithm better, recall $E(y_{11} - y_{00}|x) = \beta_{d1} + \beta_m \gamma_{d1} + \beta_{d2}$ for the linear model in the previous subsection. To see that the G algorithm yields this, observe

$$\int E(y|d_1 = 1, d_2 = 1, m_2) f(m_2|d_1 = 1) \partial m_2$$

$$- \int E(y|d_1 = 0, d_2 = 0, m_2) f(m_2|d_1 = 0) \partial m_2$$

$$= \int E(y_{11}|d_1 = 1, d_{12} = 1, m_{12}) f(m_{12}|d_1 = 1) \partial m_{12}$$

$$-\int E(y_{00}|d_1 = 0, d_{02} = 0, m_{02})f(m_{02}|d_1 = 0)\partial m_{02}$$

$$= \int (\beta_1 + \beta_{d1} + \beta_{d2} + \beta_m m_{12})f(m_{12}|d_1 = 1)\partial m_{12}$$

$$-\int (\beta_1 + \beta_m m_{02})f(m_{02}|d_1 = 0)\partial m_{02}$$

$$= \beta_{d1} + \beta_{d2} + \beta_m\{E(m_{12}|d_1 = 1) - E(m_{02}|d_1 = 0)\}$$

$$= \beta_{d1} + \beta_{d2} + \beta_m\gamma_{d1}, \qquad \text{(thanks to } e \amalg \varepsilon_1|x).$$

Although the regression (or mean-difference) approach failed to deliver the total effect $\beta_{d1} + \beta_{d2} + \beta_m\gamma_{d1}$, the G algorithm does deliver the total effect.

7.3.3   G algorithm for three or more periods

In the previous subsection, the G algorithm was introduced for two periods. This subsection generalizes the G algorithm for three or more periods. Then some remarks on implementation for dynamic treatment effects are made.

Suppose there is one more period and we thus have d_1, d_2, d_3 and m_2, m_3 such that

For this, define y_{jkl} analogously to y_{jk} and, for all j, k, l,

interim exo.: $(m_{j2}, m_{jk3}) \amalg d_{jk3}|(d_1 = j, d_{j2} = k),$ $m_{j2} \amalg d_{j2}|(d_1 = j)$

outcome exo.: $y_{jkl} \amalg d_{jk3}|(d_1 = j, d_{j2} = k),$ $y_{jkl} \amalg d_{j2}|(d_1 = j),$ $y_{jkl} \amalg d_1$

NUC: $y_{jkl} \amalg d_{jk3}|(d_1 = j, d_{j2} = k, m_{j2}, m_{jk3}),$

$y_{jkl} \amalg d_{j2}|(d_1 = j, m_{j2}),$ $y_{jkl} \amalg d_1.$

As in the two-period case, outcome exogeneity is equivalent to

$$y_{jkl} \amalg (d_1 = j, d_{j2} = k, d_{jk3}).$$

The G algorithm is

$$
\int\int E(y|d_1 = j, d_2 = k, d_3 = l, m_2, m_3) \cdot f(m_3|m_2, d_1 = j, d_2 = k)
$$
$$
\times f(m_2|d_1 = j)\partial m_3 \partial m_2
$$
$$
= \int\int E(y_{jkl}|d_1 = j, d_{j2} = k, m_{j2}, m_{jk3})
$$
$$
\times f(m_{jk3}|m_{j2}, \; d_1 = j, d_{j2} = k) \cdot f(m_{j2}|d_1 = j)\partial m_{jk3} \partial m_{j2}
$$
$$
= \int E(y_{jkl}|d_1 = j, d_{j2} = k, m_{j2}) \cdot f(m_{j2}|d_1 = j)\partial m_{j2}
$$
$$
(m_{jk3} \text{ integrated out})
$$
$$
= \int E(y_{jkl}|d_1 = j, m_{j2}) \cdot f(m_{j2}|d_1 = j)\partial m_{j2}
$$
$$
(\text{owing to } y_{jkl} \; \text{II} \; d_{j2}|(d_1 = j, m_{j2}))
$$
$$
= E(y_{jkl}|d_1 = j) = E(y_{jkl})
$$
$$
(m_{j2} \text{ integrated out and } y_{jkl} \; \text{II} \; d_1 \text{ used}).
$$

If m_2 and m_3 are binary, then considering the 2×2 cases, the G algorithm to identify $E(y_{jkl})$ is

$$
E(y|d_1 = j, d_2 = k, d_3 = l, \; m_2 = 0, m_3 = 0)
$$
$$
\times P(m_3 = 0|m_2 = 0, d_1 = j, d_2 = k) \cdot P(m_2 = 0|d_1 = j)
$$
$$
+ E(y|d_1 = j, d_2 = k, d_3 = l, \; m_2 = 0, m_3 = 1)
$$
$$
\times P(m_3 = 1|m_2 = 0, d_1 = j, d_2 = k) \cdot P(m_2 = 0|d_1 = j)
$$
$$
+ E(y|d_1 = j, d_2 = k, d_3 = l, \; m_2 = 1, m_3 = 0)
$$
$$
\times P(m_3 = 0|m_2 = 1, d_1 = j, d_2 = k) \cdot P(m_2 = 1|d_1 = j)
$$
$$
+ E(y|d_1 = j, d_2 = k, d_3 = l, \; m_2 = 1, m_3 = 1)
$$
$$
\times P(m_3 = 1|m_2 = 1, d_1 = j, d_2 = k) \cdot P(m_2 = 1|d_1 = j).
$$

Suppose the treatment is an income-enhancing policy and the response is income. Assume that d_1 is given to all poor people in the initial period, but d_2 and d_3 are given only to some poor individuals based on interim incomes. Then the G algorithm can be implemented with panel data: get d_1, d_2, d_3 sequentially from different waves. Getting m_2 and m_3 depends on whether m_t and d_t in the same wave fulfil the condition that m_t is realized before d_t or not. If yes, draw m_t from the same wave, otherwise, draw m_t from a wave between d_{t-1} and d_t. A similar reasoning prevails for y that should be realized after d_3.

More generally than three periods, consider T periods with $d_1, \ldots, d_T$, $m_2, \ldots, m_T$, and $y_{j_1 j_2 \ldots j_T}$ that is defined analogously to y_{jkl}. We have, for all $t = 2, \ldots, T$ and $\forall j_1, \ldots, j_T$,

interim exogeneity:

$$(m_{j_1 2}, \ldots, m_{j_1, \ldots j_{t-1} t}) \text{ II } d_{j_1, \ldots j_{t-1} t} | (d_1 = j_1, \ldots, d_{j_1, \ldots j_{t-2} t-1} = j_{t-1}),$$

outcome exogeneity:

$$y_{j_1 j_2 \ldots j_T} \text{ II } d_{j_1, \ldots j_{t-1} t} | (d_1 = j_1, \ldots, d_{j_1, \ldots j_{t-2} t-1} = j_{t-1}),$$

NUC:

$$y_{j_1 j_2 \ldots j_T} \text{ II } d_{j_1, \ldots j_{t-1} t} | (d_1 = j_1, \ldots, d_{j_1, \ldots j_{t-2} t-1} = j_{t-1}, m_{j_1 2}, \ldots, m_{j_1 \ldots j_{t-1} t}).$$

The G algorithm becomes

$$\int E(y | d_1 = j_1, \ldots, d_T = j_T, \ m_2, \ldots, m_T)$$

$$\times \prod_{t=2}^{T} f(m_t | m_2, \ldots, m_{t-1}, d_1 = j_1, \ldots, d_{t-1} = j_{t-1}) \partial m_t$$

where $f(m_2 | m_2, m_1, \ d_1 = j_1)$ should be construed as $f(m_2 | d_1 = j_1)$.

Implementation of G algorithm in practice is difficult, because (i) the conditional mean function has to be estimated, (ii) the conditional density of m_t must be estimated for $t = 2, \ldots, T$, and (iii) all m_t's have to be integrated out, which requires a $T - 1$ dimensional integration. As can be seen in Robins (1998, 1999) and the references therein, 'marginal structural models' and a 'structural nested models' are also available for dynamic treatment effect. The former is a dynamic generalization of the static weighting estimators that appeared in the preceding chapters, whereas the latter, in its simple version, postulates that counter-factual responses are functions of no-treatment response and covariates.

Despite a number of applications of these methods in the literature, it appears that their practicality and operational characteristics are yet to be known fully. Also, the NUC assumption, which is a selection-on-observable assumption, may not hold in a given problem. The static approaches for hidden bias may be thus generalized for dynamic cases, but it seems premature to discuss them here. Readers interested further in dynamic treatment effect can refer to Gill and Robins (2001), Lok (2001), Murphy (2003), Van der Laan and Robins (2003), and the references therein.

Appendix

Many topics have been left out from the main text, either because they digress or are too technical. This appendix puts together those topics. Also shown here are some lengthy derivations omitted in the main text. Except for Section A.1, kernel nonparametric regression, each section corresponds to each chapter.

A.1 Kernel nonparametric regression

In this section, we review kernel nonparametric regression drawing on Lee (2002) (see, for instance, Härdle (1990) for nonparametrics in general). Two methods related to kernel method are also briefly mentioned near the end of this section. There are many nonparametric methods other than the kernel methods, but for our purpose, we will concentrate on the kernel and related methods.

Assuming that $x_1, \ldots, x_N$ are iid random variables (rv) with density function $f(x)$, consider a $B(N, \pi)$ rv (binomial with N trials and π success probability) where $h > 0$:

$$\sum_{i=1}^{N} 1[|x_i - x_o| < h], \qquad \pi \equiv P(|x_i - x_o| < h) = P(x_o - h < x_i < x_o + h)$$

$$\implies E\left(\sum_{i=1}^{N} 1[|x_i - x_o| < h]\right) = N \cdot \pi,$$

$$V\left(\sum_{i=1}^{N} 1[|x_i - x_o| < h]\right) = N \cdot \pi(1 - \pi).$$

Define a 'histogram' around x_o with the interval size $2h$:

$$\hat{f}_N(x_o) \equiv \left(\frac{1}{N}\right) \sum_{i=1}^{N} (2h)^{-1} 1\left[\frac{|x_i - x_o|}{h} < 1\right]$$

$$= (Nh)^{-1} \sum_{i=1}^{N} 1\left[\frac{|x_i - x_o|}{h} < 1\right] \Big/ 2.$$

Since this is an estimator for $f(x_o)$ without parameterizing $f(x_o)$, say normal or logistic, $\hat{f}_N(x_o)$ is a 'nonparametric estimator' for $f(x_o)$. For instance, if we know that x_i follows $N(\mu, \sigma^2)$, then $f(x)$ can be estimated parametrically with

$$\tilde{f}_N(x) \equiv (s_N \sqrt{2\pi})^{-1} \exp\left\{ -\left(\frac{x - \bar{x}_N}{s_N}\right)^2 \Big/ 2 \right\}, \quad where$$

$$\bar{x}_N \equiv (1/N) \sum_i x_i, \quad s_N^2 \equiv (1/N) \sum_i (x_i - \bar{x}_N)^2.$$

In the following, we show that $\hat{f}_N(x_o)$ is consistent for $f(x_o)$.

Using the mean and variance of $\sum_{i=1}^{N} 1[|x_i - x_o| < h]$, we get

$$E\{\hat{f}_N(x_o)\} = \frac{N\pi}{N2h} = \frac{\pi}{2h}, \qquad V\{\hat{f}_N(x_o)\} = \frac{\pi(1-\pi)}{4Nh^2} = \frac{\pi}{2h} \frac{1-\pi}{2Nh}.$$

Let F denote the distribution function of x, three times continuously differentiable. With $\pi = F(x_o + h) - F(x_o - h)$, Taylor's expansion yields

$$\frac{\pi}{2h} \cong \left\{ F(x_o) + f(x_o) \cdot h + \frac{f'(x_o) \cdot h^2}{2} + \frac{f''(x_o) \cdot h^3}{6} \right\} \Big/ 2h$$

$$- \left\{ F(x_o) - f(x_o) \cdot h + \frac{f'(x_o) \cdot h^2}{2} - \frac{f''(x_o) \cdot h^3}{6} \right\} \Big/ 2h$$

$$= f(x_o) + \frac{f''(x_o) \cdot h^2}{6}.$$

Substitute this into $E\{\hat{f}_N(x_o)\}$ and $V\{\hat{f}_N(x_o)\}$ to get

$$E\{\hat{f}_N(x_o)\} \cong f(x_o) + \frac{f''(x_o) \cdot h^2}{6},$$

$$V\{\hat{f}_N(x_o)\} \cong \left\{ f(x_o) + \frac{f''(x_o) \cdot h^2}{6} \right\} \cdot \frac{1-\pi}{2Nh}.$$

If $h \to 0$ and $Nh \to \infty$ as $N \to \infty$, then as $N \to \infty$,

$$E\{\hat{f}_N(x_o)\} \to f(x_o), \qquad V\{\hat{f}_N(x_o)\} \to 0.$$

$h \to 0$ makes the bias $E\{\hat{f}_N(x_o)\} - f(x_o)$ disappear, while $Nh \to \infty$ makes the variance disappear. This implies

$$\hat{f}_N(x_o) \to^p f(x_o).$$

The role of the indicator function $1[|x_i - x_o|/h < 1]$ in $\hat{f}_N(x_o)$ is to weight the i-th observation: the weight is 1 if x_i falls within the h-distance from x_o and 0 otherwise. If we generalize this weighting idea, a smooth weight can depend on $|x_i - x_o|$. Let x be now a $k \times 1$ vector. In this case, h-distance becomes h^k-distance (e.g., the two dimensional analog of $1[\|x_i - x_o\| < h]$ is the rectangle of size $(2h)^2 = 4h^2$). A *kernel density estimator* is based upon the smooth weighting idea:

$$f_N(x_o) \equiv (Nh^k)^{-1} \sum_{i=1}^{N} K\left(\frac{x_i - x_o}{h}\right),$$

where K (called a 'kernel') is a smooth multivariate density symmetric about 0 such as the $N(0, I_k)$ density. The kernel estimator $f_N(x_o)$ includes $\hat{f}_N$ as a special case with $k = 1$ and $K(\cdot) = 1[|\cdot| < 1]/2$. Doing analogously to the earlier proof for $\hat{f}_N(x_o) \to^p f(x_o)$, we can show that $f_N(x_o) \to^p f(x_o)$. Furthermore, it holds that

$$(Nh^k)^{1/2}\{f_N(x_o) - f(x_o)\} \rightsquigarrow N\left(0, f(x_o) \int K(z)^2 dz\right),$$

which can be used to construct (point-wise) confidence intervals for $f(x_o)$.

Other than the $1[\cdot]$ and $N(0, 1)$ kernel,

$$(3/4) \cdot (1 - z^2) \cdot 1[|z| < 1]: \text{ (trimmed) quadratic kernel,}$$
$$(15/16) \cdot (1 - z^2)^2 1[|z| < 1]: \textit{quartic or biweight } \text{kernel}$$

are popular univariate kernels. For $k > 1$, 'product kernels', which consist of copies of univariate kernels such as $\prod_{j=1}^{k} \phi(z_j)$ with ϕ being the $N(0, 1)$ density, are often used.

The scalar h is called a 'bandwidth' or 'smoothing parameter', whose role is analogous to that of the interval size in a histogram. If h is too small, there is no grouping (averaging), and $f_N(x_o)$ will be too jagged as x_o varies (small bias but large variance). If h is too large, $f_N(x_o)$ will show little variation as x_0 changes (large bias but small variance). As in histogram interval-size, there is no 'best rule' for choosing h in practice. A practical rule of thumb for choosing h is $h \cong \nu \cdot N^{-1/(k+4)}$ with, say, $0.5 \le \nu \le 2.5$ if k is 1 or 2 with all components of x standardized. $N^{-1/(k+4)}$ falls in $(0.15, 0.50)$ for $N = 100$ to 10000 and $k = 1, 2$. For example, if $K(t) = \prod_{j=1}^{k} \phi(t_j)$ where $t = (t_1, \ldots, t_k)'$ is used, then,

$$K\left(\frac{x_i - x_o}{h}\right) = \prod_{j=1}^{k} \phi\left[\frac{x_{ij} - x_{oj}}{SD(x_j)\nu N^{-1/(k+1)}}\right].$$

More discussion on choosing K and h is given below.

A kernel regression estimator $r_N(x_o)$ for $\rho(x_o)$ in $y_i = \rho(x_i) + u_i$ with $E(u|x) = 0$ is

$$r_N(x_o) \equiv \frac{(Nh^k)^{-1} \sum_{i=1}^{N} K((x_i - x_o)/h)y_i}{(Nh^k)^{-1} \sum_{i=1}^{N} K((x_i - x_o)/h)} = \frac{g_N(x_o)}{f_N(x_o)},$$

where the numerator of $r_N(x_o)$ is defined as $g_N(x_o)$. Rewrite $r_N(x_o)$ as

$$\sum_{i=1}^{N} \left\{ \frac{K((x_i - x_o)/h)}{\sum_{i=1}^{N} K((x_i - x_o)/h)} \right\} \cdot y_i$$

to see that $r_N(x_o)$ *is a weighted average of y_i's where the weight is large if x_i is close to x_o and small otherwise.*

Doing analogously for $\hat{f}_N(x_o) \to^p f(x_o)$, it can be shown that

$$g_N(x_o) \to^p E(y|x_o) \cdot f(x_o)$$

which implies, when combined with $f_N(x_o) \to^p f(x_o)$,

$$r_N(x_o) \to^p \rho(x_o).$$

Also, analogously to the asymptotic normality of $(Nh^k)^{1/2}\{f_N(x_o) - f(x_o)\}$, it holds that

$$(Nh^k)^{0.5}\{r_N(x_o) - \rho(x_o)\} \rightsquigarrow N\left(0, \frac{V(u|x_o) \int K(z)^2 dz}{f(x_o)}\right).$$

To implement kernel estimation, one has to choose K and h. As for K, it is known that the choice of kernel makes little difference. But the story is quite different for h, for the choice of h makes a huge difference. When $k = 1$ or 2 a good practical alternative to the above rule-of-thumb is to draw $f_N(x)$ or $r_N(x)$ over a reasonable range for x and choose h such that the curve estimate is not too smooth (if h is too big) nor too jagged (if h is too small). If $k > 2$, this balancing act is hard to do. In this case, it is advisable to choose h by minimizing the following minimand over some range for h:

$$\sum_{i}\{y_i - r_{Ni}(x_i)\}^2, \quad where \; r_{Ni}(x_i) \equiv \frac{\sum_{j=1,j\neq i}^{N} K((x_j - x_i)/h)y_j}{\sum_{j=1,j\neq i}^{N} K((x_j - x_i)/h)};$$

$r_{Ni}(x_i)$ is a 'leave-one-out' estimator for $\rho(x_i)$. This method of choosing h is called a 'cross-validation', which works well in practice. For $f(x)$, y_i is irrelevant, and a cross-validation minimand for h is

$$(N^2 h^k)^{-1} \sum_{i} \sum_{j} K^{(2)}\left(\frac{x_i - x_j}{h}\right) - 2(N^2 h^k)^{-1} \sum_{i\neq j} K\left(\frac{x_i - x_j}{h}\right),$$

where $K^{(2)}(a) \equiv \int K(a - m)K(m)dm$.

The kernel regression estimator can be obtained by minimizing the following with respect to (wrt) a:

$$\sum_i (y_i - a)^2 \cdot K\left(\frac{x_i - x_o}{h}\right).$$

The kernel estimator may be viewed as predicting y_i locally around x_o using only the intercept a. One variation of the kernel estimator is obtained using a line (intercept and slope) centered at x_o, which is a *local linear regression* (LLR) minimizing

$$\sum_i \{y_i - a - b'(x_i - x_o)\}^2 \cdot K\left(\frac{x_i - x_o}{h}\right)$$

wrt a and b. The estimator $a_N(x_o)$ for a is the LLR estimator for $\rho(x_o)$, whereas the estimator for b is the LLR estimator for $\partial\rho(x_o)/\partial x$.

To be specific, the LLR estimator for $\rho(x_o)$ is

$$a_N(x_o) = (1, 0\ldots 0) \cdot \{X(x_o)'W(x_o)X(x_o)\}^{-1} \cdot \{X(x_o)'W(x_o)Y\},$$

where $Y \equiv (y_1, \ldots, y_N)'$, $W(x_o) \equiv diag\{K((x_1 - x_o)/h), \ldots, K((x_N - x_o)/h)\}$, and

$$X(x_o) \equiv \begin{bmatrix} 1, & (x_1 - x_o)' \\ & \vdots \\ 1, & (x_N - x_o)' \end{bmatrix}.$$

The asymptotic distribution of LLR, other than the bias, is the same as that of the (local constant) kernel method. LLR has some advantages over kernel method such as working better at the boundaries of the x-support, but it can be also too variable (e.g., Seifert and Gasser (1996)). See Fan (1996) for LLR in general.

In the νth 'Nearest Neighbor (NN)' estimator, $\rho(x_o)$ is estimated using an (weighted) average of y_i's whose x_i's fall within the νth NN of x_o, where the νth NN of x_o is the neighborhood of x_o that is just big enough to contain up to the νth closest point in terms of x. For example, with the equal weights,

$$r_{NN}(x_o) = (1/\nu) \sum_i 1[x_i \in \nu\text{th NN of } x_o] \cdot y_i$$

$$= \sum_i \{1[x_i \in \nu\text{th NN of } x_o]/\nu\} y_i = \sum_i w_i(x_o, \nu) \cdot y_i,$$

where $w_i(x_o, \nu) \equiv 1[x_i \in \nu\text{th NN of } x_o]/\nu$. Note that $\sum_i w_i(x_o, \nu) = 1$ for all x_o and ν so long as $x_o \neq x_i$ for all i. Instead of the uniform weight, we can use a smooth weighting function depending on $|x_i - x_o|$. The main difference between the NN and the kernel method is the number of observations used to estimate $\rho(x_o)$: the number varies in the kernel method because a fixed neigborhood is used, whereas the same number, ν, is used always in NN. Kernel methods and NN will be used for matching later.

A.2 Appendix for Chapter 2

A.2.1 Comparison to a probabilistic causality

In treatment effect analysis, there is a *known* cause and a response variable of interest, and estimating the effect of the cause on the response variable is the main goal. We call this 'counter-factual causality', for the concept of counter-factual is necessary. This framework fits well randomized experiments where we have control over the treatment and thus there is no dispute on what the cause is. In observational studies, however, we merely observe a number of variables 'after the fact'. Here, what the cause is and what the response is disputable.

Instead of fixing the treatment first, suppose we fix the response variable of interest, say y. In *probabilistic causality*, one tries to find a (or the) cause for y by checking whether the possible cause changes the probability distribution for y where no counter-factuals are envisioned. There are different versions for probabilistic causality. Here we briefly review Granger (1969, 1980) (non)-causality—a well known probabilistic causality in economics. This is shown to be equivalent to counter-factual causality in a special case.

With t indexing discrete time, a variable d_t is said to (probabilistically) 'non-cause' y_t if

$$P(y_t \leq a | U_{t-1}) = P(y_t \leq a | U_{t-1} \text{ without } d_{t-1}, d_{t-2}, \ldots) \quad \text{for all } a$$

where U_{t-1} is the information on all the variables in the universe up to time $t-1$. Otherwise d_t 'causes' y_t. To understood the definition better, suppose z_t represents all variables other than d_t in the world, and thus

$$U_{t-1} = \{d_{t-1}, d_{t-2}, \ldots, z_{t-1}, z_{t-2}, \ldots\}.$$

It can happen that d_t non-causes y_t but

$$P(y_t \leq a) \neq P(y_t \leq a | d_{t-1}, d_{t-2}, \ldots) \quad \text{for some } a,$$

because $\{z_t, z_{t-1}, \ldots\}$ is not conditioned on. Hence d_t is said to cause y_t if $\{d_{t-1}, d_{t-2}, \ldots\}$ still changes the probability distribution of y_t even when all the other variables ($\{z_t, z_{t-1}, \ldots\}$ in this case) are conditioned on.

Since there is no way we can account for all the variables in the world, in practice, the operational definition of non-causality becomes

$$P(y_t \leq a | I_{t-1}) = P(y_t \leq a | I_{t-1} \text{ without } d_{t-1}, d_{t-2}, \ldots) \quad \text{for all } a,$$

where I_{t-1} is the information available at hand up to time $t-1$. That is, d_t causes y_t if

$$P(y_t \leq a | I_{t-1}) \neq P(y_t \leq a | I_{t-1} \text{ without } d_{t-1}, d_{t-2}, \ldots) \quad \text{for some } a,$$

which is called the 'Granger causality of d_t on y_t'. The problem of not being able to observe U_{t-1} is not limited to probabilistic causality: in counter-factual causality for observational data, one also has to worry about unobserved variables making the T and C groups heterogenous other than in the treatment.

Since I_{t-1} is ambiguous,

$$I_{t-1} = \{y_{t-1}, y_{t-2}, \ldots, d_{t-1}, d_{t-2}, \ldots\}$$

is often taken for a simplified operational definition of the Granger causality. Furthermore, since it is cumbersome to check $P(y_t \leq a | I_{t-1})$ for all a, a further simplification is often used in practice for the non-causality:

$$E(y_t | y_{t-1}, y_{t-2}, \ldots, d_{t-1}, d_{t-2}, \ldots) = E(y_t | y_{t-1}, y_{t-2}, \ldots),$$

which may be called the 'mean non-causality'.

Going even further, instead of conditional means, 'linear projection' is often used:

$$E^*(y_t | y_{t-1}, y_{t-2}, \ldots, d_{t-1}, d_{t-2}, \ldots) = E^*(y_t | y_{t-1}, y_{t-2}, \ldots)$$

where

$$E^*(y|m) \equiv m'\{E(mm')\}^{-1}E(my),$$

and m is a random vector including 1 as a component. Both sides of the equation for non-causality in linear projection can be estimated by LSE. Since non-causality in probability implies non-causality in mean, which in turn implies non-causality in linear projection, rejecting non-causality in linear projection implies rejecting non-causality in mean and thus in probability.

As such, probabilistic causality may look as attractive as counter-factual causality. However, it has the following main problem. Consider a 'causal chain' running, say, A to C:

$$A \rightarrow B \rightarrow C.$$

In this case, B is the 'direct' or 'immediate' cause of C while A is an indirect cause. Can we then say that A really is a cause? In the counter-factual causality, there is no problem in saying that A is a cause and then estimating the effect (simply imagine a randomized experiment with an A group and a non-A group). In probabilistic causality, in principle this is impossible, as B should be in the information set. So long as B is held constant, A cannot affect C, and A cannot be a cause. This shows that the aim of probabilistic causality, which is to find the direct cause, is almost impossible to achieve and any cause found in probabilistic causality is only tentative, waiting to be negated as the information set is expanded to include a more direct cause.

Declaring whether something is a cause for something else may be less important than finding out the magnitude of a causal relation. This seems to be the position taken by counter-factual causality, whereas probabilistic causality is more about finding causes rather than measuring the effect. For a given drug and disease, counter-factual causality strives to measure the effect of the drug on the disease, whereas probabilistic causality asks whether the disease has been cured because of the drug or something else (for example, regular exercise).

If, however, we write zero counter-factual causality in terms of the observed variables, then zero counter-factual causality becomes equivalent to zero probabilistic causality in some cases. To see this, suppose the treatment and response variables are both binary, and there are only two periods, one for the cause and the other for the response (we will thus suppress the time index here). Define I_c as 'I other than d' to have a probabilistic non-causality written as

$$E(y|I_c, d) = E(y|I_c) \qquad \text{for } d = 0, 1 \iff E(y|I_c, d = 1) - E(y|I_c, d = 0) = 0.$$

If selection-on-observable holds for both potential responses (i.e., if $E(y_j|I_c, d) = E(y_j|I_c), j = 0, 1$), then zero counter-factual causality conditional on I_c is

$$E(y_1|I_c) - E(y_0|I_c) = 0 \iff E(y|I_c, d = 1) - E(y|I_c, d = 0) = 0.$$

The left-hand side of no effect is written in potential variables, and the right-hand side of no effect is written in the observed variables. The right-hand side is equal to zero probabilistic causality in the preceding display.

A.2.2 Learning about joint distribution from marginals

Although y_0 and y_1 are never observed together, we can learn about the joint distribution using the marginal distributions for y_0 and y_1, which we explore in this subsection.

One way to learn about the joint distribution of (y_0, y_1) from the marginal distributions without invoking any assumption is to use the *Fréchet bounds*, which bound the unknown joint distribution using known marginals. With the joint and marginal distribution functions for y_j denoted, respectively, as $F_{0,1}$ and F_j, we have

$$\max\{0, F_0(y_0) + F_1(y_1) - 1\} \le F_{0,1}(y_0, y_1) \le \min\{F_0(y_0), F_1(y_1)\}.$$

The bounds are sharp, and both bounds are 'proper bivariate probability distribution functions', which means

$$\lim_{y_j \to -\infty} F_{0,1}(y_0, y_1) = 0, \quad for \ j = 0, 1, \qquad \lim_{y_0 \to \infty, y_1 \to \infty} F_{0,1}(y_0, y_1) = 1,$$

$$0 \le F_{0,1}(z_0, z_1) - F_{0,1}(x_0, z_1) - F_{0,1}(z_0, x_1) + F_{0,1}(x_0, x_1)$$
$$\forall \ x_0 < z_0, \ x_1 < z_1.$$

If y_j is binary, say, indicating the event of finding a job within a certain period following a job training, then we get, for $a, b = 0, 1$,

$$\max\{0, P(y_0 = a) + P(y_1 = b) - 1\} \le P(y_0 = a, y_1 = b)$$
$$\le \min\{P(y_0 = a), P(y_1 = b)\}.$$

As an empirical example, using a randomized experimental job-training data called JTPA (Job Training Partnership Act), Heckman, Smith, and Clements (1997) obtain estimates for $P(y_0 = 1)$ and $P(y_1 = 1)$:

$$P_N(y_0 = 1) = 0.61 \quad \text{and} \quad P_N(y_1 = 1) = 0.64.$$

The difference is very small. Using the Fréchet bounds and ignoring the sampling errors for the estimates, we get

$$\max(0, \ 0.39 + 0.64 - 1) \leq P(y_0 = 0, \ y_1 = 1) \leq \min(0.39, 0.64)$$
$$\implies 0.03 \leq P(y_0 = 0, y_1 = 1) \leq 0.39,$$

the width of which is fairly large. Doing analogously, we get

$$\max(0, \ 0.61 + 0.36 - 1) \leq P(y_0 = 1, \ y_1 = 0) \leq \min(0.61, 0.36)$$
$$\implies 0 \leq P(y_0 = 1, y_1 = 0) \leq 0.36.$$

We can obtain bounds for $P(y_0 = 1, y_1 = 1)$ and $P(y_0 = 0, y_1 = 0)$ doing analogously.

One may wonder how much information is lost in the Fréchet bounds. To get some idea of this, observe the following decomposition of the mean treatment effect:

$$E(y_1 - y_0) = P(y_1 - y_0 = 1) - P(y_1 - y_0 = -1)$$
$$= P(y_0 = 0, y_1 = 1) - P(y_0 = 1, y_1 = 0).$$

This accords an interesting view: $P(y_0 = 0, \ y_1 = 1)$ means 'no job without the training but a job with the training' while $P(y_0 = 1, \ y_1 = 0)$ means 'a job without the training but no job with the training'. The former is the benefit while the latter is the loss. $E(y_1 - y_0)$ is the 'net' effect from subtracting the loss from the benefit. For the JTPA data, the mean effect is

$$E(y_1) - E(y_0) = P(y_1 = 1) - P(y_0 = 1) = 0.64 - 0.61 = 0.03.$$

However, the already derived Fréchet bounds for the benefit and loss probabilities, when put together, render

$$-0.33 \leq P(y_0 = 0, \ y_1 = 1) - P(y_0 = 1, \ y_1 = 0) \leq 0.39.$$

Although this interval includes 0.03, it is not very informative (note that the sampling errors are not accounted for).

To show the inherent difficulty of learning about the joint distribution of (y_0, y_1) given the two marginal distributions, we introduce *copula* drawing on Joe (1997). A copula is a multivariate distribution with all univariate marginals being $U[0, 1]$. Suppose we know that the marginal distributions for y_0 and y_1 are F_0 and F_1, respectively, and wonder what kind of joint distribution would have generated them. There are infinite possibilities to this query. Take any copula, say $C(u_0, u_1)$ with a single 'dependence parameter' ρ, and adopt

$$C\{F_0(y_0), F_1(y_1); \rho\}$$

as the joint distribution for (y_0, y_1). This is valid because $F_j(y_j)$ follows $U[0, 1]$, $j = 0, 1$.

An example of $C(u_0, u_1)$ is

$$J\{\Phi^{-1}(u_0), \Phi^{-1}(u_1); \rho\}, \qquad -1 < \rho < 1,$$

where $J\{\cdot, \cdot; \rho\}$ is the standard bivariate normal distribution with correlation ρ. With this normal copula, the joint distribution function for (y_0, y_1) becomes

$$J\{\Phi^{-1}(F_0(y_0)), \Phi^{-1}(F_0(y_1)); \rho\}.$$

We could have used another copula, say,

$$C(u_0, u_1) = (u_0^{-\rho} + u_1^{-\rho} - 1)^{-1/\rho}, \qquad 0 < \rho < \infty,$$

leading to the joint distribution function for (y_0, y_1), $\{F_0(y_0)^{-\rho} + F_1(y_1)^{-\rho} - 1\}^{-1/\rho}$. Even when the functional form of the copula is fixed, ρ still gives infinite possibilities. Furthermore, a copula can be indexed by multiple parameters, not just by ρ.

Since it is difficult to recover the joint distribution from two given marginals, we sometimes impose assumptions on the dependence between y_1 and y_0 in order to narrow down the joint distribution. One extreme assumption is independence of y_0 and y_1, and the other extreme is $y_1 = y_0$. In both cases, the difficult task becomes trivial. Also helpful is to impose assumptions on how d is determined. For instance, if $d = 1[y_1 > y_0]$, then we know that at least $y_1 - y_0 > 0$ given $d = 1$. In the following, we explore the 'same rank' assumption. The same rank assumption allows for heterogeneous treatment effects across individuals and includes the constant effect as a special case.

Suppose initially that we can observe both y_{0i} and y_{1i}, $i = 1, \ldots, N$, which are continuously distributed, and that y_{1i}, $i = 1, \ldots, N$, are ordered such that $y_{11} < y_{12} \cdots < y_{1N}$. The rank of y_{1i} in the T group can be written as $\sum_{j=1}^{N} 1[y_{1j} \leq y_{1i}]$. Assume the same ranks across the two groups:

$$N \cdot F_{0N}(y_{0i}) \equiv \sum_{j=1}^{N} 1[y_{0j} \leq y_{0i}] = \sum_{j=1}^{N} 1[y_{1j} \leq y_{1i}] \equiv N \cdot F_{1N}(y_{1i}) \quad \text{for all } i,$$

which means $y_{01} < y_{02} < \cdots < y_{0N}$, where F_{jN} is the empirical distribution function for group $d = j$. That is, the treatment may change y_{0i} but only in a way that preserves the order. For two individuals i and m, it may happen

$$y_{1i} - y_{0i} \neq y_{1m} - y_{0m} \qquad \text{(no constant effect)},$$

but the ranks of y_{1i} and y_{1m} in the T group will be the same as those of y_{0i} and y_{0m} in the C group.

This suggests, with only one of y_{0i} and y_{1i} observed, the individual with the same rank in the other group is taken as the counter-factual. That is, suppose the T and C groups have the same number of observations, say N_c, and the following ordered values:

$$y_{(1)} < y_{(2)} <, \ldots, < y_{(N_c)} \quad \text{for the T group,}$$
$$w_{(1)} < w_{(2)} <, \ldots, < w_{(N_c)} \quad \text{for the C group.}$$

Then $(w_{(i)}, y_{(i)})$ that comes from two different individuals is taken as (y_{0i}, y_{1i}), $i = 1, \ldots, N_c$ and the joint distribution is to be estimated with $(w_{(i)}, y_{(i)})$, $i = 1, \ldots, N_c$. In practice, when N_0 and N_1 are different, grouping may be done to achieve $N_0 = N_1$. Under the same rank condition, the rank correlation (coefficient) across the T and C groups is one. Heckman, Smith, and Clements (1997) show that high rank correlation is likely.

A.3 Appendix for Chapter 3

A.3.1 Derivation for a semi-linear model

To obtain the asymptotic distribution of b_N, apply Taylor's expansion to $p_i(a_N)$ to get

$$p_i(a_N) \simeq p_i(\alpha) + \frac{\exp(x_i'\alpha)\{1 + \exp(x_i'\alpha)\} - \exp(x_i'\alpha)\exp(x_i'\alpha)}{\{1 + \exp(x_i'\alpha)\}^2} x_i'(a_N - \alpha)$$

$$= p_i(\alpha) + \frac{\exp(x_i'\alpha)}{\{1 + \exp(x_i'\alpha)\}^2} x_i'(a_N - \alpha)$$

$$= p_i + p_i(1 - p_i)x_i'(a_N - \alpha), \quad \text{where } p_i \equiv p_i(\alpha).$$

In the b_N equation

$$b_N = \beta + \frac{N^{-1}\sum_i\{d_i - p_i(a_N)\}\{g(x_i) + u_i\}}{N^{-1}\sum_i\{d_i - p_i(a_N)\}d_i},$$

replace a_N in the denominator with α, which is innocuous for the asymptotic distribution, and then substitute the $p_i(a_N)$ expansion into the numerator to get

$$b_N = \beta + \frac{N^{-1}\sum_i\{d_i - p_i - p_i(1 - p_i)x_i'(a_N - \alpha)\}\{g(x_i) + u_i\}}{N^{-1}\sum_i(d_i - p_i)d_i}$$

$$= \beta + \frac{\left[\begin{array}{l} N^{-1}\sum_i(d_i - p_i)\{g(x_i) + u_i\} \\ -N^{-1}\sum_i\{p_i(1 - p_i)x_i'\}\{g(x_i) + u_i\}(a_N - \alpha) \end{array}\right]}{N^{-1}\sum_i(d_i - p_i)d_i}$$

$$\Longrightarrow \sqrt{N}(b_N - \beta) = E^{-1}\{(d_i - p_i)d_i\} \cdot \left[N^{-1/2}\sum_i (d_i - p_i)\{g(x_i) + u_i\} \right.$$

$$\left. - E\{p_i(1 - p_i)x_i'(g(x_i) + u_i)\}\sqrt{N}(a_N - \alpha) \right] + o_p(1).$$

Note that, with s denoting the logit score function, we have

$$\sqrt{N}(a_N - \alpha) = N^{-1/2} \sum_i I_f^{-1} s_i + o_p(1)$$

$$= N^{-1/2} \sum_i I_f^{-1}(d_i - p_i)x_i + o_p(1)$$

$$\text{where } I_f = E\{p_i(1 - p_i)x_i x_i'\}.$$

Substitute this expression for $\sqrt{N}(a_N - \alpha)$ into the preceding display to get

$$\sqrt{N}(b_N - \beta) = E^{-1}\{(d_i - p_i)d_i\} \cdot N^{-1/2} \sum_i [(d_i - p_i)\{g(x_i) + u_i\}$$

$$- L \cdot I_f^{-1}(d_i - p_i)x_i] \quad \text{where } L \equiv E\{p_i(1 - p_i)x_i'(g(x_i) + u_i)\}.$$

In $N^{-1/2} \sum_i [\cdots]$, the first term yields C_o, the second term yields $L I_f^{-1} L'$, and the cross-term is

$$-E\{(d_i - p_i)^2 (g(x_i) + u_i)x_i'\} \cdot I_f^{-1} L' = L I_f^{-1} L' \quad \text{for } E\{(d_i - p_i)^2 | x_i\} = p_i(1 - p_i).$$

Hence, twice the cross-term cancels the second variance term to yield the desired asymptotic variance for b_N.

A.3.2   Derivation for weighting estimators

For the asymptotic distribution of $\sqrt{N}\{U_N - E(y_1 - y_0 | d = 0)\}$, observe

$$\sqrt{N}\{U_N - E(y_1 - y_0 | d = 0)\} = P(d = 0)^{-1} \cdot N^{-1/2} \sum_i \left[\left(\frac{d_i}{\pi_N(x_i)} - 1\right)y_i\right.$$

$$\left. - E\left\{\left(\frac{d}{\pi(x)} - 1\right)y\right\}\right] + o_p(1).$$

On the right-hand side,

$$N^{-1/2} \sum_i \left[\left(\frac{d_i - \pi_N(x_i)}{\pi_N(x_i)}\right)y_i - E\left(\frac{d - \pi(x)}{\pi(x)}y\right)\right]$$

$$= N^{-1/2} \sum_i \left[\left\{\frac{d_i - \pi(x_i) - \{\pi_N(x_i) - \pi(x_i)\}}{\pi_N(x_i)}\right\}y_i - E\left(\frac{d - \pi(x)}{\pi(x)}y\right)\right].$$

The denominator $\pi_N(x_i)$ can be replaced with $\pi(x_i)$ without affecting the asymptotic distribution (see, e.g., Lee (1996)). Thus we need to deal with

$$N^{-1/2}\sum_i\left[\left\{\frac{d_i-\pi(x_i)}{\pi(x_i)}-\frac{\pi_N(x_i)-\pi(x_i)}{\pi(x_i)}\right\}y_i-E\left(\frac{d-\pi(x)}{\pi(x)}y\right)\right]$$

$$=N^{-1/2}\sum_i\left[\left\{\frac{d_i-\pi(x_i)}{\pi(x_i)}-\frac{\Phi(x_i'a_N)-\Phi(x_i'\alpha)}{\pi(x_i)}\right\}y_i-E\left(\frac{d-\pi(x)}{\pi(x)}y\right)\right]$$

$$=N^{-1/2}\sum_i\left[\frac{(d_i-\pi(x_i))y_i}{\pi(x_i)}-E\left\{\frac{(d-\pi(x))y}{\pi(x)}\right\}-\frac{\phi(x_i'a_{Ni}^*)x_i'y_i(a_N-\alpha)}{\pi(x_i)}\right];$$

in the last expression, Taylor's expansion with a_{Ni}^* as the 'mean value' is applied. This display is $o_p(1)$ equal to

$$N^{-1/2}\sum_i\left[\frac{(d_i-\pi(x_i))y_i}{\pi(x_i)}-E\left\{\frac{(d-\pi(x))y}{\pi(x)}\right\}-E\left(\frac{\phi(x'\alpha)x'y}{\pi(x)}\right)\cdot\eta_i\right]$$

$$\rightsquigarrow N(0,\,E(\lambda^2)),\qquad\text{where }\lambda_i\equiv\frac{(d_i-\pi(x_i))y_i}{\pi(x_i)}-E\left\{\frac{(d-\pi(x))y}{\pi(x)}\right\}$$

$$-E\left\{\frac{\phi(x'\alpha)x'y}{\pi(x)}\right\}\eta_i.$$

From this, the asymptotic distribution for U_N follows.

As for the asymptotic distribution of $\sqrt{N}\{T_N-E(y_1-y_0|d=1)\}$, observe

$$N^{-1/2}\sum_i\left[\left\{1-\frac{1-d_i}{1-\pi_N(x_i)}\right\}y_i-E\left\{\left(1-\frac{1-d}{1-\pi(x)}\right)y\right\}\right]$$

$$=N^{-1/2}\sum_i\left[\left\{\frac{1-\pi_N(x_i)-(1-d_i)}{1-\pi_N(x_i)}\right\}y_i-E\left\{\frac{1-\pi(x)-(1-d)}{1-\pi(x)}y\right\}\right].$$

Replace $\pi_N(x_i)$ in the denominator with $\pi(x_i)$ and rewrite the sum as

$$N^{-1/2}\sum_i\left[\left\{\frac{1-\pi_N(x_i)-(1-\pi(x_i))}{1-\pi(x_i)}-\frac{(1-d_i)-(1-\pi(x_i))}{1-\pi(x_i)}\right\}y_i\right.$$

$$\left.+E\left\{\frac{(1-d)-(1-\pi(x))}{1-\pi(x)}y\right\}\right].$$

Doing analogously to what was done above for the effect on the untreated, we get

$$N^{-1/2}\sum_i\left[-E\left(\frac{\phi(x'\alpha)x'y}{1-\pi(x)}\right)\eta_i-\frac{(\pi(x_i)-d_i)y_i}{1-\pi(x_i)}+E\left\{\frac{(\pi(x)-d)y}{1-\pi(x)}\right\}\right]$$

$$\rightsquigarrow N(0,E(\zeta^2)).$$

From this, the asymptotic distribution for T_N follows.

A.4   Appendix for Chapter 4

A.4.1   Non-sequential matching with network flow algorithm

Although sequential matching is computationally convenient, greedy sequential matching depends on the ordering of the observations, which is undesirable. Also, non-greedy sequential matching cannot restrict the number of times a control can be used, which may also be undesirable. Here, we examine non-sequential matching that avoids these shortcomings in sequential matching. Since the non-sequential matching in this section is time-consuming and the extra gain from using it seems to be small, we do not expect non-sequential matching to be used widely. However, understanding how it can be implemented may be useful. An easy-to-use and quick non-sequential multiple matching will be introduced in the next subsection.

In a non-sequential matching scheme, one has to consider all possible ways of pairing the controls and treated units. This is challenging to say the least. Surprisingly, algorithms to implement non-sequential matching can be found in network flow theory (Rosenbaum (1989)) where transportation cost from a point ('source') to another point ('sink') is minimized under a capacity restriction of each possible route and the cost of using the route. In the following, we explain the main idea. Bergstralh and Kosanke (1995) provide a SAS program to implement non-sequential matching. Rephann and Isserman (1994) provide an empirical example of highway effect on economic development.

Suppose there are two treated units ($N_1 = 2$) and three controls ($N_0 = 3$). Examine all possible routes from a source (origin) to the treated, then to the control subjects, and finally to a sink (destination):

		Greedy pair matching			
		$(1, \delta(1,1)) \longrightarrow$	C1	$(1,0)\searrow$	
	T1	$(1, \delta(1,2)) \longrightarrow$	C2	$(1,0)\longrightarrow$	sink
	$(1,0)\nearrow$	$(1, \delta(1,3)) \longrightarrow$	C3	$(1,0)\nearrow$	
source					
	$(1,0)\searrow$	$(1, \delta(2,1)) \longrightarrow$	C1	$(1,0)\searrow$	
	T2	$(1, \delta(2,2)) \longrightarrow$	C2	$(1,0)\longrightarrow$	sink
		$(1, \delta(2,3)) \longrightarrow$	C3	$(1,0)\nearrow$	

where (a, b) attached to each arrow means capacity a and cost b, $\delta(i, j)$ is the cost of transportation of going from Ti to Cj, and the two sinks in the rightmost column are for the same single final destination. The cost $\delta(i, j)$ is the distance (i.e., dissimilarity) between treated i and control j. For instance, for the route 'source-T1-C2-sink', the total capacity is only 1 because each edge has a capacity of 1, and the total cost is $\delta(1, 2) = 0 + \delta(1, 2) + 0$.

Imagine sending two units of cargo from the source: one should be sent to T1 and the other to T2 (at no cost) due to the capacity limitation, then to some control with the minimum cost, and then to the sink at no cost. If we choose the two routes with the minimum cost, then we find the closest control for each treated. The matching here is greedy, because each edge from a control to the sink has a capacity limit of one, that is, each control can be matched to only one treated. In general, with $N_1 \leq N_0$, sending out the total N_1 units of cargo from the source and then minimizing the total cost of transportation yields non-sequential greedy pair matching.

Suppose $(1,0)$ for the edge 'control-sink' is replaced by $(2,0)$ in the table for greedy pair matching:

		Non-greedy pair matching			
		$(1, \delta(1,1)) \longrightarrow$	C1	$(2,0) \searrow$	
	T1	$(1, \delta(1,2)) \longrightarrow$	C2	$(2,0) \longrightarrow$	sink
$(1,0) \nearrow$		$(1, \delta(1,3)) \longrightarrow$	C3	$(2,0) \nearrow$	
source					
$(1,0) \searrow$		$(1, \delta(2,1)) \longrightarrow$	C1	$(2,0) \searrow$	
	T2	$(1, \delta(2,2)) \longrightarrow$	C2	$(2,0) \longrightarrow$	sink
		$(1, \delta(2,3)) \longrightarrow$	C3	$(2,0) \nearrow$	

Two units of cargo can be sent out. T1 carries one unit and T2 carries one unit and each unit is then carried by a control to the sink. If we minimize the total cost of transporting two units, then we do a non-sequential non-greedy pair matching. The matching here is not greedy, because a control can be used twice. In general, sending out the total N_1 units of cargo and replacing $(2,0)$ with $(M,0)$, we do a non-sequential non-greedy pair matching that allows a control to be used up to M times.

Suppose $(1,0)$ for the edge 'source-T1' is replaced by $(2,0)$ in the table for greedy pair matching:

		Greedy multiple matching with predetermined control numbers			
		$(1, \delta(1,1)) \longrightarrow$	C1	$(1,0) \searrow$	
	T1	$(1, \delta(1,2)) \longrightarrow$	C2	$(1,0) \longrightarrow$	sink
$(2,0) \nearrow$		$(1, \delta(1,3)) \longrightarrow$	C3	$(1,0) \nearrow$	
source					
$(1,0) \searrow$		$(1, \delta(2,1)) \longrightarrow$	C1	$(1,0) \searrow$	
	T2	$(1, \delta(2,2)) \longrightarrow$	C2	$(1,0) \longrightarrow$	sink
		$(1, \delta(2,3)) \longrightarrow$	C3	$(1,0) \nearrow$	

Here, three units of the cargo can be sent out: T1 carries two units and T2 carries one unit. Each unit is then carried by a control to the sink. If we minimize the total cost of transporting the three units, then we do a matching where T1 is matched to two controls whereas T2 is matched to one. The matching here is greedy with a predetermined number of controls for each treated. In general, by fixing the capacity for each edge from the source to a treated, we do non-sequential multiple matching where the number of matched controls for each treated is fixed. If the capacity sum from the source to the treated is N_0, and if the total N_0 units of cargo are sent out, then all controls are used up.

In the preceding table, it was predetermined that T1 gets two controls whereas T2 gets only one. Suppose we want multiple matching without predetermining who gets more than one unit, so long as each treated gets at least one control. This can be achieved by first sending one unit to each treated and then sending the leftover units to a vertex 'extra' to redistribute the leftover units to the treated. Examine

---

| | Greedy multiple matching without predetermined control numbers | | | | | |

				$(1, \delta(1,1)) \longrightarrow$	C1	$(1,0) \searrow$
	$\longrightarrow$	$\longrightarrow$	T1	$(1, \delta(1,2)) \longrightarrow$	C2	$(1,0) \longrightarrow$ sink
$(1,0) \nearrow$		$(\infty, 0) \nearrow$		$(1, \delta(1,3)) \longrightarrow$	C3	$(1,0) \nearrow$
source $(1,0) \longrightarrow$	extra					
$(1,0) \searrow$		$(\infty, 0) \searrow$		$(1, \delta(2,1)) \longrightarrow$	C1	$(1,0) \searrow$
	$\longrightarrow$	$\longrightarrow$	T2	$(1, \delta(2,2)) \longrightarrow$	C2	$(1,0) \longrightarrow$ sink
				$(1, \delta(2,3)) \longrightarrow$	C3	$(1,0) \nearrow$

---

where which treated gets the extra unit of cargo (that is, the extra control) is determined by minimizing the total cost of transporting the three units. In general, sending out first N_1 units (one for each treated) and then some further units later, we do non-sequential multiple matching where the number of the matched controls for each treated is optimally determined such that the number is at least one for each treated. If the later shipment is $N_0 - N_1 > 0$, then all control units are used up.

In the above table, each treated is matched to at least one control because N_1 units of cargo were evenly distributed first, and each control is matched only to one treated (thus, a greedy matching) with the edge from Cj to the sink being $(1,0)$. By sending out the total N_0 ($>N_1$) units, each treated is matched to at least one control and each control is matched to only one treated, to result in a greedy full matching. If $(1,0)$ in the edges from the controls to the sink is replaced by $(M,0)$, then each control can be used up to M times and the matching is not greedy, but the matching may not be full.

A.4.2   Greedy non-sequential multiple matching

The preceding non-sequential matching is time-consuming. This section presents a greedy non-sequential multiple matching with a varying number of matched controls (MMV), drawing on Lee and Lee (2004a). Some authors who require restrictions on the number of matched controls per treated may not call MMV a matching. In MMV, it is possible that a few treated subjects monopolize all controls. However barring such extreme cases, MMV can be implemented as fast as sequential pair matching can be.

To implement MMV, instead of finding the best matched control(s) for each treated, we do the opposite and *find the best matched treated for each control*. This requires consideration of only $N_0 N_1$ operations, because there are N_1 pairs to consider for each control. When each control finds its best matched treated, we 'turn the table around' and list each treated and its matched controls, whose number can range from zero to N_0.

MMV can be implemented in three simple steps: with $j = 1$,

1. For a control j, obtain $|x_j - x_i| \; \forall i \in T$.

2. If $|x_j - x_i| > caliper \; \forall i \in T$, then go to Step 3. Otherwise, find i minimizing the difference to 'store' control j in C_i, the comparison group for treated i.

3. If $j = N_0$, then stop; otherwise, replace j with $j + 1$ and go to Step 1.

When this algorithm is done, each C_i could be empty or filled with a number of controls. MMV is optimal in the sense that each control is matched to its closest treated and the number $|C_i|$ of matched controls for treated i is determined optimally by this consideration.

The essential reason why MMV can be implemented so easily is that there is *no restriction on the number of matched controls*. If we impose restriction, then the above simple algorithm for MMV no longer is optimal. To see this, suppose $N_1 = 3$, $N_0 = 4$, and there are three levels of distance $|x_j - x_i|$ (low, medium, high) with the caliper size falling in between medium and high:

	low (<caliper)	medium (<caliper)	high (>caliper)
C_1			C1
C_2	C2, C3		
C_3		C4	

where C1, C2, C3, C4 denote the four controls. Treated 1 has no matched control, treated 2 has two and treated 3 has one. If we want to impose pair-matching restriction on MMV, then we discard C3 from C_2. However, this may not be optimal, because C3 may fall in 'row C_1 and column medium', to become the matched control for treated 1. Algorithms based on the network-flow idea can give this, but the algorithm for MMV cannot.

The question is thus whether we want to restrict the number of matched controls. In the extreme situation where a single treated gets all controls, MMV breaks down. Otherwise, it is hard to think of a reason to do so. In practice, one may do MMV first to see how evenly dispersed the controls are across the matched treated units. If this is not too one-sided, then MMV can be used.

A mean treatment effect estimator after MMV is, as appeared in Subsection 4.1.1,

$$T_N = N_{1u}^{-1} \sum_{i \in T_u} \left(y_i - |C_i|^{-1} \sum_{m \in C_i} y_{mi} \right).$$

In Subsection 4.1.3, it was mentioned that the variance of T_N may be estimated with

$$V_N \equiv N_{1u}^{-2} \sum_{i \in T_u} \left\{ y_i^2 - 2y_i \left(|C_i|^{-1} \sum_{m \in C_i} y_{mi} \right) + |C_i|^{-2} \sum_{m \in C_i} y_{mi}^2 \right.$$
$$\left. + |C_i|^{-1}(|C_i| - 1) \left(|C_i|^{-1} \sum_{m \in C_i} y_{mi} \right)^2 \right\};$$

a heuristic justification for V_N is the following. Under the null hypothesis of no effect, $E(T_N) = 0$. Observe then, writing $E(\cdot | i \in T_u)$ just as $E(\cdot)$,

$$E(T_N^2) = N_{1u}^{-1} E\left[\left\{ y_i - |C_i|^{-1} \sum_{m \in C_i} y_{mi} \right\}^2 \right]$$

$$= N_{1u}^{-1} E\left[y_i^2 - 2y_i \cdot |C_i|^{-1} \sum_{m \in C_i} y_{mi} + \left\{ |C_i|^{-1} \sum_{m \in C_i} y_{mi} \right\}^2 \right]$$

$$= N_{1u}^{-1} \left[E(y_i^2) - 2E(y_i)E(y_{mi} | m \in C_i) + E\left\{ |C_i|^{-1} \sum_{m \in C_i} y_{mi} \right\}^2 \right]$$

$$= N_{1u}^{-1} [E(y_i^2) - 2E(y_i)E(y_{mi} | m \in C_i) + |C_i|^{-1} E(y_{mi}^2 | m \in C_i)$$
$$+ |C_i|^{-2} |C_i|(|C_i| - 1) \{E(y_{mi} | m \in C_i)\}^2]$$

$$= N_{1u}^{-1} [E(y_i^2) - 2E(y_i)E(y_{mi} | m \in C_i) + |C_i|^{-1} E(y_{mi}^2 | m \in C_i)$$
$$+ |C_i|^{-1}(|C_i| - 1) \{E(y_{mi} | m \in C_i)\}^2]$$

$$\simeq N_{1u}^{-2} \sum_{i \in T_u} \left\{ y_i^2 - 2y_i \left(|C_i|^{-1} \sum_{m \in C_i} y_{mi} \right) + |C_i|^{-2} \sum_{m \in C_i} y_{mi}^2 \right.$$
$$\left. + |C_i|^{-1}(|C_i| - 1) \left(|C_i|^{-1} \sum_{m \in C_i} y_{mi} \right)^2 \right\}.$$

V_N would work better as $|C_i|$ gets larger.

In the empirical part of Lee and Lee (2004a), the effect of job training on reemployment by certain time is analyzed with the same data on Korean women used in Lee and Lee (2005). The result is (t-values are in (·))

$$-0.092 \ (-6.57) \quad \text{for greedy sequential pair matching}$$
$$-0.087 \ (-6.21) \quad \text{for greedy non-sequential pair matching}$$
$$\text{(network flow algorithm)}$$
$$-0.087 \ (-5.80) \quad \text{for MMV.}$$

The first two t-values were obtained using V_{pN} in Subsection 4.1.3 and the last t-value was obtained using V_N above. The effect is significantly negative in all three matchings and the MMV result is almost the same as the greedy non-sequential pair matching.

Recall the worry that MMV would break down if a few treated units monopolize all controls. The following table shows the percentage of the treated who get 1 control, 2 controls, and so on in MMV.

Percentage of treated units with varying number of controls									
#controls: 1	2	3	4	5	6	7	8	9	10+
% treated 41.9	26.5	15.9	9.0	3.1	2.4	0.8	0.2	0.2	0.1

In this table, 41.9% of the treated get only one control, 26.5% get two controls, and etc. Most treated units get only one to six controls, dismissing the worry.

A.4.3 Nonparametric matching and support discrepancy

When we examined treatment effect estimators with matching in Subsection 4.1.1, an estimator for the effect on the treated was

$$N_1^{-1} \sum_{i \in T} \left(y_i - \sum_{j \in C} w_{ij} y_j \right), \qquad \sum_{j \in C} w_{ij} = 1 \ \forall i \quad \text{and} \quad w_{ij} \geq 0 \ \forall i, j.$$

This is a two-stage nonparametric estimator: the counter-factual $E(y_0|x, d = 1)$ is estimated in the first stage with $\sum_{j \in C} w_{ij} y_j$, and the effect on the treated is estimated in the second stage. Weighting can be also applied to the second stage (i.e., instead of $N_1^{-1} \sum_{i \in T} (\cdot)$, we may use $\sum_{i \in T} \omega_i \times (\cdot)$ where ω_i is a weight for treated i). When we examined the estimator T_{wN} that uses a kernel weighting, we deferred showing the asymptotic distribution, which is taken up now in this section drawing on Lee (1997). Also some other related issues raised in Heckman, Ichimura, and Todd (1997, HIT from now on) will be discussed here.

Define the 'y_0-comparison-group-bias conditional on x':

$$B_1(x) \equiv E(y_0|x, d=1) - E(y_0|x, d=0)$$
$$\Longleftrightarrow E(y_0|x, d=1) = E(y_0|x, d=0) + B_1(x),$$

and observe

$$E(y_0|d=1) = \int \{E(y_0|x, d=0) + B_1(x)\} f(x|d=1) dx$$
$$= \int E(y_0|x, d=0) f(x|d=1) dx + B_1,$$
$$\text{where } B_1 \equiv \int B_1(x) f(x|d=1) dx.$$

From this, the effect on the treated is

$$E(y_1 - y_0|d=1) = E(y|d=1) - \int E(y_0|x, d=0) f(x|d=1) dx - B_1.$$

Thus, under $B_1 = 0$ that is implied by $B_1(x) = 0 \ \forall x$, the effect on the treated is identified by this display. Note that B_1 can be zero even if $B_1(x) \neq 0$ for some x. HIT show a case where indeed the average of $B_1(x)$ over some range of x becomes zero.

For $E(y_1|d=1)$, let

$$E_N(y_1|d=1) \equiv \frac{\sum_i d_i y_i}{\sum_i d_i} = \frac{N^{-1} \sum_i d_i y_i}{N^{-1} \sum_i d_i} (\to^p E(y_1|d=1))$$
$$\Longrightarrow E_N(y_1|d=1) - E(y_1|d=1) = \frac{N^{-1} \sum_i d_i (y_i - E(y|d=1))}{N^{-1} \sum_i d_i}.$$

Since $N^{-1} \sum_i d_i \to^p P(d=1)$, we have

$$\sqrt{N}\{E_N(y_1|d=1) - E(y_1|d=1)\} = \frac{(1/\sqrt{N}) \sum_i d_i \{y_i - E(y|d=1)\}}{N^{-1} \sum_i d_i}$$
$$= P(d=1)^{-1}(1/\sqrt{N}) \sum_i d_i \{y_i - E(y|d=1)\} + o_p(1).$$

As for $E(y_0|d=1)$, define

$$f(x, j) \equiv f(x|d=j) \cdot P(d=j) \quad \text{for } j = 0, 1.$$

$E(y_0|d=1)$ can be estimated (up to B_1) in two stages. First, for each treated i, estimate $E(y_0|x_i, d=0)$ with

$$E_N(y_0|x_i, d=0) \equiv \frac{\sum_{j, j \neq i} K((x_j - x_i)/h)(1 - d_j) y_j}{\sum_{j, j \neq i} K((x_j - x_i)/h)(1 - d_j)},$$

where K is a kernel and h is a bandwidth. Second, average $E_N(y_0|x_i, d = 0)$ over the treated to get

$$E_N(y_0|d = 1) \equiv \frac{\sum_i d_i E_N(y_0|x_i, d = 0)}{\sum_i d_i} (\to^p E(y_0|d = 1) - B_1).$$

Hence,

$$E_N(y_1|d = 1) - E_N(y_0|d = 1) \to^p E(y_1 - y_0|d = 1) + B_1.$$

The estimator T_{wN} is $E_N(y_1|d = 1) - E_N(y_0|d = 1)$ that can be written as

$$\frac{N^{-1}\sum_i d_i\{y_i - E_N(y_0|x_i, d = 0)\}}{N^{-1}\sum_i d_i}.$$

This appeared as $\hat{\tau}_1$ in Subsection 3.4.3, which means that the asymptotic variance of T_{wN} in the following paragraph should be equal to the semiparametric efficiency bound V_1 in Subsection 3.4.3 if proposition 4 in Hahn (1998), which states the semiparametric efficiency of $\hat{\tau}_1$, indeed holds.

As for the asymptotic distribution of T_{wN}, Lee (1997) shows that

$$\sqrt{N} \cdot \{E_N(y_1|d = 1) - E_N(y_0|d = 1) - E(y_1 - y_0|d = 1) - B_1\}$$
$$\rightsquigarrow N\left(0, P(d = 1)^{-2} \cdot E\left[d\{y_1 - E(y_1|d = 1) + \int E(y_0|x, d = 0)f(x|d = 1)dx\right.\right.$$
$$\left.\left. -E(y_0|x, d = 0)\} - (1 - d)\{y_0 - E(y_0|x, d = 0)\}\frac{f(x, 1)}{f(x, 0)}\right]^2\right).$$

The reason to have B_1 explicitly in the asymptotic distribution is that there is a scope for 'sensitivity analysis', where we can initially carry out a statistical inference with $B_1 = 0$, and then allow B_1 to change around zero to see how non-zero comparison-group bias affects the inference. This kind of sensitivity analysis is a way to deal with hidden bias and appears in Chapter 6.

One major problem in matching is the support problem of only partially overlapping supports of $x|(d = 0)$ and $x|(d = 1)$ distributions. When this problem is present, there may not be a good comparison group for some x. We already saw some extreme cases where the supports did not overlap at all, and as the consequence, matching was not feasible. In light of the support problem, we re-examine the preceding nonparametric matching allowing for comparison group bias *and* support discrepancy in the following.

For the treatment effect on the treated $E(y_1 - y_0 | d = 1)$, redefine the parameter of interest as

$$E(y_1 - y_0 | x \in S, d = 1) = \frac{\int_S E(y_1 - y_0 | x, d = 1) \cdot f(x|d = 1)dx}{\int_S f(x|d = 1)dx},$$

(i.e., x is integrated out only over S) where

$$S \equiv S_0 \cap S_1, \qquad S_j \equiv \text{support of } x|(d = j), \quad j = 0, 1.$$

Recall $B_1(x) = E(y_0 | x, d = 1) - E(y_0 | x, d = 0)$, and define its unconditional version for S:

$$B_S \equiv \frac{\int_S \{E(y_0 | x, d = 1) - E(y_0 | x, d = 0)\} f(x|d = 1)dx}{\int_S f(x|d = 1)dx}.$$

With B_S, the parameter of interest $E(y_1 - y_0 | x \in S, d = 1)$ can be rewritten as

$$\frac{\int_S \{E(y_1 | x, d = 1) - E(y_0 | x, d = 0)\} f(x|d = 1)dx}{\int_S f(x|d = 1)dx} - B_S$$

$$= E(y_1 | x \in S, d = 1) - \frac{\int_S E(y_0 | x, d = 0) f(x|d = 1)dx}{\int_S f(x|d = 1)dx} - B_S$$

$$= E(y_1 | x \in S, d = 1) - M_1 - B_S,$$

$$\text{where } M_1 \equiv \frac{\int_S E(y_0 | x, d = 0) f(x|d = 1)dx}{\int_S f(x|d = 1)dx}.$$

In M_1, the conditioning is on $d = 0$ while the integrating density has $d = 1$. A consistent estimator for $E(y_1 | x \in S, d = 1)$ is

$$E_N(y_1 | x \in S, d = 1) \equiv \frac{\sum_i d_i 1[x_i \in S] \cdot y_i}{\sum_i d_i 1[x_i \in S]}.$$

The asymptotic distribution for this is

$$\sqrt{N} \{ E_N(y_1 | x \in S, d = 1) - E(y_1 | x \in S, d = 1) \}$$

$$\rightsquigarrow P(d = 1, x \in S)^{-1} (1/\sqrt{N}) \sum_i d_i 1[x_i \in S] \{ y_i - E(y_1 | x \in S, d = 1) \}.$$

As for M_1, we need a two-stage procedure. First, for each treated i with $x_i \in S$, estimate $E(y_0 | x_i, d = 0)$ with $E_N(y_0 | x_i, d = 0)$, and then average $E_N(y_0 | x_i, d = 0)$ over the T group with $x_i \in S$ to get

$$E_N(y_0 | x \in S, d = 1) \equiv \frac{\sum_i d_i 1[x_i \in S] E_N(y_0 | x_i, d = 0)}{\sum_i d_i 1[x_i \in S]} \rightarrow^p M_1.$$

Then

$$E_N(y_1|x \in S, d = 1) - E_N(y_0|x \in S, d = 1) \to^P E(y_1 - y_0|x \in S, d = 1) + B_S.$$

The asymptotic distribution for this estimator is

$$\sqrt{N}\{E_N(y_1|x \in S, d=1) - E_N(y_0|x \in S, d=1) - E(y_1 - y_0|x \in S, d=1) - B_S\}$$

$$\rightsquigarrow N\left(0,\ P(d=1, x \in S)^{-2} \cdot E\left[1[x \in S]\left[d\{y_1 - E(y_1|x \in S, d=1)\right.\right.\right.$$

$$\left.\left.\left. +M_1 - E(y_0|x, d=0)\} - (1-d)\{y_0 - E(y_0|x, d=0)\}\frac{f(x,1)}{f(x,0)}\right]^2\right]\right).$$

HIT decompose the comparison group bias (or selection bias)

$$B \equiv E(y_0|d = 1) - E(y_0|d = 0)$$

into three terms:

$$B = \int_{S_1} E(y_0|x, d = 1)f(x|d = 1)dx - \int_{S_0} E(y_0|x, d = 0)f(x|d = 0)dx$$

$$= \int_{S_1 \setminus S} E(y_0|x, d = 1)f(x|d = 1)dx$$

$$- \int_{S_0 \setminus S} E(y_0|x, d = 0)f(x|d = 0)dx \quad (\equiv B_d)$$

$$+ \int_S E(y_0|x, d = 0) \cdot \{f(x|d = 1) - f(x|d = 0)\}dx \quad (\equiv B_f)$$

$$+ \int_S \{E(y_0|x, d = 1) - E(y_0|x, d = 0)\} \cdot f(x|d = 1)dx \quad (\equiv B_t).$$

$B_d \neq 0$ is due to the problem of non-overlapping supports, B_f is due to imbalance of x across the two groups on the common support, and B_t is the comparison group bias (or selection bias) on S. Matching only on $x \in S$ makes $B_f \simeq 0$ and the selection-on-observable assumption rules out B_t, thus leaving only B_d in B.

Suppose d denotes participation, not necessarily getting the treatment. In the job-training experiment data used in HIT, there were both nonpartici-pants and participants without treatment. The latter were randomized out despite participation $d = 1$. This enabled HIT to estimate B consistently: $\int_{S_1} E(y_0|x, d = 1)f(x|d = 1)dx$ was estimated with the randomized-out participants, and $\int_{S_0} E(y_0|x, d = 0)f(x|d = 0)dx$ was estimated with the non-participants.

HIT found that, in their data analysis, B_d and B_f were far bigger than B_t in the absolute magnitude. However, because B_d and B_f are of the opposite signs, they cancelled each other to some extent. This phenomenon of the opposite signs is due to the fact that the $d = 0$ group put most observations on $S_0 \backslash S$, which makes B_d negative and B_f positive. HIT also found that although B_t was small, it was not small compared with the true treatment effect measured with the experimental data.

A.5 Appendix for Chapter 5

A.5.1 Some remarks on LATE

The subsection makes three remarks on LATE. Recall the notations and three assumptions (a), (b), and (c) in Subsection 5.6.3.

First, instead of the monotonicity (c) $d_1 \geq d_0$, suppose $d_0 = 0$ always. Then $d = zd_1$ from $d = (1 - z)d_0 + zd_1$, and thus $d = 1 \iff (z = 1, d_1 = 1)$. Since $d_0 = 0$, we get $P(d_1 - d_0 = -1) = 0$ as the monotonicity does. Then, recalling the equation for $E\{(d_1 - d_0)(y_1 - y_0)\}$ in Subsection 5.6.3,

$$
\begin{aligned}
E(y|z = 1) - E(y|z = 0) &= E(y_1 - y_0|d_1 - d_0 = 1) \cdot P(d_1 - d_0 = 1) \\
&= E(y_1 - y_0|d_1 = 1) \cdot P(d_1 = 1) \\
&= E(y_1 - y_0|d_1 = 1, z = 1) \cdot P(d_1 = 1|z = 1) \\
&\quad \text{owing to (b) } z \text{ II } (y_0, y_1, d_0, d_1) \\
&= E(y_1 - y_0|d = 1) \cdot P(d = 1|z = 1) \\
&\quad \text{owing to } d = 1 \iff (z = 1, d_1 = 1).
\end{aligned}
$$

Hence,

$$
E(y_1 - y_0|d = 1) = \frac{E(y|z = 1) - E(y|z = 0)}{E(d|z = 1)};
$$

the effect on the treated is identified as Imbens and Angrist (1994) show. The condition '$d_0 = 0$ always' is, however, restrictive. In the example on the effects of exercise on health, there can be many persons who exercise without education or encouragement (i.e., $d_0 = 1$).

Second, without the monotonicity, take $E(\cdot|z = 0)$ on $y = y_0 + (y_1 - y_0)d$ to get

$$
\begin{aligned}
E(y|z = 0) &= E(y_0|z = 0) + E(y_1 - y_0|z = 0, d = 1) \cdot P(d = 1|z = 0) \\
&= E(y_0|z = 0) + E(y_1 - y_0|z = 0, d_0 = 1) \cdot P(d = 1|z = 0) \\
&= E(y_0) + E(y_1 - y_0|d_0 = 1) \cdot P(d = 1|z = 0) \quad \text{owing to (b)} \\
&= E(y_0) + E(y_1 - y_0|d_1 = 1) \cdot P(d = 1|z = 0) \\
&\quad + \{E(y_1 - y_0|d_0 = 1) - E(y_1 - y_0|d_1 = 1)\} \cdot P(d = 1|z = 0).
\end{aligned}
$$

Analogously,

$$
\begin{aligned}
E(y|z = 1) &= E(y_0|z = 1) + E(y_1 - y_0|z = 1, d = 1) \cdot P(d = 1|z = 1) \\
&= E(y_0) + E(y_1 - y_0|d_1 = 1) \cdot P(d = 1|z = 1).
\end{aligned}
$$

Subtract the last equation of the preceding display from this equation to get

$$E(y|z=1) - E(y|z=0) = E(y_1 - y_0|d_1 = 1)$$
$$\times \{P(d=1|z=1) - P(d=1|z=0)\}$$
$$+ \{E(y_1 - y_0|d_1 = 1) - E(y_1 - y_0|d_0 = 1)\} \cdot P(d=1|z=0).$$

Divide through $E(d|z=1) - E(d|z=0)$ to get

$$\text{Wald Est.} = E(y_1 - y_0|d_1 = 1) + \frac{E(y_1 - y_0|d_1 = 1) - E(y_1 - y_0|d_0 = 1)}{E(d|z=1) - E(d|z=0)}$$
$$\times P(d=1|z=0).$$

Since $E(y_1 - y_0|d_1 = 1) = E(y_1 - y_0|\text{compliers, always takers})$, this shows that, without the monotonicity, the Wald estimator is different from the effect on the compliers and always-takers by the magnitude of the second expression. If there is no always-taker, then the Wald estimator is the effect on the compliers that is the effect on the treated because $P(d=1|z=0) = 0$.

Third, although LATE can be estimated with the Wald estimator, differently from $E(y_1 - y_0)$ and $E(y_1 - y_0|d=1)$, the LATE subpopulation $d_1 - d_0 = 1$ is not identified. In other words, the subjects who would change their treatment as the instrument changes cannot be seen. The Wald estimator shows the effect on the compliers, but we will not know how big the subpopulation of compliers is or who belongs to it. Another problem of LATE is that the subpopulation depends on the instrument at hand, which is not ideal because we would prefer a constant parameter as the instrument changes. See, however, Angrist (2004) who tries to link LATE to $E(y_1 - y_0)$ by restricting parameters in

$$E(y_0|d_0, d_1) = \alpha_0 + \beta_{00}d_0 + \beta_{01}d_1 \quad \text{and} \quad E(y_1|d_0, d_1) = \alpha_1 + \beta_{10}d_0 + \beta_{11}d_1.$$

Note that the linear specifications here are not restrictions because there are three groups (never takers, compliers, and always takers) and three parameters in each conditional mean.

In Angrist's (1990) Vietnam era draft lottery example, $d=1$ if the person serves in the military and 0 otherwise, and $z=1$ if a high draft-priority lottery number is drawn and 0 otherwise (z is in fact not binary in Angrist (1990)). The four sub populations are:

> Always Takers: $d_1 = 1$, $d_0 = 1$: join the military anyway,
> Never Takers: $d_1 = 0$, $d_0 = 0$: never join the military,
> Compliers: $d_1 = 1$, $d_0 = 0$: join the military only if drafted,
> Defiers: $d_1 = 0$, $d_0 = 1$: join the military only if not drafted.

The LATE sub population, the compliers, is likely to be large in this example. But there are examples where the size of the LATE sub population is hard to gauge. For instance, in estimating the effects of fertility d (number of children) on a female labor market outcome y (d and y are likely to be determined jointly, making d endogenous), Angrist and Evans (1998) use twin birth at the second birth as an instrument for d, because twin birth gives an exogenous increase to d. In this example, the subpopulation $d_1 - d_0 = 1$ is those couples who have three kids only because of a twin birth at the second birth.

A.5.2   Outcome distributions for compliers

By using instruments, not just the mean effect for the compliers is identified, but the entire marginal distributions of y_0 and y_1 for the compliers. This was shown by Imbens and Rubin (1997). Abadie (2002) proposes a number of bootstrap-based nonparametric tests for the equality of the two marginal distributions. These are examined in this subsection.

Recall that monotonicity rules out defiers. Hence the population consists of never takers, compliers, and always takers. Denote the population probability for these types, respectively, as p_n, p_c, and p_a. It is important to note that only never takers have $d = 0$ when $z = 1$. Also, only always takers have $d = 1$ when $z = 0$. Because the population is randomly dichotomized with $z = 0$ and $z = 1$, the proportion of the never takers in the $z = 1$ subpopulation ($P(d = 0|z = 1)$) is the same as that in the $z = 0$ subpopulation. Thus we have

$$p_n = P(d = 0|z = 1), \qquad p_a = P(d = 1|z = 0), \qquad p_c = 1 - p_n - p_a.$$

Note that p_n is not $P(d = 0, z = 1)$ because never takers contribute also to $P(d = 0, z = 0)$.

Observe

$$E(y|z = 0, d = 0) = E(y|z = 0, d = 0, \text{complier}) \cdot P(\text{complier}|z = 0, d = 0)$$
$$+ E(y|z = 0, d = 0, \text{never taker}) \cdot P(\text{never taker}|z = 0, d = 0)$$
$$= E(y_0|z = 0, d_0 = 0, d_1 = 1) \cdot P(\text{complier}|z = 0, d = 0)$$
$$+ E(y_0|z = 0, d_0 = 0, d_1 = 0) \cdot P(\text{never taker}|z = 0, d = 0)$$
$$= E(y_0|d_0 = 0, d_1 = 1)\frac{p_c}{p_c + p_n} + E(y_0|d_0 = 0, d_1 = 0)\frac{p_n}{p_c + p_n}.$$

Replace $E(y_0|d_0 = 0, d_1 = 0)$ with $E(y|z = 1, d = 0)$ to get

$$E(y|z = 0, d = 0)$$
$$= E(y_0|d_0 = 0, d_1 = 1)\frac{p_c}{p_c + p_n} + E(y|z = 1, d = 0)\frac{p_n}{p_c + p_n}.$$

Solve this for $E(y_0|d_0 = 0, d_1 = 1)$:

$$E(y_0|d_0 = 0, d_1 = 1) = \frac{p_c + p_n}{p_c}E(y|z = 0, d = 0) - \frac{p_n}{p_c}E(y|z = 1, d = 0);$$

all terms on the right-hand side are identified. In this derivation, we used y_0 and y. If we replace y_0 and y with $1[y_0 \le t]$ and $1[y \le t]$, respectively, then the marginal distribution of y_0 for compliers is identified:

$$P(y_0 \le t | \text{complier})$$
$$= \frac{p_c + p_n}{p_c} P(y \le t | z = 0, d = 0) - \frac{p_n}{p_c} P(y \le t | z = 1, d = 0).$$

Doing analogously,

$$E(y | z = 1, d = 1) = E(y | z = 1, d = 1, \text{complier}) \cdot P(\text{complier} | z = 1, d = 1)$$
$$+ E(y | z = 1, d = 1, \text{always taker}) \cdot P(\text{always taker} | z = 1, d = 1)$$
$$= E(y_1 | z = 1, d_0 = 0, d_1 = 1) \cdot P(\text{complier} | z = 1, d = 1)$$
$$+ E(y_1 | z = 1, d_0 = 1, d_1 = 1) \cdot P(\text{always taker} | z = 1, d = 1)$$
$$= E(y_1 | d_0 = 0, d_1 = 1) \frac{p_c}{p_a + p_c} + E(y_1 | d_0 = 1, d_1 = 1) \frac{p_a}{p_a + p_c}.$$

Replace $E(y_1 | d_0 = 1, d_1 = 1)$ with $E(y | z = 0, d = 1)$ to get

$$E(y | z = 1, d = 1)$$
$$= E(y_1 | d_0 = 0, d_1 = 1) \frac{p_c}{p_a + p_c} + E(y | z = 0, d = 1) \frac{p_a}{p_a + p_c}.$$

Solve this for $E(y_1 | d_0 = 0, d_1 = 1)$:

$$E(y_1 | d_0 = 0, d_1 = 1) = \frac{p_a + p_c}{p_c} E(y | z = 1, d = 1) - \frac{p_a}{p_c} E(y | z = 0, d = 1).$$

Replace y_1 and y with $1[y_1 \le t]$ and $1[y \le t]$, respectively, to get

$$P(y_1 \le t | \text{complier})$$
$$= \frac{p_a + p_c}{p_c} P(y \le t | z = 1, d = 1) - \frac{p_a}{p_c} P(y \le t | z = 0, d = 1).$$

Observe, $h(y) = dh(y_1) + (1 - d)h(y_0)$ for any function $h(\cdot)$. Doing in the same way as we did for LATE in subsection 5.6.3, we get

$$E(h(y) | z = 1) - E(h(y) | z = 0)$$
$$= E\{h(y_1) - h(y_0) | d_0 = 0, d_1 = 1\} \cdot P(d_0 = 0, d_1 = 1).$$

Hence, recalling $E(d | z = 1) - E(d | z = 0) = P(d_0 = 0, d_1 = 1)$,

$$E\{h(y_1) - h(y_0) | d_0 = 0, d_1 = 1\} = \frac{E(h(y) | z = 1) - E(h(y) | z = 0)}{E(d | z = 1) - E(d | z = 0)}.$$

Replace $h(\cdot)$ with $1[\cdot \le t]$ to get

$$P(y_1 \le t | \text{complier}) - P(y_0 \le t | \text{complier}) = \frac{P(y \le t | z = 1) - P(y \le t | z = 0)}{E(d | z = 1) - E(d | z = 0)}.$$

Because $E(d|z = 1) - E(d|z = 0) > 0$ in the LATE assumptions, we get

$$sign\{P(y_1 \leq t|\text{complier}) - P(y_0 \leq t|\text{complier})\}$$
$$= sign\{P(y \leq t|z = 1) - P(y \leq t|z = 0)\}.$$

If the sign is zero or negative $\forall t$, then the (first-order) *stochastic dominance* of F_{c1} over F_{c0} holds:

$$F_{c1}(t) \leq F_{c0}(t) \ \forall t \qquad \text{(with inequality holding for some } t\text{)}$$

where F_{cj} denotes the marginal distribution for y_j given compliers. In other words, $y_1|(d_0 = 0, d_1 = 1)$ tends to be greater than $y_0|(d_0 = 0, d_1 = 1)$.

Abadie (2002) proposes a 'Kolmogorov-Smirnov' type nonparametric test for $F_{c0}(t) = F_{c1}(t) \ \forall t$ versus the stochastic dominance of F_{c1} over F_{c0}. The test statistic is

$$KS_N \equiv \left(\frac{N_0 N_1}{N}\right)^{1/2} \sup_{t \in R} \{\hat{F}_{c0}(t) - \hat{F}_{c1}(t)\},$$

where $\hat{F}_{cj}(t)$ is the empirical distribution function for the group with $z = j$. The asymptotic distribution is approximated by bootstrap in Abadie (2002) who proves the bootstrap consistency. The bootstrap here proceeds as follows. First, from the pooled sample of size N, draw randomly N times with replacement to get a pseudo sample of size N. Second, assign the first N_0 of them to the C group and the remaining N_1 to the T group, and apply the same estimation to the pseudo sample to get a pseudo test statistic KS_N^*. Third, repeat this B times (e.g., $B = 500$) to get B-many pseudo test statistics $KS_{N1}^*, \ldots, KS_{NB}^*$. Fourth, compute the bootstrap p-value $B^{-1} \sum_{j=1}^{B} 1[KS_{Nj}^* > KS_N]$ and reject the null hypothesis if this p-value is smaller than a chosen significance level, say, 5%.

Abadie (2002) also proposes two more tests

$$\left(\frac{N_0 N_1}{N}\right)^{1/2} \sup_{t \in R} |\hat{F}_{c0}(t) - \hat{F}_{c1}(t)|,$$

$$\left(\frac{N_0 N_1}{N}\right)^{1/2} \sup_{t \in R} \int_{-\infty}^{t} \{\hat{F}_{c0}(y) - \hat{F}_{c1}(y)\}dy.$$

In the former, $F_{c1} = F_{c1} \ \forall t$ versus $F_{c1} \neq F_{c1}$ for some t are tested for. In the latter, the *second-order stochastic dominance* of F_{c1} over F_{c0} is tested for:

$$\int_{-\infty}^{t} \{F_{c0}(y) - F_{c1}(y)\}dy \geq 0 \ \forall t.$$

Note that no covariates are controlled for in the above three tests.

A.5.3   Median treatment effect

In the main text, we focused on the average effect $(1/N)\sum_i(y_{1i} - y_{0i})$, its conditional version, or its population version. A minor reason for this is that the mean is attractive relating to the total $\sum_i(y_{1i} - y_{0i})$ and we can talk about an increase or decrease of the total 'welfare'. The major reason for focusing on the mean is the linearity of the mean functional:

$$E(y_1 - y_0) = E(y_1) - E(y_0).$$

Other than for the mean, linearity does not hold in general. For example, even if we get the two marginal medians, we cannot get the median of $y_1 - y_0$. One trivial case for median functional to be linear is the constant effect $y_{1i} - y_{0i} = \beta$ for all i, which implies

$$Med(y_1) - Med(y_0) \ (= Med(y_0 + \beta) - Med(y_0) = \beta) = Med(y_1 - y_0).$$

Other than the two reasons cited above for the mean (and the popularity of mean in our daily life), it is hard to think of a good reason to focus on the mean. One of the best known disadvantage of the mean is its sensitivity to outliers: it is possible that $(1/N)\sum_i(y_{1i} - y_{0i})$ is positive, but only one individual (outlier) gains $(y_{1i} - y_{0i} > 0)$ while all the others lose $(y_{1m} - y_{0m} < 0$, for all $m \neq i)$. From a politician's viewpoint, a (treatment or) policy that gives small gains to the majority of the people could be more attractive than a policy that gives large gains to a minority group. In this case, whether the median of $y_1 - y_0$ is positive or not is of interest. More generally, taking into account the cost side of the policy, we may want to know whether an α-th quantile of $y_1 - y_0$ is positive or not. That is, quantiles are as much of an interest as is the mean. In this subsection, we present Lee's (2000) result for the median, which is a first step toward learning about $Med(y_1 - y_0)$ from $Med(y_1)$ and $Med(y_0)$.

Define

$$Med(y_0) \equiv m_0, \qquad Med(y_1) \equiv m_1, \quad and \quad m \equiv m_1 - m_0;$$
$$w_0 \equiv y_0 - m_0, \qquad w_1 \equiv y_1 - m_1.$$

Assume that (w_0, w_1) has a density $f(w_0, w_1)$ that is continuous and positive around $(0, 0)$. We look for conditions under which the following holds:

$$M0: \ m_1 = m_0 \ \text{implies} \ Med(y_1 - y_0) = 0;$$
$$M1: \ m_1 > m_0 \ \text{implies} \ Med(y_1 - y_0) > 0.$$

The case with '$<$' is analogous and thus omitted. M1 does not mean $m_1 - m_0 = Med(y_1 - y_0)$; M1 only means

$$sign(m_1 - m_0) = sign(Med(y_1 - y_0)).$$

For the four quadrants on the (w_0, w_1) plane, denote the probability masses as p_1, p_2, p_3 and p_4, respectively. From the very fact that the density f is centered at (m_0, m_1), it follows that

$$p_1 + p_4 = 0.5 \quad \text{and} \quad p_1 + p_2 = 0.5.$$

Subtract the second equation from the first to get $p_2 = p_4$. Analogously, we get $p_1 = p_3$. Using these simple equations, Theorem 1 in Lee (2000) shows

> M0 holds iff $P(w_1 < w_0 < 0) = P(0 < w_0 < w_1)$;
> M1 holds iff $P(w_1 < w_0 - m,\ w_0 < 0) < P(w_0 - m < w_1,\ 0 < w_0)$.

Due to $p_1 = p_3$ and $p_2 = p_4$, M0 is equivalent to

$$P(w_0 < w_1 < 0) = P(0 < w_1 < w_0);$$

analogously, M1 is equivalent to

$$P(w_0 - m < w_1 < 0) > P(0 < w_1 < w_0 - m).$$

To understand the conditions better, in the (w_0, w_1) plane, split each quadrant into two triangles to get eight equal-sized 'octants'. In essence, M0 holds *if the second octant has the same probability mass as the sixth octant.* Due to a non-zero probability mass of (w_0, w_1) around $(0, 0)$, M1 follows as well. The condition for M0 is weaker than, e.g., central symmetry $f(w_0, w_1) = f(-w_0, -w_1)$ and exchangeability $f(w_0, w_1) = f(w_1, w_0)$. If M0 holds, then we can conclude no median treatment effect when $m = 0$, despite that $y_{0i} \neq y_{1i}$ is certainly possible at the individual level.

A special case for the conditions for M0 and M1 is

$$\text{under no effect}: y_{0i} = \psi(\alpha_i, u_{0i}), \quad y_{1i} = \psi(\alpha_i, u_{1i}),$$
$$u_{0i}, u_{1i} \text{ are iid given } \alpha_i,$$
$$\text{under some effect}: y_{0i} = \psi(\alpha_i, u_{0i}), \quad y_{1i} = \zeta\{\psi(\alpha_i, u_{1i})\},$$

where $\zeta(z) > z$, and $\zeta(z_1) \geq \zeta(z_2)$ if $z_1 \geq z_2$; an example for $\zeta(\cdot)$ is $\exp(\cdot)$. In this case, under no treatment effect, y_{0i} and y_{1i} are exchangeable, which implies the same marginal distribution for y_{0i} and y_{1i} (and thus the same marginal median). Under some effect, y_{1i} is a monotonic transformation of $\psi(\alpha_i, u_{1i})$ such that $\zeta\{\psi(\alpha_i, u_{1i})\} > \psi(\alpha_i, u_{1i})$. In this sense, y_1 becomes bigger than y_0 'on average'. For a given i, since $u_{0i} \neq u_{1i}$ in general, we can have $\zeta\{\psi(\alpha_i, u_{1i})\} < \psi(\alpha_i, u_{0i})$. This special case looks somewhat restrictive in terms of the conditions imposed on the function $\zeta(\cdot)$; Theorem 1 relaxes this type of restriction, while not being specific on how y_{0i} and y_{1i} are generated.

Although not presented here, the findings in Lee (2000) for quantiles suggest that it would be difficult to learn about the quantiles of $y_1 - y_0$ from the marginal quantiles. Even for the median, the above presentation shows only that, under the 'equal octant probability' assumption, if $m_1 > (=, <)m_0$, then $Med(y_1 - y_0) > (=, <)0$. That is, examining the T and C groups separately and comparing their quantiles will tell little of the corresponding quantile of $y_1 - y_0$ in general, although this is what is often done in practice.

A.6 Appendix for Chapter 6

Earlier, in Chapter 3, we showed briefly that post-treatment covariates affected by the treatment should not be controlled for so as to avoid diluting the treatment effect. This tenet holds in general despite an exception shown in Chapter 6. Here, we examine this in further detail, which may also serve as a 'warm up' for the dynamic treatment effect in Chapter 7.

A.6.1 Controlling for affected covariates in a linear model

Suppose we have observational data and we are worried about 'selection-on-unobservables'

$$E(y_j|d, x, \varepsilon) = E(y_j|x, \varepsilon) \quad \text{for all } x, \varepsilon$$

but

$$E(y_j|d, x) \neq E(y_j|x) \text{ for some } x, \quad j = 0, 1,$$

and there is a post-treatment variable m which may be a good 'proxy' for the unobservable variable ε. Recall the following 'x-omitted' causal diagram with different notations, dubbed 'proxy (iii)' in Chapter 3:

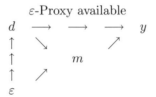

In this diagram, ε is a common factor causing hidden bias. Since m stands in between ε and y, it is tempting to control for m instead of ε. However there is a trade-off: not controlling for m leads to a hidden bias, but controlling for m can dilute the effect of d on y, because of the indirect effect of d on y, though m is not accounted for.

One example is: d is an education program where students participate voluntarily, y is GPA in the third year, m is a test score in the second year, and ε is ability. Although ability should have been controlled for before the program was administered, suppose that it was not done, and high-ability students self-selected into the program. The second year test can be used as a proxy for ability after the treatment is given. Not controlling for m means imbalance in ability across the two groups, whereas controlling for m yields only the incremental (direct) effect relative to the second year test. It is possible that m is a lagged y, that is, GPA in the second year.

To see the trade-off better, let m_0 and m_1 be the two potential variables for the effect of d on m. Suppose

$$d_i = \alpha_1 + x_i'\alpha_x + \varepsilon_i, \qquad E(\varepsilon|x) = 0,$$
$$m_{0i} = \gamma_1 + x_i'\gamma_x + e_{0i}, \qquad m_{1i} = \gamma_1 + \gamma_d + x_i'\gamma_x + e_{1i}$$
$$E(e_0|x) = E(e_1|x) = 0,$$
$$y_0 \text{ SF} : y_{0i} = \beta_1 + \beta_m m_{0i} + x_i'\beta_x + u_i,$$
$$y_1 \text{ SF} : y_{1i} = \beta_1 + \beta_d + \beta_m m_{1i} + x_i'\beta_x + u_i, \qquad E(u|x) = 0,$$

where α, β, γ are parameters and ε, e_0, e_1, u are mean-zero error terms. The equations for (y_0, y_1) include the constant-effect assumption, which is restrictive but invoked here to simplify the discussion.

Suppose that ε is related to e_j but not to u directly in the sense

$$\varepsilon \rightarrow e_j \rightarrow u.$$

This establishes how m_j is a good *proxy* for ε:

$$E(y_j|d, x, m_j) = E(y_j|x, m_j) :$$

this is $d \perp y_j|(x, m_j)$ (i.e., $\varepsilon \perp u|(x, e_j)$). Assume this mean independence (or its stronger version $d \amalg y_j|(x, m_j)$).

From the latent model, the effect of d on m is

$$E(m_1 - m_0|x) = \gamma_d$$

and the direct effect of d on y is

$$E(y_1 - y_0|m_0 = m_o, m_1 = m_o, x) = \beta_d.$$

This effect is dubbed 'direct', because the indirect effect of d on y through m is ruled out by conditioning on $m_0 = m_o$ and $m_1 = m_o$. This conditioning may look strange but one has to imagine subjects with $(d, x, m_0, m_1, y_0, y_1)$: the conditional mean is for those with x and $m_0 = m_1 = m_o$.

Substitute the m_1 and m_0 equations into the y_1 and y_0 equation to get

$$y_0 \text{ RF for } d_0 : \quad y_{0i} = \beta_1 + \beta_m(\gamma_1 + x_i'\gamma_x + e_{0i}) + x_i'\beta_x + u_i$$
$$= \beta_1 + \beta_m\gamma_1 + x_i'(\beta_x + \beta_m\gamma_x) + \beta_m e_{0i} + u_i,$$
$$y_1 \text{ RF for } d_1 : \quad y_{1i} = \beta_1 + \beta_d + \beta_m(\gamma_1 + \gamma_d + x_i'\gamma_x + e_{1i}) + x_i'\beta_x + u_i$$
$$= \beta_1 + \beta_m\gamma_1 + \beta_d + \beta_m\gamma_d + x_i'(\beta_x + \beta_m\gamma_x) + \beta_m e_{1i} + u_i.$$

From this, the total effect of d on y is

$$E(y_1 - y_0|x) = \beta_d + \beta_m\gamma_d.$$

The latter term $\beta_m\gamma_d$ is the indirect effect of d on y through m.

Although we consider $(d, x, m_0, m_1, y_0, y_1)$ for each individual, what is observed is (d, x, m, y) where

$$
\begin{aligned}
m_i &= d_i m_{1i} + (1 - d_i) m_{0i} = \gamma_1 + \gamma_d d_i + x_i' \gamma_x + e_i, \\
&\quad \text{where } e_i = d_i e_{1i} + (1 - d_i) e_{0i}, \\
y_i &= d_i y_{1i} + (1 - d_i) y_{0i} = \beta_1 + \beta_d d_i + \beta_m (d_i m_{1i} + (1 - d_i) m_{0i}) + x_i' \beta_x + u_i \\
&\Longrightarrow y \ \text{SF}: \ y_i = \beta_1 + \beta_d d_i + \beta_m m_i + x_i' \beta_x + u_i.
\end{aligned}
$$

Here, we are using the usual econometric terminology 'SF' although this is not really structural—the latent y_1 and y_0 models are the real structural models.

Turning to how to identify the total effect, substitute the m equation into the y SF to get

$$
\begin{aligned}
y \ \text{RF for } d: \ y_i &= \beta_1 + \beta_d d_i + \beta_m (\gamma_1 + \gamma_d d_i + x_i' \gamma_x + e_i) + x_i' \beta_x + u_i \\
&= \beta_1 + \beta_m \gamma_1 + (\beta_d + \beta_m \gamma_d) d_i + x_i' (\beta_x + \beta_m \gamma_x) + \beta_m e_i + u_i.
\end{aligned}
$$

Also, substitute the d equation into the y SF to get

$$
\begin{aligned}
y \ \text{RF for } m: \ y_i &= \beta_1 + \beta_d (\alpha_1 + x_i' \alpha_x + \varepsilon_i) + \beta_m m_i + x_i' \beta_x + u_i \\
&= \beta_1 + \beta_d \alpha_1 + \beta_m m_i + x_i' (\beta_x + \beta_d \alpha_x) + \beta_d \varepsilon_i + u_i.
\end{aligned}
$$

From the y-RF for d, we get

$$
\begin{aligned}
E(y|d = 1, x) &= \beta_1 + \beta_m \gamma_1 + \beta_d + \beta_m \gamma_d + x'(\beta_x + \beta_m \gamma_x) \\
&\quad + E(\beta_m e_1 + u|d = 1, x), \\
E(y|d = 0, x) &= \beta_1 + \beta_m \gamma_1 + x'(\beta_x + \beta_m \gamma_x) + E(\beta_m e_0 + u|d = 0, x).
\end{aligned}
$$

Hence,

$$
\begin{aligned}
E(y|d = 1, x) - E(y|d = 0, x) &= \beta_d + \beta_m \gamma_d + E(\beta_m e_1 + u|d = 1, x) \\
&\quad - E(\beta_m e_0 + u|d = 0, x),
\end{aligned}
$$

where the error term conditional mean difference is the bias due to not controlling for m. The relation between e_j and ε (i.e., e_j and d) is the culprit. Integrating out x, the marginal version does not equal $\beta_d + \beta_m \gamma_d$ in general.

From the y SF,

$$
\begin{aligned}
E(y|d = 1, m &= m_o, x) - E(y|d = 0, m = m_o, x) \\
&= E(y_1|d = 1, m_1 = m_o, x) - E(y_0|d = 0, m_0 = m_o, x) \\
&= E(y_1|m_1 = m_o, x) - E(y_0|m_0 = m_o, x) = \beta_d.
\end{aligned}
$$

Here, only the direct effect of d on y is identified whereas the indirect effect of d on y through m is missed. In short, not controlling for m yields a bias for the total effect, whereas controlling for m renders only the direct effect.

A.6.2   Controlling for affected mean-surrogates

The findings in the previous subsection are not artefacts of the linear models, which were used only to help understand the main points easily. In this subsection, we make the same points without the linear model assumption.

Suppose

d is determined by x and ε (and some error term unrelated to e_j and u),

and ε is an unobserved confounder for y_j in the sense that

$$E(y_j|d, x, \varepsilon) = E(y_j|x, \varepsilon) \quad \text{for all } x \text{ and } \varepsilon,$$

but

$$E(y_j|d, x) \neq E(y_j|x) \quad \text{for some } x, \ j = 0, 1.$$

Also suppose ε is an unobserved confounder for m_j in the sense that

$$m_j \amalg d|(x, \varepsilon), \quad \text{but} \quad m_j \text{ is not independent of } d \text{ given only } x, \ j = 0, 1.$$

The assumption of ε being the unobserved confounder for y_j can be strengthened using $\amalg$ instead of $\perp$, although the weaker mean-based version will do.

Suppose m_0 and m_1 *are the mean surrogate for* ε in the sense that

$$E(y_j|d, m_j, x) = E(y_j|m_j, x), \qquad j = 0, 1;$$

this is the same as the proxy assumption in the preceding subsection. Rosenbaum (1984) defines a stronger version: m_1 and m_0 are a *surrogate for* ε if

$$y_j \amalg \varepsilon|(m_j, x), \qquad j = 0, 1.$$

The surrogacy and the above two assumptions—ε being an unmeasured confounder for m_j and y_j—was illustrated in the linear model of the preceding section with $\varepsilon \to e_j \to u$ where ε does not influence u if m_j and x are fixed (i.e., if e_j and x are fixed).

Define the (total mean) effect of d on y as

$$\tau = \int E(y_1 - y_0|x) F_x(\partial x),$$

where x is integrated out with the distribution F_x for the population (i.e., the pooled sample), and ∂ instead of d is used for the integral to prevent confusion.

To identify τ, if we control only for x in the two group means, then we would be getting

$$\tau_x \equiv E(y_1|d = 1, x) - E(y_0|d = 0, x).$$

After this step, x would be integrated out using the distribution for the pooled sample. The integrated version is

$$E(\tau_x) = \int \{E(y_1|d = 1, x) - E(y_0|d = 0, x)\} F_x(\partial x).$$

If we control for m as well as x to get τ, then we would be getting

$$\tau_{mx} \equiv E(y_1|d = 1, m_1 = m, x) - E(y_0|d = 0, m_0 = m, x).$$

Letting $F_{m,x}$ denote the joint distribution for m and x in the pooled sample, the integrated version is

$$E(\tau_{mx}) = \int \{E(y_1|d = 1, m_1 = m, x) - E(y_0|d = 0, m_0 = m, x)\} F_{m,x}(\partial m, \partial x).$$

Observe (the mean surrogacy is used for $E(\tau_x)$ and $E(\tau_{mx})$ in the following display)

$$
\begin{aligned}
\tau &= \int E(y_1|x) F_x(\partial x) - \int E(y_0|x) F_x(\partial x) \\
&= \Big\{ \int E(y_1|m_1 = m, x) F_{m_1|x}(\partial m) \\
&\quad - \int E(y_0|m_0 = m, x) F_{m_0|x}(\partial m) \Big\} \cdot F_x(dx),
\end{aligned}
$$

$$
\begin{aligned}
E(\tau_x) &= \int \{E(y|d = 1, x) - E(y|d = 0, x)\} F_x(\partial x) \\
&= \Big\{ \int E(y_1|d = 1, m_1 = m, x) F_{m_1|d=1,x}(\partial m) \\
&\quad - \int E(y_0|d = 0, m_0 = m, x) F_{m_0|d=0,x}(\partial m) \Big\} \cdot F_x(\partial x) \\
&= \Big\{ \int E(y_1|m_1 = m, x) F_{m|d=1,x}(\partial m) \\
&\quad - \int E(y_0|m_0 = m, x) F_{m|d=0,x}(\partial m) \Big\} F_x(\partial x),
\end{aligned}
$$

$$E(\tau_{mx}) = \left\{ \int E(y_1|d=1, m_1=m, x) F_{m|x}(\partial m) \right.$$

$$\left. - \int E(y_0|d=0, m_0=m, x) F_{m|x}(\partial m) \right\} F_x(\partial x)$$

$$= \left\{ \int E(y_1|m_1=m, x) F_{m|x}(\partial m) \right.$$

$$\left. - \int E(y_0|m_0=m, x) F_{m|x}(\partial m) \right\} \cdot F_x(\partial x).$$

Thus, τ, $E(\tau_x)$, and $E(\tau_{mx})$ differ only in terms of the (x-conditioned) m-weighting function, $F_{m_j|x}$, $F_{m|d=j,x}$, and $F_{m|x}$, respectively. Because ε is an unobserved confounder for m_j, the three m-weighting functions—thus the three effects—are different in general, which suggests failure in identifying τ with $E(\tau_x)$ or $E(\tau_{mx})$. If d has no effect on m in the strongest sense $m_1 = m_0$, then $\tau = E(\tau_x) = E(\tau_{mx})$.

Rosenbaum (1984) defines a parameter

$$E(\nu_{mx}) \equiv \int \{E(y_1|m_1=m, x) - E(y_0|m_0=m, x)\} F_{m,x}(\partial m, \partial x),$$

$$\text{where } \nu_{mx} \equiv E(y_1|m_1=m, x) - E(y_0|m_0=m, x).$$

$E(\nu_{mx})$ is nothing but the direct effect (or 'net effect') of d on y, and $E(\nu_{mx})$ equals $E(\tau_{mx})$ under the (mean) surrogacy. We get

$$\underset{total\ effect}{\tau} = \underset{indirect\ effect}{\{\tau - E(\nu_{mx})\}} + \underset{direct\ effect}{E(\nu_{mx})}.$$

Rosenbaum (1984) also rewrites $\tau - E(\tau_{mx})$ into two terms:

$$\underset{indirect\ effect}{\{\tau - E(\nu_{mx})\}} + \underset{bias\ in\ observational\ study}{\{E(\nu_{mx}) - E(\tau_{mx})\}},$$

Since randomization assures $\tau_{mx} = \nu_{mx}$, the second term is relevant only to observational studies.

In summary, parametric or nonparametric, the regression function difference or its integrated version cannot identify the total effect of d on y when there is an unobserved confounder ε despite that a surrogate m_j for ε in the sense $E(y_j|d, m_j, x) = E(y_j|m_j, x)$ is available.

A.7   Appendix for Chapter 7

A.7.1   Regression models for discrete cardinal treatments

In this subsection, we explore the link between the treatment effect framework and the usual regression models. This has been done already to some extent, but here we look closer for discrete cardinal treatments. The treatment effect of interest is $\mu_j - \mu_0 \equiv E(y_j - y_0)$ where $\mu_j \equiv E(y_j)$, $j = 0, 1, ..., J$; there are $J + 1$ cardinal levels of treatment.

Under cardinality, we may parameterize μ_j as

$$\mu_j = \beta_1 + \beta_2 j;$$

the intercept β_1 is irrelevant for $\mu_j - \mu_0$. Recalling $\sum_{j=0}^{J} d_{ji} = 1$,

$$\sum_{j=0}^{J} d_{ji}\mu_j = \beta_1 \sum_{j=0}^{J} d_{ji} + \beta_2 \sum_{j=0}^{J} d_{ji}j = \beta_1 + \beta_2 d_i, \quad \text{where } d_i = \sum_{j=0}^{J} d_{ji}j.$$

With $u_i = \sum_{j=0}^{J} d_{ji}u_{ji}$, we get

$$y_i = \beta_1 + \beta_2 d_i + u_i$$

which is nothing but a simple linear model with a cardinal regressor d.

Observe

$$COV(d, u) = E\left(\sum_{j=0}^{J} d_j j \cdot \sum_{j=0}^{J} d_j u_j\right) = \sum_{j=0}^{J} j \cdot E(d_j u_j) \quad \text{because } d_j d_k = 0 \,\forall\, j \neq k.$$

If we have randomized data, then $E(d_j u_j) = 0 \,\forall j$. However, randomization is stronger than necessary, for

$$\sum_{j=0}^{J} j \cdot COV(d_j, u_j) = 0$$

is enough for the LSE of y_i on d_i.

Functional forms for μ_j other than linear can also be accommodated: e.g., if $\mu_j = \exp(\beta_1 + \beta_2 j)$, then

$$\sum_{j=0}^{J} d_{ji}\mu_j = \sum_{j=0}^{J} d_{ji}\exp(\beta_1 + \beta_2 j) = \exp(\beta_1 + \beta_2 d_i).$$

To understand the second equality, let $d_{mi} = 1$ without loss of generality and observe

$$\sum_{j=0}^{J} d_{ji}\exp(\beta_1 + \beta_2 j) = \exp(\beta_1 + \beta_2 m) = \exp\left(\beta_1 + \beta_2 \sum_{j=0}^{J} d_{ji}j\right).$$

Hence we get a nonlinear model $y_i = \exp(\beta_1 + \beta_2 d_i) + u_i$.

We can also allow μ_j in $y_{ji} = \mu_j + u_{ji}$ to depend on covariates x_i. Now using the notation μ_{ji} instead of μ_j, suppose

$$E(y_{ji}|x_i) = \mu_{ji} = \beta_1 + \beta_2 j + \beta_3' x_i + \beta_4' x_i j, \quad E(u_{ji}) = 0 \quad \text{and} \quad E(u_{ji}|x_i) = 0.$$

In this specification, the treatment effect $\mu_{ji} - \mu_{0i}$ varies across i due to x_i:

$$\mu_{ji} - \mu_{0i} = (\beta_2 + \beta_4' x_i) \cdot j.$$

Then we get

$$\sum_{j=0}^{J} d_{ji} \mu_{ji} = \beta_1 + \beta_2 d_i + \beta_3' \sum_{j=0}^{J} d_{ji} x_i + \beta_4' \sum_{j=0}^{J} d_{ji} x_i j$$

$$= \beta_1 + \beta_2 d_i + \beta_3' x_i \sum_{j=0}^{J} d_{ji} + \beta_4' x_i \sum_{j=0}^{J} d_{ji} j$$

$$= \beta_1 + \beta_2 d_i + \beta_3' x_i + \beta_4' d_i x_i$$

$$\implies y_i = \beta_1 + \beta_2 d_i + \beta_3' x_i + \beta_4' d_i x_i + u_i,$$

which is a linear model. On the right-hand side, there are d, x, and the interaction term between d and x.

A.7.2   Complete pairing for censored responses

Consider a treatment (say, a job training) and a response variable that is a duration (say, unemployment duration). As usual, the duration is right-censored at a censoring point c_i, and the observed response is

$$y_i = \min\{c_i, (1 - d_i)y_{0i} + d_i y_{1i}\}.$$

Define a non-censoring indicator $q_i \equiv 1[(1 - d_i)y_{0i} + d_i y_{1i} \leq c_i]$. What is observed is

$$d_i, q_i, x_i, y_i, \qquad i = 1, \ldots, N,$$

and there are N_0 controls and N_1 treated subjects. The covariate x may include the treatment duration (i.e., training duration). Assume that $(y_0, y_1) \amalg d | x$ and

$$y_j | x \text{ follows a continuous distribution } F_{j|x} \text{ on } [0, \infty), \qquad j = 0, 1.$$

Also assume $(y_0, y_1, d) \amalg c | x$. It is possible to allow for 'potential' censoring points c_0 and c_1, but so long as $c_0 | x$ and $c_1 | x$ follow the same distribution, this generality makes little difference in the following where the structure and notations are analogous to those of Subsection 3.5.

Suppose x is discrete for a while with the support points x_r, $r = 1, \ldots, R$. Lee (2003c) proposes to test for

$$H_0 : F_{0|x}(\cdot) = F_{1|x}(\cdot) \equiv F(\cdot|x)$$

with

$$L_N \equiv (N_0 N_1)^{-1} \sum_{j \in T} \sum_{i \in C} 1[x_i = x_j]\{1[y_j < y_i]q_j - 1[y_j > y_i]q_i\}.$$

The test statistic L_N has a number of desirable characteristics. First, it is invariant to increasing monotonic transformations of y, (e.g., taking ln on y does not alter the test). Second, L_N is robust to outliers, because only the sign of $y_j - y_i$ matters and the contribution of each datum is essentially the same across the observations. Third, no regression function nor any distribution need to be specified nor to be estimated for L_N.

To understand the idea of L_N, examine the comparability of y_j and y_i that is restricted due to the right-censoring:

y_j	y_i	comparability
not censored	not censored	yes always
censored	not censored	yes only for $y_j > y_i$
not censored	censored	yes only for $y_j < y_i$
censored	censored	no always

In the case y_j is censored whereas y_i is not, if $y_j > y_i$, then we know that the true duration of subject j is longer than that of subject i. The opposite case can be understood analogously.

It is because of the restricted comparability that we do not compare $y_j - y_i$ directly as in the complete pairing in Section 3.5. Instead, only that which is the greater is looked at in L_N. This results in the above null hypothesis, instead of the usual null hypothesis $E(y_1 - y_0|x) = 0 \ \forall x$. As mentioned in Subsection 2.2.2, however, $F_{0|x} = F_{1|x}$ is also an interesting null hypothesis *per se*.

To see that L_N is centered at 0 when the H_0 holds, let π_{1r} be $P(x = x_r)$ in the T group, and let π_{0r} be $P(x = x_r)$ in the C group. With a slight abuse of notation, let $F(\cdot|x)$ denote the distribution function as well. Define $F_c(\cdot|x)$ as the distribution function for $c|x$. Also define $S(\cdot|x) \equiv 1 - F(\cdot|x)$ and $S_c(\cdot|x) \equiv 1 - F_c(\cdot|x)$. Then, under the H_0,

$$E(L_N) = E\{1[x_i = x_j] \left(1[y_j < y_i] \, 1[y_j < c_j]\right\}$$
$$- E\{1[x_i = x_j] \, 1[y_j > y_i] \, 1[y_i < c_i])\}.$$

Examine the first term:

$$\sum_r E_{(c_j,y_j)|x_r}[E\{1[x_i = x_r]\,1[y_j < y_i]\,1[y_j < c_j]\,|x_j = x_r, c_j, y_j\}]\pi_{1r}$$

$$= \sum_r E_{(c_j,y_j)|x_r}\{S(y_j|x_r)1[y_j < c_j]\pi_{0r}\}\pi_{1r}$$

$$= \sum_r \int S(y_j|x_r)S_c(y_j|x_r)dF(y_j|x_r)\pi_{0r}\pi_{1r}.$$

Analogously, the second term is

$$\sum_r E_{(c_i,y_i)|x_r}[E\{1[x_j = x_r]\,1[y_j > y_i]\,1[y_i < c_i]\,|x_i = x_r, c_i, y_i\}]\pi_{0r}$$

$$= \sum_r E_{(c_i,y_i)|x_r}\{S(y_i|x_r)1[y_i < c_i]\pi_{1r}\}\pi_{0r}$$

$$= \sum_r \int S(y_i|x_r)S_c(y_i|x_r)dF(y_i|x_r)\pi_{0r}\pi_{1r}.$$

Thus, the two terms are equal and $E(L_N) = 0$ under the H_0.

As for the asymptotic distribution of L_N under the H_0, with $\lambda \equiv \lim_{N\to\infty} N_0/N$, it holds that

$$N^{1/2}L_N \rightsquigarrow N\{0, \lambda^{-1}\psi_0 + (1-\lambda)^{-1}\psi_1\},$$

where consistent estimators for ψ_0 and ψ_1 are

$$\hat{\psi}_0 \equiv N_0^{-1}\sum_{a\in C}\left[N_1^{-1}\sum_{b\in T}1[x_a = x_b]\{1[y_b < y_a]q_b - 1[y_b > y_a]q_a\}\right]^2,$$

$$\hat{\psi}_1 \equiv N_1^{-1}\sum_{a\in T}\left[N_0^{-1}\sum_{b\in C}1[x_a = x_b]\{1[y_a < y_b]q_a - 1[y_a > y_b]q_b\}\right]^2.$$

Suppose now that x is continuous with dimension $k \times 1$. In this case, use, instead of L_N,

$$M_N \equiv (N_0N_1)^{-1}\sum_{j\in T}\sum_{i\in C}h^{-k}K\left(\frac{x_i - x_j}{h}\right)\{1[y_j < y_i]q_j - 1[y_j > y_i]q_i\},$$

where K is a kernel and h is a bandwidth. Let g_1 denote the density for x in the T group and g_0 denote the density for x in the C group. It holds that

$$N^{1/2}M_N \rightsquigarrow N\{0, \lambda^{-1}\phi_0 + (1-\lambda)^{-1}\phi_1\},$$

where consistent estimators for ϕ_0 and ϕ_1 are

$$\hat{\phi}_0 \equiv N_0^{-1} \sum_{a \in C} \left[N_1^{-1} \sum_{b \in T} h^{-k} K((x_b - x_a)/h)\{1[y_b < y_a]q_b - 1[y_b > y_a]q_a\} \right]^2,$$

$$\hat{\phi}_1 \equiv N_1^{-1} \sum_{a \in T} \left[N_0^{-1} \sum_{b \in C} h^{-k} K((x_b - x_a)/h)\{1[y_a < y_b]q_a - 1[y_a > y_b]q_b\} \right]^2.$$

The mixed (continuous/discrete) x cases can be handled as in Section 3.5.

As a by-product, we may obtain an asymptotic confidence interval (CI) for 'location and scale treatment effect' under the same unknown distributional shape. Suppose that the treatment changes only the scale and location of y_0: $y_1 = \alpha + \sigma y_0$ for some constants α and σ. Then the null hypothesis of no effect is $H_0 : \alpha = 0$ and $\sigma = 1$. As is well known (e.g., Lehmann (1986)), we can construct CI's by inverting the testing procedure. For example, with x continuous, a 95% asymptotic CI for (α, σ) is

$$\{(\alpha, \sigma) : |N^{1/2} M_{\alpha\sigma}|/\{AV(N^{1/2} M_{\alpha\sigma})\}^{1/2} < 1.96\},$$

$$\text{where } M_{\alpha\sigma} \equiv (N_0 N_1)^{-1} \sum_{j \in T} \sum_{i \in C} h^{-k} K \left(\frac{x_i - x_j}{h} \right)$$

$$\times \{1[y_j < \alpha + \sigma y_i]q_j - 1[y_j > \alpha + \sigma y_i]q_i\},$$

where $AV(N^{1/2} M_{\alpha\sigma})$ denotes a consistent estimator for the asymptotic variance of $N^{1/2} M_{\alpha\sigma}$ which can be obtained replacing y_i with $\alpha + \sigma y_i$ in the above asymptotic variance estimator for $N^{1/2} M_N$.

If one desires a single treatment effect number, say, the proportional increase in y_1 relative to y_0 where y is $\ln(duration)$, then, postulate $y_1 = y_0 + \beta$ instead of $y_1 = \alpha + \sigma y_0$. In this case, no effect is $H_0 : \beta = 0$, and a 95% asymptotic CI is

$$\{\beta : |N^{1/2} M_\beta|/\{AV(N^{1/2} M_\beta)\}^{1/2} < 1.96\},$$

$$\text{where } M_\beta \equiv (N_0 N_1)^{-1} \sum_{j \in T} \sum_{i \in C} h^{-k} K \left(\frac{x_i - x_j}{h} \right)$$

$$\times \{1[y_j < y_i + \beta]q_j - 1[y_j > y_i + \beta]q_i\}.$$

References

Aakvik, A. (2001). Bounding a matching estimator: The case of a Norwegian training program. *Oxford Bulletin of Economics and Statistics*, **63**, 115–43.

Abadie, A. (2002). Bootstrap tests for distributional treatment effects in instrumental variable models. *Journal of the American Statistical Association*, **97**, 284–92.

—— (2003). Semiparametric instrumental variable estimation of treatment response models. *Journal of Econometrics*, **113**, 231–63.

—— (2005). Semiparametric difference-in-differences estimators. *Review of Economic Studies*, 72, 1–19.

—— Angrist, J., and Imbens, G. (2002). Instrumental variables estimates of the effect of subsidized training on the quantiles of trainee earnings. *Econometrica*, **70**, 91–117.

—— and Imbens, G. (2002). Simple and bias-corrected matching estimators for average treatment effects, unpublished paper.

Agodini, R. and Dynarski, M. (2004). Are experiments the only option? A look at dropout prevention programs. *Review of Economics and Statistics*, **86**, 180–94.

Allison, P. D. and Long, J. S. (1990). Departmental effects on scientific productivity. *American Sociological Review*, **55**, 469–78.

Angrist, J. D. (1990). Lifetime earnings and the Vietnam era draft lottery: Evidence from social security administrative records. *American Economic Review*, **80**, 313–35.

—— (2001). Estimation of limited dependent variable models with dummy endogenous regressors: Simple strategies for empirical practice. *Journal of Business and Economic Statistics*, **19**, 2–16.

Angrist, J. D. (2004). Treatment effect heterogeneity in theory and practice. *Economic Journal*, **114**, C52–C83.

—— and Evans, W. N. (1998). Children and their parent's labor supply: Evidence from exogenous variation in family size. *American Economic Review*, **88**, 450–77.

—— and Imbens, G. (1995). Two-stage least squares estimation of average causal effects in models with variable treatment intensity. *Journal of the American Statistical Association*, **90**, 431–42.

—— Imbens, G. W., and Rubin, D. B. (1996). Identification of causal effects using instrumental variables. *Journal of the American Statistical Association*, **91**, 444–55.

—— and Krueger, A. B. (1991). Does compulsory school attendance affect schooling and earnings? *Quarterly Journal of Economics*, **106**, 979–1014.

———— (1999). Empirical strategies in labor economics. In *Handbook of Labor Economics 3A* (ed. O. Ashenfelter and D. Card), North-Holland.

———— (2001). Instrumental variables and the search for identification: From supply and demand to natural experiments. *Journal of Economic Perspectives*, **15**, 69–85.

—— and Lavy, V. (1999). Using Maimonides' rule to estimate the effect of class size on scholastic achievement. *Quarterly Journal of Economics*, **114**, 533–75.

Battistin, E. and Rettore, E. (2002). Testing for programme effects in a regression discontinuity design with imperfect compliance. *Journal of the Royal Statistical Society, Series A*, **165**, 39–57.

Behrman, J. R., Cheng, Y., and Todd, P. E. (2004). Evaluating pre-school programs when length of exposure to the program varies: A nonparametric approach. *Review of Economics and Statistics*, **86**, 108–32.

Bergstralh, E. J. and Kosanke, J. L. (1995). Computerized matching of cases to controls. *Technical Report 56*, Mayo Foundation.

Berk, R. A. and de Leeuw, J. (1999). An evaluation of California's inmate classification system using a generalized regression discontinuity design. *Journal of the American Statistical Association*, **94**, 1045–52.

Bertrand, M., Duflo, E., and Mullainathan, S. (2004). How much should we trust differences-in-differences estimates. *Quarterly Journal of Economics*, **119**, 249–75.

Besley, T. and Case, A. (2004). Unnatural experiments? Estimating the incidence of endogenous policies. *Economic Journal*, **110**, F672–F694.

Black, S. E. (1999). Do better schools matter? Parental evaluation of elementary education. *Quarterly Journal of Economics*, **114**, 577–99.

Bound, J. (1989). The health and earnings of rejected disability insurance applicants. *American Economic Review*, **79**, 482–503.

Card, D. (1990). The impact of the Mariel Boatlift on the Miami labor market. *Industrial and Labor Relations Review*, **43**, 245–57.

—— and Krueger, A. B. (1994). Minimum wage and employment: A case study of the fast-food industry in New Jersey and Pennsylvania. *American Economic Review*, **84**, 772–93.

——— (2000). Minimum wage and employment: A case study of the fast-food industry in New Jersey and Pennsylvania: Reply. *American Economic Review*, **90**, 1397–420.

Corak, M. (2001). Death and divorce: The long-term consequences of parental loss on adolescents. *Journal of Labor Economics*, **19**, 682–715.

Cox, D. R. (1972). Regression models and life tables. *Journal of the Royal Statistical Society, Series B*, **34**, 187–202.

Dawid, A. P. (1979). Conditional independence in statistical theory. *Journal of the Royal Statistical Society, Series B*, **41**, 1–31.

Dehejia, R. H. and Wahba, S. (1999). Causal effects in nonexperimental studies: Reevaluating the evaluation of training programs. *Journal of the American Statistical Association*, **94**, 1053–62.

——— (2002). Propensity score-matching methods for nonexperimental causal studies. *Review of Economics and Statistics*, **84**, 151–61.

Donohue III, J. J., Heckman, J. J., and Todd, P. E. (2002). The schooling of southern blacks: The roles of legal activism and private philanthropy, 1910–1960. *Quarterly Journal of Economics*, **117**, 225–68.

Eberwein, C., Ham, J. C., and Lalonde, R. J. (1997). The impact of being offered and receiving classroom training on the employment histories of disadvantaged women: Evidence from experimental data. *Review of Economic Studies*, **64**, 655–82.

Eissa, N. (1995). Taxation and labor supply of married women: The tax reform act of 1986 as a natural experiment. NBER working paper 5023.

Eissa, N. and Liebman, J. B. (1996). Labor supply response to the earned income tax credit. *Quarterly Journal of Economics*, **111**, 605–37.

Fan, J. (1996). *Local Polynomial Modeling and its Applications*. Chapman and Hall.

Fraker, T. and Maynard, R. (1987). The adequacy of comparison group designs for evaluations of employment-related programs. *Journal of Human Resources*, **22**, 194–227.

Freedman, D. (1999). From association to causation: Some remarks on the history of statistics. *Statistical Science*, **14**, 243–58.

Friedberg, R. M. and Hunt, J. (1995). The impact of immigrants on host country wages, employment and growth. *Journal of Economic Perspectives*, **9**, 23–44.

Friedlander, D. and Robins, P. K. (1995). Evaluating program evaluations: New evidence on commonly used nonexperimental methods. *American Economic Review*, **85**, 923–37.

Frölich, M. (2003). *Programme Evaluation and Treatment Choice*. Springer-Verlag.

Gastwirth, J. L., Krieger, A. M., and Rosenbaum, P. R. (1998). Dual and simultaneous sensitivity analysis for matched pairs. *Biometrika*, **85**, 907–20.

Gill, R. and Robins, J. M. (2001). Causal inference for complex longitudinal data: The continuous case. *Annals of Statistics*, **29**, 1785–811.

Gordis, L. (2000). *Epidemiology*. Saunders.

Granger, C. W. J. (1969). Investigating causal relations by econometric models and cross-spectral methods. *Econometrica*, **37**, 424–38.

—— (1980). Testing for causality: A personal viewpoint. *Journal of Economic Dynamics and Control*, **2**, 329–52.

Gruber, J. (1994). The incidence of mandated maternity benefits. *American Economic Review*, **84**, 622–41.

Gu, X. S. and Rosenbaum, P. R. (1993). Comparison of multivariate matching methods: Structures, distances, and algorithms. *Journal of Computational and Graphical Statistics*, **2**, 405–20.

Hahn, J. (1998). On the role of the propensity score in efficient semiparametric estimation of average treatment effects. *Econometrica*, **66**, 315–31.

—— Todd, P., and van der Klaauw, W. (2001). Identification and estimation of treatment effects with a regression-discontinuity design. *Econometrica*, **69**, 201–9.

Ham, J. C. and Lalonde, R. J. (1996). The effect of sample selection and initial conditions in duration models: Evidences from experimental data on training. *Econometrica*, **64**, 175–205.

Härdle, W. (1990). *Applied Nonparametric Regression*. Cambridge University Press.

Heckman, J. J. (1979). Sample selection bias as a specification error. *Econometrica*, **47**, 153–61.

——(1996). Comment. *Journal of the American Statistical Association*, **91**, 459–62.

——(1997). Instrumental variables: A study of implicit behavioral assumptions used in making program evaluations. *Journal of Human Resources*, **32**, 441–62.

——(2001). Accounting for heterogeneity, diversity, and general equilibrium in evaluating social programmes. *Economic Journal*, **111**, F654–F699.

—— Hohmann, N., and Smith, J. (2000). Substitution and dropout bias in social experiments: A study of an influential social experiment. *Quarterly Journal of Economics*, **115**, 651–94.

—— and Hotz, V. (1989). Choosing among alternative nonexperimental methods for estimating the impact of social program: The case of manpower training. *Journal of the American Statistical Association*, **84**, 862–74.

—— Ichimura H., Smith J., and Todd, P. E. (1998). Characterizing selection bias using experimental data. *Econometrica*, **66**, 1017–98.

———— and Todd, P. E. (1997). Matching as an econometric evaluation estimator: Evidence from evaluating a job training program. *Review of Economic Studies*, **64**, 605–54.

—— Lalonde R. J., and Smith, J. A. (1999). The economics and econometrics of active labor market programs. In *Handbook of Labor Economics 3B* (ed. O. C. Ashenfelter and D. Card), North-Holland.

—— Smith J., and Clements, N. (1997). Making the most out of program evaluations and social experiments: Accounting for heterogeneity in program impacts. *Review of Economic Studies*, **64**, 487–535.

Heckman, J. J., Tobias J. L., and Vytlacil, E. (2003). Simple estimators for treatment parameters in a latent-variable framework. *Review of Economics and Statistics*, **85**, 748–55.

——— and Vytlacil, E. J. (1999). Local instrument variables and latent variable models for identifying and bounding treatment effects. *Proceedings of National Academy of Science*, **96**, 4730–4.

Hirano, K., Imbens, G. W., and Ridder, G. (2003). Efficient estimation of average treatment effects using the estimated propensity score. *Econometrica*, **71**, 1161–89.

Holland, P. W. (1986). Statistics and causal inference. *Journal of the American Statistical Association*, **81**, 945–60.

Hotz, V. J., Mullin, C. H., and Sanders, S. G. (1997). Bounding causal effects using data from a contaminated natural experiments: Analyzing the effects of teenage childbearing. *Review of Economic Studies*, **64**, 575–603.

Hsu, J. C. (1996). *Multiple Comparisons: Theory and Methods*. Chapman and Hall.

Imbens, G. W. (2000). The role of the propensity score in estimating dose-response functions. *Biometrika*, **87**, 706–10.

——— (2003). Sensitivity to exogeneity assumptions in program evaluation. *American Economic Review, Papers and Proceedings*, **93**, 126–32.

——— (2004). Nonparametric estimation of average treatment effects under exogeneity: A review. *Review of Economics and Statistics*, **86**, 4–29.

——— and Angrist, J. D. (1994). Identification and estimation of local average treatment effects. *Econometrica*, **62**, 467–75.

——— and Rubin, D. B. (1997). Estimating outcome distributions for compliers in instrumental variables models. *Review of Economic Studies*, **64**, 555–74.

Joe, H. (1997). *Multivariate Models and Dependence Concepts*. Chapman and Hall.

Kang, C. H., Lee, M. J., and Park, C. S. (2005). Effects of ability mixing in high school on adulthood earnings: Quasi-experimental evidence from South Korea, unpublished paper.

Krueger, A. B. and Whitmore, D. M. (2001). The effect of attending a small class in the early grades on college-test taking and middle school test results: Evidence from Project Star. *Economic Journal*, **111**, 1–28.

Lalonde, R. J. (1986). Evaluating the econometric evaluations of training programs with experimental data. *American Economic Review*, **76**, 604–20.

Lechner, M. (1999). Nonparametric bounds on employment and income effects of continuous vocational training in East Germany. *Econometrics Journal*, **2**, 1–28.

——(2000). An evaluation of public-sector sponsored continuous vocational training programs in East Germany. *Journal of Human Resources*, **35**, 347–75.

——(2001). Identification and estimation of causal effects of multiple treatments under the conditional independence assumption. In *Econometric Evaluation of Labor Market Policies* (ed. M. Lechner and F. Pfeiffer), Physica-Verlag.

——(2002). Program heterogeneity and propensity score matching: An application to the evaluation of active labor market policies. *Review of Economics and Statistics*, **84**, 205–20.

Lee, M. J. (1996). *Methods of Moments and Semiparametric Econometrics for Limited Dependent Variable Models*. Springer-Verlag.

——(1997). Nonparametric estimation of treatment effects under comparison group bias, unpublished paper.

——(2000). Median treatment effect in randomized trials. *Journal of the Royal Statistical Society, Series B* (Series B) **62**, 595–604.

——(2002). *Panel Data Econometrics: Methods-of-Moments and Limited Dependent Variables*. Academic Press.

——(2003a). Complete pairing, propensity score, and endogeneity test for binary selection models, unpublished paper.

——(2003b). Treatment effect and sensitivity analysis for self-selected treatment and selectively observed response, unpublished paper.

——(2003c). Nonparametric test and estimation of treatment effects for randomly censored responses, presented at the Australian Econometric Society Meeting at Sydney.

——(2004). Selection correction and sensitivity analysis for ordered treatment effect on count response. *Journal of Applied Econometrics*, **19**, 323–37.

Lee, M. J. and Kobayashi, S. (2001). Proportional treatment effects for count response panel data: Effects of binary exercise on health care demand. *Health Economics*, **10**, 411–28.

Lee, M. J. and Lee, S. J., (2004a). Job-training effects with dropouts: Partial likelihood, matching, and causality, unpublished paper.

—— —— (2004b). Sensitivity analysis of job-training effects on reemployment for Korean women, unpublished paper.

—— —— (2005). Analysis of job-training effects on Korean women. *Journal of Applied Econometrics*, forthcoming.

Lehmann, E. L. (1986). *Testing Statistical Hypotheses*. 2nd ed. Wiley.

Lok, J. J. (2001). Statistical modelling of causal effects in time. Ph.D. thesis. Free University, Amsterdam, the Netherlands.

Lu, B., Zanutto, E., Hornik, R., and Rosenbaum, P. R. (2001). Matching with doses in an observational study of a media campaign against drug abuse. *Journal of the American Statistical Association*, **96**, 1245–53.

Ludwig, J., Duncan, G. J., and Hirschfield, P. (2001). Urban poverty and juvenile crime: Evidence from a randomized housing-mobility experiment. *Quarterly Journal of Economics*, **116**, 655–79.

Madrian, B. C. (1994). Employment-based health insurance and job mobility: Is there evidence of job-lock? *Quarterly Journal of Economics*, **109**, 27–54.

Manski, C. F. (1995). *Identification Problems in the Social Sciences*. Harvard University Press.

—— (2003). *Partial Identification of Probability Distributions*. Springer-Verlag.

—— Sandefur, G. D., McLanahan, S., and Powers, D. (1992). Alternative estimates of the effect of family structure during adolescence on high school graduation. *Journal of the American Statistical Association*, **87**, 25–37.

Marcantonio, R. J. and Cook, T. D. (1994). Convincing quasi-experiments: The interrupted time series and regression-discontinuity designs. In *Handbook of Practical Program Evaluation* (ed. J. S. Wholey, H. P. Hatry, and K. E. Newcomer), Jossey-Bass Publishers, San Francisco.

Meyer, B. D. (1995). Natural and quasi-experiments in Economics. *Journal of Business and Economic Statistics*, **13**, 151–61.

—— Viscusi, W. K., and Durbin, D. L. (1995). Workers' compensation and injury duration: Evidence from a natural experiment. *American Economic Review*, **85**, 322–40.

Michalopoulos, C., Bloom, H. S., and Hill, C. J. (2004). Can propensity-score methods match the findings from a random assignment evaluation of mandatory welfare-to-work programs? *Review of Economics and Statistics*, **86**, 156–79.

Murphy, S. A. (2003). Optimal dynamic treatment regimes. *Journal of the Royal Statistical Society, Series B*, **65**, 331–55.

Pearl, J. (2000). *Causality.* Cambridge University Press.

Pepper, J. V. (2000). The intergenerational transmission of welfare receipt: A nonparametric bound analysis. *Review of Economics and Statistics*, **82**, 472–88.

Pierce, D. A. (1982). The asymptotic effect of substituting estimators for parameters in certain types of statistics. *Annals of Statistics*, **10**, 475–8.

Rephann, T. and Isserman, A. (1994). New highways as economic development tools: An evaluation using quasi-experimental matching methods. *Regional Science and Urban Economics*, **24**, 723–51.

Robins, J. M. (1998). Structural nested failure time models. In *Survival Analysis*, vol. 6, *Encyclopedia of Biostatistics* (ed. P. Armitage and T. Colton), Wiley.

—— (1999). Marginal structural models versus structural nested models as tools for causal inference. In *Statistical Models in Epidemiology: The Environment and Clinical Trials* (ed. M. E. Halloran and D. Berry), Springer, 95–134.

—— Mark S. D., and Newey W. K. (1992). Estimating exposure effects by modelling the expectation of exposure conditional on confounder. *Biometrics*, **48**, 479–95.

Robinson, P. M. (1988). Root-N consistent semiparametric regression. *Econometrica*, **56**, 931–54.

Rosenbaum, P. R. (1984). The consequences of adjustment for a concomitant variable that has been affected by the treatment. *Journal of the Royal Statistical Society, Series B*, **147**, 656–666.

—— (1987). Sensitivity analysis for certain permutation inferences in matched observational studies. *Biometrika*, **74**, 13–26.

—— (1989). Optimal matching for observational studies. *Journal of the American Statistical Association*, **84**, 1024–32.

—— (1991). A characterization of optimal designs for observational studies. *Journal of the Royal Statistical Society, Series B*, **53**, 597–610.

Rosenbaum, P. R. (2002). *Observational Studies*, 2nd ed. Springer-Verlag.

—— and Rubin, D. B. (1983a). The central role of the propensity score in observational studies for causal effects. *Biometrika*, **70**, 41–55.

Rosenbaum, P. R. and Rubin, D. B. (1983b). Assessing sensitivity to an unobserved binary covariate in an observational study with binary outcome. *Journal of the Royal Statistical Society, Series B*, **45**, 212–18.

——— (1985). Constructing a control group using multivariate matched sampling methods that incorporate the propensity score. *American Statistician*, **39**, 33–8.

Rosenzweig, M. R. and Wolpin, K. I. (1980). Life cycle labor supply and fertility: Causal inferences from household models. *Journal of Political Economy*, **88**, 328–48.

——— (2000). Natural 'natural experiments' in economics. *Journal of Economic Literature*, **38**, 827–74.

Rosner, B. (1995). *Fundamentals of Biostatistics*. Duxbury Press.

Rubin, D. B. (1974). Estimating causal effects of treatments in randomized and nonrandomized studies. *Journal of Educational Psychology*, **66**, 688–701.

Seifert, B. and Gasser, T. (1996). Finite-sample variance of local polynomials: Analysis and solution. *Journal of the American Statistical Association*, **91**, 267–75.

——— (2000). Data adaptive ridging in local polynomial regression. *Journal of Computational and Graphical Statistics*, **9**, 338–60.

Shadish, W. R., Cook, T. D., and Campbell, D. T. (2002). *Experimental and Quasi-Experimental Designs for Generalized Causal Inference*. Houghton Mifflin Company.

Smith, H. (1997). Matching with multiple controls to estimate treatment effects in observational studies. *Sociological Methodology*, **27**, 325–53.

Stock, J. H. and Watson, M. W. (2003). *Introduction to Econometrics*. Addison-Wesley.

Thun, M. J., Peto, R., Lopez, A. D., Monaco, J. H., Henley, S. J., Heath, C. W., and Doll, R. (1997). Alcohol consumption and mortality among middle-aged and elderly U.S. adults. *New England Journal of Medicine*, **337**, 1705–14.

Triest, R. K. (1998). Econometric issues in estimating the behavioral response to taxation: A nontechnical introduction. *National Tax Journal*, **51**, 761–73.

Van der Klaauw, V. (2002). Estimating the effect of financial aid offers on college enrollment: A regression-discontinuity approach. *International Economic Review*, **43**, 1249–87.

Van der Laan, M. J. and Robins, J. (2003). *Unified Methods for Censored Longitudinal Data and Causality.* Springer-Verlag.

Vella, F. and Verbeek, M. (1998). Whose wages do unions raise? A dynamic model of unionism and wage determination for young men. *Journal of Applied Econometrics*, **13**, 163–83.

Vytlacil, E. (2002). Independence, monotonicity, and latent index models: An equivalence result. *Econometrica*, **70**, 331–41.

Wagner, J. (2002). The causal effects of exports on firm size and labor productivity: First evidence from a matching approach. *Economics Letters*, **77**, 287–92.

White, J. R. and Froeb, H. F. (1980). Small-airways dysfunction in non-smokers chronically exposed to tobacco smoke. *New England Journal of Medicine*, **302**, 720–23.

Wooldridge, J. M. (2002). *Econometric Analysis of Cross-Section and Panel Data.* MIT Press.

Zhao, Z. (2004). Using matching to estimate treatment effects: Data requirement, matching metrics, and Monte Carlo evidence. *Review of Economics and Statistics*, **86**, 91–107.

Index

surrogate, 224
switching regression, 9

T group, *see* treatment group
TD, *see* triple differences
total effect, 183
treatment duration, 177
treatment group, 10
treatment intervention effect, 8, 24
treatment profile, 181
treatment self-selection
      effect, 24

triple differences, 111
two-stage LSE, 133

varying effect, 31, 32, 200

Wald estimator, 62, 134, 137, 141
weighting, 65
weighting estimator, 102, 142,
      177, 190
worst-case bound, 164, 165

zero comparison-group bias, 51